SEXUAL HAPPINESS

A Practical Approach

Maurice Yaffé
Senior Clinical Psychologist,
York Clinic, Guy's Hospital, London

Elizabeth Fenwick

Consultant Editor
Raymond C. Rosen, Ph.D,
Associate Professor of Psychiatry,
Rutgers Medical School, New Jersey

Illustrated by
Charles Raymond

HENRY HOLT AND COMPANY
NEW YORK

Editor Richard Dawes

Art editor Philip Lord

First published in the United States in 1988 by Henry Holt and
Company, Inc., 115 West 18th Street, New York, New York 10011.

First published in Great Britain in 1986
by Dorling Kindersley Limited, London.

Library of Congress Catalog Card Number:

87-45839

ISBN 0-8050-0691-5

First American Edition

Printed in Italy
10 9 8 7 6 5 4 3 2 1

ISBN 0-8050-0691-5

Contents

Contents

PART TWO: MEN

Introduction

Why yet another book about sex? Sexual relationships and the difficulties arising from them assume major importance in many people's lives. Yet it is only in the last 15 years that reliable short-term and direct-treatment procedures have been available, and it has taken this long to evaluate their effectiveness and relative merits. Since the spread of the AIDS virus there has also been a need for greater awareness about how our sex lives can affect our health, and what we can do to make sex safer.

Resolving sexual problems

This book deals with the rich and diverse pattern of human sexuality, but places special emphasis on its problems and their resolution. Most people do not in fact have clearly defined sexual problems, but have instead nagging difficulties. Examples of such difficulties, which nearly always affect the partner's enjoyment of sex too, are an inability to relax, a reluctance to engage in adequate foreplay or afterplay, the loss of sexual desire, or simply problems in keeping the relationship alive.

It makes sense to confront sexual problems in the context of the relationship itself, and the structure of this book reflects this aim. What is offered here is the opportunity to see problems from both sides of the sexual divide, for *Sexual Happiness: A Practical Approach* is essentially two books in one. With two sections of equal length – one for men, the other for women – it highlights in an easy-to-use form the differences and similarities between the feelings of each about sex. This comparison is the first step towards removing the obstacles that limit your enjoyment of sex.

Authoritative guidance

What distinguishes this book from most other sex manuals is that, besides offering this balanced view of sexual problems, it proposes clinically tried and tested solutions to them. The questionnaires and charts that form the first two parts of the book are based on this body of practical knowledge and enable you not only to look at your own difficulties but to understand your partner's feelings more fully. By recognizing the patterns of behaviour that restrict sexual development you will be better able to help one another attain greater satisfaction.

A plan for sexual development

This book is arranged systematically and it makes sense to use it similarly. The structure of the men's section of the book is the same as that of the women's. The first part, YOUR SEXUAL PROFILE, will provide you with a picture of where you currently stand in terms of sexual adjustment and competence. According to your scores for the questionnaires, you will be guided to relevant sections of the book, including the PROBLEM CHARTS that form the second part. These will help you to diagnose your sexual difficulties and either offer immediate advice or direct you to the third part, IMPROVING YOUR SEX LIFE, where self-help therapy programmes are described. Whether you happen to be in your teens, the prime of life, or well advanced in years, are about to experience your first sexual encounter or have had such adventures many times before, you will find here practical advice. This is a book for everyone, irrespective of their age, race or sexual orientation.

The questions in the charts are designed to pinpoint the particular characteristics of your problem, allowing you to examine your situation with some of the insight of the trained therapist. Accurate and early pinpointing is an important part of overcoming sexual difficulties and this rigorous self-scrutiny will help minimize frustration and prevent disappointment during the subsequent therapy programs.

Using the book as a couple
If your partner has made use of the book too – always, it must be stressed, at his or her own pace and without coercion – you should both understand enough about how the other probably feels to look at

your difficulties together. The next step is to bring about real changes in your sexual relationship by using the third part of the book.

Enriching your sex life

The aim of this section is to help you get the most out of sex, whether you feel you have problems or not. IMPROVING YOUR SEX LIFE offers detailed step-by-step instructions on how to tackle specific difficulties, using techniques that have had wide success. Here you are offered practical means of eliminating or relieving the anxiety and guilt that contribute to and sustain sexual problems.

As you progress with the exercises, you will find that the changes in your relationship are no longer simply a response to problems but represent an open-ended development. Once you have dealt with the major difficulties you can go on improving the quality of your sex life together as much as you both want, whether this takes the form of finding better positions for intercourse, exploring your partner's erogenous zones, or simply learning how to relax and enjoy sex more.

Barriers to forming relationships

The fourth and fifth parts of this book are intended, respectively, for those who have a steady partner and those who do not. Normally, practical books on sex are aimed specifically at those in a relationship, but we acknowledge that there are many people who, for various reasons, do not have a partner. Often, these reasons are related to sex. Clinical experience has shown repeatedly that once a sexual concern has been resolved, relationships are sought out more confidently.

Long-term difficulties

Of course, established relationships themselves can conceal entrenched sexual problems. With this in mind, the fourth part of the book, THE WOMAN/MAN WITH A STEADY PARTNER, explores the issues of compatibility and communication and helps the user gain a better understanding of her or his partner's sexuality. In addition, the potentially destructive problems of sexual boredom, infidelity, and jealousy are confronted in depth. Finally, the full choice of contraceptive methods is covered, as are the lovemaking positions suitable in pregnancy.

The needs of the single person

The fifth part, THE SINGLE WOMAN/MAN, contains a wealth of material relevant to both those who do not have a steady partner by choice and those who are single because they cannot integrate their social and sexual skills. Advice is likewise given to everyone who has difficulty in finding or choosing a suitable partner and to those who are embarking on a new, or their first, sexual relationship.

The appendices suggest guidelines for safer sexual practices, give advice about conditions which may have an adverse effect on sexual functioning, and provide a brief survey of sexually transmitted diseases, along with information on testing for AIDS. Finally, the Resource Guide suggests further reading and advises you on where you can obtain professional help for sexual problems.

You will undoubtedly deprive yourself of some very enjoyable experiences if you just skim through this book without using it with your partner. The same is true – should you be unhappy about being alone – if you do not act on the advice for the single person. But by making sure you follow the intended sequence of the book, and practising conscientiously the relevant exercise programs, you will be taking a positive step towards lasting sexual fulfilment.

SEXUAL
HAPPINESS
A Practical Approach

PART ONE
WOMEN

YOUR SEXUAL PROFILE

Your answers to the following questionnaires together form your sexual profile, a complete picture of the attitudes and behavior that shape your relationships and determine how much enjoyment you get and give in sex. By collating your scores for the questionnaires in the form of a chart, you can create your sexual profile. Instructions on how to do this are given on pp.24-5.

The answer to each question in the questionnaires on pp.14-22 carries a score. By checking your total score for a questionnaire against the **What you should do** box that follows it, you will obtain an assessment of where you stand in the particular area of your sex life under examination. The questionnaire on p.23, while contributing to an overall view of your sexual identity, is not rated in this way, and serves simply to establish your orientation.

A low or medium score for a questionnaire indicates that a particular aspect of your sexual experience is limiting your happiness. An appropriate course of action is suggested where necessary, the first step of which is usually to study other sections of the book. Often the situation is indeed remediable, and you can change almost any aspect of your sex life that is a problem. This book aims to help you do so.

SEXUAL KNOWLEDGE

How much do you know about sex and sexual physiology?

Indicate by a T or F in the box whether the following statements are true or false. Compare your total score with the ratings following the questionnaire.

1 Masturbation is bad because it leads to a loss of interest in sex with a partner. ☐

2 Intercourse during menstruation is harmless and often relieves menstrual cramp. ☐

3 The menopause need not reduce a woman's desire for sex. ☐

4 A condom gives some protection against AIDS. ☐

5 Most women who masturbate can reach orgasm this way. ☐

6 As a man grows older he takes longer to reach orgasm. ☐

7 Simultaneous orgasm is necessary for satisfactory sex. ☐

8 The penis's head is its most sensitive part. ☐

9 If a man has an erection on waking in the morning it means that he wants sex. ☐

10 Just thinking about sex is enough to give any man an erection. ☐

11 It is very painful for a man not to have an orgasm once he is sexually aroused and erect. ☐

12 Some women can have several orgasms in quick succession. ☐

13 Most homosexuals like to dress in women's clothes now and then. ☐

14 A breastfeeding woman cannot conceive. ☐

15 A potent man (i.e. capable of intercourse) must be fertile. ☐

16 Female sterilization can be reversed in every case. ☐

17 Conception is most likely around the middle of your menstrual cycle. ☐

18 For birth control, douching is useless. ☐

19 A circumcised penis is less sensitive. ☐

20 If your partner fails to get an erection or loses it, he does not really want you. ☐

For key to answers, see p.19.

Give yourself a point for each correct answer.

WHAT YOU SHOULD DO

High rating (16-20) Your knowledge is sound. Now try the questionnaire TECHNIQUE, p.21, to make sure that your ability as a lover matches your grasp of theory. Check wrong answers (see below).

Medium rating (9-15) Check wrong answers (see below) to remedy gaps in your knowledge. You should also benefit from answering the questionnaire TECHNIQUE, p.21.

Low rating (0-8) Check wrong answers (see below) and see TECHNIQUE, p.21.

You will find full answers to the questions as follows: Question 1 – p.46; 2 – p.49; 3 – p.42; 4 – p.136; 5 – p.86; 6 – p.125; 7 – p.69; 8 – p.93; 9 – p.125; 10 – p.125; 11 – p.123; 12 – p.104; 13 – p.129; 14 – p.138; 15 – p.139; 16 – p.137; 17 – p.139; 18 – p.137; 19 – p.93; 20 – p.125.

SEX DRIVE

How strong is your appetite for sex?

For each question, circle the score to the right of your answer.
Compare your total score with the ratings following the questionnaire.

1 If you are under 55, do you have sex:

More than three times a week?	2
Once or twice a week?	1
Less than once a week?	0

If you are 55 or over, do you have sex:

More than once a week?	2
Seldom or never?	0
Once or twice every couple of weeks?	1

2 Did you first have sexual intercourse:

Before most of your friends?	2
About the same time as your friends?	1
Rather later than your friends?	0

3 How often do you masturbate?

Once or twice a week	1
Several times a week	2
Seldom or never	0

4 Do you become sexually excited:

Quickly and easily?	2
Fairly easily?	1
Only after a great deal of stimulation?	0

5 On average, how long after sexual stimulation begins do you climax?

Five minutes	2
About a quarter of an hour	1
I seldom or never reach orgasm	0

6 Do you think about sex:

Several times a day?	2
Seldom or never?	0
Most days?	1

7 How often do you suggest sex?

Often	2
Sometimes	1
Seldom or never	0

8 Have you been sexually involved with more than one person at a time:

Seldom?	1
Several times?	2
Never?	0

9 Are you aroused by erotic magazines?

Always	2
Sometimes	1
Never	0

10 If your partner suggests sex, do you:

Nearly always respond gladly?	2
Respond more often than not?	1
Respond, if at all, from kindness or apathy?	0

WHAT YOU SHOULD DO

High rating (16-20) Your sex drive is strong, but if you have problems with your partner, see WHAT IS WRONG WITH YOUR RELATIONSHIP?, p.115. If you are troubled because you lack a partner, see WHY ARE YOU SINGLE?, p.138.

Medium rating (9-15) Consult ARE YOU SEXUALLY SATISFIED?, p.116, to establish how closely your sexual needs match your partner's.

Low rating (0-8) If your partner wants sex far more often than you do, see LACK OF INTEREST, p.128, and DEALING WITH A SEX-DRIVE DISCREPANCY, p.122.

PSYCHOLOGICAL WELL-BEING
Can you enjoy sex without anxiety or guilt?

For each question, circle the appropriate score. Compare your total score with the ratings following the questionnaire.

	YES	NO		YES	NO
1 Do you feel sex is unimportant and has never played a large part in your life?	0	1	**6** Are you afraid of intercourse because you think it might be painful or even damage you physically?	0	1
2 Are you a solitary person, unable or unwilling to get emotionally close to others?	0	1	**7** Do you find sex messy? Are you repelled by the sight and feel of semen or vaginal fluid, for example, or do you have to bathe immediately after sex?	0	1
3 Do you worry that you may not be able to satisfy your partner sexually?	0	1	**8** Do you worry so much about AIDS that you have considered giving up sex?	0	1
4 Do fears about getting pregnant spoil sex for you, even when you are taking adequate precautions?	0	1	**9** Do you feel very vulnerable in sexual relationships – afraid that your partner might leave you?	0	1
5 Were you brought up to feel that there is nothing to be ashamed of in sex?	1	0	**10** Are you completely sure about your preference for heterosexual relationships to lesbian ones, or vice versa?	1	0

WHAT YOU SHOULD DO

High rating (8-10)
You are able to relax and respond naturally in a sexual situation. However, sexual functioning is very easily thrown off balance, so wherever you scored 0 on a question, consult the appropriate section of the book for advice (see the key following **Low rating**).

Medium rating (5-7)
Fear or guilt about sex probably makes it hard for you to enjoy a sexual relationship fully. Consult the appropriate sections of the book about questions for which you scored 0 (see the key following **Low rating**).

Low rating (0-4)
Your capacity for, and interest in, sex are limited by a lack of psychological balance. Various sections of the book deal with factors which commonly influence psychological health and attitudes to sex. Consult them as follows on questions for which you scored 0:

Question 1 – LACK OF INTEREST, p.28; 2 – **Fear of intimacy**, p.77; 3, 4 – NEGATIVE FEELINGS, p.30; 5 – LOW SELF-ESTEEM, p.34; 6 – **Dealing with anxiety about sex**, , p.77; 7, 8, 9 – NEGATIVE FEELINGS, p.30; 10 – HETEROSEXUALITY/HOMOSEXUALITY CONFLICTS, p.50.

SATISFACTION

Are you satisfied with your sex life?

For each question, circle the appropriate score. Compare your
total score with the ratings following the questionnaire.

	YES	NO		YES	NO
1 Are you getting as much sex as you would like?	1	0	**6** Is sex usually as good as you had imagined it would be?	1	0
2 Are you getting the kind of sex you like, so that you usually do the things you most enjoy?	1	0	**7** Is sex always or frequently disappointing?	0	1
3 Does your usual sexual partner still arouse you?	1	0	**8** Do you usually feel relaxed and happy after sex?	1	0
4 Do you think sex is a thoroughly overrated activity?	0	1	**9** Does your partner show you as much tenderness and affection as you would like when you have sex?	1	0
5 Do you normally anticipate sex with great pleasure?	1	0	**10** Is your usual partner too sexually demanding?	0	1

WHAT YOU SHOULD DO

High rating (8-10)
You seem happy with both the quality and quantity of your sex life. If you have a steady partner, answer together the questionnaire ARE YOU SEXUALLY SATISFIED?, p.116. This will indicate your sexual compatibility, and show you how your partner's satisfaction compares with yours. You should also try the questionnaire COMPATIBILITY, p.112.

Medium rating (5-7)
Ask yourself whether the main source of dissatisfaction is your relationship with a particular person or whether you perhaps have an unrealistic idea of how great sex ought to be. The questionnaires COMPATIBILITY, p.112, and ARE YOU SEXUALLY SATISFIED?, p.116, will prove useful in the former case. In the latter case, the problem chart UNFULFILLED EXPECTATIONS, p.32, will help you gain a more realistic

view of sex. ENRICHING YOUR SEX LIFE, p.54, and BECOMING MORE RESPONSIVE, p.90, will also help you.

Low rating (0-4)
Besides consulting the questionnaires COMPATIBILITY, p. 112, and ARE YOU SEXUALLY SATISFIED?, p.116, which may identify problem areas in your relationship, you should see the problem chart UNFULFILLED EXPECTATIONS, p.32, since your low level of satisfaction may well be due in part to a fantasy view of sex. Part of your problem may also be that you have not learned how to ask for what you want. In this connection, IMPROVING YOUR SELF-ESTEEM, p.79, will help you. The next step is to improve the quality of your experience by studying ENRICHING YOUR SEX LIFE, p.54, and BECOMING MORE RESPONSIVE, p.90.

SENSUALITY

How important is bodily contact to you in a loving relationship?

For each question, circle the appropriate score. Compare your total score with the ratings following the questionnaire.

	YES	NO		YES	NO
1 Do you enjoy having your body caressed by your partner?	1	0	**6** If you cannot sleep or are feeling low does it help to be held by or to hold someone?	1	0
2 Do you enjoy caressing your partner?	1	0	**7** Does prolonged foreplay make you feel irritated or frustrated?	0	1
3 Do you find it hard to be physically demonstrative with people you like?	0	1	**8** Do you often initiate sex in order to enjoy being held?	1	0
4 Do you tend to touch people occasionally when you are talking with them?	1	0	**9** Do you often hug or kiss a lover simply to show affection, when you are not feeling like sex?	1	0
5 Given the choice, would you rather you and your partner slept in separate beds?	0	1	**10** Is it important to you to be held and caressed after making love?	1	0

WHAT YOU SHOULD DO

High rating (8-10)
Sensuality and physical closeness, both vital in making rewarding sexual relationships, come easily to you. ENRICHING YOUR SEX LIFE, p.54, will help you to make the most of your ability to give and receive affection.

Medium rating (5-7)
You have the capacity for enjoying physical intimacy but have not developed it fully. Study the exercises in GIVING YOURSELF PLEASURE, p.86, and BECOMING MORE RESPONSIVE, p.88.

Low rating (0-4)
A certain physical reserve may be causing a lack of warmth in your relationships. The problem chart NEGATIVE FEELINGS, p.30, and **Fear of intimacy**, p.77, may help you to understand why you avoid closeness. See also BECOMING MORE RESPONSIVE, p.90.

COMMUNICATION

How well can you communicate – both verbally and non-verbally – with your sexual partner?

For each question, circle the appropriate score. Compare your
total score with the ratings following the questionnaire.

	YES	NO		YES	NO
1 Do you ever ask your sexual partner if there is anything he particularly likes or dislikes when you make love?	1	0	**6** Are you comfortable about making the first move if you want sex?	1	0
2 Do you find it hard to tell your partner if he does something you particularly like or dislike during sex?	0	1	**7** If you had an erotic dream about your partner, could you describe it to him without feeling embarrassed?	1	0
3 Are you able to tell your partner you are not in the mood for sex without making him feel rejected?	1	0	**8** Would you be embarrassed to ask a new partner to wear a condom to reduce the risk of AIDS?	0	1
4 If you do not want to make love because your partner has hurt you, can you explain that it is impossible to feel in the mood for it when you are upset?	1	0	**9** Are you afraid to get angry or be critical of your partner because you believe that to do so would destroy the relationship?	0	1
5 Do you often fake orgasm rather than tell your partner he is not giving you the right kind of stimulation?	0	1	**10** When you do get angry, do your quarrels take a long time to resolve and leave you both feeling bitter?	0	1

WHAT YOU SHOULD DO

High rating (8-10)
You clearly communicate well with your partner, and are able to make your needs felt and to understand his. ENRICHING YOUR SEX LIFE, p.54, may help you to derive even more pleasure from your easy relationship.

Medium rating (5-7)
You probably find it hard to talk with your partner about sex without becoming embarrassed. Consequently, when sexual difficulties arise, your inhibition may lead you to ignore them, so that they become more entrenched. If this is the case for you, LEARNING TO COMMUNICATE, p.120, should help you.

Low rating (0-4)
Your sex life is almost certainly suffering because, like many women, you find it hard to ask your sexual partner for what you want. LEARNING TO COMMUNICATE, P.120, will be of assistance here, and you should also study **Learning to be more assertive,** p.81, which will help you to improve other areas of your life.

CONFIDENCE

How do you rate your sex appeal and ability as a lover?

For each question, circle the appropriate score. Compare your total score with the ratings following the questionnaire.

	YES	NO		YES	NO
1 At a party or in a group of people do you usually stay with the women because you are shy with men?	0	1	**6** Do you feel it is more important to please your partner than to make sure you have sexual satisfaction yourself?	0	1
2 Do you deliberately dress in an unprovocative way to avoid attracting male attention?	0	1	**7** When you do develop a close relationship do you continually demand reassurance that you are loved?	0	1
3 If you are single, would you take the initiative in getting to know, or even asking for a date, someone you were attracted to?	1	0	**8** Do you find it hard to believe that anyone can really love you?	0	1
4 If someone you do not know well, or do not much care for, makes a pass at you, can you deal with it without getting angry, upset, or embarrassed?	1	0	**9** Do you often get jealous or upset when your partner enjoys someone else's company?	0	1
5 Do you regard yourself as sexually attractive?	1	0	**10** Do you feel quite comfortable and relaxed about being seen naked by your sexual partner?	1	0

WHAT YOU SHOULD DO

High rating (8-10)

You are very confident in your sexual relationships. However, if your partner's confidence, or that of the men you meet, does not match up to your own, you may encounter difficulties. If you cannot usually resolve these, you need a man who is as self-assured as you are or at least one who does not cling to the traditional role of male dominance.

Medium rating (5-7)

Your slight lack of confidence may make you shy and may even give others the impression that you are unfriendly. If you think this is the case, consult the problem chart LOW SELF-ESTEEM, p.34, which will direct you to helpful features.

Low rating (0-4)

A poor self-image may be hampering you. Consult the problem chart LOW SELF-ESTEEM, p.34. If jealousy is a particular problem for you, see JEALOUSY, p.134. But if your diffidence is so severe that you never or rarely form a relationship, see the problem chart DIFFICULTY IN FINDING A PARTNER, p.144.

TECHNIQUE

How capable are you of arousing and satisfying a partner?

For each question, circle the appropriate score. Compare your total score with the ratings following the questionnaire.

	YES	NO		YES	NO
1 Do you know which are your partner's 'erogenous zones' – the parts of his body which he particularly likes to be touched?	1	0	**6** Do you ever take the sexual initiative and make love to your partner?	1	0
2 Do you caress your partner?	1	0	**7** Are you skilled in masturbating your partner to orgasm?	1	0
3 Do you know how to tighten your vaginal muscles around your partner's penis?	1	0	**8** Do you use your tongue and mouth to stimulate your partner's penis or bring him to orgasm?	1	0
4 If your partner is tired, or not feeling as sexually excited as you, can you usually arouse him?	1	0	**9** Do you get upset or angry about your partner's problems – if he cannot get an erection or loses it, for example?	0	1
5 Do you often fake orgasm?	0	1	**10** Do you feel that you convey your enjoyment of sex to your partner?	1	0

WHAT YOU SHOULD DO

High rating (8-10)
You are clearly a competent sexual partner. But lovemaking is a complex skill. Therefore, if your scores for the questionnaires SENSUALITY, p.18, and COMMUNICATION, p.19, are considerably lower than your score here, you probably need to develop your ability to make your partner feel emotionally, as well as physically, fulfilled. Follow the advice given in the ratings guides.

Medium rating (5-7)
You may well have inhibitions that are diminishing your ability as a lover. Consult the problem chart NEGATIVE FEELINGS, p.30, to establish if this is so. It may be, though, that your real problem is simply inexperience. The problem chart UNFULFILLED EXPECTATIONS, p.32, will direct you to helpful features.

Low rating (0-4)
Do not be discouraged by your low score. Sexual technique can be learned and it is never too late. Examine your feelings about sex by studying the problem charts NEGATIVE FEELINGS, p.30, and UNFULFILLED EXPECTATIONS, p.32. However, if your problems seem predominantly a matter of competence as a lover rather than of attitude, you should turn to STIMULATION TECHNIQUES, p.57, SEXUAL POSITIONS, p.63, and BECOMING, MORE RESPONSIVE, p.90.

BROADMINDEDNESS

How tolerant of sexual freedom and experimentation are you?

For each question, circle the appropriate score. Compare your total score with the ratings following the questionnaire.

	YES	NO		YES	NO
1 Do you always make love in the dark?	0	1	**6** Do erotic episodes in movies or books usually make you feel embarrassed or uncomfortable?	0	1
2 Do you have oral sex with your partner, or would you like to?	1	0	**7** Does the idea of having intercourse during your period seem distasteful?	0	1
3 Do you enjoy trying new positions for intercourse?	1	0	**8** Would you think less of a friend if you discovered that she was a lesbian?	0	1
4 Have you ever suggested to your partner an unfamiliar sexual activity that you heard of or read about?	1	0	**9** Would you agree to it if your partner suggested anal intercourse?	1	0
5 Do you sometimes masturbate simply because you enjoy it, without thinking of it as a substitute for sex with a partner?	1	0	**10** Would you try partner-swapping if invited to?	1	0

WHAT YOU SHOULD DO

High rating (8-10)

You have a very tolerant attitude to sexual self-expression. However, are you quite sure your interest in novelty does not conceal a degree of boredom with your present sex life? If your rating for the questionnaire SATISFACTION, p.17, is not equally high, turn to the problem chart UNFUL-FILLED EXPECTATIONS, p.32, which suggests possible reasons for dissatisfaction and features which will help you remedy it. If you answered "Yes" to questions nine or ten you might be a little more cautious in your approach to sex. Both of these are 'high risk' activities as far as AIDS is concerned. The use of a condom and spermicide can reduce the dangers, but the safest sexual relationships are those in which neither partner has any other sexual contacts. Resist pressure to be 'broadminded' if it involves doing anything you feel is dangerous or anything that simply does not appeal to you.

Medium rating (5-7)

You are probably reasonably happy with your cautious outlook on sex. However, if you find you have lost some of your enthusiasm, turn to the problem chart LACK OF INTEREST, p.23. Perhaps you have never found sex as exciting as you would like it to be, in which case the problem chart UNFULFILLED EXPECTATIONS, p.32, may help you.

Low rating (0-4)

Your low score suggests that you are rather prudish about sex, and perhaps even find it sinful or shameful. The problem chart NEGATIVE FEEL-INGS, p.30, examines common misgivings about sex and will help you develop an outlook that does not limit your sexual happiness so severely.

ORIENTATION

Are your sexual inclinations heterosexual, homosexual, or somewhere between the two?

Read through the statements and choose the one that most accurately describes you.
If you have no sexual experience, try to imagine what your inclinations might be.

	RATING		RATING
I am sexually aroused only by, and have sex only with, men.	A	I have sex with both men and women, but my fantasies are more often about women.	E
I am sexually aroused by men, but have occasional fantasies of sex with women.	B	I prefer women and have little interest in men as sexual partners.	F
I prefer sex with men, but have occasional lesbian encounters.	C	I am sexually aroused only by, and have sex only with, women.	G
I am equally aroused by men and women and enjoy sex with both.	D		

WHAT YOU SHOULD DO

Your choice among the above statements gives you a rating on a scale of sexual orientation adapted from the one devised by the sexologist Alfred Kinsey. To check your rating, turn to the key on p.164. The ratings are not value judgments; if you are comfortable with your orientation, you need do nothing about it. But if you find it hard to reconcile your sexual inclinations with other areas of your life, study the problem chart HETEROSEXUALITY/HOMOSEXUALITY CONFLICTS, p.50.

KEY TO SEXUAL KNOWLEDGE QUESTIONNAIRE (p.14)

TRUE: Questions 2, 3, 4, 5, 6, 8, 12, 17, 18
FALSE: Questions 1, 7, 9, 10, 11, 13, 14, 15, 16, 19, 20

THE SEXUAL PROFILE CHART

Using the blank chart on p.162 (or a photocopy), indicate your score for each of the questionnaires by marking the appropriate point on the rating scale. Join the points to create your sexual profile.

Your rating for sexual satisfaction is the touchstone of this exercise. What you will probably find is that alongside factors that contribute to your satisfaction there are others that are clearly limiting it.

Your scores for the four questionnaires on the right-hand side of the chart – **Psychological well-being**, **Confidence**, **Broadmindedness**, and **Sex drive** – reflect your fundamental attitudes to sex. High scores here indicate that you are sexually confident, while low scores suggest that you are perhaps inhibited in this area or have little interest in sex. (These factors are often linked, since a consistent lack of enthusiasm can conceal powerful inhibitions.) The questionnaires on the left-hand side of the chart – **Sensuality**, **Communication**, **Technique**, and **Sexual knowledge** – deal with those aspects of your sexual identity that are likely to affect your ability to be close to a partner and determine the degree of your sexual competence.

Low scores in any part of your profile chart indicate problems, and advice is given in the ratings guides following the questionnaires. A serious imbalance in your scores is also a cause for concern. For example, it is possible to enjoy high confidence which conceals from you a poor grasp of sexual technique or an inability to understand another person's feelings.

It is possible for you to score low in one area without your being aware of the need – or simply the scope – for improvement in another. In this connection, it is particularly important to realize that while you may score low on the right-hand side and nevertheless feel sexually satisfied, your partner may remain unfulfilled. Accordingly, a lack of sexual confidence or a narrow-minded outlook may well underlie an inability to express warmth to your partner or may create difficulties in the practical aspects of lovemaking. Such problems will be reflected in low scores in the relevant areas on the left of the chart.

In a similar way you may be untroubled by a low score in an area on the left that is less important to you than to your partner. You may, for example, score low for technique or sensuality since, being brought up to believe that the man is always the active partner, many women do not realize how much their own understanding of a man's sexuality can enhance sex for both partners.

SAMPLE PROFILE CHARTS

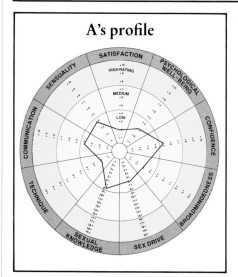

A's profile

It is not surprising that *A* gains little satisfaction from sex. She was raised in a family where the subject was rarely mentioned, and never openly discussed. *A*'s sex life has never been active, but she has always told herself that it is because she is not interested. However, the ratings on the right of her profile show that there is more wrong than simply a lack of interest. Her low scores for broadmindedness and psychological well-being suggest that her outlook on sex is so negative that it suppresses her natural desires and almost certainly impedes any sexual relationships she tries to make. The low scores on the 'activity' side of her profile suggest that she brings little enthusiasm to love-making.

The problem charts LACK OF INTEREST, p.28, NEGATIVE FEELINGS, p.30, and LACK OF AROUSAL, p.36, should help *A* to discover whether her sex drive is naturally low or whether she is burying feelings that she finds frightening or unacceptable. The features recommended in the charts will help her develop her sexuality, or at least find ways of bridging the sex-drive gap that has so often caused problems.

B's profile

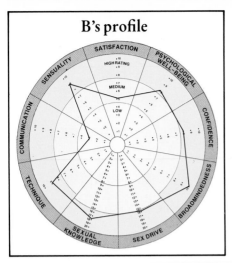

The right-hand side of *B*'s profile shows that she has a strong sex drive, and there is little evidence of problems, while on the left-hand side her ratings indicate that she is a sensual and skillful lover. And yet her satisfaction rating is puzzlingly low.

The only clue is a poor rating for communication. In fact *B* has never had an orgasm during intercourse, but, being of a romantic nature, with a 'moonlight and roses' view of sex, she cannot bring herself to discuss the problem and try to resolve it with her partner. Instead, she repeatedly resorts to affairs in an attempt to find the magic touch that will help her achieve orgasm.

Clearly, sex has never matched *B*'s fantasy view of it, but the problem charts UNFULFILLED EXPECTATIONS, p.32, and FAILURE TO REACH ORGASM, p.40, will help her to gain a more realistic attitude and to tackle her immediate problem. But she will also need to improve her ability to communicate if she is to achieve any real sexual rapport with her partner. LEARNING TO COMMUNICATE, p.120, will help her to do so.

C's profile

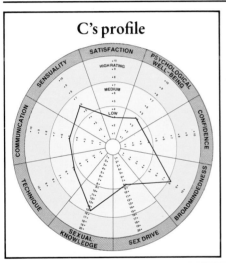

C is married, with two children. Her satisfaction rating is poor, and she believes this is because her sex drive is low so that she meets continual pressure from her husband. Although *C* is reasonably broadminded the other ratings on the right-hand or 'attitude' side are low, suggesting ambivalence about her own sexuality. *C* has always had close emotional relationships with other women and, since being married, she has become aware – reluctantly – that sexually she is drawn to women rather than to men.

The problem chart HETEROSEXUALITY / HOMO-SEXUALITY CONFLICTS, p.50, and the feature LESBIAN-ISM, p.107, will help *C* to fully acknowledge her feelings. But, if she decides that she wants to try to make a success of her marriage, she will need to reach a compromise with her husband that takes account of their very different approaches to sex. ENRICHING YOUR SEX LIFE, p.54, may help *C* and her partner to establish a relationship that does not rely so heavily on intercourse for sexual satisfaction.

D's profile

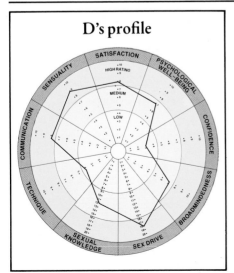

D is just beginning her first sexual relationship. She is a quiet girl whose natural reserve has led her to have very few boyfriends and to be a late starter in sex. To her surprise, she enjoys sex greatly and rates her satisfaction as high. However, she is obviously inexperienced, as her scores for sexual knowledge and technique – medium and low, respectively – indicate.

But the fact that the other ratings on the left-hand or 'activity' side of her profile are high and that the right-hand side shows a positive and enthusiastic attitude to sex suggests that, although *D* currently lacks confidence, she is likely to be able to make a success of her future sexual relationships.

D's profile should reassure her that she has good prospects for sexual happiness and no reason to continue feeling unsure of herself. The features UNDERSTANDING A MAN'S FEEL-INGS, p.124, and ENRICHING YOUR SEX LIFE, p.54, will help to give her the sexual expertise she lacks, while the problem chart LOW SELF-ESTEEM, p. 34, will help her understand the reasons for her rather poor self-image and gain greater confidence.

PROBLEM CHARTS

Each of the following self-diagnostic problem charts will help you track down the reasons for a particular kind of sexual difficulty and offer you advice on resolving it. By means of a logically constructed network of questions to be answered either with a YES or a NO, the charts will lead you to conclusions based on authoritative research and expert opinion. Always begin at the first question and follow through to the correct endpoint for your special set of circumstances. The endpoint that you reach will either provide brief advice or, more often, refer you to other parts of the book where the problem is discussed in greater detail and self-help programs are given. Follow up cross-references in every case, so as not to miss further advice. In a few instances you will be advised to make use of a related problem chart or, occasionally, to seek professional help.

LACK OF INTEREST

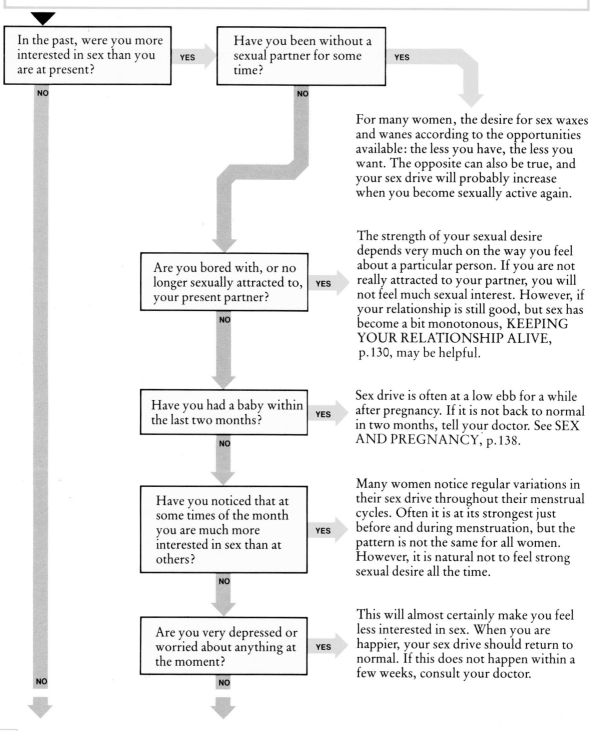

In the past, were you more interested in sex than you are at present?

YES → Have you been without a sexual partner for some time?

YES → For many women, the desire for sex waxes and wanes according to the opportunities available: the less you have, the less you want. The opposite can also be true, and your sex drive will probably increase when you become sexually active again.

NO →

Are you bored with, or no longer sexually attracted to, your present partner?

YES → The strength of your sexual desire depends very much on the way you feel about a particular person. If you are not really attracted to your partner, you will not feel much sexual interest. However, if your relationship is still good, but sex has become a bit monotonous, KEEPING YOUR RELATIONSHIP ALIVE, p.130, may be helpful.

NO →

Have you had a baby within the last two months?

YES → Sex drive is often at a low ebb for a while after pregnancy. If it is not back to normal in two months, tell your doctor. See SEX AND PREGNANCY, p.138.

NO →

Have you noticed that at some times of the month you are much more interested in sex than at others?

YES → Many women notice regular variations in their sex drive throughout their menstrual cycles. Often it is at its strongest just before and during menstruation, but the pattern is not the same for all women. However, it is natural not to feel strong sexual desire all the time.

NO →

Are you very depressed or worried about anything at the moment?

YES → This will almost certainly make you feel less interested in sex. When you are happier, your sex drive should return to normal. If this does not happen within a few weeks, consult your doctor.

NO →

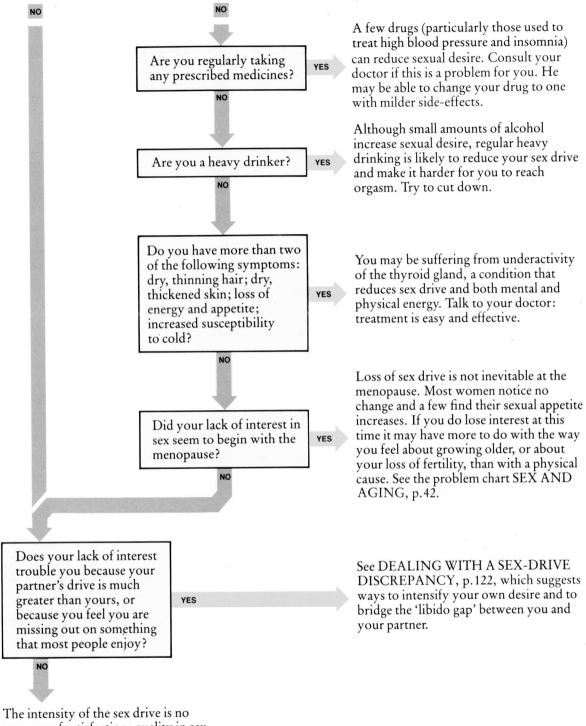

Are you regularly taking any prescribed medicines? — YES → A few drugs (particularly those used to treat high blood pressure and insomnia) can reduce sexual desire. Consult your doctor if this is a problem for you. He may be able to change your drug to one with milder side-effects.

NO

Are you a heavy drinker? — YES → Although small amounts of alcohol increase sexual desire, regular heavy drinking is likely to reduce your sex drive and make it harder for you to reach orgasm. Try to cut down.

NO

Do you have more than two of the following symptoms: dry, thinning hair; dry, thickened skin; loss of energy and appetite; increased susceptibility to cold? — YES → You may be suffering from underactivity of the thyroid gland, a condition that reduces sex drive and both mental and physical energy. Talk to your doctor: treatment is easy and effective.

NO

Did your lack of interest in sex seem to begin with the menopause? — YES → Loss of sex drive is not inevitable at the menopause. Most women notice no change and a few find their sexual appetite increases. If you do lose interest at this time it may have more to do with the way you feel about growing older, or about your loss of fertility, than with a physical cause. See the problem chart SEX AND AGING, p.42.

NO

Does your lack of interest trouble you because your partner's drive is much greater than yours, or because you feel you are missing out on something that most people enjoy? — YES → See DEALING WITH A SEX-DRIVE DISCREPANCY, p.122, which suggests ways to intensify your own desire and to bridge the 'libido gap' between you and your partner.

NO

The intensity of the sex drive is no measure of satisfaction: quality in sex matters much more than quantity. Everyone has different needs, but if your needs are met, and you meet your partner's, then your sex life is good.

NEGATIVE FEELINGS

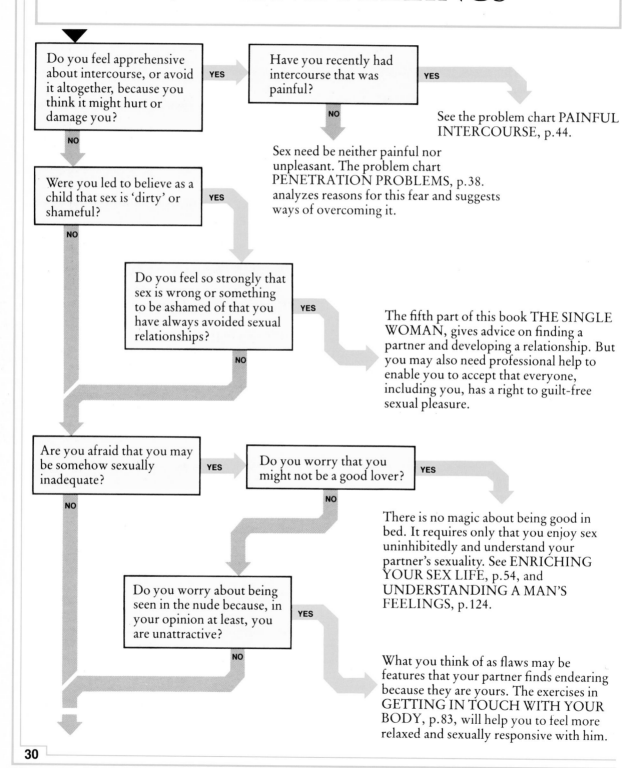

Do you feel apprehensive about intercourse, or avoid it altogether, because you think it might hurt or damage you?

YES →

Have you recently had intercourse that was painful?

YES →

See the problem chart PAINFUL INTERCOURSE, p.44.

NO ↓

Sex need be neither painful nor unpleasant. The problem chart PENETRATION PROBLEMS, p.38. analyzes reasons for this fear and suggests ways of overcoming it.

NO ↓

Were you led to believe as a child that sex is 'dirty' or shameful?

YES →

Do you feel so strongly that sex is wrong or something to be ashamed of that you have always avoided sexual relationships?

YES →

The fifth part of this book THE SINGLE WOMAN, gives advice on finding a partner and developing a relationship. But you may also need professional help to enable you to accept that everyone, including you, has a right to guilt-free sexual pleasure.

NO ↓

NO ↓

Are you afraid that you may be somehow sexually inadequate?

YES →

Do you worry that you might not be a good lover?

YES →

There is no magic about being good in bed. It requires only that you enjoy sex uninhibitedly and understand your partner's sexuality. See ENRICHING YOUR SEX LIFE, p.54, and UNDERSTANDING A MAN'S FEELINGS, p.124.

NO ↓

NO ↓

Do you worry about being seen in the nude because, in your opinion at least, you are unattractive?

YES →

What you think of as flaws may be features that your partner finds endearing because they are yours. The exercises in GETTING IN TOUCH WITH YOUR BODY, p.83, will help you to feel more relaxed and sexually responsive with him.

NO ↓

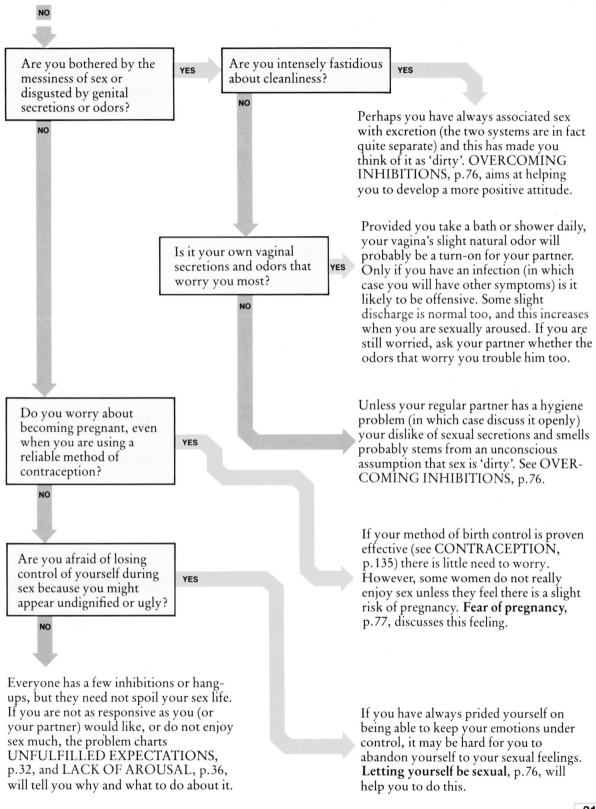

NO

Are you bothered by the messiness of sex or disgusted by genital secretions or odors?

YES →

Are you intensely fastidious about cleanliness?

YES →

NO ↓

Perhaps you have always associated sex with excretion (the two systems are in fact quite separate) and this has made you think of it as 'dirty'. OVERCOMING INHIBITIONS, p.76, aims at helping you to develop a more positive attitude.

Is it your own vaginal secretions and odors that worry you most?

YES →

Provided you take a bath or shower daily, your vagina's slight natural odor will probably be a turn-on for your partner. Only if you have an infection (in which case you will have other symptoms) is it likely to be offensive. Some slight discharge is normal too, and this increases when you are sexually aroused. If you are still worried, ask your partner whether the odors that worry you trouble him too.

NO ↓

Do you worry about becoming pregnant, even when you are using a reliable method of contraception?

YES →

Unless your regular partner has a hygiene problem (in which case discuss it openly) your dislike of sexual secretions and smells probably stems from an unconscious assumption that sex is 'dirty'. See OVER-COMING INHIBITIONS, p.76.

NO ↓

Are you afraid of losing control of yourself during sex because you might appear undignified or ugly?

YES →

If your method of birth control is proven effective (see CONTRACEPTION, p.135) there is little need to worry. However, some women do not really enjoy sex unless they feel there is a slight risk of pregnancy. **Fear of pregnancy**, p.77, discusses this feeling.

NO ↓

Everyone has a few inhibitions or hang-ups, but they need not spoil your sex life. If you are not as responsive as you (or your partner) would like, or do not enjoy sex much, the problem charts UNFULFILLED EXPECTATIONS, p.32, and LACK OF AROUSAL, p.36, will tell you why and what to do about it.

If you have always prided yourself on being able to keep your emotions under control, it may be hard for you to abandon yourself to your sexual feelings. **Letting yourself be sexual**, p.76, will help you to do this.

WOMEN ♀ **2** PROBLEM CHARTS

UNFULFILLED EXPECTATIONS

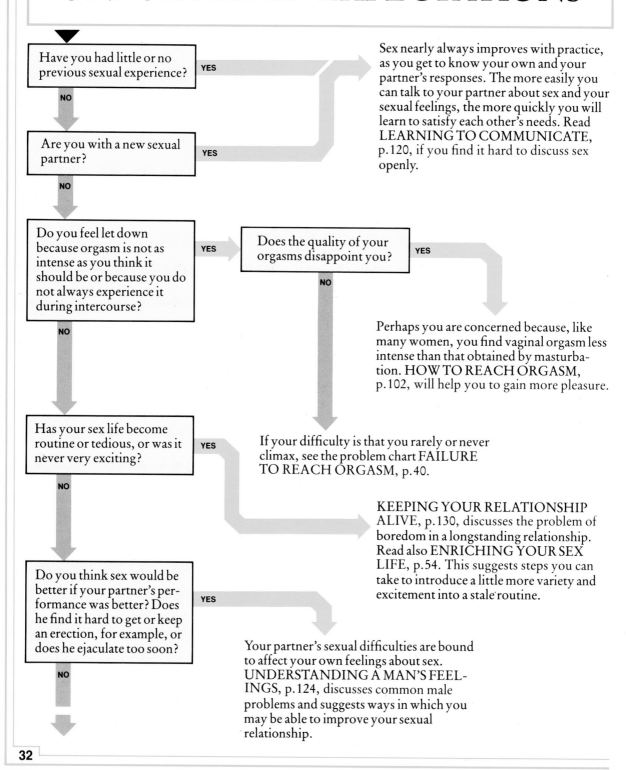

Have you had little or no previous sexual experience?   YES

Sex nearly always improves with practice, as you get to know your own and your partner's responses. The more easily you can talk to your partner about sex and your sexual feelings, the more quickly you will learn to satisfy each other's needs. Read LEARNING TO COMMUNICATE, p.120, if you find it hard to discuss sex openly.

NO

Are you with a new sexual partner?   YES

NO

Do you feel let down because orgasm is not as intense as you think it should be or because you do not always experience it during intercourse?   YES

Does the quality of your orgasms disappoint you?   YES

NO

Perhaps you are concerned because, like many women, you find vaginal orgasm less intense than that obtained by masturbation. HOW TO REACH ORGASM, p.102, will help you to gain more pleasure.

NO

Has your sex life become routine or tedious, or was it never very exciting?   YES

If your difficulty is that you rarely or never climax, see the problem chart FAILURE TO REACH ORGASM, p.40.

NO

KEEPING YOUR RELATIONSHIP ALIVE, p.130, discusses the problem of boredom in a longstanding relationship. Read also ENRICHING YOUR SEX LIFE, p.54. This suggests steps you can take to introduce a little more variety and excitement into a stale routine.

Do you think sex would be better if your partner's performance was better? Does he find it hard to get or keep an erection, for example, or does he ejaculate too soon?   YES

Your partner's sexual difficulties are bound to affect your own feelings about sex. UNDERSTANDING A MAN'S FEELINGS, p.124, discusses common male problems and suggests ways in which you may be able to improve your sexual relationship.

NO

NO

Has intercourse always been less pleasurable for you than the 'petting' of your first sexual encounters? **YES**

'Petting' and foreplay provide much of the physical intimacy that is, for many women, one of the most satisfying aspects of sex. If they are brief, and intercourse is over quickly, lovemaking may be disappointing. The answer is to take the lead in making sex more intimate and prolonged. See **Pleasuring each other**, p.91.

NO

Do you feel that your partner should know what pleases you sexually without your having to tell him? **YES**

This suggests that you are a romantic at heart, but in matters of sex it is safer to be a realist, taking steps to make things better rather than expecting them always to be perfect. LEARNING TO COMMUNICATE, p.120, will be helpful if you have always found it hard to talk about sex or to tell your partner what you enjoy or dislike about sex with him.

NO

Is your partner less caring, loving, and responsive than you would like? **YES**

For most women, the emotional side of a relationship is at least as important as the physical. **Fear of intimacy**, p.77, discusses the difficulties some women have in expressing feelings. It may help you develop a closeness in your relationship that will make it more fulfilling.

NO

Most women's enjoyment of sex is dependent on their feelings for their partner. If you are unsure about these, the chances are that sex together will be disappointing. Improving your relationship in other areas or dealing with problems that have been worrying you may be what is needed to make your sex life more fulfilling. The questionnaires COMPATIBILITY, p.112, and ARE YOU SEXUALLY SATISFIED?, p.116, will help you to do this.

LOW SELF-ESTEEM

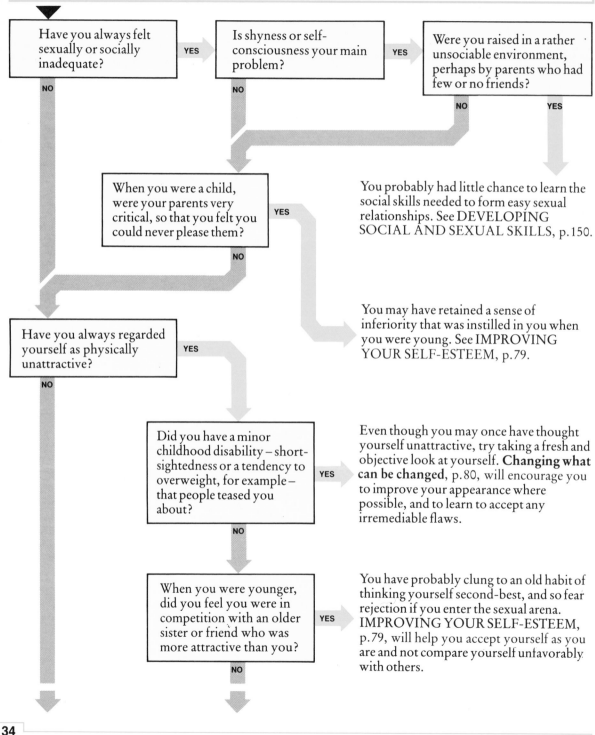

Have you always felt sexually or socially inadequate?

YES → Is shyness or self-consciousness your main problem?

YES → Were you raised in a rather unsociable environment, perhaps by parents who had few or no friends?

YES → You probably had little chance to learn the social skills needed to form easy sexual relationships. See DEVELOPING SOCIAL AND SEXUAL SKILLS, p.150.

When you were a child, were your parents very critical, so that you felt you could never please them?

YES → You may have retained a sense of inferiority that was instilled in you when you were young. See IMPROVING YOUR SELF-ESTEEM, p.79.

Have you always regarded yourself as physically unattractive?

YES → Did you have a minor childhood disability – short-sightedness or a tendency to overweight, for example – that people teased you about?

YES → Even though you may once have thought yourself unattractive, try taking a fresh and objective look at yourself. **Changing what can be changed**, p.80, will encourage you to improve your appearance where possible, and to learn to accept any irremediable flaws.

When you were younger, did you feel you were in competition with an older sister or friend who was more attractive than you?

YES → You have probably clung to an old habit of thinking yourself second-best, and so fear rejection if you enter the sexual arena. IMPROVING YOUR SELF-ESTEEM, p.79, will help you accept yourself as you are and not compare yourself unfavorably with others.

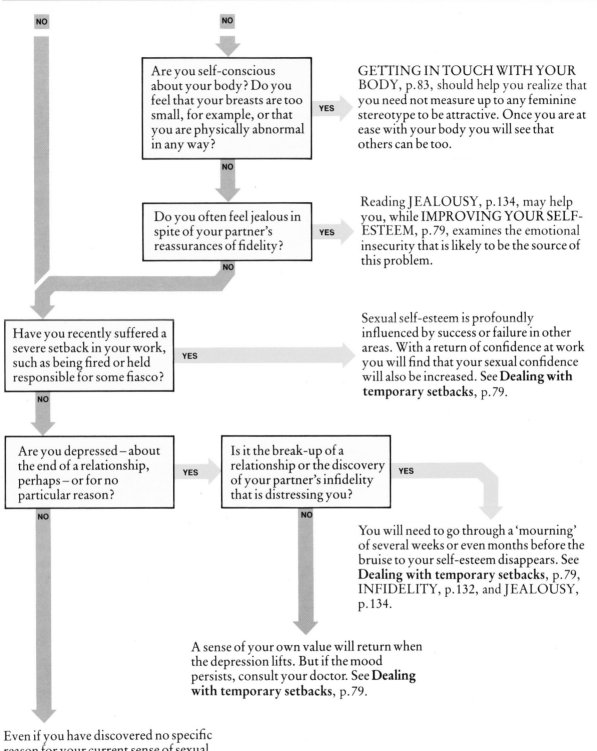

Are you self-conscious about your body? Do you feel that your breasts are too small, for example, or that you are physically abnormal in any way?

YES → GETTING IN TOUCH WITH YOUR BODY, p.83, should help you realize that you need not measure up to any feminine stereotype to be attractive. Once you are at ease with your body you will see that others can be too.

NO

Do you often feel jealous in spite of your partner's reassurances of fidelity?

YES → Reading JEALOUSY, p.134, may help you, while IMPROVING YOUR SELF-ESTEEM, p.79, examines the emotional insecurity that is likely to be the source of this problem.

NO

Have you recently suffered a severe setback in your work, such as being fired or held responsible for some fiasco?

YES → Sexual self-esteem is profoundly influenced by success or failure in other areas. With a return of confidence at work you will find that your sexual confidence will also be increased. See **Dealing with temporary setbacks**, p.79.

NO

Are you depressed – about the end of a relationship, perhaps – or for no particular reason?

YES → Is it the break-up of a relationship or the discovery of your partner's infidelity that is distressing you?

YES → You will need to go through a 'mourning' of several weeks or even months before the bruise to your self-esteem disappears. See **Dealing with temporary setbacks**, p.79, INFIDELITY, p.132, and JEALOUSY, p.134.

NO

NO

A sense of your own value will return when the depression lifts. But if the mood persists, consult your doctor. See **Dealing with temporary setbacks**, p.79.

Even if you have discovered no specific reason for your current sense of sexual inadequacy, you may find that IMPROVING YOUR SELF-ESTEEM, p.79, will help to restore your confidence.

WOMEN ♀ 2 PROBLEM CHARTS

LACK OF AROUSAL

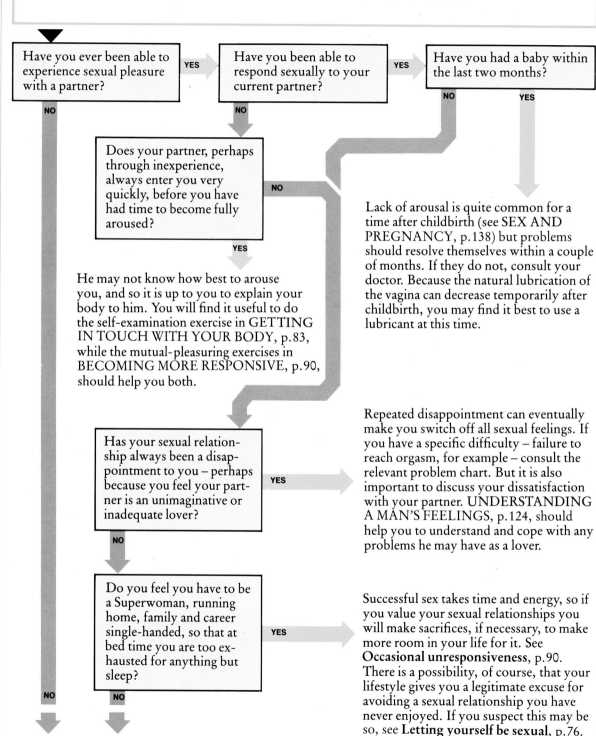

Have you ever been able to experience sexual pleasure with a partner?

YES → Have you been able to respond sexually to your current partner?

YES → Have you had a baby within the last two months?

Does your partner, perhaps through inexperience, always enter you very quickly, before you have had time to become fully aroused?

Lack of arousal is quite common for a time after childbirth (see SEX AND PREGNANCY, p.138) but problems should resolve themselves within a couple of months. If they do not, consult your doctor. Because the natural lubrication of the vagina can decrease temporarily after childbirth, you may find it best to use a lubricant at this time.

He may not know how best to arouse you, and so it is up to you to explain your body to him. You will find it useful to do the self-examination exercise in GETTING IN TOUCH WITH YOUR BODY, p.83, while the mutual-pleasuring exercises in BECOMING MORE RESPONSIVE, p.90, should help you both.

Has your sexual relationship always been a disappointment to you – perhaps because you feel your partner is an unimaginative or inadequate lover?

YES → Repeated disappointment can eventually make you switch off all sexual feelings. If you have a specific difficulty – failure to reach orgasm, for example – consult the relevant problem chart. But it is also important to discuss your dissatisfaction with your partner. UNDERSTANDING A MAN'S FEELINGS, p.124, should help you to understand and cope with any problems he may have as a lover.

Do you feel you have to be a Superwoman, running home, family and career single-handed, so that at bed time you are too exhausted for anything but sleep?

YES → Successful sex takes time and energy, so if you value your sexual relationships you will make sacrifices, if necessary, to make more room in your life for it. See **Occasional unresponsiveness**, p.90. There is a possibility, of course, that your lifestyle gives you a legitimate excuse for avoiding a sexual relationship you have never enjoyed. If you suspect this may be so, see **Letting yourself be sexual**, p.76.

Does your sexual mood vary, so that at some times you are far less easily aroused than at others?

YES →

Many women find that they are less easily aroused at a particular stage – often in the middle – of their menstrual cycle. Fatigue, stress, depression, and certain drugs will also temporarily reduce your own responsiveness. Consult your doctor about the possible side-effects of drugs you are taking.

NO

Boredom with a long-term relationship may be your problem. If so, see KEEPING YOUR RELATIONSHIP ALIVE, p.130. But for most women a failure to become aroused by a particular partner is a sign that they do not feel emotionally close enough. Unresolved anger or resentment against your partner may have made you switch off sexually. The questionnaire COMPATIBILITY, p.112, may show you where there is room for improvement in your relationship.

This suggests that you feel guilty about sex, although less so if you can convince yourself that it is a duty and not a pleasure. An excessive desire to please indicates that you are also insecure in your relationship with men. The exercises in GIVING YOURSELF PLEASURE, p.86, should help you begin to derive guilt-free enjoyment of sex. Then study **Letting yourself be sexual**, p.76. Finally, IMPROVING YOUR SELF-ESTEEM, p.79, will consolidate these benefits by teaching you how to be more self-assured in the area of sex and, in particular, to accept that you have a right to pleasure.

When you make love, do you tend to think exclusively of what will please your partner rather than trying to satisfy your own sexual needs?

YES

NO

Were you brought up to feel guilty or ashamed about your body or about sex?

YES →

Before you can be truly responsive to your partner, you will need to come round to the opposite view of sex: that it is a source of pleasure and a way of forming the closest of bonds between two people in a loving relationship. The self-examination exercises in GETTING IN TOUCH WITH YOUR BODY, p.83, and the mutual-pleasuring exercises in BECOMING MORE RESPONSIVE, p.90, are the first practical steps you should take . Study also OVERCOMING INHIBITIONS, p.76.

NO

Have you always been uninterested in sex?

YES

NO

Your main difficulty is probably lack of interest (see LACK OF INTEREST, p.28), rather than lack of arousal. This does not matter if your partner is not very interested in sex either, but, if his sex drive is much higher than yours, DEALING WITH A SEX-DRIVE DISCREPANCY, p.122, may help you.

If you have always been sexually unresponsive, you may need professional help to help you discover and dispel whatever is blocking your sexuality. Perhaps, for example, you are afraid of becoming too close to another person. See **Long-term unresponsiveness**, p.90.

PENETRATION PROBLEMS

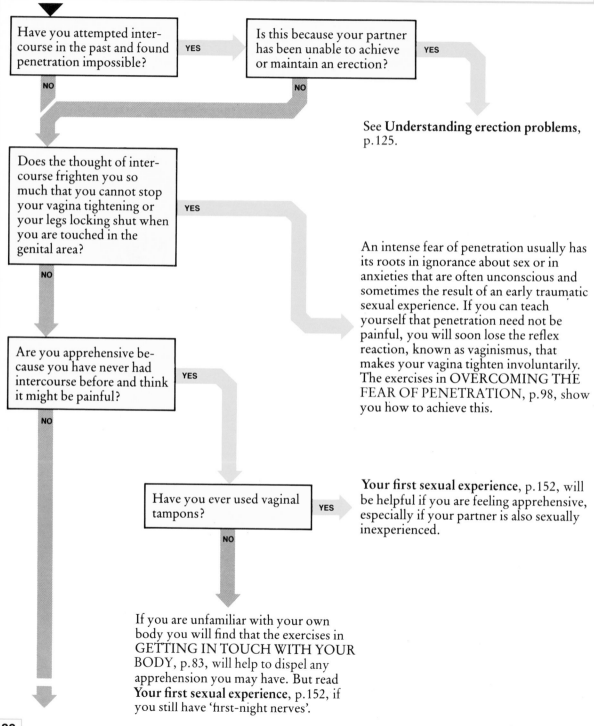

Have you attempted intercourse in the past and found penetration impossible?

YES →

Is this because your partner has been unable to achieve or maintain an erection?

YES →

NO ↓

NO ↓

See **Understanding erection problems**, p.125.

Does the thought of intercourse frighten you so much that you cannot stop your vagina tightening or your legs locking shut when you are touched in the genital area?

YES →

NO ↓

An intense fear of penetration usually has its roots in ignorance about sex or in anxieties that are often unconscious and sometimes the result of an early traumatic sexual experience. If you can teach yourself that penetration need not be painful, you will soon lose the reflex reaction, known as vaginismus, that makes your vagina tighten involuntarily. The exercises in OVERCOMING THE FEAR OF PENETRATION, p.98, show you how to achieve this.

Are you apprehensive because you have never had intercourse before and think it might be painful?

YES →

NO ↓

Have you ever used vaginal tampons?

YES →

NO ↓

Your first sexual experience, p.152, will be helpful if you are feeling apprehensive, especially if your partner is also sexually inexperienced.

If you are unfamiliar with your own body you will find that the exercises in GETTING IN TOUCH WITH YOUR BODY, p.83, will help to dispel any apprehension you may have. But read **Your first sexual experience**, p.152, if you still have 'first-night nerves'.

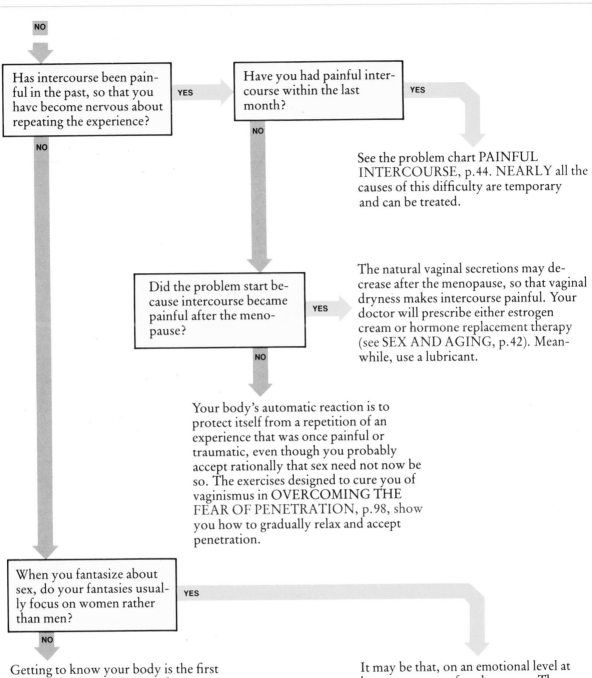

NO

Has intercourse been painful in the past, so that you have become nervous about repeating the experience?

Have you had painful intercourse within the last month?

YES

YES

NO

See the problem chart PAINFUL INTERCOURSE, p.44. NEARLY all the causes of this difficulty are temporary and can be treated.

Did the problem start because intercourse became painful after the menopause?

YES

The natural vaginal secretions may decrease after the menopause, so that vaginal dryness makes intercourse painful. Your doctor will prescribe either estrogen cream or hormone replacement therapy (see SEX AND AGING, p.42). Meanwhile, use a lubricant.

NO

Your body's automatic reaction is to protect itself from a repetition of an experience that was once painful or traumatic, even though you probably accept rationally that sex need not now be so. The exercises designed to cure you of vaginismus in OVERCOMING THE FEAR OF PENETRATION, p.98, show you how to gradually relax and accept penetration.

When you fantasize about sex, do your fantasies usually focus on women rather than men?

YES

NO

Getting to know your body is the first step toward eliminating any fears you may have about sex. Do the exercises in GETTING IN TOUCH WITH YOUR BODY, p.83, and study OVERCOMING THE FEAR OF PENETRATION, p.98. These will confirm that you are physically normal and that there is no reason why sex should be either painful or unpleasant.

It may be that, on an emotional level at least, you want a female partner. The questionnaire ORIENTATION, p.23, and the feature LESBIANISM, p.107, will help you decide where your true sexual preferences lie.

WOMEN ♀ 2 PROBLEM CHARTS

FAILURE TO REACH ORGASM

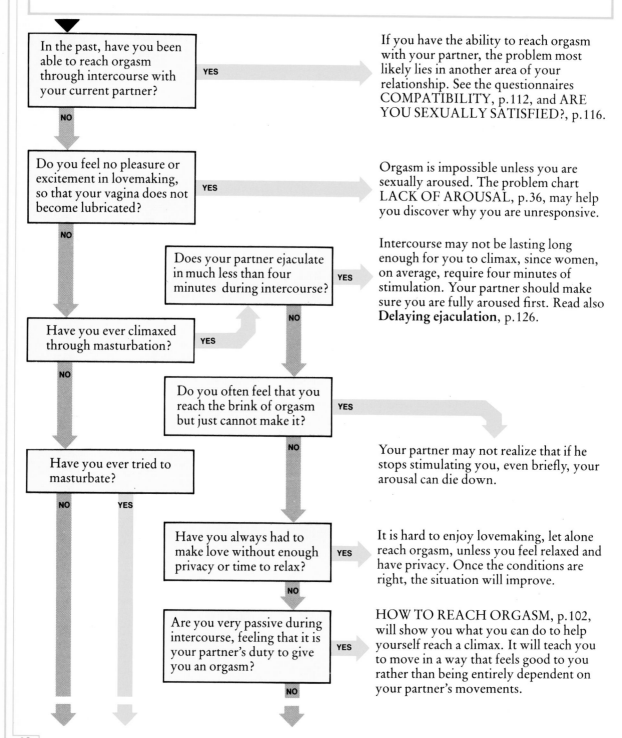

In the past, have you been able to reach orgasm through intercourse with your current partner? YES →

If you have the ability to reach orgasm with your partner, the problem most likely lies in another area of your relationship. See the questionnaires COMPATIBILITY, p.112, and ARE YOU SEXUALLY SATISFIED?, p.116.

NO ↓

Do you feel no pleasure or excitement in lovemaking, so that your vagina does not become lubricated? YES →

Orgasm is impossible unless you are sexually aroused. The problem chart LACK OF AROUSAL, p.36, may help you discover why you are unresponsive.

NO ↓

Does your partner ejaculate in much less than four minutes during intercourse? YES →

Intercourse may not be lasting long enough for you to climax, since women, on average, require four minutes of stimulation. Your partner should make sure you are fully aroused first. Read also **Delaying ejaculation**, p.126.

NO ↓

Have you ever climaxed through masturbation? YES →

Do you often feel that you reach the brink of orgasm but just cannot make it? YES →

NO ↓

Have you ever tried to masturbate?

NO   YES

Your partner may not realize that if he stops stimulating you, even briefly, your arousal can die down.

Have you always had to make love without enough privacy or time to relax? YES →

It is hard to enjoy lovemaking, let alone reach orgasm, unless you feel relaxed and have privacy. Once the conditions are right, the situation will improve.

NO ↓

Are you very passive during intercourse, feeling that it is your partner's duty to give you an orgasm? YES →

HOW TO REACH ORGASM, p.102, will show you what you can do to help yourself reach a climax. It will teach you to move in a way that feels good to you rather than being entirely dependent on your partner's movements.

NO ↓

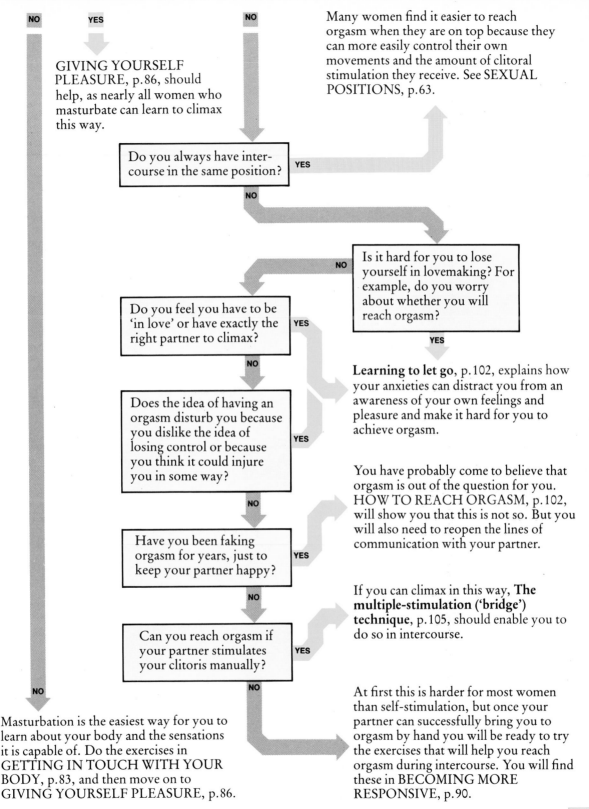

NO   **YES**   **NO**

GIVING YOURSELF PLEASURE, p.86, should help, as nearly all women who masturbate can learn to climax this way.

Many women find it easier to reach orgasm when they are on top because they can more easily control their own movements and the amount of clitoral stimulation they receive. See SEXUAL POSITIONS, p.63.

Do you always have intercourse in the same position?   **YES**

NO

Is it hard for you to lose yourself in lovemaking? For example, do you worry about whether you will reach orgasm?   **NO**

Do you feel you have to be 'in love' or have exactly the right partner to climax?   **YES**

YES

Learning to let go, p.102, explains how your anxieties can distract you from an awareness of your own feelings and pleasure and make it hard for you to achieve orgasm.

NO

Does the idea of having an orgasm disturb you because you dislike the idea of losing control or because you think it could injure you in some way?   **YES**

You have probably come to believe that orgasm is out of the question for you. HOW TO REACH ORGASM, p.102, will show you that this is not so. But you will also need to reopen the lines of communication with your partner.

NO

Have you been faking orgasm for years, just to keep your partner happy?   **YES**

If you can climax in this way, The multiple-stimulation ('bridge') technique, p.105, should enable you to do so in intercourse.

NO

Can you reach orgasm if your partner stimulates your clitoris manually?   **YES**

NO   **NO**

Masturbation is the easiest way for you to learn about your body and the sensations it is capable of. Do the exercises in GETTING IN TOUCH WITH YOUR BODY, p.83, and then move on to GIVING YOURSELF PLEASURE, p.86.

At first this is harder for most women than self-stimulation, but once your partner can successfully bring you to orgasm by hand you will be ready to try the exercises that will help you reach orgasm during intercourse. You will find these in BECOMING MORE RESPONSIVE, p.90.

SEX AND AGING

Do you have a partner?   YES

NO

Do you still have a good sex life together?   YES

NO

There is no reason for your sexual activity to cease, although your sex life may change a little as you grow older. There is a general slowing down, so that both you and your partner will take longer, and need more direct stimulation, to become aroused. Lovemaking is likely to become more leisurely and relaxed, with greater emphasis on the intimacy and comfort of a loving relationship and less on orgasm.

Is this because intercourse is sometimes painful?   YES

NO

Sometimes thinning of the vagina's lining and a decrease in its natural lubrication make intercourse painful. Your doctor may prescribe an estrogen cream or hormone replacement therapy (see below) to restore the vaginal lining, but a lubricant may be adequate. Sex itself helps to retard the effects of aging.

Is it because you have lost interest?   YES

NO

Age in itself does not usually bring about a serious loss of interest in sex (see the problem chart LACK OF INTEREST, p.28, for other causes). And while you and your partner may accept that your need for sex has diminished, remember that there is no physical bar to sex in old age and no reason for you to stop giving and receiving the affection which will help you remain close.

Is it because your partner seems no longer interested?   YES

NO

Sexual activity tends to decline more rapidly in men than in women. Often, though, a man's apparent loss of interest is based on worry about his performance. See **Men's fears about aging**, p.125.

The problem may be that you have not accepted that both you and your partner now take longer to become aroused and reach orgasm. If you can adjust to these changes, sex will once again be enjoyable.

NO

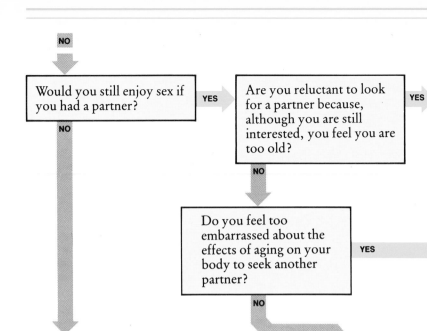

NO

Would you still enjoy sex if you had a partner?

YES

Are you reluctant to look for a partner because, although you are still interested, you feel you are too old?

YES

Do not be frightened of seeking a partner because you think you are too old, and still less because anybody else suggests that you might be. Age has little to do with sexuality, attitude, everything. As long as you think of yourself as sexual, you are, and sex can still form an important part of your life.

NO

NO

Do you feel too embarrassed about the effects of aging on your body to seek another partner?

YES

You need never feel too old for sex. However, if it has never played a large part in your life you will probably feel less and less sexual need as you grow older. Conversely, it is those who have always been sexually active who are likely to continue enjoying sex into old age.

Perhaps you never felt really good about your body when you were younger, and the way you feel now may reflect this. Try the exercises in GETTING IN TOUCH WITH YOUR BODY, p.83, and remember that faces age more quickly than bodies, so that an honest appraisal of your body may be reassuring. Unless you are seriously overweight, diet in moderation only, because your skin will have lost some of its elasticity.

NO

HORMONE REPLACEMENT THERAPY

If you have severe menopausal symptoms (hot flushes, night sweats and vaginal soreness) your doctor may suggest hormone replacement therapy. The treatment must be given under medical supervision and the hormones (estrogen and progestogen) can be given separately or combined in a pill, or as an implant beneath the skin, the effects of which last for about six months. Testosterone can be added to the implant for women who notice a loss of sex drive at the menopause. Besides effectively relieving menopausal symptoms, HRT has other health benefits. The estrogen gives protection against osteoporosis (a thinning of the bones which affects some postmenopausal women) and arterial disease, from which women rarely suffer before the menopause.

It is difficult, but certainly not impossible, for the older woman who wants to continue her sex life to find a partner. Your best plan is to concentrate on making friends and keeping up social contacts, since some of these may well provide lovers. But even if finding a partner proves difficult, do not try to stifle your sexual feelings. Masturbation will go some way to meeting your needs and will keep you in good sexual trim until you can have sex with a partner again.

WOMEN ♀ 2 PROBLEM CHARTS

43

PAINFUL INTERCOURSE

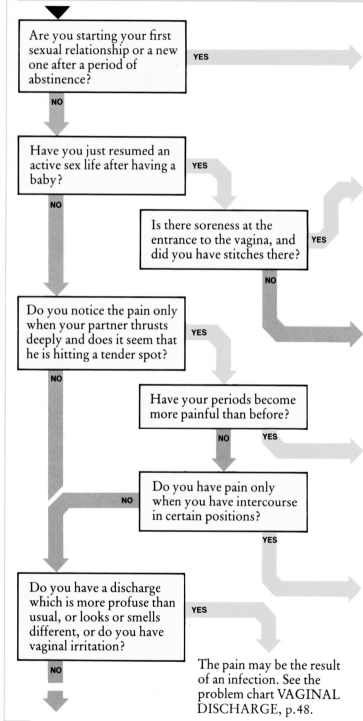

Are you starting your first sexual relationship or a new one after a period of abstinence?

YES → You may be slightly bruised or sore after the unaccustomed sexual activity. Give your body a few days to recover before you have intercourse again.

NO ↓

Have you just resumed an active sex life after having a baby?

YES ↓

NO ↓

Is there soreness at the entrance to the vagina, and did you have stitches there?

YES → Soreness after stitches persists for much longer than many doctors realize. If you still have pain after you have had your six-week check-up, ask your doctor whether healing is complete. Your natural vaginal lubrication will be less than usual for a while, especially if you are breast-feeding, and a lubricant will make intercourse more comfortable.

NO ↓

Do you notice the pain only when your partner thrusts deeply and does it seem that he is hitting a tender spot?

YES → Apprehension about resuming intercourse after childbirth is natural, but it may make you tense and lead to discomfort or pain. Your partner should apply a lubricant to his penis and enter you very gently and slowly.

NO ↓

Have your periods become more painful than before?

NO ↓   YES →

Several medical conditions – for example, endometriosis, fibroids, and pelvic inflammatory disease – can cause pain during intercourse. See SEX AND HEALTH, p.156.

Do you have pain only when you have intercourse in certain positions?

NO ←

YES → The pain may be caused by pressure on an ovary during intercourse, a condition which may arise if you have a retroverted (tipped back) uterus. A different position may solve the problem, but if it does not and the pain remains severe, your doctor may suggest an operation to adjust the position of your uterus.

Do you have a discharge which is more profuse than usual, or looks or smells different, or do you have vaginal irritation?

YES → The pain may be the result of an infection. See the problem chart VAGINAL DISCHARGE, p.48.

NO ↓

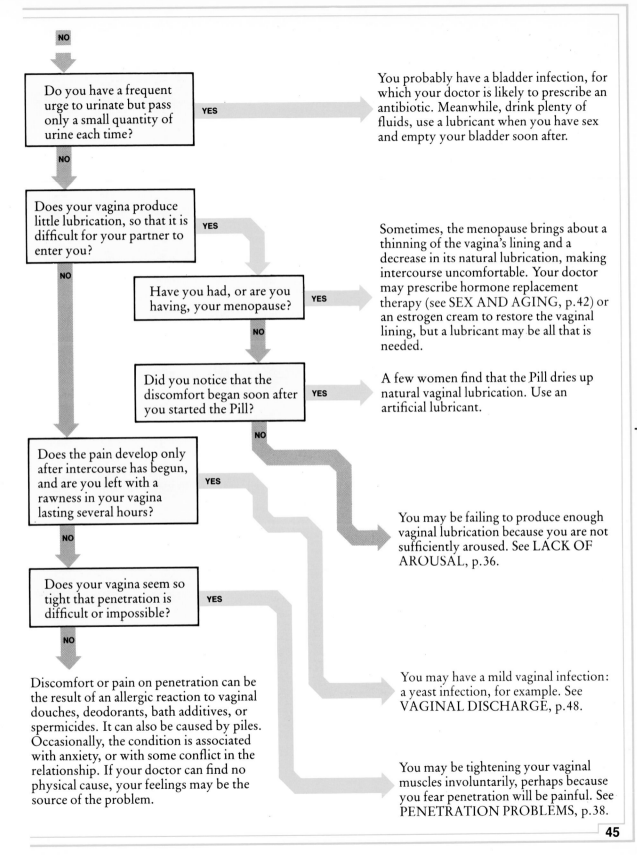

NO

Do you have a frequent urge to urinate but pass only a small quantity of urine each time?

YES → You probably have a bladder infection, for which your doctor is likely to prescribe an antibiotic. Meanwhile, drink plenty of fluids, use a lubricant when you have sex and empty your bladder soon after.

NO

Does your vagina produce little lubrication, so that it is difficult for your partner to enter you?

YES

Have you had, or are you having, your menopause?

YES → Sometimes, the menopause brings about a thinning of the vagina's lining and a decrease in its natural lubrication, making intercourse uncomfortable. Your doctor may prescribe hormone replacement therapy (see SEX AND AGING, p.42) or an estrogen cream to restore the vaginal lining, but a lubricant may be all that is needed.

NO

Did you notice that the discomfort began soon after you started the Pill?

YES → A few women find that the Pill dries up natural vaginal lubrication. Use an artificial lubricant.

NO

Does the pain develop only after intercourse has begun, and are you left with a rawness in your vagina lasting several hours?

YES → You may be failing to produce enough vaginal lubrication because you are not sufficiently aroused. See LACK OF AROUSAL, p.36.

NO

Does your vagina seem so tight that penetration is difficult or impossible?

YES

Discomfort or pain on penetration can be the result of an allergic reaction to vaginal douches, deodorants, bath additives, or spermicides. It can also be caused by piles. Occasionally, the condition is associated with anxiety, or with some conflict in the relationship. If your doctor can find no physical cause, your feelings may be the source of the problem.

You may have a mild vaginal infection: a yeast infection, for example. See VAGINAL DISCHARGE, p.48.

You may be tightening your vaginal muscles involuntarily, perhaps because you fear penetration will be painful. See PENETRATION PROBLEMS, p.38.

WOMEN ♀ 2 PROBLEM CHARTS

45

MASTURBATION ANXIETY

Are you afraid that masturbation may be mentally or physically harmful?

YES → None of the old myths about the harmful effects of masturbation is true. Nor does it matter how much you do it.

NO ↓

Even though you know it is not harmful, do you feel ashamed or guilty about masturbating?

YES → It can be hard to overcome guilt instilled in you as a child. It may reassure you to know that the majority of women masturbate, although many suffer the same irrational guilt. GETTING IN TOUCH WITH YOUR BODY, p.83, should help you to relax and enjoy masturbation instead of feeling embarrassed or ashamed about it.

NO ↓

Are you afraid that if you masturbate you will be unable to reach orgasm through intercourse?

YES → The opposite is true, for you are far more likely to have an orgasm with a partner if you can when you masturbate.

NO ↓

Do you worry because, although you climax when you masturbate, you are seldom able to do so during intercourse?

YES → If you usually masturbate in a particular way (for example, with your legs tightly closed) you will probably climax more easily in this position during intercourse. Experiment by masturbating in positions similar to those you might adopt to make love – kneeling or lying on your back, for example – and use gentler, more diffuse stimulation. See HOW TO REACH ORGASM, p.102.

NO ↓

Do you believe masturbation is only permissible when you have no opportunity of sex with a partner?

YES → Masturbation can be a substitute for intercourse when, for example, you have no partner, or when your partner does not feel like sex and you do. And at times it may simply feel good to be able to satisfy your needs in your own way without having to consider anyone else. You are not taking anything away from your relationship by masturbating.

NO ↓

Masturbation is the easiest way a woman can discover her sexual responsiveness. It also keeps alive the interest that otherwise withers away without regular sex. See GIVING YOURSELF PLEASURE, p.86.

VAGINAL IRRITATION

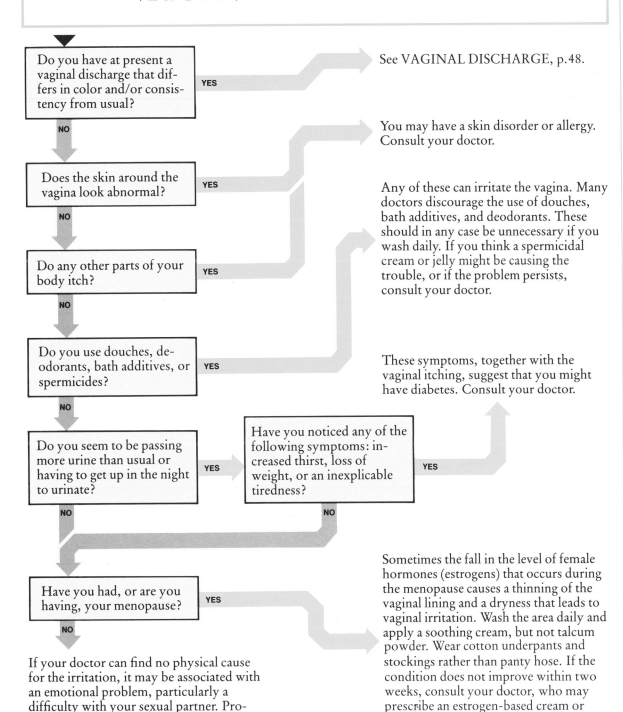

Do you have at present a vaginal discharge that differs in color and/or consistency from usual?

YES → See VAGINAL DISCHARGE, p.48.

NO ↓

Does the skin around the vagina look abnormal?

YES → You may have a skin disorder or allergy. Consult your doctor.

NO ↓

Do any other parts of your body itch?

YES → Any of these can irritate the vagina. Many doctors discourage the use of douches, bath additives, and deodorants. These should in any case be unnecessary if you wash daily. If you think a spermicidal cream or jelly might be causing the trouble, or if the problem persists, consult your doctor.

NO ↓

Do you use douches, deodorants, bath additives, or spermicides?

YES ↗

NO ↓

Do you seem to be passing more urine than usual or having to get up in the night to urinate?

YES → Have you noticed any of the following symptoms: increased thirst, loss of weight, or an inexplicable tiredness?

YES → These symptoms, together with the vaginal itching, suggest that you might have diabetes. Consult your doctor.

NO ↓

NO ↓

Have you had, or are you having, your menopause?

YES → Sometimes the fall in the level of female hormones (estrogens) that occurs during the menopause causes a thinning of the vaginal lining and a dryness that leads to vaginal irritation. Wash the area daily and apply a soothing cream, but not talcum powder. Wear cotton underpants and stockings rather than panty hose. If the condition does not improve within two weeks, consult your doctor, who may prescribe an estrogen-based cream or hormone replacement therapy (see p.43) to help restore the vaginal lining.

NO ↓

If your doctor can find no physical cause for the irritation, it may be associated with an emotional problem, particularly a difficulty with your sexual partner. Professional counseling may help you. See VAGINAL DISCHARGE, p.48.

VAGINAL DISCHARGE

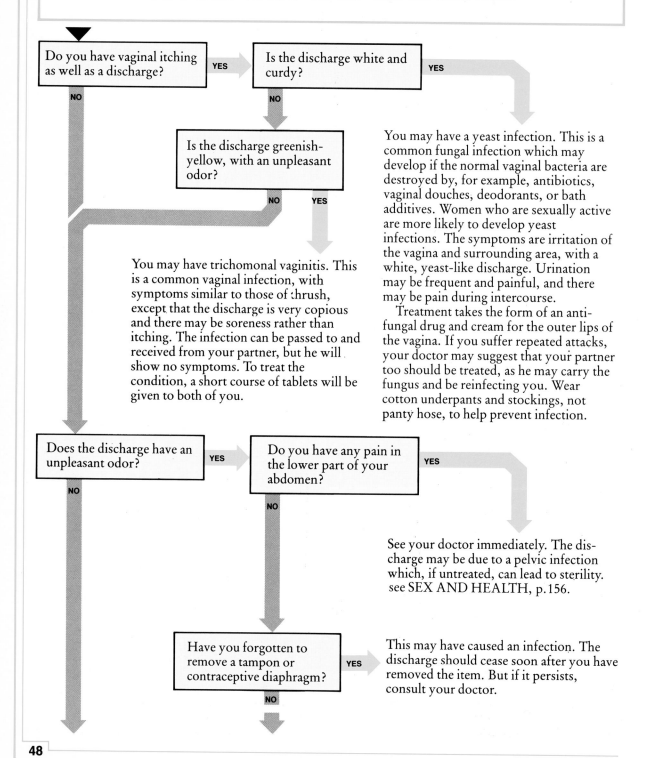

Do you have vaginal itching as well as a discharge?
YES / NO

Is the discharge white and curdy?
YES / NO

Is the discharge greenish-yellow, with an unpleasant odor?
NO / YES

You may have a yeast infection. This is a common fungal infection which may develop if the normal vaginal bacteria are destroyed by, for example, antibiotics, vaginal douches, deodorants, or bath additives. Women who are sexually active are more likely to develop yeast infections. The symptoms are irritation of the vagina and surrounding area, with a white, yeast-like discharge. Urination may be frequent and painful, and there may be pain during intercourse.

Treatment takes the form of an anti-fungal drug and cream for the outer lips of the vagina. If you suffer repeated attacks, your doctor may suggest that your partner too should be treated, as he may carry the fungus and be reinfecting you. Wear cotton underpants and stockings, not panty hose, to help prevent infection.

You may have trichomonal vaginitis. This is a common vaginal infection, with symptoms similar to those of thrush, except that the discharge is very copious and there may be soreness rather than itching. The infection can be passed to and received from your partner, but he will show no symptoms. To treat the condition, a short course of tablets will be given to both of you.

Does the discharge have an unpleasant odor?
YES / NO

Do you have any pain in the lower part of your abdomen?
YES / NO

See your doctor immediately. The discharge may be due to a pelvic infection which, if untreated, can lead to sterility. see SEX AND HEALTH, p.156.

Have you forgotten to remove a tampon or contraceptive diaphragm?
YES / NO

This may have caused an infection. The discharge should cease soon after you have removed the item. But if it persists, consult your doctor.

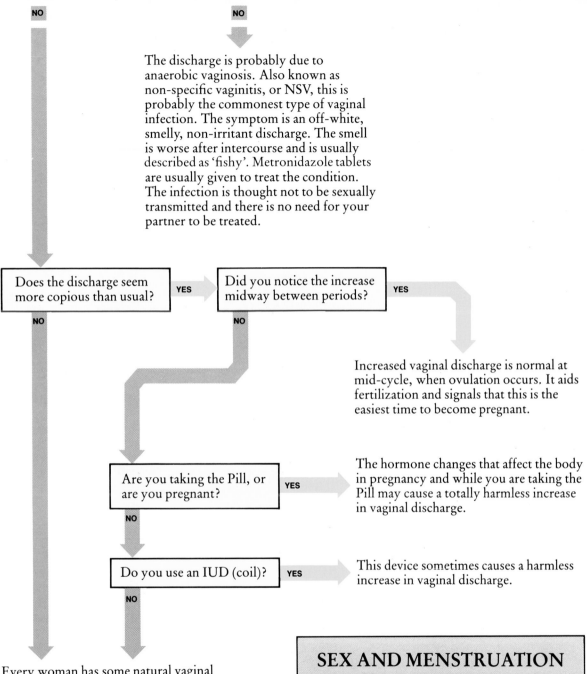

NO NO

The discharge is probably due to anaerobic vaginosis. Also known as non-specific vaginitis, or NSV, this is probably the commonest type of vaginal infection. The symptom is an off-white, smelly, non-irritant discharge. The smell is worse after intercourse and is usually described as 'fishy'. Metronidazole tablets are usually given to treat the condition. The infection is thought not to be sexually transmitted and there is no need for your partner to be treated.

Does the discharge seem more copious than usual? YES Did you notice the increase midway between periods? YES

NO NO

Increased vaginal discharge is normal at mid-cycle, when ovulation occurs. It aids fertilization and signals that this is the easiest time to become pregnant.

Are you taking the Pill, or are you pregnant? YES The hormone changes that affect the body in pregnancy and while you are taking the Pill may cause a totally harmless increase in vaginal discharge.

NO

Do you use an IUD (coil)? YES This device sometimes causes a harmless increase in vaginal discharge.

NO

Every woman has some natural vaginal discharge which, although it is odorless and colorless, may dry on underwear as a yellow or brownish stain. If you are sexually aroused you will produce more discharge than usual. Naturally, if you have just had intercourse and your partner ejaculated inside you, the discharge will be more copious since it will include semen.

SEX AND MENSTRUATION

If you and your partner want to have intercourse during your period, it is perfectly harmless. In fact, if you suffer menstrual cramps you will probably find that sex will help to relieve these. You may prefer to wear a diaphragm, if you have one, to stem the flow; otherwise lie on a towel.

WOMEN ♀ 2 PROBLEM CHARTS

HETEROSEXUALITY/ HOMOSEXUALITY CONFLICTS

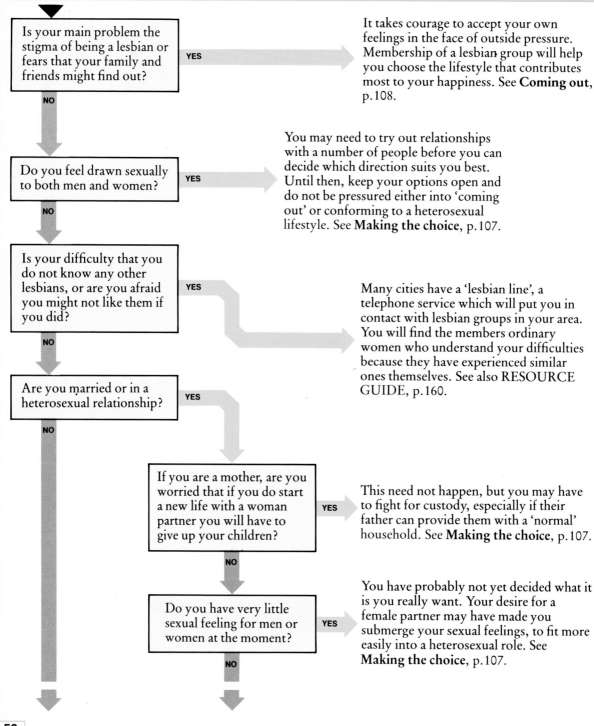

Is your main problem the stigma of being a lesbian or fears that your family and friends might find out?

YES → It takes courage to accept your own feelings in the face of outside pressure. Membership of a lesbian group will help you choose the lifestyle that contributes most to your happiness. See **Coming out**, p.108.

NO ↓

Do you feel drawn sexually to both men and women?

YES → You may need to try out relationships with a number of people before you can decide which direction suits you best. Until then, keep your options open and do not be pressured either into 'coming out' or conforming to a heterosexual lifestyle. See **Making the choice**, p.107.

NO ↓

Is your difficulty that you do not know any other lesbians, or are you afraid you might not like them if you did?

YES → Many cities have a 'lesbian line', a telephone service which will put you in contact with lesbian groups in your area. You will find the members ordinary women who understand your difficulties because they have experienced similar ones themselves. See also RESOURCE GUIDE, p.160.

NO ↓

Are you married or in a heterosexual relationship?

YES ↓

NO ↓

If you are a mother, are you worried that if you do start a new life with a woman partner you will have to give up your children?

YES → This need not happen, but you may have to fight for custody, especially if their father can provide them with a 'normal' household. See **Making the choice**, p.107.

NO ↓

Do you have very little sexual feeling for men or women at the moment?

YES → You have probably not yet decided what it is you really want. Your desire for a female partner may have made you submerge your sexual feelings, to fit more easily into a heterosexual role. See **Making the choice**, p.107.

NO ↓

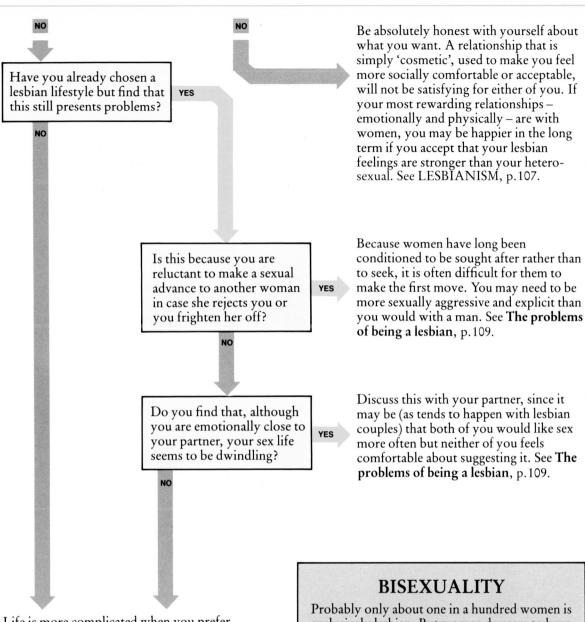

NO

NO

Have you already chosen a lesbian lifestyle but find that this still presents problems?

YES

NO

Be absolutely honest with yourself about what you want. A relationship that is simply 'cosmetic', used to make you feel more socially comfortable or acceptable, will not be satisfying for either of you. If your most rewarding relationships – emotionally and physically – are with women, you may be happier in the long term if you accept that your lesbian feelings are stronger than your heterosexual. See LESBIANISM, p.107.

Is this because you are reluctant to make a sexual advance to another woman in case she rejects you or you frighten her off?

YES

NO

Because women have long been conditioned to be sought after rather than to seek, it is often difficult for them to make the first move. You may need to be more sexually aggressive and explicit than you would with a man. See **The problems of being a lesbian**, p.109.

Do you find that, although you are emotionally close to your partner, your sex life seems to be dwindling?

YES

NO

Discuss this with your partner, since it may be (as tends to happen with lesbian couples) that both of you would like sex more often but neither of you feels comfortable about suggesting it. See **The problems of being a lesbian**, p.109.

Life is more complicated when you prefer women to men, but if you can accept yourself happily, others will eventually do so too. LESBIANISM, p.107, should reassure you that being a lesbian is a positive alternative to being heterosexual.

BISEXUALITY

Probably only about one in a hundred women is exclusively lesbian. But women do seem to have a greater ability to enjoy both homosexual and heterosexual relationships, and more women than men describe themselves as bisexual. The Women's Movement may have played some part in the greater ease with which women seem able to accept bisexuality. Many otherwise heterosexual women become involved in the movement on ideological grounds, and find a good deal of emotional, and sometimes physical, satisfaction in the close same-sex relationships which it fosters.

3

IMPROVING YOUR SEX LIFE

The aim of this part of the book is to help you develop your full sexual potential, discover ways of enhancing and sustaining a good sex life, and derive more enjoyment if it is currently unsatisfying. The advice given is relevant to any woman, married or single, regardless of age or experience.

However good your sex life, it can be fun to try something new, to experiment a little. This helps to keep your interest in each other alive, and ensures that your relationship will continue to be as sensual as it ever was. There is never a need to feel too old, or that you have been together too long, to make any changes. It is even possible that you may get more pleasure from the activities suggested than you would have done when you were younger and less sure of yourself and your partner.

This section also deals with some of the difficulties that take the edge off sexual enjoyment. However longstanding a sexual problem is, do not feel that it is too late to try to resolve it. You will almost certainly experience a marked improvement in your sex life, or overcome your problems altogether, if you follow the recommended self-help programs.

ENRICHING YOUR SEX LIFE

A large part of being a good sexual partner is being able to keep sex vital and interesting by discovering the activities that give you and your lover repeated pleasure. For a woman to simply say yes is not enough. It is quite possible for a man to have sex with a woman who is compliant but uninvolved, but the experience will not mean much to him on any but a physical level. And even on that level it will not be as sensual, as exciting, or as satisfying as it could have been with a skillful and responsive woman. Later in this feature and in those that follow we examine the skills you need to become just such a partner. At the very least they will make your sex life more varied and probably more satisfying.

However, real sexual happiness demands more than technical ability. It depends on your having positive feelings about your own sexuality and that of your lover. Below are listed the most important of the attitudes that contribute to sexual fulfilment for a woman and her partner:

☐ *Attraction and affection.* Sex provides only a limited range of sensations. What lifts it out of the ordinary for most people is the quality of the relationship involved and, for good sex, this is the prime ingredient. It is very important to be strongly attracted to your partner as an individual and not just as a representative of the opposite sex. This sexual chemistry is something which cannot be explained easily and for which there is no real substitute. It is also vital that affection, honesty, and trust exist between you, for these qualities create the background you need in order to explore and develop your sexuality together.

☐ *Willingness to take the initiative.* This means making the first sexual move sometimes, not always leaving it to your partner. Seduce him occasionally: ask him to lie back and enjoy your caresses and take the on-top position so that you control the pace and intensity of lovemaking. But it does not mean taking over completely. Few men or women would be comfortable with a complete role reversal and flexibility is after all the aim.

☐ *Involvement and enthusiasm.* Never be afraid to show by the way you look and sound that you are enjoying what happens to you when you make love. If you do not do so already, learn to think of sex as something you do for mutual pleasure, not something done to you. BECOMING MORE RESPONSIVE, p.90, will help you to do this.

☐ *Imagination.* Being able to apply imagination to your sex life is especially important in a long-term relationship. Boredom can blunt the edge of sexual enjoyment, even with a partner you care for. Use your imagination to introduce variety into your sexual routine so that even though most of it remains familiar, there is also an element of adventure. (See INCREASING YOUR PLEASURE, p.74.)

Resistance to innovation

At the time the Kinsey report on female sexuality was published in 1953, fewer than half the women interviewed had experienced anything other than the traditional man-on-top position during intercourse. Although it is now much more common for couples to draw on a range of sexual positions, some women still feel that it is somehow wrong to depart in any way from the 'missionary' position. Similarly, some women have a restrictive outlook on all sexual activity that departs from what they feel is normal.

If you prefer always to stick to the same few well-tried activities during sex, ask yourself what is preventing you from being more adventurous. It may simply be because your partner has never suggested it, for it is still usually the man who initiates any new sexual practice. However, if you have always been resistant to changes he has suggested it may be because you are embarrassed by the thought of looking ridiculous or undignified. Or you may be afraid that if you agree to experiment, your partner's demands might escalate so that you will eventually be expected to try something you would be really unhappy about – anal intercourse, for example.

It may help to bear the following points in mind if you feel you would like to incorporate into your sex life some of the activities listed on p.56.

☐ Most human sexual activity is reassuringly ordinary. Because sex is nearly always a private affair, people's knowledge of it is limited to their own experience or to what they have read or heard. Bizarre sexual practices are rare and although there are positions more unusual and acrobatic than those shown later in this part of the book, for most people they would be neither comfortable nor particularly stimulating.

☐ If your partner suggests a new sexual activity that you cannot greet enthusiastically, try not to reject it out of hand. Say instead that you are not ready to try it yet, but regard his suggestion as something to be thought about and, possibly, to eventually agree to.

☐ Do not approach any new sexual activity as a challenge, or something designed to test you, but only as a possible source of pleasure. The only failure you face is the failure to enjoy it. But be guided by your own instincts. A new experience is not necessarily a good experience, and if you really dislike the idea of something, do not do it. If you try something new and find that you do not enjoy it, avoid repeating it.

☐ Do not believe that sex is never a laughing matter. In fact, it is quite likely that when you try something new you will be slightly awkward, perhaps even comic, but does it matter with only the two of you sharing the joke?

△ **Lasting sexual pleasure**
When the initial excitement has passed, sexual fulfillment depends on the development of true mutual affection.

ASSESSING YOUR SEXUAL REPERTOIRE

The checklist overleaf will help you determine the scope of your sexual experience and, because it may include possibilities that you think would be fun but have never tried, will widen your horizons. It also gives you a chance to judge the degree of pleasure you are currently getting from sex and to test the balance of giving and receiving between you and your steady partner (if you have one). If your preferences include things you enjoy doing for a partner as well as things you like to have done for you, you are likely to be able to maintain a satisfactory relationship.

On a 0–4 scale, indicate in the columns provided: first, how much you enjoy the activity, and, secondly, how often you do it. The list is selective, so feel free to add other activities you perform that are not included.

Checking your ratings

Ideally you should find that activities to which you have assigned a high enjoyment rating also have a high frequency rating. If not, ask yourself why not. On the other hand, if there are any activities to which you have assigned a higher rating for frequency than

for enjoyment, give some serious thought to the question of why this is so. Are you doing something you do not particularly like chiefly to please your partner? If so, this is a healthy and productive attitude – but only up to a point. The frequent practice of any kind of sexual activity that you dislike may not only cause resentment but can even lead to an inability to make love with any enthusiasm.

A balanced relationship

It is important to check the balance between you and your partner. Why not study the above list together so as to consider how well your responses match each other? Items 2, 6, 8, 10, 12, 14, 22, and 24 are things you can do to arouse and please your partner. Items 3, 7, 9, 11, 13, 15, 23, and 25 are things your partner can do to you. Your frequency ratings and levels of enjoyment for each of these two sets of activities should be similar, if not exactly the same. If they are not, what is the reason? Does one of you tend to be the giver, the other the recipient of pleasure? If this is the case, you will probably both find a better balance between your roles more fulfilling.

While you are using the checklist you might also consider activities which you feel you would enjoy very much, but which, for some reason, you have never tried. These, of course, would attract a high enjoyment rating but nil for frequency. Then you should discuss your lack of fulfilment in these areas with your partner, particularly if it is his reluctance that has prevented experimentation.

ENJOYMENT RATING				FREQUENCY RATING			
Very high 4	Low 1			Regularly 4	Seldom 1		
High 3	Nil 0			Often 3	Never 0		
Medium 2				Sometimes 2			
	ENJOY-MENT	FRE-QUENCY			ENJOY-MENT	FRE-QUENCY	
1 'French kissing' (tongues in each other's mouths).				**14** Giving your partner an orgasm by manual stimulation.			
2 'Petting' (fondling your partner's clothed body).				**15** Being manually stimulated to orgasm by your partner.			
3 Having your partner fondle your clothed body.				**16** Having intercourse with your partner on top.			
4 Seeing your partner naked.				**17** Having intercourse with you on top.			
5 Being seen naked by your partner.				**18** Having intercourse in a side-by-side position.			
6 Caressing your partner's naked body.				**19** Having intercourse in a rear-entry position.			
7 Having your naked body caressed.				**20** Having intercourse in a sitting position.			
8 Kissing your partner's chest and nipples.				**21** Having intercourse in a standing position.			
9 Having your partner kiss your breasts and nipples.				**22** Fondling or kissing your partner's buttocks and anus.			
10 Exploring and stroking your partner's genitals.				**23** Having your buttocks and anus fondled or kissed.			
11 Having your partner explore and stroke your genitals.				**24** Using oral stimulation to bring your partner to orgasm.			
12 Licking and kissing your partner's genitals.				**25** Being brought to orgasm by oral stimulation.			
13 Having your partner lick and kiss your genitals.							

STIMULATION TECHNIQUES

The lovemaking techniques described below are usually called 'foreplay' and most couples use them to arouse each other before intercourse. Foreplay is often thought of as something which is primarily, even exclusively, the concern of the man; something he has to do to 'prime' his partner for intercourse. It is usually assumed too that the man does not, or should not, need any such stimulation, that he is always ready for action, come what may. This is misguided, for men often need direct stimulation, especially as they grow older, to become aroused. Moreover, this attitude deprives men of a whole range of sexual sensations quite different from those of intercourse.

You can both employ stimulation techniques, not only as foreplay but as an alternative to intercourse. They are valuable when intercourse is out of the question because, for example, one of you has an infection or you prefer not to make love during your period. You might also want to enjoy them with your partner simply because you are in the mood for variety or because they happen to suit the time, or the place, better that day.

Taking the initiative

If you are habitually uneasy about sex and find the thought of making love to your partner in this way perplexing or frightening, you might feel more comfortable approaching it as a formal exercise to begin with. Concentrate, at least for the time being, on the exercise programs in BECOMING MORE RESPONSIVE, p.90. Probably though, you will not need any special instructions on how to caress your partner, because for most people it is instinctive to want to hug, kiss and caress the person you care for. But what does have to be learned, because it is something no woman can know entirely intuitively, is the technique of genital stimulation. This involves arousing your partner as skillfully as possible with your hands or your mouth, prolonging his sexual excitement, and finally bringing him to orgasm.

Stimulating the penis manually

Knowing how to stimulate the penis is one of the most valuable skills a woman can possess. Your partner is the best person to teach you how to do this. He will almost certainly have masturbated, so he will know the most sensitive places and the pressure and rhythm that most effectively arouse him. Ask him to guide your hand at first until you get it right. The following advice will give you a good grounding in this art if you are too inhibited to ask for help or he is too inhibited to show you. But you will get further more quickly if you can talk freely to each other.

1 If you are right-handed, position yourself on your partner's right side and grip the penis firmly, with your thumb nearest his navel. If you are left-handed, position yourself on the left. But in either position you may find that you can also effectively stimulate the penis with the other hand. If so, you can apply firmer pressure with your thumb to the sensitive area on the uppermost side of the erect penis. This part of the head is known as the frenulum and the technique is useful if your partner has trouble in achieving or maintaining an erection. A lubricant will enhance his sensations in any position and is particularly recommended if he has erection difficulties.

▽ **Choosing a position**
Experiment to find a position that allows you to provide effective stimulation without becoming tired or uncomfortable.

2 Now move your hand up and down on the penis in a regular rhythm. Experiment to see whether your partner prefers you to use long or short strokes. Grip firmly – the most common mistake women make is to be too gentle or tentative.

3 By slowing the rhythm, you will prolong his pleasure; by speeding it up you will intensify it and bring him to orgasm sooner. The pace of stimulation that he will want as he approaches ejaculation will probably be much faster than he would normally thrust during intercourse.

4 Continue the stimulation until ejaculation is completely over, when you will feel his tension relax. Immediately after ejaculation the penis

◁ **Developing a rhythm**
Whether your partner wants you to use fast or slow strokes, he will almost certainly prefer a smooth rhythm to a halting one.

▽ **Cupping your breasts**
You can provide tender pleasure for your partner and yourself by cupping your breasts around his penis so that he can thrust gently between them.

usually feels extremely sensitive, so he will not want you to continue touching it then.

As you grow more adept at masturbating your partner, you will learn to recognize the signs that his climax is imminent. His muscles will tense up, most noticeably in his thighs, and his breathing will become faster. The testes will be drawn up tight to the body and may be swollen. The head of the penis will increase in size slightly and its color may deepen. You may notice one or two drops of pre-ejaculatory fluid ooze from the tip.

Other manual techniques

The technique described above is probably the most effective way of bringing your partner to orgasm by hand. But there are many other manual techniques for stimulating his penis, and the only limits are those of your imagination. Try for example, rolling it between your palms, squeezing it and letting go, gently stroking the sensitive tip with your fingers, or brushing your fingertips from side to side against the frenulum, vibrating it gently. By experimenting you will gain a wider repertoire of techniques or at least discover what your partner likes best.

ORAL SEX

You can use your mouth and tongue in various ways during lovemaking, but the term 'oral sex' normally refers specifically to oral-genital contact. Stimulation of the male genitals in this way is known as fellatio, while oral stimulation of the female genitals is known as cunnilingus.

Oral sex is something that most men enjoy but many women feel uncomfortable about, so that it can be a source of tension. It is perhaps the most intimate of sex acts, implying a total acceptance of each other, both emotionally and physically. For this reason, it can be extremely satisfying for both the giver and the recipient. Oral sex is also a very effective means for both arousing and bringing your partner to orgasm.

Nevertheless, oral stimulation still marks for many women the borderline between what is and what is not acceptable in sex. If you are reluctant to try it, this may be partly because you do not know quite what is expected of you, but it is also very likely that you have an inhibition which is based on one of several common fears about oral sex. These are discussed below.

Fear of body odor

Perhaps the worst anxiety for a woman is that she will smell or taste bad to her partner, or that he will smell or taste bad to her. But, provided your genitals are kept clean by daily bathing, they will have only the normal healthy odor of sexual arousal, which will be both pleasant and exciting for your partner. It is easy to check this yourself by gathering a little of your vaginal lubricant on your finger after you have bathed and smelling or tasting it. This should reassure you that it is in no way offensive. (If it does smell bad, you probably have a vaginal infection and should see your doctor.) Do not use vaginal deodorants, douches, or bath additives. They are totally unnecessary and may even bring about vaginal irritation.

Fear of ejaculation

Although semen, like vaginal fluid, is harmless and almost odorless and tasteless, many women, even if they enjoy oral sex, dislike the idea of swallowing it or even having their partner ejaculate in their mouth. They may also worry about infection by the HIV (AIDS) virus. Most doctors believe that although there is a theoretical risk of transmitting the disease during oral sex it is a very small one, possibly because saliva usually contains a substance which inactivates the virus. However, someone who has mouth sores, infections, or bleeding gums (which are all quite common) may be at risk if an infected partner ejaculates in their mouth.

However, oral sex need not result in orgasm, and is often a way of arousing each other prior to intercourse. If your partner does want to ejaculate, he can signal to you when he is about to do so, and you can withdraw and stimulate him by hand for the last few seconds. A safer solution is for him to wear a condom during oral sex (see **Guidelines for safer sex**, p.157).

Fear of choking

How much of your partner's penis you take into your mouth is entirely up to you. When you first try fellatio you will probably prefer just to kiss or lick the head until you feel more comfortable. Even when you become more confident, you will probably not be able to let it touch the back of your throat without gagging. This is a perfectly natural reaction and one which your partner is sure to understand. If you remain nervous about choking, you can encircle the base of the penis with your hand, to act as a brake to his thrusting.

Fellatio

If you would like to stimulate your partner's penis orally but are unsure of exactly what to do, the following instructions will help.

1 Begin by treating your partner's penis like an ice-cream cone. Hold the shaft in one hand and swirl your tongue gently around the tip.

2 Now explore the shaft, running your tongue around the ridge where it meets the head and vibrating it gently against the frenulum.

3 Open your mouth, ensuring your lips cover your teeth, and take in the whole head of the penis.

4 Move your mouth up and down on the penis, with as long a stroke as feels comfortable for both of you. Your partner can indicate the rhythm he prefers by guiding your head with his hands, but he should be careful not to force your head down any farther than you want. It is best if he does not thrust at this stage, so that you retain control.

5 Make an extension of your mouth by encircling the lower part of the penis with your thumb and forefinger, moving mouth and hand up and down on it in the same rhythm. As you become more confident you will probably want to take more into your mouth. Because your hand is acting as a 'stop' your partner will not be able to thrust too deeply and make you feel you will choke. Keep up a steady rhythm and a firm pressure, remembering to keep your teeth well apart.

6 Gradually increase your speed. If you are used to stimulating your partner to orgasm by hand you will recognize the signs that he is about to ejaculate. At this stage you can withdraw if you do not want him to ejaculate in your mouth, and bring him to a climax manually or switch to intercourse.

△ **Taking it slowly**
If you have never tried oral sex before, you will probably prefer just to kiss your partner's penis to begin with, rather than suck it.

Precautions against discomfort ▷
Remember, if you want to take your partner's penis in your mouth, that the head is particularly sensitive. Keep your teeth well apart and purse your lips to stimulate it.

Fear of choking ▷
You can allay any anxiety you might have about choking by encircling the penis with one or more fingers. This limits penetration whether you are moving up and down or your partner is thrusting.

Cunnilingus

Since the tongue is softer than the fingers, it can be used to provide gentler stimulation of the clitoris and the vaginal lips. Your partner can probably give you intense pleasure in this way, but it is important to let him know what is most stimulating, since the range of sensations experienced through the clitoris and the surrounding area is very wide.

△ **Oral foreplay**
By kissing the area around your vaginal entrance your partner will probably sharpen your anticipation and provide indirect but intense stimulation of the clitoris.

△ **Penetration with the tongue**
Having your partner penetrate your vagina with his tongue may prove highly arousing, but many women prefer attention to the clitoris.

Positions for oral stimulation

Any position in which both partners are able comfortably to reach and stimulate each other's genitals is suitable for simultaneous fellatio and cunnilingus. But while such positions can be very exciting, the difficulty of giving and receiving pleasure at the same time often diminishes the enjoyment. Many couples find that they enjoy oral sex considerably more if they take it in turn to play the active role.

△ **Positions for oral stimulation**
The '69' position allows mutual oral-genital contact and can be intensely exciting. Many couples, however, prefer to take turns in giving each other oral stimulation, as it is easier to concentrate on either giving or receiving pleasure than to do both simultaneously.

ANAL SEX

The idea of anal sex arouses strong feelings – nearly always negative – in many women. But it need not mean anal intercourse. The simplest and commonest form of anal stimulation is known as postillionage and means gently touching your partner's anus during intercourse or oral sex. Alternatively, a finger can be inserted in the rectum. If you try this, lubricate your finger well first and be quite sure you have no jagged nails. You will probably find that by slipping your finger in about two inches and pressing against the front wall with a slight downward pressure, you will be able to stimulate his prostate gland. Many men find this intensely exciting. You may also enjoy his finger in your rectum when you are highly aroused.

Anal intercouse, if suggested at all, is nearly always initiated by the man, and often at a time when normal intercourse is for some reason – a vaginal infection, for example – out of the question. Or it may be something he just wants to try once, to satisfy his curiosity. It is an activity to avoid,

however, if there is any chance of your partner being infected with AIDS. The lining of the rectum is thin, delicate and easily damaged, and this means that the HIV (AIDS) virus is more easily transmitted during anal intercourse than during any other form of sexual activity.

If this is an activity you both want to try, the risks are reduced if your partner always wears a strong condom. Also use plenty of a spermicide or lubricant containing nonoxynol-9, which has been shown to kill the HIV virus. He should enter you slowly and gently, inserting just the head of his penis, and be prepared to stop immediately if you ask him to. It will be more comfortable if you bear down slightly to relax your anal sphincter. You may also find it easier to be on top, so that you can control the entry of his penis yourself.

Never have vaginal intercourse after anal sex unless your partner has washed his penis well, otherwise you risk transferring an infection from the anus to the vagina.

SEXUAL POSITIONS

There are six basic groups of positions for intercourse, within which there are innumerable variations that differ only in minor details such as the relative position of the limbs.

Some of the positions are especially appropriate for particular situations – during pregnancy, for example. Others are strictly for fun, with no special value except that of novelty, but you may find them worth trying on occasion.

The value of experimentation

Do not feel you have to go entirely by the book when you try a new position. If it feels awkward, make small adjustments until it is right for both of you. You will probably find that, no matter how many of them you try, you will keep coming back to the few that give you and your partner the most mutual pleasure. If you prefer this approach, it does not mean that you are unadventurous, but that you have experimented enough to know what you like. (The obvious times for experimentation are at the beginning of a new relationship when you want to explore each other's bodies and search out each other's preferences, and after you have been together a long time and want to enliven your lovemaking by trying something new.)

Remember that:

☐ Your partner will be able to enter you more easily if your thighs are widely spread. A pillow beneath your hips should make entry easier too.

☐ Positions in which your knees are bent up to your chest give the deepest penetration.

☐ Positions in which your legs are closed give maximum stimulation to the penis.

☐ Change to a woman-on-top position if you want to postpone your partner's orgasm, as most men find this less stimulating.

MAN-ON-TOP POSITIONS

The man-on-top positions, and in particular the 'missionary', in which the man lies between the woman's slightly parted legs, are probably the most widely used group of positions. They give the man almost total control during intercourse, allowing the woman very little freedom of movement.

Deep penetration ▷
In this position, the vulva faces downward to a greater degree than in the more common knees-flexed postures, providing extra stimulation for the clitoris. Penetration is deep and the entrance to the vagina is narrowed, so that the penis also receives considerable stimulation.

Moving in rhythm ▷
*This deep-penetration position is useful if
your partner's penis is short. The vaginal
opening is slack, but the clitoris receives
good stimulation and you are able to move
in rhythm with your partner.*

▽ **'Split-level' position**
*In this 'split-level' position you lie on the
bed while your partner stands or kneels
beside it. By lifting you, he can alter the
angle of penetration.*

◁ **Penetration from above**
This position is moved into with ease from the one shown at the top of the facing page. It retains deep penetration, with the penis entering from almost directly above. You will probably get intense pleasure from holding your partner tight by clasping your feet around his neck while he bears down on the vagina.

▽ **Creating friction on the penis**
With your legs closed, the vaginal lips exert considerable friction on the penis. You may experience the very pleasurable sensation of seizing the penis, while the clitoris also receives strong stimulation.

WOMAN-ON-TOP POSITIONS

Many couples find the woman-on-top positions particularly satisfying. They give you a chance to make love to your partner, and to control both depth of penetration, which can be helpful if you are apprehensive through lack of experience, and the tempo of lovemaking. These positions are good if you are pregnant or your partner is much heavier than you.

Intense stimulation ▷
Of all the woman-on-top positions this probably offers the best combination of intense stimulation with ease of movement for the woman. Your up-and-down motion is less tiring than horizontal movements with your body extended.

◁ **Astride, face-to-face**
This position, which can be very exciting for both partners, allows your partner to fondle your breasts and clitoris and lets you enjoy each other's face. You can make side-to-side or back-and-forth movements, or can rotate on the penis. To intensify genital sensations for both partners, you should lean back slightly.

◁ Ease of movement
Positions in which the man lies on his back are generally relaxing for him. In this position, both penetration and stimulation of the penis are moderate, so that it is easier for him to delay ejaculation. Being on top, you can make vigorous and highly exciting movements with ease.

Working together ▷
Physical intimacy is guaranteed in this position, but movement for both partners demands considerable exertion of the trunk and thighs. This effort in itself, though, can be very exciting as it gives a strong feeling of striving together for orgasm.

REAR-ENTRY POSITIONS

This group of positions allows penetration while lying, standing, sitting, or kneeling, and it is possible in certain of them for the woman to be on top. You need not bear the man's weight and so have considerable freedom to move. Most offer the advantage that your partner can fondle your breasts and clitoris during intercourse, and nearly all are comfortable when you are in late pregnancy.

◁ **Pushing and pulling**
Here, your partner can thrust vigorously by gripping your waist (in itself pleasurable for both of you) and pushing and pulling you up and down. Alternatively, you can provide the stimulation by moving in the way that feels best for you.

◁ Rear entry with man kneeling
Most rear-entry positions are physiologically natural in that the vagina is well aligned with the erect penis. However, many women feel that to kneel, especially with the head lowered, is too submissive or too animal-like. Your partner can compensate for the closeness you may miss by stroking your breasts and back.

Rear entry with man standing ▷
If you kneel on the bed and your partner stands beside it, penetration is deep and the slightly upturned vagina creates strong friction.

SIMULTANEOUS ORGASM

A couple who know their own and each other's sexual responses well can pace intercourse so that they reach a climax at more or less the same moment. However, some couples become obsessional about this, watching each other's level of arousal and trying to control their own, in the belief that simultaneous orgasm is so special that it is worth striving for above all else.

But concentrating so earnestly on timing is likely to distract you from your own sensations – perhaps so much so that you fail to climax at all. Furthermore, you will be better able to enjoy your partner's pleasure at orgasm if you are not fully involved in your own. Simultaneous orgasm is fine if it happens, but regard it as just one kind of sexual experience.

SIDE-BY-SIDE POSITIONS

For relaxed, unhurried lovemaking, side-by-side positions are ideal, and couples often fall comfortably asleep locked together after making love this way. Side-by-side intercourse works well in pregnancy too, or if either of you is very heavy. A drawback for the woman is that her clitoris gets little stimulation from the pressure of the man's body, but in some variants it can be stimulated manually.

△ **Lying on your side**
This intimate and relaxed position can be achieved by rolling over from the man-on-top position. However, to begin intercourse in this way, you should raise your uppermost leg so that your partner can enter you from the side. By placing his thigh between yours, he can increase clitoral stimulation.

△ **Comfortable prolonged intercourse**
With both partners on their sides, rear entry is easy. This position is comfortable, so that it is suitable for prolonged intercourse. To gain deeper penetration your partner should hold the upper half of his body away from yours.

◁ **Relaxed intimacy**
The 'spoons' position gives a relaxed closeness and considerable freedom of movement for both partners. Absence of pressure on you from your partner's weight makes this position particularly suitable when you are in late pregnancy.

VARYING POSITION

It is natural to change position several times during intercourse. But trying too many variations will tend to break the flow of your lovemaking and make it seem more like gymnastics than a tender experience. Whatever position you choose, do not be content to remain passive all the time. By moving your hips, and tightening and relaxing your vaginal muscles, you will intensify the pleasurable sensations for both you and your partner.

SITTING POSITIONS

Although the sitting positions allow neither partner much movement or direct genital stimulation, many couples find them erotic, partly because of their novelty and partly because they provide a strong sense of intimacy. They are also restful positions that can be used when you want intercourse again after a tiring first bout.

Sitting, woman astride ▷
Sitting positions in which the couple face each other are psychologically stimulating and strong on novelty, if somewhat restrictive of movement. But, by stretching his arms out behind him to support himself, your partner can thrust or at least make it easier for you to move on his penis.

◁ **Using a chair**
A chair gives support for your partner's back, allowing him to embrace you and to caress your body. The position is intimate but little movement is possible, so that orgasm is unlikely for either partner unless you are adept in the use of your vaginal muscles.

STANDING POSITIONS

As with the sitting positions, the main benefit here is novelty. However, penetration is often difficult, especially if you are much shorter, and you may need to stand on something to effect it.

△ **Agile interlude**
Considerable agility and strength are required in this position and it is likely to be no more than a brief variant of the position shown on the right. Your partner can support you as shown here, if you are light, or by placing one or both hands under your buttocks.

△ **Basic standing position**
This is the simplest standing position, often used when a couple want to dispense with the preliminaries. In order to keep the penis from slipping out, you will probably have to close your legs. If your partner wants to thrust vigorously it is best to lean against a wall.

INCREASING YOUR PLEASURE

The following checklist suggests activities you and your partner might try if you want to introduce some novelty into a relationship which has become stale. They are meant to introduce variety into a sexual routine, not simply to become part of that routine, for used too often they easily lose their stimulus.

You may not like all the ideas suggested. For example, although some women find it very exciting to share their sexual fantasies with their partner, others would consider this an intolerable invasion of privacy. Use your own judgment, and regard this list as merely a starting point to stimulate your imagination to find new activities you both enjoy.

☐ Take a bath or shower together.

☐ Make love in the dark if you usually prefer some light and vice versa.

☐ Make love somewhere other than the bed – on a chair, sofa, or rug, perhaps.

☐ Make love at an unusual time. Come home from work at lunchtime, for example.

☐ Use a mirror to watch yourselves making love.

☐ Make love outdoors if you can find a private place.

☐ Create a sensual atmosphere with music and candlelight.

☐ Enjoy a meal and wine in bed.

☐ Read an erotic novel or poetry to each other in bed, or watch a sexy video together.

☐ Give each other a massage with scented body oils, and use feathers, velvet, fur, and other textures to give a variety of sensations to the skin.

☐ Tell your partner your favorite fantasy. If your own fantasy life does not seem exciting, read Nancy Friday's book *My Secret Garden* (see RESOURCE GUIDE, p.160) which describes a wide variety of female erotic fantasies.

☐ Use a vibrator (see below).

☐ Perhaps the most valuable boost you can give to your lovemaking is to give it enough time, so that it can be as leisurely, sensuous, and prolonged as you like. Plan for it as you would plan for any other worthwhile activity. It is no compliment to your partner, but a threat to your enjoyment, if sex is usually a last-minute activity, squeezed in after the late movie.

VIBRATORS

Masturbation with a vibrator is probably the easiest means of all for a woman to achieve orgasm. A vibrator can produce such subtle but intense stimulation of the clitoris that even a woman who has difficulty achieving an orgasm manually can climax with the help of one. Since the sensitive head of the penis also responds well to this form of stimulation, a vibrator is a doubly useful aid for a couple who want to inject some variety into mutual pleasuring.

Vibrators are battery- or electricity-powered. The battery-operated kind tend to be noisier and less powerful, but are useful when you are traveling. The best investment is probably an electrically-powered machine with interchangeable heads that can be used to massage the whole body as well as to stimulate the clitoral area. You should avoid the type of vibrator that fits over your hand since in the majority of cases they fail to provide adequate stimulation and can be tiring to use.

It is not necessary to choose a penis-shaped vibrator and, in fact, few women use vibrators to stimulate the vagina internally. Choose a model that does not heat up too quickly and, preferably, one that offers more than one speed.

Using a vibrator
The following instructions will guide you if using a vibrator is new to you and will help the woman who already uses one to get the best out of it. You will be better prepared if you read GIVING YOURSELF PLEASURE, p.86, first and make sure that you understand the structure of the clitoris.

1 Apply lubricant to the clitoral area and angle the vibrator so that only the tip touches the clitoris. Now, holding the vibrator lightly, apply gentle pressure – first on the shaft, through the hood, then directly on the shaft, and finally on the glans, through the hood again. (You will probably find the stimulation too strong for the exposed glans.)

2 Build up a rhythm, creating as much sensation as you can bear, by moving the vibrator from the shaft to the glans, allowing the hood to slip back over the glans each time before you apply the vibrator.

3 The glans will grow increasingly sensitive, but continue to stimulate it unless it becomes very uncomfortable, when you should apply lighter pressure. Eventually you should feel the hot flush of an imminent climax. Do not stop the vibrator, but continue stimulating the clitoris right through the vaginal contractions of orgasm and until these have died away. It is best when using the vibrator not to try to reach orgasm. Instead, just let yourself go with the sensations and do not attempt to resist them. Use the fantasy and deep-breathing exercises suggested on p. 104, too, if you want to increase your arousal.

Choosing a vibrator ▷
The choice of vibrators is extensive. While many of them seem to have been inspired by phallus worship, the size does not have a great bearing on efficiency. But the shape of the head is important, since it does most of the work in genital stimulation.

▽ Using a vibrator
Either you or your partner can use a vibrator to stimulate your clitoris. You may find that what you enjoy most is indirect pressure through the folds of the vaginal lips, or (right) using the tip to stimulate the vaginal entrance.

AIDS PRECAUTIONS
To avoid the risk of AIDS, vibrators – and any other sex toys that you use – should never be shared unless they are cleaned thoroughly after use. The HIV virus is destroyed by ordinary household disinfectant or bleach, and also by dish-detergent diluted in hot water.

OVERCOMING INHIBITIONS

Inhibitions are feelings that interfere with your enjoyment of sex and make it hard for you to be responsive to your partner. In extreme cases they can lie behind a woman's inability to reach orgasm or even make her feel that sex is so fearful or distasteful that it must be avoided altogether.

Many of the hang-ups that women have about sex arise because the old attitudes about what a woman ought or ought not to feel die hard. The concept of 'looseness' or 'cheapness' is applied only to women. Implicit in it are the notions that women are sexual commodities and that it is their responsibility to exercise sexual self-restraint. Given such a poor deal, many women naturally find it hard to stop exercising control and give themselves freely in adult sexual relationships, while others eventually feel so guilty that they bury their desire for sex altogether.

Letting yourself be sexual

The aim of the self-help program below is to make you look at some of the feelings of guilt or anxiety about sex that you have acquired and that may be limiting your enjoyment. It is designed to help you to 're-program' yourself, to modify inappropriate attitudes and patterns of behavior, and possibly to replace them with new and more flexible ones.

If you think of yourself as someone who has little interest in or desire for sex, you probably need to give yourself 'permission' to be sexual, to believe that sexual pleasure is something that everyone, including you, has a right to enjoy. This need never mean that you have to violate your own feelings in any way or do anything you do not want to do. The following notes will help you.

☐ *Develop your fantasy life.* This is a good place to start, because it is safe to let your inhibitions go in imagination. If you find it hard to fantasize, use sexually explicit writing or images to stimulate your imagination. Do not worry if your fantasies include people other than your partner, or activities (group sex, for example) that you would avoid in reality. Fantasy is a way of experimenting with feelings you have not fully acknowledged, but it does not necessarily represent your true sexual preferences or indicate that you would ever act on them.

☐ *Learn to like your body.* Embarrassment about her body, a fear of not being desirable enough, are among the strongest factors inhibiting a woman's sex drive. Unless you feel good about your body, it will be hard for you to believe that anyone else can desire or admire it. The exercises in GETTING IN TOUCH WITH YOUR BODY, p.83, and GIVING YOURSELF PLEASURE, p.86, are an important part of this program. They will help you feel comfortable with the way you look and show you that sex can be a source of pleasure.

☐ *Be selfish.* Try at least to be more selfish than you are at present. It is almost a compulsion for some women to neglect their own feelings, to be so concerned with whether or not they are pleasing their partner, that they scarcely give a thought to how they themselves feel. Next time you make love, try not to think about your partner's reactions, but focus entirely on your own.

☐ *Do not be a spectator.* If you have always had difficulty in accepting your own sexual feelings you probably tend to stand back mentally when making love, disassociating yourself by thinking about other things and wondering whether you will reach orgasm, rather than feeling what is happening. When you make love, concentrate on the sensations you experience and be aware all the time of your partner's body as you touch him and yours as he touches you. The exercises in the **Program for improving responsiveness**, p.91, will help you to practise this.

☐ *Give up control.* If you are sexually inhibited, you are probably disturbed by the idea of losing control during lovemaking, of being seen in an unflattering light by your partner. Occasionally, a woman will hold herself back because she is afraid that she might enjoy sex too much if she abandoned herself to it and that it might even make her promiscuous, threatening her steady relationship.

Maybe you have always made love in silence because it seems to draw less attention to you, or because you feel it is somehow wrong to let yourself go or show enjoyment. One way to overcome this is to practise a deliberate loss of self-control during sex. Respond to your feelings by moving, breathing more loudly or heavily, or yelling – in short, show the pleasure you feel in any way you like. If you have never behaved like this before, you will feel self-conscious at first, so start very gradually. It is probably easiest to do it first when you masturbate, and later to try it during sex with your partner.

☐ *Examine your attitudes.* Take a fresh look, in the light of subsequent experience, at the sexual attitudes you acquired when you were much younger. Do you have an uneasy feeling, for example, that 'nice' girls do not enjoy sex? Or that sex matters more to men than to women? Or were you made to feel, when you were a child, that sex is something to feel embarrassed, ashamed, or even guilty about? Are your preconceptions, in fact, an emotional response that is hard to justify rationally?

☐ *Become a hedonist.* A common characteristic of women who feel inhibited or guilty about sex is that they cannot help believing that pleasure of any kind for its own sake is wrong. If you always feel guilty about relaxing instead of working, or spending money on occasional luxuries, you almost certainly feel uneasy about enjoying life too much. Try to make yourself more receptive to pleasure by creating more time and space in your life for sensual enjoyment – of food, music, pictures, erotic literature, or the occasional massage or sauna, for example. This should make it easier for you to regard sex as another source of legitimate pleasure.

Dealing with anxiety about sex

Fears and anxieties about sex are as destructive of your enjoyment as guilt, and likewise make you hold back, preventing the relaxation that is essential for arousal and full responsiveness. Often, such fears are rooted in ignorance, in which case understanding a little more about sex may be all that is needed to dispel them. Below we examine some of the sexual fears that most commonly afflict women.

Fear of penetration

For some women there is a rational basis for such fears. If you suffered a traumatic sexual experience, or a painful gynecological examination, for example, you may well be apprehensive about intercourse. Often, though, a woman mistakenly believes that her vagina is too small, or that intercourse will in some

indefinable way damage her physically. But, whatever its origin, fear of pain is likely to be self-perpetuating. It tends to make a woman tighten up in order to resist penetration so that real pain is much more likely. Ways of dealing with this particular anxiety are discussed in OVERCOMING THE FEAR OF PENETRATION, p.98.

'Performance anxiety'

Because they are traditionally the passive partner, many women are unsure exactly what is expected of them in bed. The only thing a woman can be certain about is that she is 'supposed' to have an orgasm every time – a false expectation which is very unlikely to be fulfilled. If she does not climax, her 'performance anxiety' may well increase, inhibiting still more her responsiveness and her capacity to reach orgasm.

Worries about whether or not you are 'good in bed' are best alleviated by reading ENRICHING YOUR SEX LIFE, p.54, and in particular the introductory section. If your anxiety centers on the fact that you find it difficult or impossible to reach orgasm, or if you are unsure whether what you experience is orgasm or not, read HOW TO REACH ORGASM, p.102. You will find that these anxieties will diminish when you acquire a deeper understanding of sex and your own responses.

Fear of pregnancy

The feeling that you run the risk of an unwanted pregnancy will almost certainly spoil your enjoyment of sex, but the risk can be minimized so much nowadays that it can almost be ignored. CONTRACEPTION, p.135, will help you choose a method that suits you and is highly reliable.

Yet, despite taking every reasonable precaution, you may still feel concerned about the possibility of pregnancy. If this is the case, it may be that for you sex is inseparably bound up with reproduction. You may actually need to feel you risk pregnancy to be able to enjoy sex properly. The above program should, over a period of a few weeks, help you to change your attitude so that you can regard sex as a source of pleasure and not exclusively as the means of reproduction.

Fear of intimacy

Within the framework of a close relationship, sex is safe: you can communicate your needs and show your feelings without fear of rejection or ridicule. Intimacy involves honesty, trust, and commitment, and for some people these are easier to establish than for others. If you have been hurt or rejected in previous relationships you may now want to hold back to make yourself less vulnerable. And if you were raised in a family in which feelings were seldom shown or discussed and each member tended to live in emotional isolation, you will find it hard to develop a close relationship in adult life.

If you want to feel closer to your partner, the following suggestions will help. Because you are attempting to change a very fundamental part of your nature you will need a high degree of determination, but the rewards, in your sexual and your emotional life, will be correspondingly great.

☐ Choose the right partner, or at least minimize your chances of choosing the wrong one. See MAKING A LASTING RELATIONSHIP, p.148, which shows how you can sabotage your own chances of success by investing in a relationship that is almost certainly doomed to failure.

☐ Set aside some time when you can talk daily to your partner about what has happened to you during the day and discuss problems. Make a special effort to talk about what matters most to you and do not avoid emotional or sexual issues. LEARNING TO COMMUNICATE, p.120, will help you here.

☐ Let your partner see the 'bad' side of you. It is easy to let anyone know the good things about you, but much more difficult to expose aspects of yourself about which you feel worried, guilty or ashamed. However, it is revealing these failings that makes for true intimacy.

☐ Show your feelings. Affectionate touching is the most straightforward way of demonstrating a need to be close. Show anger, too, if you feel it, but not in a destructive way. See **Dealing with anger**, p.121.

☐ Give your partner the opportunity to do things for you, letting go of your emotional independence a little. Ask for things sometimes, acknowledging that you have needs and allowing your partner to meet them.

☐ Spend time together on leisure activities. Do not use excuses such as the pressure of work to avoid spending time alone with your partner.

☐ Do not distance yourself, by provoking a quarrel, for example, whenever you sense that your partner is getting too close to you.

☐ Do not focus on your partner's shortcomings or least attractive features so that you lose sexual interest in him as soon as you feel you are becoming more involved than you want to be.

☐ The sensate-focusing exercises on pp.91-95 are designed to foster intimacy. However, it is important to realize that these exercises provide you with an excellent opportunity for self-sabotage, for employing all the tactics to avoid intimacy which contribute to your problem. Do not allow yourself to be too tired or too busy to do them, or to remember past injustices and notice physical imperfections as soon as you begin to feel emotional and physical satisfaction.

ANXIETY ABOUT SEXUAL ODORS AND SECRETIONS

If you are bothered by the inevitable smells and messiness of sex, it may be because you have come to associate sex with excretion. The two functions are, in fact, quite separate and if the genitals are kept clean by daily washing they do not normally smell. When you are sexually aroused though, your genitals do have a characteristic odor, and so do a man's. Most people find this not only pleasant, but exciting. Furthermore, the sexual secretions – vaginal fluid and semen – are harmless and with little odor or taste. A bath or shower together before you have sex, as well as relaxing you, should dispel any anxiety you have about offending your partner.

IMPROVING YOUR SELF-ESTEEM

To have self-esteem is to feel that you are worth something. A poor self-image affects not only the way you behave toward other people – shyness and jealousy are nearly always the result of low self-esteem, for example – but also the way they behave toward you, because people tend to accept you at your own self-evaluation. A lack of self-esteem puts you at a disadvantage in social situations, because fear of being rejected usually makes you overeager to please others and very reluctant to risk giving offence. And, naturally, your self-esteem has a direct bearing on your confidence about attracting and retaining sexual partners.

Causes of low self-esteem

Timidity and a sense of the inevitability of failure may be built into a woman's personality as the result of an upbringing by parents who were too strict, over critical, or even unloving. A child will accept her parents' view of her; if they do not make her feel good, lovable and successful, it is not surprising that she grows up believing she is of little worth. Often, too, a woman's self-image is colored by childhood teasing that made her believe she was unattractive, or by unsuccessful adolescent experiences of sex.

Even a normally self-confident woman may suffer a temporary loss of self-esteem if she fails in an area that is important to her. A setback at work or the break-up of a relationship will diminish her sexual confidence as well as affecting her general mood.

Furthermore, women are still coerced, often very subtly, into believing that it is not feminine to feel that they really matter. They are brought up to be givers rather than takers, to satisfy other people's needs before, or even rather than, their own. The notion of service is a poor basis for a satisfactory sex life, and yet it is an attitude that many – perhaps most – women hold to some degree. If your self-esteem is low, if you have always felt that it is perfectly reasonable always to put yourself second, then it will prove rewarding to learn to be more assertive.

Dealing with temporary setbacks

When you have suffered a major blow to your self-esteem it is important first of all to try to see your failure in perspective, as only part of you and your life, not the whole of it. Focus on other areas in which you have had more success. For the time being, concentrate your energies on something at which you are unlikely to fail and which will restore your self-image. For example, after a relationship has come to an end, you may find it helps to immerse yourself in your work more than usual.

Remember that after any loss of prestige or self-esteem, whether at work or in a relationship, you may be tempted to embark on an affair simply because it seems to be the easiest and quickest way to soothe your bruised ego. Such rebound affairs are a risky way to deal with the problem because they are likely to lead to another failure. It is probably better to wait until you have regained your emotional equilibrium.

If, in two or three months, you still lack sexual confidence, your problem may be more deep-seated. The program that follows is designed to help you overcome such difficulties.

PROGRAM FOR IMPROVING YOUR SELF-ESTEEM

This program will help you to build up your self-esteem and begin to accept yourself as a sexually desirable woman. Other parts of the book are important complements to the program, and you will be directed to these at certain points.

1 ASSESSMENT

Assess your strengths and weaknesses by compiling two lists. First, list your good points, intellectual and emotional as well as physical; secondly, list your faults – the things about yourself that you wish were different or could be improved. Bear in mind the following suggestions:

☐ Try to be specific. Do not simply put down 'good-natured' or 'unattractive,' for example. Work out what makes you consider yourself positively good-natured (you like children, you are kind and tolerant, for example) or negatively unattractive (you are overweight, your hair is mousy, you have a short temper, etc).

☐ Do not be tempted to overlook or minimize your strengths. Nearly every woman will write down 'poor complexion' if she happens to have one, but far fewer will remember to give themselves credit for a clear skin.

☐ Include among your strong points attributes or skills not directly related to sexual competence. Are you a good cook, for example, or do you play a sport well? Similarly, if someone else has a talent that you admire and that you believe would give you more self-confidence if you had it – an ability to play a musical instrument, or to speak a foreign language, or skill with computers, for example – list it among your weaknesses.

Now analyze your lists, beginning by comparing them. Are the weaknesses far more numerous than the strengths? If so, why? Perhaps you are being unfair to yourself. A poor self-image may be making you so self-critical that you have dismissed some of your good points as unworthy of mention.

Examine your list of strengths. Are you making good use of those you do have? If there are situations in which you shine, how often do you find yourself in them? If you have a good eye for a ball and enjoy tennis, for example, have you joined a club? Do you even play regularly? And what about your best features? If you are tall, inspect your posture, for a round-shouldered slouch cancels out the advantage of height. If your eyes are one of your most attractive features, have you learned how to emphasize their appeal with make-up and how to use them to your best advantage? (See **Eye contact**, p.150.)

Finally, examine your list of faults. Delete the ones you can do nothing about. For example, you cannot make yourself six inches taller, however much you would like to. Even so, your list will still contain a number of things you can change if you are willing to invest time and energy.

2 SELF-IMPROVEMENT

The second element of the program will enable you to improve your appearance and develop greater self-assurance.

Changing what can be changed
It is in the area of your appearance that changes are most easily made and most readily appreciated by yourself and others. A woman who lacks self-esteem is often tempted to dwell on her physical imperfections. But to say 'I'm not bothered about how I look' covers up what is probably your real fear:

'Even if I did make an effort it would probably make no difference'. The answer to this defensive strategy is that a little effort will almost certainly pay off. Women are at an enormous advantage if they want to change their looks, since the scope for improvement is so vast – through clothes, make-up, and hairstyle – that it is no exaggeration to say that no woman need be entirely unattractive.

Change the cut or the color of your hair if you think a different style would flatter you more. Remember too that most women, unless they have a ravishing complexion, look better with a little make-up, provided that it is used skillfully. At the very least, make the best of your eyes. If you wear spectacles, do they improve your appearance? If not, why not try contact lenses? Lose weight if you need to, wash your hair more often, and try electrolysis if you have more than a down of facial hair.

Next, look at your clothes. If your aim has always been to blend invisibly with your surroundings, try to draw a little attention to yourself. Do not buy anything which does not flatter you and which you cannot feel really good in. Magazines, advertisements, and store windows will all give you a sense of style which you can go on to develop for yourself. Try to buy at stores that suit the image you would like to present. When shopping for clothes, be experimental – you do not have to buy what you try on. Consider styles and colors you have never worn before rather than going always for what you 'know' suits you best. You may well be pleased with something quite different from what you always imagined to be right for you. Try using perfume if you have not done so before. This will soon become a pleasantly recognizable part of your image, but avoid the temptation to use too much if you are unused to it – a hint is all you need.

A timetable for improvements
There is no need to make all these changes at the same time. In fact, it is best to introduce them gradually over about six months, to give yourself and everyone else a while to adjust to them. This approach will also give you time to get used to other people's changed reaction to you. You will start to be noticed, and this, although it will boost your self-esteem, may embarrass you at first if you have always been shy.

At the same time that you are modifying the way you look, tackle the other points on your list of strengths and weaknesses. Some of these goals – learning to play a sport, for example – may be long-term ones, so give yourself plenty of time to achieve them and then you will not so easily become disheartened or impatient for change.

This is also the time to think about the way you behave with other people. Often people who feel insecure or inadequate try to compensate by being the sort of person who is always right. The easiest way of doing this is by being hypercritical of others, trying continually to prove them wrong, which usually has a damaging effect on relationships. If you recognize this tendency in yourself, accept the fact that you will sometimes be wrong and that no one will think any the worse of you for it.

Finally, remember that the most important change is a change in your attitude to yourself. Try to think of yourself in terms of your positive qualities, and define yourself by them. Try not to be self-critical. People with low self-esteem tend to be perfectionists and so there is a built-in possibility of failure about everything they do. Congratulate yourself on the things you achieve and be tolerant of your occasional failures.

Valuing what cannot be changed
Get to know and like your face and body as they really are. Women are so frequently reminded by the media of what constitutes the ideal of feminine beauty that it is hard for them not to feel self-conscious or dissatisfied if, as is almost certainly the case, they do not measure up to it. Few people are either physically perfect or expect physical perfection in their lovers. The exercises in GETTING IN TOUCH WITH YOUR BODY, p.83, will help you gain a more positive view of yourself as you are.

Learning to overcome shyness
Over 80 per cent of people questioned in a recent survey said they had felt shy at some time or in some situations, and of these over 40 per cent admitted that shyness was a constant problem for them. So the chances are strong that the person you are too timid to talk to feels much the same as you.

Do not automatically label yourself 'shy'. Instead, regard yourself only as feeling shy in certain situations – in large groups, for example, or with attractive strangers. Giving up the label is the first step toward overcoming the problem itself.

Have faith in your likeability. Shy people usually lack the social skill to make others believe that they are worth knowing. Believe it yourself, and you will spread the idea. For this very important part of the program, turn to DEVELOPING SOCIAL AND SEXUAL SKILLS, p.150.

Try not to concentrate on your own feelings of self-consciousness, or to brood about what people think of you. Instead, give your entire attention to anyone you talk to or to any situation, whether sexual or not, that you find yourself in. Some psychologists suggest that an excellent way to overcome shyness is to become involved in a social or political cause. Involvement of this sort provides an opportunity to make a fresh start as an unshy person in a non-sexual situation. Having interests in common with others should make it easier to form relationships with them, and in working toward something you feel strongly about you will probably forget your self-consciousness.

Finally, make sure you pick the right sexual partner. Many women seem deliberately to sabotage their self-esteem by choosing partners who lower it even more. Not many women are happy with a lover who is critical or rejecting and a partnership based on love and support is essential for anyone whose self-esteem is fragile or for whom self-consciousness is a problem.

Learning to be more assertive
Assertiveness can be a difficult thing for a woman to learn because in the traditional man-woman partnership it is the man who is the dominant, assertive partner, the one who makes all the major decisions, while the woman is the passive, submissive one. If you are truly comfortable in this role, fine. But the danger in being too compliant and accommodating is that your relationships will never be as satisfying, sexually and emotionally, as they might be. And the simple reason is that you are, or act as if you were, unable to tell a partner, friend or colleague, what you really want.

Practise saying no to suggestions you normally, though unwillingly, say yes to. If you have fallen into a pattern of habitually doing something you dislike just because you think it is expected of you – seeing too much of your partner's, or even your own, relatives when you have little in common, for example – break the habit. If your partner regularly pressures you into watching his favorite TV program, invite him to watch yours next time. Assertiveness is not the same as aggressiveness. It simply means expressing the way you feel and implies no criticism of your partner or others for feeling or wanting something different.

Do not be afraid to ask for things you want. Start by requesting small favors of friends – the loan of something, for example. Or ask a friend to pick up something for you if he or she is going shopping. Sometimes even these small requests will not be granted (other people can choose to be assertive too) but part of learning assertiveness is being able to accept an occasional rebuff without interpreting it as a serious rejection.

Practise making decisions and, when they are minor, do not spend time worrying about whether they are right or wrong. A good starting point is to resolve never to say, 'I don't really mind' when you are asked whether you prefer one thing to another. If you have a preference, make it known. Even if you really do not care, make a firm, immediate decision.

Take deliberate risks by acting out of character sometimes. It helps if you can think of it as 'acting'. Allow yourself to seem to lose your temper, for example, if the occasion is right and everyone knows you are a woman who never loses her temper. Their impression to date may well be that you do not dare to show your anger, and their realization that you can show anger, when appropriate, may do wonders for your reputation and your self-confidence.

Make the effort to do something you find difficult, such as striking up a conversation with a stranger or making a justified complaint. Sometimes you may get the snub or even the hostile reaction you dread, but most often you will receive a satisfactory response and a boost to your self-esteem.

When you have gained confidence and feel more comfortable about asking for what you want among acquaintances and friends, introduce a little more assertiveness into your sexual relationships. You may find this difficult if it involves discussions about sex and your sexual feelings, but LEARNING TO COMMUNICATE, p.120, will help you overcome the problem.

Assessing your progress

After you have worked on the above program for three months, check your progress by answering once again the questionnaire CONFIDENCE, p.20. Compare your result with your previous rating. Has there been any improvement? Check whether your answers pinpoint any specific area you can work on. Concentrate on the section **Learning to be more assertive** if your rating is still low.

Remember that you are trying to change ideas about yourself that you have probably held for most of your life. Do not be discouraged if, like most old habits, they die hard. If you are determined to change and to give up an outdated view of yourself, and if you are willing to take a few risks and expose yourself to a few minor disappointments, you will almost certainly win through.

Improving your appearance ▷
Your voice and your manner contribute strongly to the impression you make on others, but your appearance is of undeniable importance – at least in an initial encounter. Any improvements you make to the way you look will stimulate the interest of others and boost your confidence.

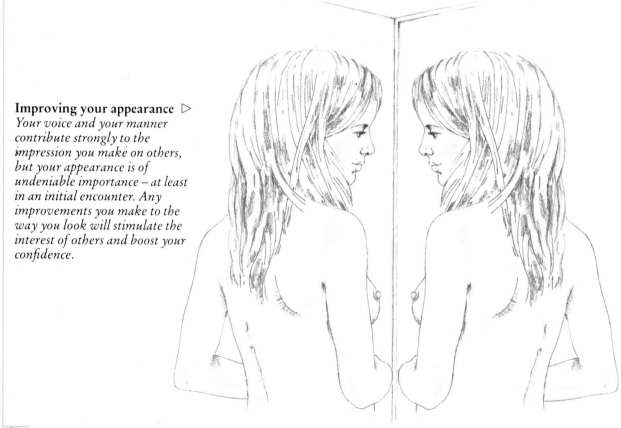

GETTING IN TOUCH WITH YOUR BODY

For most couples, the sight and feel of each other's bodies is one of the special joys of lovemaking. Yet it can be difficult to believe that another person, however loving, can accept and enjoy your body if you are uncomfortable or unhappy about it.

The idealized woman

It is perhaps not surprising that many women attach so much importance to bodily perfection, so widespread is the ideal image created by the mass media and the fashion world. However, it is clear that such stereotypes have nothing to do with the chemistry of attraction between lovers. Your sexual appeal to whoever finds you attractive is very much your own. It may even depend to an extent which would surprise you on the very characteristics which you regard as flaws. Your partner may find such qualities endearing because they form part of your uniqueness.

There is a further reason why it is important to feel confident about the way you look. Confidence is, in itself, an attractive quality, and an infectious one. If you can be unselfconscious about your nakedness rather than trying to conceal it by undressing in the dark or hiding beneath the bedclothes, you will find that your lover will happily accept you as you are.

For many women, the simple fact of unfamiliarity with their own bodies creates a barrier to physical intimacy with a partner. If you grew up without a clear idea of what your genitals are like, you may well feel uncomfortable or vulnerable at the thought of a lover exploring them.

The two exercises below are designed to make your body more familiar to you, and to help you accept it for what it is instead of longing for what you feel would be a more attractive one. They are also the first step toward making you more aware of your body as a source of pleasure.

PROGRAM FOR INCREASING BODILY AWARENESS

1 SELF-EXAMINATION EXERCISE

It is best to do this exercise in complete quiet and privacy after a bath or shower.

1 Undress in front of a full-length mirror. Now examine your body carefully, from head to toes. Imagine that you are seeing yourself for the first time.

2 Watch yourself kneeling, bending, and moving around. Stand, then sit, with your legs apart, then together. Look over your shoulder to see the curve of your back and the set of your buttocks.

3 Notice what is special about you; not perfect, but special. These are the characteristics (peculiarities, if you prefer) that make your body appealing and unique in the eyes of anyone who is attracted to you.

4 Like everyone else, you have a mixture of good and not-so-good features. Look at your body again, but focus your attention on your best points. Gloss over the things you dislike, regarding them as only a part of the whole. Accept them, but do not think of yourself exclusively in terms of them.

5 Now pay special attention to the features that most worry you. Try to look at them with a completely fresh eye, shedding, if you can, all preconceptions. The scales may show that you are a few pounds overweight, for example, but is this extra weight really visible – and more important, even if it is, could it not be attractive rather than a failing? Your breasts may be smaller, or larger, than you have always wanted, but a lover will not share your view of them. He will see them as part of you and completely suited to the rest of your body.

6 With a hand-mirror, and in as good a light and as comfortable a position as possible, look at your genitals. If you are unfamiliar with their structure, use the illustrations on p.84 to help you identify the different parts. Do not worry if your genitals are not like what you see there. Like your face and the rest of your body, they are unique and there is considerable variation in their size, color, shape and configuration from woman to woman.

7 The next stage is to explore your genitals by touch as well as visually. Do not move on to this stage until you feel quite comfortable about simply looking at

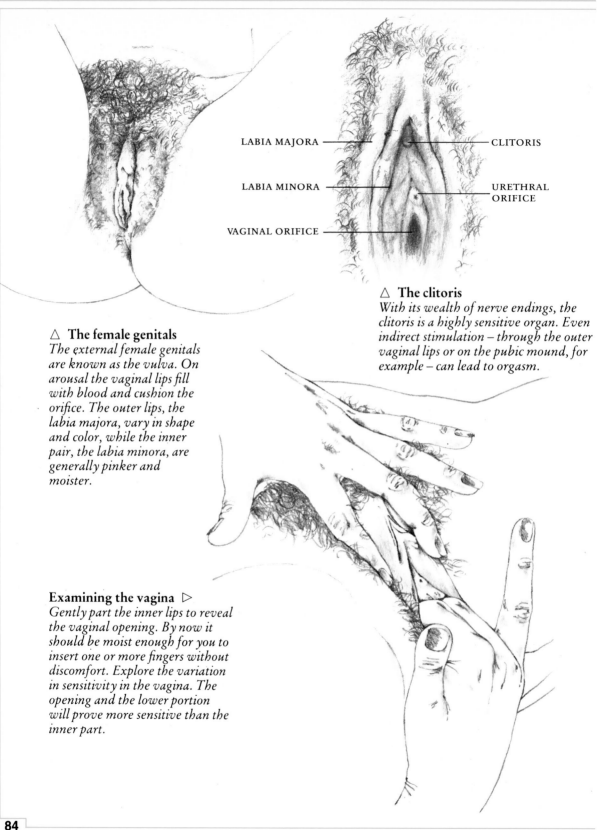

LABIA MAJORA —————— CLITORIS

LABIA MINORA —————— URETHRAL
ORIFICE

VAGINAL ORIFICE ——————

△ **The clitoris**
With its wealth of nerve endings, the clitoris is a highly sensitive organ. Even indirect stimulation – through the outer vaginal lips or on the pubic mound, for example – can lead to orgasm.

△ **The female genitals**
The external female genitals are known as the vulva. On arousal the vaginal lips fill with blood and cushion the orifice. The outer lips, the labia majora, vary in shape and color, while the inner pair, the labia minora, are generally pinker and moister.

Examining the vagina ▷
Gently part the inner lips to reveal the vaginal opening. By now it should be moist enough for you to insert one or more fingers without discomfort. Explore the variation in sensitivity in the vagina. The opening and the lower portion will prove more sensitive than the inner part.

them. There is no need to hurry this process if you do not find it easy. The important thing is to repeat it, however briefly, as often as you can.

___

8 Now start to explore the whole area with your fingers. You will already have identified your clitoris, which is situated at the point where the inner vaginal lips join together at the front. To see it properly though, you will need to pull back the hood of skin which covers it. The clitoris will be revealed as a small pink knob about half an inch long. It is extremely sensitive, so touch it gently.

___

9 Next, run your fingers along the inner and outer vaginal lips and back along the perineum (the area between the vagina and the anus) to find out which parts feel most sensitive.

___

10 With your fingers, explore the entrance to your vagina, separating the inner lips to expose the opening. The area just around the entrance, and the outermost third of the vaginal passage itself, are more sensitive to touch than the inner two-thirds, which contain nerve-endings that respond only to pressure.

Assessing your progress

Do you now feel more relaxed and positive about your body when you look in the mirror? And do you feel you would be equally at ease with a sexual partner? If so, you have made good progress. You can, if you like, increase your body awareness still more by going on to do with your partner the exercises in **Pleasuring each other**, p.91.

You perhaps managed the first part of the program with no difficulty but found that you 'blocked' when you reached step 6, in which you were asked to explore your genitals. If so, remember that you need make only the slightest progress for the next step to become easier. Once you have overcome your initial reluctance, much of the apprehension will disappear. You may find it easier to take this difficult step if you distance yourself a little, standing over a mirror rather than holding it up close to your genitals. Other parts of the book may be helpful too, particularly OVERCOMING INHIBITIONS, p.76, and IMPROVING YOUR SELF-ESTEEM, p.79.

2 VAGINAL AWARENESS

The second part of this program for increasing body awareness consists of the Kegel exercises, which are used to strengthen the pubococcygeal (or PC) muscle. This is actually a group of muscles in a large band which encircles the vagina and the urethra. The exercises were originally developed simply to help women suffering from mild stress incontinence – that is, they tended to pass very small quantities of urine when they laughed, coughed, or ran.

It was discovered however, that the Kegel exercises offer a variety of side-benefits. You can use them, as is suggested here, to increase your awareness of vaginal sensations, and practising them will intensify the sensations of intercourse for both you and your partner. Because the PC muscle is among those that contract at orgasm, the Kegel exercises also play a part in the program designed to help women who have difficulty in reaching orgasm (see HOW TO REACH ORGASM, p.102). The exercises are helpful too in regaining vaginal muscle tone after childbirth, and useful for the post-menopausal woman because, by increasing the bloodflow to the vaginal area, they help to maintain the natural vaginal lubrication.

The Kegel exercises are easy, can be practised anywhere and at any time, and do not depend on your having a partner. Even if you had some difficulty in practising the latter half of the self-examination exercise above you can still start the following exercises. They will increase your familiarity with your body and its sensations, and so may make genital exploration easier. Practise the exercises three times a day and do steps 2-5 ten times at each session.

___

1 To locate the pubococcygeal muscle, urinate sitting with your legs apart and stop the flow of urine abruptly several times. It is the PC muscle that you are using when you do this.

___

2 Tighten the muscle for three seconds, relax it for three seconds, and then tense it again. You may not be able to hold the tension for the full three seconds at first, but you will soon develop this ability as the muscle grows stronger. Try not to tighten your abdominal muscles at the same time.

___

3 Now tighten and relax the muscle ten times as quickly as you can, so that it seems to 'flutter'. You will probably need to practise for a while in order to be able to control the muscle in this way.

___

4 The next step is to contract the muscle long and steadily as though you were trying to draw an object into your vagina. Hold the contraction for three seconds.

___

5 The final step is to bear down, as if emptying the bowels, but pushing more through the vagina than the anus. Hold the tension for three seconds.

GIVING YOURSELF PLEASURE

In doing the previous exercises in GETTING IN TOUCH WITH YOUR BODY, p.83, you probably discovered differences in sensitivity in different parts of your genitals. The exercises below explore this variation, teaching you how to stimulate yourself to produce the most pleasurable sensations.

Masturbation is something many women find hard to admit to. This remains the case even though, in a major survey in the 1970s, over 60 per cent of women questioned had masturbated at some time and nearly 70 per cent of the married women continued to do so within marriage. For many women, masturbation is not simply a substitute for intercourse, but a long-term feature of their sex life.

Barriers to enjoyment

Despite the fact that there is no rational reason to feel guilt or shame about masturbation – and none of the notions about the physical or psychological damage it does has any foundation in fact – many women suffer from these feelings. If you have never masturbated, and you have been referred to this part of the book in order to increase your sexual responsiveness or because you have never had an orgasm, you will probably find you have a built-in resistance to the idea. If so, it may help first of all to examine the benefits of masturbation.

☐ Masturbation is the easiest way to discover the best kinds of stimulation. Once you know how to give yourself pleasure you can show your partner how to please you.

☐ It is a very reliable way for you to learn how to reach orgasm. Only very few of the women who masturbate fail to reach a climax by means of it.

☐ Whether or not you have a partner, and whether or not you both want sex at the same time and with the same frequency, you can retain your sexual vitality and release tension by masturbating.

Starting to masturbate

To do these exercises successfully you must be free from the fear of interruption or distraction, so make sure you have complete privacy. You should also allow yourself ample time for them. Use some lubricant (massage or baby oil for example, but not Vaseline) to intensify the sensations and minimize the possibility of skin irritation. Practise for 10-20 minutes four or five times a week. You may or may not reach orgasm, but it does not matter either way, for the aim at this stage is just to explore the sensations.

1 Touch and stroke the inner and outer vaginal lips and the surrounding area. Experiment with different kinds of pressure and vary the rhythm.

2 Now explore the clitoris: the shaft, the glans (tip), and the hood of skin which covers them. You may need to pull back this hood in order to touch the clitoris.

3 Start with a light touch and gradually increase the pressure. You will find you can use intense pressure more comfortably if you rub through the folds of skin either side of the clitoris rather than directly on it. Try to increase and decrease sensation by varying the pressure.

4 Holding the shaft of the clitoris between your index and middle fingers, try rubbing up and down or from side to side. Then, using a circular motion, apply firm pressure with two fingers over the whole clitoral area as if you were massaging a muscle beneath the skin.

5 If the preceding technique produces sensation in your clitoris that is too intense, spread the pressure by using the palm or heel of your hand instead.

6 Should rubbing and pressure both fail to provide strong stimulation, cup your hand over the clitoral area and vibrate it, or brush your fingers rapidly to and fro across the clitoris.

Assessing your progress

Once you can do these exercises without anxiety, guilt, or embarrassment, and have discovered how to arouse at least some pleasurable sensations, you are ready to go on to the next stage, below. If, after six weeks, you feel you have made no progress, try the next stage anyway, since you will probably find that the stronger stimulation that is involved makes it easier for you to become aroused.

◁ **Stroking the vaginal lips**
By varying the rhythm of the stimulation and the amount of pressure you apply, you will discover a wide range of pleasurable sensations.

◁ **Indirect stimulation**
The tip, or glans, of the clitoris is particularly sensitive. You may find that you can only bear to touch it through the hood of skin that covers it.

▽ Using the heel of the hand
With the heel of your hand on the clitoris and the pubic bone either side of it, apply firm pressure while making a circular rubbing movement.

▽ Brushing with the fingers
An alternative method of stimulating the clitoris, if both rubbing and pressure fail, is to brush your fingers rapidly back and forth across it.

The following exercises show you to how to build up the intensity of genital sensation until you reach orgasm. As with the previous exercises, practise for 10-20 minutes per session, four or five times a week.

1 Using a lubricant, first stroke the outer vaginal lips gently and then gradually transfer your attention to the clitoris.

2 Stimulate the clitoris through the hood, then pull this up so that you can stimulate the shaft and glans directly. Develop a regular rhythm, applying firm pressure to the shaft but lighter pressure to the glans.

3 The glans will probably grow increasingly sensitive as you become more aroused. You may even find that you cannot bear to stimulate it directly. If this happens, reduce the sensation a little, either by concentrating on the shaft instead of the glans, or by applying pressure through the hood or the vaginal lips. Maintain, as far as possible, the same rhythm and type of stimulation.

4 Eventually you will feel a wave of warmth sweep over you. This is not orgasm, but usually precedes it. It is important to continue stimulation, in the same way and with the same rhythm. If you stop, the sensations will die away and it may be hard to regain them. Orgasm itself – a rapid series of contractions deep within your vagina – will probably follow. It is best to continue stimulating yourself until these contractions have completely ceased. You should not concentrate in this exercise on reaching orgasm, but just allow it to happen.

Assessing your progress
By practising this exercise you will probably soon be able to reach orgasm quite easily every time you masturbate, or at least experience the pre-orgasmic suffusion of warmth. If you still do not climax, or feel you need a little extra stimulation to push you over the edge into orgasm, try using a vibrator. Masturbation techniques with this powerful aid are described in greater detail in INCREASING YOUR PLEASURE, p.74.

▽ Concentrating on pleasure
Apply a lubricant to the vaginal area to reduce the risk of soreness. Then stroke the outer lips gently, focusing exclusively on the sensations.

▽ Stimulating the clitoris
Touch the clitoris through the hood and then, if the sensations are not too intense, with the hood retracted.

BECOMING MORE RESPONSIVE

One of the most important components of a couple's sexual happiness is the woman's responsiveness. It is perfectly possible for a man to have sex with a woman who is unresponsive and therefore unaroused, but it will not give either partner much pleasure. Since a man's enjoyment depends to an extent on the woman's, your partner will see your sexual excitement as a measure of your desire for him; your failure to become aroused or feel fulfilled as his inadequacy as a lover.

It is easy to see, given this tendency in men, how the term 'frigidity' has come to be used pejoratively by them. The description implies emotional coldness, and suggests not only that a woman does not like sex but that she does not like men either. It is an easy defense for a man who has failed to interest or arouse a woman to decide that she is 'frigid', thus neatly transferring the blame from him to her.

Occasional unresponsiveness

A woman is very much governed by circumstances in her sexual response to a man. You are unlikely to show much warmth if you are feeling resentful or angry with your partner, for example. This is why it is seldom a good idea to resort to sex in order to patch up quarrels. If the issue has not been properly resolved first, and the relationship restored to a more friendly footing, you may feel used and probably even less responsive.

Nor will you be able to relax and enjoy sex easily if the demands of your professional, domestic, or social life leave you so exhausted that all you want to do at bedtime is sleep. Try to plan your life better if your energy for sex is being drained in other ways. It may seem ridiculous to make a date with your own partner, and to treat it as something around which other activities and obligations have to fit. But it is worthwhile, and sometimes it is the only way a busy couple can ensure that their sex life is a real source of pleasure to both of them.

Lack of privacy and fear of interruption also contribute to a lack of responsiveness. Therefore, if you have small children who tend to wander in and out of your room in the night, fix a lock to your bedroom door. It will do the children no harm if they occasionally have to rattle for a moment or two when they need you, and it will make you feel much more relaxed.

Long-term unresponsiveness

The temporary blocks to responsiveness mentioned above make most women hold back on occasion. But sometimes a woman unwittingly erects permanent barriers to sexual feelings. In some cases, this mental resistance is so strong that she cannot respond to anyone sexually.

More usually, though, unresponsiveness develops in a particular relationship or set of circumstances. The reason may be, for example, that your partner has a sexual problem which has, over the years, made sex so disappointing that you have 'switched off' sexually. When this happens, you need to learn to recognize and respond to the feelings that you have long suppressed, or perhaps have not yet even started to experience.

The training program described below is designed to gradually awaken your sexual feelings. It is important also to understand, and try to dispel, whatever negative attitudes to sex have made you set up such fierce defenses against it. OVERCOMING INHIBITIONS, p.76, may help you deal with such feelings, but if sexual unresponsiveness has been a long-term problem you will probably benefit from the help of a professional therapist as well. You will be wise too to seek professional help if there is intense strain or there are important unresolved problems in your relationship.

By its very nature, the following program needs the cooperation of a willing partner. It is unlikely to be successful if there is a reservoir of bad feelings between you, or a lack of trust, especially if these problems have contributed to your lack of responsiveness in the first place.

The program consists of four exercises, which you should do in the order in which they are given. But read through the instructions for all the exercises before you start the program, so that you both realize what is involved.

The first two exercises, **Pleasuring each other** and **Genital pleasuring**, teach you simply how to give and receive pleasure. Although these exercises are an important part of several self-help therapy programs, any couple can benefit from this sort of tender and imaginative sex play. It allows them to rediscover all the sensations of which their bodies are capable without setting themselves the usual goals of intercourse and orgasm.

PROGRAM FOR IMPROVING RESPONSIVENESS

1 PLEASURING EACH OTHER

This exercise, like the following one, is known as a 'sensate-focusing' exercise because it helps you focus on the sensations that are produced when you gently explore and caress each other's bodies. But it is important that you do not have intercourse or, at first, genital contact. This takes the heat out of the situation so that there is no reason for you to feel anxious about your ability to enjoy sex. You cannot fail, because you are not being asked to succeed – only to experience. In order to be as relaxed as possible, make sure that you have plenty of time and that there is no risk of interruption. Both of you should be naked, and for many couples a warm bath or shower together can be a relaxing preliminary.

Try to practice **Pleasure in giving**, the first stage of this exercise, at least three times a week for at least two weeks before going on to the next stage, **Pleasure in receiving**. In both cases it is a good idea to alternate your activities so that the person who is first to give pleasure at one session becomes first to receive it at the next.

Pleasure in giving

Caressing another person's body need not have any overt sexual content, which is why, during this first exercise, you are asked to avoid genital stimulation. You may find that the pleasure for both of you is increased if the active partner lubricates his or her hands with body lotion.

---

1 Start the session with your partner lying face down while you kneel either beside or astride him. Begin by fondling and stroking his whole body, working your

▽ **Relaxing your partner**
Massage sessions usually begin with the back, because attention to this area rarely fails to produce a sense of ease. You may choose simply to stroke your partner's back or to brush the skin lightly with your fingertips rather than massage it. But, whatever your preference, the face-down position will help your partner to relax.

way down from his head to his toes. During this time, you are in control. Explore or kiss his body in any way that feels good to you. Your partner can gently push your hand away if you do something he does not enjoy.

2 After 10 minutes (or longer if you like) change places. Now just relax and enjoy the sensations while your partner caresses and massages you. Feel what is happening to you and focus your attention on each spot he touches. Try not to stand back mentally and watch him.

3 Change position so that your partner can lie on his back while you gently stroke his face and body. (You should not touch his genitals at this stage.)

4 Now lie back while, avoiding your breasts and genitals, he pleasures you. Do not try to direct or guide him, but if he does something you find uncomfortable, gently move his hand.

5 If you feel at all tense or anxious, ask him to stop for a while until you feel relaxed again.

Being pleasured in this way may make either of you feel sexually aroused or simply so relaxed that you soon fall asleep. The ban on intercourse may seem hard on your partner if he ends the session full of tension, but it is, from your point of view, and ultimately his, important. If he wants to, your partner should relieve his tension by masturbating.

Pleasure in receiving

After practising the first stage for at least two weeks, move on to the second, below. This is similar except that here the emphasis is on the reactions of the person being caressed rather than on those of the active partner. Instead of simply accepting the attention, the passive partner gives positive feedback to the other about what feels particularly enjoyable. The ban on intercourse and touching the genitals is still in force.

Receiving pleasure ▷
Concentrate only on the enjoyment you derive from your partner's touch, putting aside any feeling of selfishness, since his turn will come. If you carry out the exercises conscientiously, both of you will learn to give and receive pleasure fully.

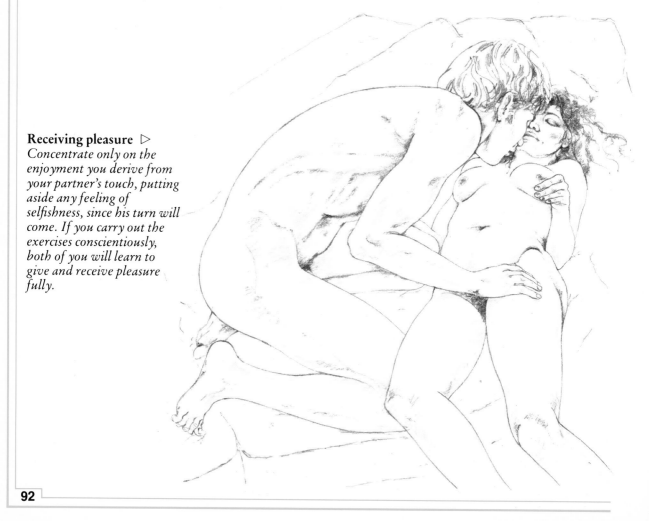

1 Lie as before, first face down, then face up, while your partner pleasures you. Let him know what feels especially good, either in words or gestures. Guide his hand with yours if you want. If he kisses you in a certain spot or in a way that is particularly pleasurable, tell him. Concentrate on your own feelings and try not to worry about whether he might be getting tired or bored.

2 Now caress your partner, as before, but try to discover the most sensitive parts of his body (excluding his genitals) and the kind of stimulation he most enjoys. He may, for example, prefer a firmer or more vigorous touch than you yourself would respond to.

3 Finally, at the end of the session, tell each other how you both felt and discuss what most pleased each of you.

Assessing your progress

If, after practicing the exercises for two or three weeks, you both enjoy them and feel at ease together when doing them, you are ready to progress to the next part of the program, **Genital pleasuring**.

However, if you felt an insurmountable resistance to doing the exercises, it is probably because you feel threatened by the idea of a close relationship (see **Fear of intimacy**, p.77). In this case, and also if you had little or no feelings, psychotherapy is recommended in order to lower your defenses.

If you found it was much easier and more enjoyable to caress your partner than to be caressed, it is possible that guilt about sex is inhibiting your responsiveness. Or it may be that you are afraid your partner does not find you attractive, or that the exercise bores him. Either reaction prevents you from concentrating on your own feelings.

It may be, however, that deeply entrenched in you is the idea that it is the woman's role to give sexual pleasure, rather than to receive it. Try to ask your partner specifically for what you want, letting him do only what you request, over at least the next four sessions.

Perhaps you find it easier to lie back and be caressed rather than to take an active role. If you feel this way, examine your feelings closely to see whether hostility or ambivalence toward your partner is making it hard for you to show tenderness and affection. Answer the questionnaires COMPATIBILITY, p.112, and ARE YOU SEXUALLY SATISFIED?, p.116, and see the problem chart WHAT IS WRONG WITH YOUR RELATIONSHIP?, p.119.

2 GENITAL PLEASURING

Here the emphasis is on focused pleasure rather than on the more diffused sensations of body-contact explored in the preceding exercise. You are now ready to take turns arousing each other by touching and caressing the genitals as well as the rest of the body. Once again though, stop short of intercourse. Aim to 'tease' – caressing, then withdrawing your hand – rather than to develop rhythmic stimulation that could lead to orgasm. Simply concentrate on enjoying what you are feeling.

1 Lie on your back, so that your partner can stroke your whole body and can easily cup your breasts and kiss and gently suck the nipples.

2 He should now explore your belly and genitals, and run his fingers through your pubic hair. Ask him to pause if you start to feel tense or anxious, but try to continue these caresses for several minutes.

3 Your partner should now concentrate on your vaginal entrance, gently stroking it. He should also explore the perineum (the area between your vagina and your anus) which is very sensitive in most women. Next, he can touch your clitoris – but very softly, since it is highly sensitive. A lubricant will make this gentle stimulation easier. All the time, focus on the sensation and tell him what feels good. If you feel at all tense, indicate this so that he can caress another part of your body for a while instead.

4 Change places and stroke your partner's chest and belly, running your fingers through his pubic hair, and caressing the inner part of his thighs.

5 Move gradually to his testes, squeezing them very gently. Run your fingers up and down the length of his penis. Discover the areas that are the most sensitive. These will probably be the head and, in particular, the frenulum – the ridge on the underside. (It makes no difference to the sensitivity of the penis if it is circumcized.) Play with his penis, then take your hands away and let his erection subside. It will return when you stimulate him again.

6 Lean back between your partner's thighs and guide his fingers so that they stimulate your clitoris in the way you like best. In this position he can caress the rest of your body with his free hand. Remember that since you have no visible sign as evident as his erection, it may be difficult for him to know what feels good for you unless you tell him.

Vaginal fullness ▷
*By inserting a finger while
he strokes your clitoris with
his other hand, your partner
can create for you the
sensation of vaginal fullness
that is often missed when
you receive only external
stimulation.*

▽ **Guiding your partner**
*You will enable your partner
to give you maximum
pleasure if you guide his
hand as he explores your
body. It will also help to tell
him exactly what feels best.*

7 Change places so that you are sitting and your partner is lying between your legs. By guiding your hand as it stimulates his penis, he can show you the pressure and the tempo that he finds most arousing. Again, it is easier for both of you if he can reinforce his actions with a precise description of what he wants you to do.

Orgasm is not the object of this exercise, but if either of you becomes very highly aroused continue manual stimulation until it is reached. Once you both feel quite comfortable doing the exercise, you might try increasing arousal by using your mouth and tongue on each other's genitals. Even if you do not want to try this, it is worth examining what you feel about the idea. It is possible that part of your reluctance stems from simply not knowing what to do. If this is the case, see **Oral sex**, p.59, which discusses the subject in more detail.

Assessing your progress

If the exercise has gone well, you will probably have enjoyed intense pleasure without any of the anxiety that may have seemed an inescapable part of previous sexual experiences. However, a major stumbling block for many women in this exercise is worries about the appearance of her genitals, or their natural products. **Anxiety about sexual odors and secretions**, p.78, may be reassuring if this is a problem for you.

You may have found that you could not prevent yourself from feeling tense and anxious when you were doing the exercise, or that you switched off by thinking of something quite irrelevant instead of focusing on your feelings. If so, distract yourself next time by using erotic fantasies while your partner stimulates you. You have to be selfish and concentrate entirely on your own feelings if you want to succeed here.

Stimulating your partner by hand ▷
Having adopted a position that is comfortable, let your partner guide your hand in order to show you the rhythm and pressure that he enjoys most.

3 NON-DEMAND INTERCOURSE

If the first two exercises in the training program have gone well, you will have learned both how to give pleasure and to respond deeply to your partner's attentions. The following exercise goes a stage further, giving you the opportunity to discover more about your vaginal sensations and to become used to the feel of your partner's penis inside you.

Again, the exercise demands that you put your own needs first. Your partner plays a passive role, allowing you to use his erection to find out more about your own sexual needs and to gratify them. This part of the program may be difficult if your partner has a sexual problem too, since it demands good ejaculatory control on his part and an ability to sustain an erection (see UNDERSTANDING A MAN'S FEELINGS, p.124).

1 Caress each other until you feel aroused and your partner has a firm erection. If your vaginal lubrication seems very slight, lubricate his penis with saliva or an artificial lubricant.

2 Now kneel astride your partner, facing him. Gently lower yourself onto his erect penis, guiding it with one hand.

3 Stay still for a few moments, concentrating on how it feels to have the penis inside you. Then use your vaginal muscles to squeeze it. Finally, begin to move slowly up and down.

4 Experiment by leaning forward or backward, in order to alter the angle of penetration. You may find that there is a marked increase in sensation in particular positions.

5 Next try lifting yourself almost entirely off your partner's penis and then coming down again. Often it is the withdrawal and re-entry of the head of the penis in the vaginal opening that produces the most intense sensations.

Continue to exercise until you are tired. As this exercise gives your partner much less stimulation than regular intercourse, he may well lose his erection. If this happens, withdraw and stimulate him manually until it returns. If, on the other hand, he rapidly becomes very excited, rest for a while (though you need not withdraw) until he has calmed down. At the end of the exercise he will probably want to continue intercourse until he reaches a climax, which he should do.

Assessing your progress

If each time you repeat this exercise you feel you have enjoyed a little more vaginal sensation and become more aroused, you have made good progress. But do not expect to reach orgasm, at least for the first two or three weeks you do the exercise. All that matters is that you should enjoy the feelings of intercourse itself. Progress may be slow, but if you feel you are making any at all, keep going.

If you become very anxious when you do the exercise, finding it very difficult to let yourself go, it may be that you have too much concern for your partner's feelings and too little for your own. Do you fear, for example, that your partner might reject you if you do not give him pleasure, or that it is only by pleasing him that you will be accepted and loved? The questionnaire CONFIDENCE, p.20, should help you to decide whether or not you undervalue yourself in this way.

If you feel you are making no headway despite having performed the exercises conscientiously, you will do best to seek the help of a professional therapist to discover why this is. It is possible that your problem lies in hidden feelings about your partner.

4 INTERCOURSE TO ORGASM

The final exercise in this program is straightforward intercourse, in any position you like. Maintain the same approach that you employed in the preceding exercise, focusing on your sensations and discovering which are the most pleasurable. (STIMULATION TECHNIQUES, p.57, and SEXUAL POSITIONS, p.63, describe ways in which you can become even more sexually responsive.) Keep the emphasis on pleasure rather than orgasm. Sometimes intercourse will lead to orgasm, sometimes not. If failure to climax becomes a problem that worries or frustrates you, turn to the feature HOW TO REACH ORGASM, p.102, which examines this difficulty and offers advice.

VAGINAL MUSCLE TONING

Some sex therapists recommend the Kegel exercises described on p.85 for enhancing orgasm and general sexual responsiveness. These are designed to tone and strengthen those vaginal muscles that contract at orgasm. They are simple, take very little time, and can be done unobtrusively at any spare moment.

Varying the angle of penetration ▷
By leaning back you will increase the friction between the vagina and the penis. Leaning forward will produce a gentler angle of penetration and is better for relaxed intercourse.

▽ **Intensifying the sensations**
Move up and down so that the head of your partner's penis makes repeated and highly pleasurable contact with the sensitive opening of the vagina.

OVERCOMING THE FEAR OF PENETRATION

Most men and women accept that a woman's first sexual experience will probably be painful. If it is, it is nearly always because of this expectation. If you anticipate being hurt it is natural to tighten your vagina against the pain, and this reaction itself often makes intercourse difficult, if not painful. In some cases, intercourse becomes impossible.

Usually, a woman's fears about her sexual initiation are founded on folklore rather than on fact. The most common anxieties are discussed below.

Fears about the hymen

The hymen is a thin membrane which stretches across part of the vaginal entrance. A few women believe that it forms a total barrier to intercourse. But the extent to which it blocks the opening varies greatly, and there is, except in some rare cases, an opening through which the menstrual flow can pass. In an adolescent girl this is usually large enough to admit a finger. 'Petting' and the use of internal tampons tend to widen the opening even more, with the result that by the time she first has sex the hymen has usually virtually disappeared.

Although, in romantic fiction, rupture of the hymen at first intercourse is a dramatic, painful, and bloody affair, the membrane is in fact sometimes elastic enough to stretch without tearing at all. Even if it does tear, it is so thin that rupture is not particularly painful and, because the hymen has a relatively meager amount of blood, there is seldom much bleeding. Very occasionally the hymen may be especially tough or extensive, so that penetration is difficult. This can be a problem for the woman who begins intercourse relatively late in life, because the hymen, like all tissues, tends to become less elastic.

A related myth is that the absence of the hymen proves the loss of virginity. But the hymen varies in structure so much from woman to woman, and, as we have seen, is so easily torn or stretched in various ways, that it can be difficult for even a doctor to establish, by examining it, whether or not a woman has had intercourse. It is certainly impossible for a man who has sex with her to know in this way whether or not she is a virgin.

Worries about vaginal size

If you are a virgin you may worry about whether your vagina is too small for your partner's penis.

Perhaps you have inserted a tampon and believe that, because it fits neatly, your vagina must have a similar diameter. In fact, the vagina is very distensible and shapes itself to whatever it contains.

In their normal state the vaginal walls are collapsed, with no space between them. But the muscles of the vagina are elastic and the skin which lines it folded and ridged so that it can stretch as much as necessary, whether in intercourse or in childbirth.

Fear of painful intercourse

The inner two-thirds of the vagina are so free of pain-sensitive nerve endings that it is possible to carry out a minor operation in that area without an anesthetic. There is a sensitivity to pressure but the sensations which arise when the penis presses on the vaginal walls are felt as pleasurable.

If you find your first or early experiences of intercourse do hurt you, it is probably because your nervousness, or your partner's inexperience, prevents you from becoming highly aroused, so that there is insufficient vaginal lubrication. There are, however, a few medical conditions which can make sex painful (see the problem chart PAINFUL INTERCOURSE, p.44).

If you are anticipating making love for the first time and are suffering from 'first night nerves', the following suggestions should help you relax.

☐ If you have never used a tampon, try to stretch your vaginal opening a little by inserting a finger, and then, when you can do this easily, two.

☐ The first time you have intercourse, and thereafter whenever necessary, your partner should apply an artificial lubricant to his penis to supplement your vaginal lubrication. This will make penetration easier and lessen the possibility of soreness if your vagina tends not to become very wet.

☐ You will find that entry is easiest if your knees are bent and your thighs are spread wide (see SEXUAL POSITIONS, p.63).

☐ As your partner enters you, bear down slightly, as though trying to push something out of your vagina. This makes it impossible to tighten up the vaginal muscles at the same time and so easier for him. If your partner is sexually inexperienced too, it will probably be best for you both if you guide his penis into you with one hand while holding your inner vaginal lips apart with the other.

Vaginismus

Very rarely, the fear of penetration, or of even being touched in the genital area, is so intense that it causes an automatic and instantaneous tightening of the muscles surrounding the vaginal entrance. This condition, which is beyond the woman's control and makes intercourse difficult or impossible, is known as vaginismus.

Sometimes this fear is life-long and can be the result of a sexually repressive upbringing that produces an irrational anxiety or guilt about sex. A woman with such feelings has probably never been able to bring herself to use tampons, or allowed a doctor to give her an internal examination. More often, though, vaginismus is a condition that starts after a painful or traumatic sexual experience. It is natural for anyone who has been hurt to tense up in anticipation of pain. Unfortunately, the vaginal muscles can easily become conditioned to respond in this way whenever penetration is attempted, and whether or not there is still any reason for it.

If you suffer from vaginismus, your first step is to consult your doctor to make sure that there is no physical reason why sex is difficult or painful. If this is confirmed, you should start the program below.

PROGRAM FOR OVERCOMING VAGINISMUS

Before starting the program, read through the earlier part of this feature if you have not done so already. You will find that your ideas about your genitals are the product of a fearful imagination and have no foundation in fact.

You will almost certainly feel at least a little tense when you start to do these exercises. It may help to take a bath or shower first, or simply to lie down and relax for a while. You can do the steps of the exercise at any pace that feels comfortable. Some you may need to repeat several times before you go on to the next, and sometimes you may have to push yourself a little to take the next step.

You can practise steps 1-7 whether or not you have a partner. These are the most important, because by the time you have completed them you will have discovered that penetration need not be painful and much of your anxiety will have gone.

1 With the aid of a hand-mirror, look closely at your genitals. Part the inner vaginal lips with your fingers so that you can see the entrance clearly.

Using a mirror ▷
Having ensured that you have complete privacy and adequate time for the exercise, use a hand-mirror to familiarize yourself with the appearance of your genitals.

2 Now touch the entrance for a little while with the tip of your finger.

3 Next, lubricate your finger and insert just the very tip. When you do this, bear down a little, as though you are trying to push something out of your vagina. Leave your finger there for a couple of minutes to get used to the feel of it.

4 Insert the finger gently, as far as the first joint. Again, bear down slightly as you insert it. This may be difficult, but once you have accomplished this step, everything else will follow.

5 If you feel your vaginal muscles tightening, stop, deliberately tighten them around your finger, and then relax them again. By repeating this several times you will begin to feel you have some control over them. Your feelings of anxiety will disappear as you become used to the sensation of having something in your vagina.

6 Repeat steps 4 and 5 several times, each time inserting the finger a little farther, until you can push the whole of it in. Take a few deep breaths each time you begin to feel tense.

7 Now try to insert two fingers, using plenty of lubrication. Do this gradually, as you did with one finger, inserting at first just the tips. Each time you do the exercise, try to push them in a little farther than the previous time.

By now, even if you have no partner and so cannot do the second half of the exercise, you will have overcome your fear of penetration to an extent which should make it possible for you to have sex when the occasion arises. Nevertheless, it is important that you tell your new partner about the fear you have managed to overcome. He will probably readily accept that you must take intercourse very gradually, following the steps outlined below, which comprise the remainder of the exercise.

▽ **Overcoming fear by stages**
Once you have been able to accept the tip without pain, insert the finger as far as the first joint, and relax with it inside you.

Involving your partner ▷
Ask your partner to insert a well-lubricated finger by gentle stages. Tense your vaginal muscles and then relax them if you feel they are tightening involuntarily.

8 Your partner should insert just the tip of a well-lubricated finger in your vagina.

9 Guiding his hand, ask him to insert more of his finger. Stop, just as you did with your own finger, if you feel the muscles tightening around it and tighten and relax them deliberately a few times. Go on doing this until you can quite comfortably help him insert all of his finger. Let him keep it there for a while without moving it.

10 Your partner should now move his finger gently in and out. Relax as much as you can while he does this. Bear down and then tighten and relax your vaginal muscles around his finger as he moves.

11 Repeat steps 9 and 10, but this time your partner should use two well-lubricated fingers.

12 You are now ready to take the final step in the program – intercourse. You can choose any position you like, but if you are on top (see SEXUAL POSITIONS, p.63) you will have most control. In this way you can lower yourself onto your partner's erect penis as slowly as you like, and control the

depth of penetration. Your partner should lubricate his penis thoroughly beforehand.

13 At first, ask your partner not to move, and become accustomed to the feel of his penis inside you. Then begin to move if you want to, and again practise tightening and relaxing your vaginal muscles.

14 Next time you do the exercise your partner should begin to thrust (although you must ask him to do so gently at first) and eventually the thrusting can continue to orgasm.

Assessing your progress

You may have experienced intense relief when you first realized you were able to tolerate penetration, even if only by one finger, without pain or discomfort. After this breakthrough, you were probably able to complete the program quite rapidly. If you made no progress, the most likely reason is that you have a deep-seated fear of sex or intercourse that needs to be confronted before treatment can be successful. If this is the case, psychotherapy will probably help you.

WOMEN ♀ 3 IMPROVING YOUR SEX LIFE

101

HOW TO REACH ORGASM

So much stress has been put on the importance of the female orgasm that it has come to overshadow every other aspect of lovemaking. You may feel a failure as a woman, or your partner may feel he is inadequate as a lover, if you do not reach a climax every time you have sex. But to focus narrowly on orgasm, regarding it as a matter of success or failure, is to undervalue the broad and varied pleasures of sex and to spoil them through anxiety. The more concerned you are about the possibility of failure, the more your own fears will affect your ability to experience sexual pleasure. Indeed, it is this very anxiety that often plays a large part in inhibiting orgasm.

The ease with which a woman achieves orgasm and the intensity of the experience vary widely from woman to woman and in the same woman from time to time. A very few women never reach orgasm, however intensely they are stimulated, while at the other end of the scale are those whose orgasmic 'threshold' is so low that they need only slight stimulation in order to reach a climax. For the latter, simply fantasizing about sex may be enough. And there are also many women who are not sure whether what they experience is an orgasm or not. What is much more usual, though, is the ability to reach orgasm sometimes, or with some partners.

The value of masturbation

Almost every woman can reach a climax if she stimulates herself. If you have never had an orgasm, even through masturbation, or if you are uncertain whether what you experience is an orgasm or not, your best plan is to begin the exercises suggested in GIVING YOURSELF PLEASURE, p.86. These will help you to get to know the way your own body responds. Because masturbation is the easiest way for a woman to reach orgasm, it is the best way to prepare yourself for it with a partner. Once you can reach a climax through self-stimulation, you are ready to move on to the self-help program below. This is designed for the many women who, although they can experience orgasm easily through masturbation, seldom or never do so during intercourse.

Understanding orgasm

To understand why reaching a climax is difficult or impossible during sex with a partner, you need to know a few key facts about the female orgasm.

☐ Orgasm is a reflex reaction usually triggered off by stimulation of the clitoris, in which muscular contractions are felt deep within the vagina as a series of intense pulsations. Like many reflexes, orgasm can be inhibited, and its intensity will vary according to your psychological state. There are inevitably times when, without realizing it, you are limiting the strength of your climax, or preventing it entirely.

☐ Almost every woman can reach orgasm through stimulation of the clitoris alone, which is the most common method of masturbation. The clitoris corresponds in some ways to the head of the penis but is even more sensitive.

☐ Few women can reach orgasm through penile thrusting alone, since the inner two-thirds of the vagina usually transmit very little sensation. The walls of the outermost third are very sensitive to pressure, however, and most sensitive of all is the vaginal entrance and the surrounding area.

☐ Clitoral stimulation by itself produces an orgasm that feels intense and focused. During intercourse, the presence of the penis seems to make the sensations feel more diffuse. This difference may explain why some women, used to climaxing through masturbation, are uncertain whether or not what they experience during intercourse is, in fact, orgasm. Physiologically, though, the reflex reaction that occurs in the vagina is the same however it is produced.

☐ A woman needs continuous stimulation in order to reach orgasm. No matter how near she is to it, the sensations will die away if stimulation stops.

Learning to let go

Orgasm depends on your ability to 'let go'. Tiredness, anxiety, tension – all of these make it difficult for you to do so. There will be times when, even though you may need the physical and emotional comfort that comes from making love, one or more of these factors will prevent you from reaching orgasm. Do not take this seriously; it is to be expected and, in any case, their influence is normally temporary.

A far more decisive factor in determining whether or not, and how often, you reach orgasm is your relationship with your partner. For nearly all women anger is incompatible with orgasm. If, for some reason, you feel hostility or resentment toward your partner, you may hold back emotionally, perhaps without even realizing it, so that your normal sexual responsiveness is inhibited and you find it hard to let go. Good sex depends more than anything else on good relationships, particularly for women, who usually find it harder than men to separate their sexual response from the rest of their emotional life.

For a few women, though, an inability to reach orgasm may be part of a negative attitude to sex that makes it hard to enjoy it at all. Such emotional obstacles to enjoyment are discussed in **Letting yourself be sexual**, p.76. Some are particularly likely to underlie repeated failure to reach orgasm. It may be, for example, that you are the kind of person who likes to be in control of yourself, to remain unemotional, whatever happens. If so, the idea of being carried away by an orgasm may seem very frightening. Or it may be that you are inhibited because the loss of control involved in having an orgasm might make you look unattractive, un-dignified, even ridiculous, to your lover.

Creating the right mood for orgasm

The following notes will help you identify factors which may be preventing you from getting into the right frame of mind for orgasm.

☐ Guarantee yourself time and privacy when you have sex so that you do not feel rushed or worry about interruptions. If you have young children, but do not like locking them out of your room at night, arrange for them to spend an occasional couple of hours in the evening or at the weekend with a friend.

☐ Try not to discuss major worries such as work, money, or the children's schooling, or broach subjects which are possible sources of friction, for at least half an hour before you go to bed.

☐ Make up quarrels before bedtime, but not in bed. If your partner tries to use sex to make up after a quarrel it will probably increase your resentment and turn you off even more.

☐ If you are feeling tense, practise relaxation exercises before you make love, or try to 'psych' yourself into a more receptive frame of mind. In fact, though, sex itself can be one of the best ways of reducing tension. If you do let go enough to reach a climax, all the better, but do not expect it to always happen or dwell on it when it does not.

☐ Concentrate on your own feelings during sex. Women are often so concerned with pleasing their partner or so worried that he is becoming impatient over their failure to reach orgasm that they cannot fully experience their own sensations. Try to focus on what you are feeling to the exclusion of all else.

The right kind of stimulation

If you seldom experience orgasm nowadays, and particularly if you used to with previous partners, it could be that you are not getting the right kind of stimulation. Your partner perhaps believes, as many men do, that if he thrusts long and hard enough you will eventually reach a climax. And you too may share the delusion that you would be able to reach orgasm if only your partner could stave off ejaculation longer.

Such notions are mistaken. First, since there is likely to be little direct stimulation of the clitoris during intercourse, penetration is not, for many women, the most efficient means of achieving orgasm, although it may be the most satisfying emotionally. Secondly, very prolonged intercourse can be counterproductive, since after a time the vagina stops producing its natural lubrication and you may become sore. With the right kind of stimulation you will be able to reach a climax even if intercourse lasts for only five minutes, perhaps even less. But without adequate stimulation you will probably fail to climax however long it continues.

Aids to achieving orgasm

You may find that the following suggestions will help you to reach a climax during intercourse.

☐ The most important thing to realize is that the more excited you are before intercourse begins, the more likely you are to have an orgasm. Try to prolong foreplay, getting your partner to caress your whole body and particularly the clitoral area until your inner vaginal lips feel engorged and swollen and you have an intense longing to feel his penis inside you. The mistake most men persist in making is to assume that a woman is fully aroused simply because she has started to produce the lubrication that makes penetration easier. Vaginal lubrication occurs at an early stage of sexual excitement and does not necessarily mean that you are near to full arousal, far less orgasm.

MULTIPLE ORGASM

While most men require a period of recovery after they have ejaculated before they are capable of erection and orgasm again, many women have no such refractory period. They can, if stimulation continues, reach orgasm again almost immediately. Intense stimulation – manual, oral, or with a vibrator – may even bring on several orgasms in quick succession.

However, even if you have a capacity for multiple orgasm, it does not follow that you need more than one to satisfy you. It simply means that you can vary your approach occasionally. For example, ask your partner to stimulate you to a climax before you have intercourse, so that you can have a second orgasm when he is inside you.

☐ Experiment with different positions. It is often easiest for a woman to reach orgasm in a position in which she herself has some control over the movements she makes and therefore the stimulation she receives. A woman-on-top position (see SEXUAL POSITIONS, p.63) is effective for many women, but it is best to discover for yourself what feels right for you.

☐ Is the position in which you masturbate very different from the position in which you usually have intercourse? Do you always lie on your back, or on your stomach, for example? Are your legs usually apart, or do you keep them together? If you have learned, through masturbation, how to have an orgasm in a particular position, the pattern may have become so established that it is hard to change. It may help to adopt instead a position that approximates more closely to your usual intercourse position, so that you get used to having an orgasm this way. You might also try changing your intercourse position so that it is similar to the one in which you masturbate.

☐ Do you fantasize when you masturbate? And do you feel guilty about using the same sort of fantasies as an aid to orgasm during sex with your partner? Your fantasies are your own, and a very private affair. Most people have them, and they do not indicate any disloyalty to your partner or cause any harm to the relationship. If erotic fantasies have always helped you to reach orgasm when you masturbate, they will probably do the same during intercourse. You might try making your partner the central figure in your masturbation fantasies and then begin to carry these over into intercourse. This approach is likely to both increase your sexual responsiveness to your partner and alleviate any guilt you feel about fantasizing during sex with him.

☐ Tension, often unconscious, is sometimes the cause of a woman's failure to reach orgasm. If you are tense you will find you hold your breath and tighten your muscles. When you do this you cut yourself off from sensation instead of being fully aware of it.

One simple way to overcome tension is to practise deep breathing. The exercise is similar to the one taught as a preparation for childbirth in which the aim is to stop you tensing up in anticipation of pain. Take slow, deep breaths, letting each one out slowly as a deep sigh from the back of your throat. You can vary the sound, but do not force it out. Practise any time you have privacy and then, when it begins to feel natural, while you are masturbating.

☐ Some positions provide more clitoral stimulation than others, either through pressure on the whole clitoral area by the man's pubic bone, or through the pulling of the hood of the clitoris during thrusting. SEXUAL POSITIONS, p.63, describes positions in which there is a good degree of clitoral stimulation.

☐ Practise the Kegel exercises recommended on p.81. Some sex therapists believe that toning up the pelvic floor muscles, which contract at orgasm, produces a stronger and more enjoyable climax.

☐ The minimum entry technique is a form of intercourse which, although it may not provide your partner with as much stimulation as he would like, will probably be very arousing for you. In a man-on-top position he should raise himself on his hands and move just the tip of the penis in and out of your vaginal lips, so that there is a slight pull on them at each stroke.

☐ The maximum withdrawal technique also pulls strongly on the vaginal lips and stimulates the sensitive entrance, producing intense sensations. Your partner should withdraw his penis as far as he can with each thrust, so that its head makes repeated contact with the vaginal lips.

Choose a position in which your partner can comfortably withdraw his penis to the tip between thrusts. This will provide intense stimulation of the vaginal lips.

☐ Try to move your body so as to increase vaginal sensation during intercourse. The exercise in **Non-demand intercourse**, p.96, recommends that you use your vaginal muscles to squeeze the penis as it thrusts in and out and move your pelvis up and down to increase friction on the vaginal walls. These movements will make you more aroused and therefore more likely to experience orgasm. A 'corkscrew' movement of your partner's penis, which brings it into closer contact with the vaginal walls, is also likely to be more stimulating than straight thrusting.

☐ The dual-stimulation technique may provide the direct clitoral stimulation during intercourse that you need in order to reach orgasm. Choose a side-by-side, woman-on-top, or rear-entry position (see SEXUAL POSITIONS, p.63) in which either you or your partner can easily reach your clitoris with a hand. This extra stimulation may be all you need to tip you over into orgasm. This approach is the most likely to succeed if all else fails, and it forms the basis of the 'bridge' technique described below.

☐ A few women find it helps, when they approach the peak of excitement and feel an orgasm is imminent, to act as though they were actually already experiencing one. They contract their vaginal muscles deliberately, exaggerate their movements, and moan out loud. This role-playing is not an attempt to deceive themselves or their partners, but it may release inhibitions so that the body can respond with a real orgasm in the wake of the simulated one.

☐ Many women find that pressure on the G-spot – a small pressure-sensitive area about half-way up the front wall of the vagina – produces sensations strong enough to trigger orgasm. The G-spot is stimulated during intercourse in any position in which the penis presses upward against this frontal wall. Rear-entry positions are particularly suitable (see SEXUAL POSITIONS, p.63). G-spot stimulation in any of the man-on-top positions is increased by putting a pillow beneath your hips. Your partner can stimulate the area more directly by slipping his right middle finger, palm upward into your vagina, and bending his other fingers so that the knuckles press against your clitoris. He should then move his finger gently in and out, pressing on the front wall of your vagina.

Multiple-stimulation ('bridge') technique

If none of the suggestions already mentioned has worked for you, but you know that you can reach orgasm when you masturbate, you will probably find the 'bridge' technique helpful. This is a method devised by the American sex therapist Helen Kaplan for the very many women who need a lot of clitoral stimulation to reach orgasm.

Nearly all women who reach orgasm when they masturbate will be able to do so if they receive additional clitoral stimulation while the penis is in the vagina. The basis of the 'bridge' technique is for one partner to give clitoral stimulation up to the point of orgasm, but to allow the thrusting of the penis to be the final trigger to orgasm. Clitoral stimulation is stopped progressively further from orgasm. But as a regular routine this method of reaching orgasm has its limitations, notably that one or other partner has continually to provide such stimulation manually, which will detract from the freedom to enjoy his or her own sensations. Nor will it develop a woman's capacity to climax during ordinary intercourse.

◁ **The 'bridge' technique**
*A period of manual stimulation
of the clitoris by either partner
during intercourse makes it
easier to climax in response to
your partner's thrusting.*

Faking orgasm

All the advice given above is much easier to benefit
from if you can talk easily and freely to your partner
about sex. But perhaps until now there has been no
real necessity for you to put your cards on the table
and tell your partner that you do not always (or ever)
reach a climax.

A great many women find it easier to fake orgasms
(usually very convincingly) than to admit that they
do not have them. Sometimes it is because this would
seem an admission of failure, producing a sense of
inadequacy, but in some cases it is because they are
protecting their partner's ego, since they are afraid
that the truth might make *him* feel inadequate. And
for women who are less than enthusiastic about sex,
faking orgasm may seem to be the easiest way of
getting the whole thing over as quickly as possible.

If you have been pretending in the past, but want
to make changes and try the 'bridge' technique
described above, the first and most important step is
to tell your partner the truth, for you will need his
cooperation. But the exercise will not work unless
you fully recognize and accept your body's
responses.

Obviously, the longer you have practised such
deception, the harder it may be to acknowledge it. If
you do choose to own up, do your best not to make
your admission sound like an accusation. The most
positive attitude is not to say 'You've never given me
an orgasm', but something like, 'I don't think I've
ever really had an orgasm. Do you think we could try
something that might help?' Try never to think, or to
let your partner think, of your orgasm as his sole
responsibility, for it is yours too.

Assessing your progress

After you have practised the 'bridge' technique two
or three times a week for several weeks you will
probably find you need less and less clitoral
stimulation to reach orgasm, and may even have
reached the point where you need no 'priming' at all.
But many women – so many, in fact, that this may be
said to be the normal pattern – continue to need at
least some stimulation of the clitoris if they are to
climax. Do not worry if, during some sessions, your
partner becomes so aroused that he cannot hold back
any longer and thrusts to ejaculation. What matters
most is that he should want you to succeed, and be
pleased by your success. However good your
progress though, do not expect to reach orgasm every
time you make love.

If, on the other hand, you have had no success at all
after several weeks, seek further help (see RE-
SOURCE GUIDE, p.160). A sex therapist will help
you resolve the underlying inhibitions that prevent
you from climaxing during intercourse.

LESBIANISM

If you are heterosexual, you probably accept the fact without question, for you are simply doing what is generally expected of you. But if you suspect that you are drawn to women rather than to men you will probably not be able to acknowledge your feelings with similar ease. Indeed, so strong is the assumption that there is only one 'normal' life a woman can lead that many women are very slow to discover that they have lesbian tendencies. In many cases they marry, have children, and go through the motions of a heterosexual life before they start to question their own feelings and decide that such a lifestyle is not what they really want.

According to the Kinsey report on female sexuality (1953) about one in five single women and one in ten married women eventually has some homosexual experience, although probably only between a half and one per cent of women are exclusively lesbian. And yet the Hite report, published in 1976, revealed that many women who had no homosexual experience were curious about what sex would be like with a woman, or suspected it might prove more satisfying than their heterosexual relationships. Probably about 15 per cent of women have occasional lesbian fantasies, but few of these seek such experiences in reality.

Making the choice

If you have doubts about your true orientation, try to analyze your feelings about both men and women.

If you are still in your teens, and have had little experience of men, do not assume that because you have had some lesbian feelings or even encounters these will necessarily set the pattern for your adulthood. As you meet men and gain more confidence, your heterosexual feelings may grow.

It may be, though, that your feelings are so strong and unmistakable that there really is no choice for you; that lesbianism is the obvious and inevitable way of life. Even so, it can be painful to acknowledge these feelings and give them a name, and even more so to allow others to know. Other people's assumptions that lesbianism is 'second best' or that lesbians are strident, aggressive man-haters make it hard to feel either pride or joy in your own sexuality. (The questionnaire ORIENTATION, p.23, should help you decide where your true preference lies, and the following notes may also be helpful.)

☐ Get in contact with your nearest lesbian support group or befriending service (see RESOURCE GUIDE, p.160) if you decide that your inclinations are exclusively or predominantly lesbian. More than anything else, this will dispel the sense of isolation that comes from believing that no one else around you feels the same as you. It will also help you to build up a more realistic and positive idea of lesbianism, because you will discover that the women you meet do not conform to the stereotypes. Above all, they will not see being a lesbian as fraught with insoluble problems, and yet they will appreciate the difficulties, for they will have confronted them themselves.

☐ Remember that you do not have to be 100 per cent straight or lesbian. You may need to try out a variety of relationships with people of both sexes to discover what suits you best. Do not let yourself be pressured by others into committing yourself one way or the other until you are sure.

☐ Lesbianism is more than a simple matter of a sexual preference for other women. It is usually more concerned with forming relationships than with simply having sex, and involves a whole lifestyle built around such friendships.

☐ If you have children already, you will not necessarily have to give them up if you separate from their father, although you can expect to meet prejudice in the courts if you seek custody. As a lesbian mother you will meet the same kind of difficulties that any parent, single or married, faces but, in addition, any problems your children have will be assumed to be a result of your personal life. Children will accept a lesbian 'family' more easily if they know others in the same position. It is the feeling that they are different and isolated that makes things most difficult for them.

Coming out

To 'come out' – to admit that you are a lesbian – may jeopardize your job, restrict your career options, and may alienate your family and friends. But it also means that you will be able to live a fuller life and dispense with secrecy.

Coming out is not necessarily a matter of making a public announcement to a fanfare of trumpets. It need only mean living the life you want to lead openly – just dropping the pretence that you are 'straight', and no longer manufacturing fictitious heterosexual involvements as a cover.

When you do tell anyone close to you that you are a lesbian, you are not making a 'confession'. You are doing nothing to be ashamed of, only sharing the facts of a very important part of your life with someone who matters to you. So be confident, be happy, and be proud, but, particularly with your parents, be sensitive too. In one survey nearly 50 per cent of the lesbians questioned believed that their parents understood the situation. Relatives, like close friends, normally care for you and want your happiness. If it is apparent that the way of life you have chosen makes you happy, they will probably be able to respect your feelings.

It is very unlikely in any case that the news will come as a surprise to those who are close to you. Once the facts are put before them they may realize that they have known, even if they have not acknowledged it, for some time. Be guided by the cues they give you. Some people are just not capable of assimilating this kind of knowledge about their own family or friends and, if this really is the case, it may be kinder not to force it on them. But if they genuinely want to know, and they care for you, they will make it as easy as they can for you to tell them.

Be prepared, when you do come out, to meet attitudes varying from the incredulous to the openly hostile. You may be told you cannot really be a lesbian because you are too pretty or too feminine. And if, like many lesbians, it has taken time and some heterosexual experience before you have discovered your true direction, you are quite likely to be told that your only problem is that you have not yet met the right man, or that it is the failure of your relationships with men that has forced you to become a lesbian.

You should also be aware that although many heterosexual women get on well with gay men, perhaps because the situation gives both parties an opportunity for friendship without sexual complications, some heterosexual men may take it as a personal affront to discover that you are lesbian. For the man who likes to 'score', you may represent both a threat and a challenge to his ego.

The benefits of being a lesbian

Sex is very important to some lesbians, less so to others, as is the case with heterosexual women. Both emotionally and physically, women are often natu-rally attuned to one another and know instinctively how to please each other. By contrast, heterosexual men and women have to learn how to do this. And so you will probably find there are benefits in your sexual relationships with women that are perhaps less easily available to heterosexual women. The most important of these advantages are:

☐ Sex may be more emotionally satisfying. Tenderness and affection play a vital part in nearly all lesbian relationships. Intimate body contact – hugging, kissing, touching – which is the element heterosexual women value highly, and often fail to find, in lovemaking, is at the very heart of lesbian sex. Here, it is an end in itself rather than just a prelude to 'real' sex – that is, intercourse. Lesbian sex is less predictable than its heterosexual counterpart, where intercourse and orgasm are regarded as goals to be attained at all costs. Women are more likely than a heterosexual couple to spend on occasion a whole lovemaking session enjoying non-genital sex – kissing, caressing, and touching each other – without feeling that they have to provide orgasm for each other.

☐ Lack of orgasm is less likely to be a problem if you are lesbian. Most women reach orgasm much more easily through clitoral stimulation than vaginal penetration. And most lesbian sexual activity focuses on clitoral stimulation in the form of oral sex, mutual masturbation by hand, or – less often – tribadism (rubbing gently against each other). Moreover, a woman, through her experience and knowledge of her own sensations, may be more adept than a man at bringing another woman to a climax.

☐ Women tend to be more sexually honest with each other – it is rare for a woman to fake orgasm with another – so if one partner does have difficulty in reaching orgasm, the couple are more likely to try to solve the problem than resort to deception or ignore it.

☐ Sex may be more prolonged, since between women it is not so limited by orgasm as heterosexual intercourse often is. One orgasm need not signal the end of lovemaking, whereas a man may not be able to have a second orgasm or may lose interest altogether after the first.

☐ Women are not so fond of casual affairs as men. Relationships which are entirely based on sexual attraction usually hold little appeal for them.

However, this is an attitude which does not always operate to a lesbian couple's advantage. A woman may be very aware of the dangers of infidelity and try to avoid them. But if she does become involved with someone else, it is quite likely that it will be at a fairly deep emotional level, and this may be more damaging to the relationship than a purely physical affair.

The problems of being a lesbian

Just as the sexual benefits of a lesbian relationship stem from the fact that both partners have a female outlook, so does the main drawback. The most fundamental difficulty lesbian couples have to cope with in their sexual relationships is that they may both find it impossible not to behave like women and will continue to hold traditional female attitudes. In such cases, the relationship often comprises two 'passive' partners, neither feeling entirely comfortable about taking the lead sexually in what is, traditionally, the male way.

This dilemma can be particularly acute in long-established relationships. Sex in a lesbian partnership tends to fall off quite rapidly and many couples have sex less often than either heterosexual couples or gay men. One survey of couples who had been together longer than ten years found that 47 per cent of lesbians had sex once a month or less, compared with 15 per cent of married couples and 33 per cent of male homosexual couples.

It is likely that this rapid falling off in sexual activity is a result of the conditioning that all women receive, whatever their sexual orientation. What seems to happen is that, even if she is interested in sex, neither woman wants to be the partner who usually suggests or initiates it. As a consequence, they may both be waiting for the other to make the first sexual advance, and so will tend to make love less often than one, or both, want.

If you feel that this is happening to you, talk about it to your partner. You will probably discover that it is not lack of interest that is eroding your sex life, but that the active role is lying vacant. Once you are sure of this it should be possible to work out between you some way of sharing responsibility so that you can halt this loss of sexual intimacy.

The same reluctance can cause difficulties for the unattached lesbian too in that she may find it difficult to make sexual relationships at all. A woman cannot easily mistake the signs of a man's sexual interest in her. But, apart from in lesbian groups or meeting places, when you are sexually interested in another woman you may feel inhibited about making the first move if you are unsure about her orientation.

Even if you do show interest you have to rely on subtle signs – eye contact or intensity of interest in what she is saying – and she may not pick up on them. These signs are open to misinterpretation too, and may be seen merely as tokens of friendship rather than of sexual attraction. It is common for a woman not to recognize the sexual cues she is given by another woman or to be afraid to follow them up.

Often, your sexual interest in another woman is awakened only when you realize that she is interested in you. The relationship can then build on this mutuality. But, unless one of you is brave enough to take the lead, the first encounter may fail to develop into anything.

Coming to terms with your feelings ▷
So dominant is the heterosexual lifestyle as a role-model that some women recognize their lesbian orientation only after years of marriage and child-rearing.

4

THE WOMAN WITH A STEADY PARTNER

Being part of a couple implies emotional commitment as well as sexual attachment and most couples prefer their relationship to be sexually exclusive. Monogamy is still the ideal most people strive for, even if it is not always achieved, and they expect of it both emotional security and physical satisfaction. Many of the problems you will face as a couple and which are discussed in this part of the book will arise simply because you have made this commitment to each other; they seem to be the most inescapable facts of a shared life. Few long-term partners will not experience, at some time or other, the overfamiliarity that can lead to boredom, or at least to a sexual wistfulness. Many will experience jealousy, or have to deal with the threat of infidelity.

The final section deals with contraception, with the problems of the couple who want to have a child but have so far been unable to, and offers guidance to the woman who is pregnant or has recently given birth.

COMPATIBILITY

For most couples, being compatible means being able to live together in a pleasurable and satisfying way. This is possible when their personalities and viewpoints are reasonably similar or complement each other so well that there is seldom serious conflict. The qualities that make for compatibility in a relationship are discussed more fully in MAKING A LASTING RELATIONSHIP, p. 148.

Yet it is quite possible to live together happily even though you may not seem, in theory, altogether compatible. Indeed no couple who live together for any length of time will see eye to eye on every issue, or always have the same needs at the same time. As important and valuable as compatibility of temperament is being able to deal with issues as they arise and to resolve them by making the necessary shifts of attitude before the whole relationship is jeopardized.

If you can do this, it will benefit your sex life as well as your overall happiness. The couple who get along well in other ways and who are loving and committed to each other will not normally allow sexual differences or difficulties to sour the rest of their relationship. Sex therapists have found, too, that while most sexual problems can be resolved successfully if a couple's general relationship is close and loving, therapy is less likely to succeed if there is hostility between them.

Certain areas of a shared life are especially vital to the health of a relationship, but may at times be abundant sources of friction. The questionnaire that follows explores these crucial areas, allowing you to see how well you have adjusted to each other's needs. You can answer on your own, but it is better to both do it, each keeping your own score.

HOW WELL DO YOU SUIT EACH OTHER?

1 How much of your leisure time do you spend with your partner?

Most	2
Some	1
Little or none	0

2 How many of your friends are mutual friends whose company you both enjoy?

Some	1
Few or none	0
Most	2

3 If your partner wants to spend a quiet evening at home together do you usually:

Not mind?	1
Welcome and enjoy it?	2
Feel bored?	0

4 If you have dinner in a restaurant with just your partner do you find:

It is a good opportunity to talk?	2
It is quite pleasant but not stimulating?	1
You have got very little to say to each other?	0

5 If your work began to make heavy inroads on your time together would you:

Welcome it?	0
Try to alter your timetable?	2
Decide there was little you could do?	1

6 Of your three main interests how many does your partner share?

All three	2
One or two	1
None	0

7 How often do you vacation together?

Usually	1
Always	2
Rarely	0

8 If your partner is clearly worried about something, does he usually:

Talk about it if you press him?	1
Discuss it with you?	2
Refuse to talk about it?	0

9 When you talk about what you have been doing, thinking, or feeling, how often does your partner seem interested?

Always _____ 2

Seldom _____ 0

Sometimes _____ 1

10 Do disagreements with your partner most often lead to:

A spirited argument? _____ 1

Serious or prolonged hostility? _____ 0

Discussion? _____ 2

11 How often do you quarrel fiercely over trivial issues?

Seldom or never _____ 2

Occasionally _____ 1

Often _____ 0

12 Are you ever concerned because your partner is much more of a spendthrift (or more careful with money) than you are?

Never _____ 2

Sometimes _____ 1

Continually _____ 0

13 If an expensive item (a car or furniture, for example) is needed for use by both of you, how often do you have what you consider a fair say in choosing it?

Always _____ 2

Seldom or never _____ 0

Sometimes _____ 1

14 Do you feel you have less say than you would like in deciding how unallocated money is spent?

No _____ 2

Slightly _____ 1

What I would like is seldom considered _____ 0

15 Are you in agreement about domestic expenditure?

Completely _____ 2

Not at all _____ 0

To some extent _____ 1

16 Do you ever feel lonely or resentful because your partner seems to have a greater need for solitude than you do?

Seldom or never _____ 2

Sometimes _____ 1

Often _____ 0

17 Does your partner 'crowd' you so that you have little or no time for yourself?

Seldom or never _____ 2

Sometimes _____ 1

Most of the time _____ 0

18 Would you like to spend more time doing things without your partner?

Much more _____ 0

A little more _____ 1

Not at all _____ 2

19 How often do problems arise because your partner resents you seeing other people or doing things without him?

Seldom or never _____ 2

Occasionally _____ 1

Often _____ 0

20 How often does jealousy cause problems between you?

Occasionally _____ 1

Often _____ 0

Seldom or never _____ 2

21 Do you feel that you spend too much time with your partner's parents or that his views about things that concern only the two of you are too much influenced by theirs?

Not at all _____ 2

A little _____ 1

Far too much _____ 0

22 Do you wish your partner was:

More ambitious? _____ 0

Less ambitious? _____ 0

Neither? _____ 2

(continued)

23 Does your job ever disrupt your time together?		**26** If you have no children, do you agree about whether or when to start a family?	
Sometimes	1	Completely	2
Often	0	Not at all	0
Seldom	2	With reservations	1

24 Does your partner's job ever disrupt your time together?		**27** If you have children, do you feel that your partner's attitude toward their rearing is:	
Seldom	2	About right?	2
Sometimes	1	Too strict?	0
Often	0	Too easygoing?	0

25 Do you and your partner agree about a woman's right to work if she wants to?		**28** Have you ever seriously considered ending your relationship?	
Completely	2	Often	0
With reservations	1	Once or twice	1
Not at all	0	Never	2

RATING

High rating (36-56)

This suggests that you are content in your relationship, and that it meets most, if not all, of your emotional needs. You probably feel you have room to grow within it too.

Medium rating (25-35)

This indicates that your relationship has a good chance of permanence. However, if you scored low in a particular group of questions, consult the detailed analysis below.

Low rating (0-24)

This suggests that dissatisfaction with your day-to-day life together is very likely to spill over into your sex life. Couples who argue a lot tend to have a less active and less satisfying sex life. Look through your answers to discover where the major difficulties lie. Does your partner score low on the same questions? If so, you probably both need to make adjustments in those areas. If there is a subtle difference between your scores, it may be that one partner is making *all* the adjustments.

ANALYSIS OF THE QUESTIONS

Questions 1-7 deal with companionship.
Companionship is one of the most important things you can give each other. An American survey published in 1983 indicated that couples who spend less time together are less satisfied and are more liable to break up than more companionable couples.

You are more likely to be happy and to develop a more intimate relationship if you have mutual friends and interests. If you spend too much time away from each other you risk loosening the bonds of intimacy. The main danger for the couple who spend little of their free time together is that they may come to find that most of the time they do spend together is concerned largely with domestic trivia and problems, the least appealing aspects of a shared life.

Companionship seems to be an area in which the homosexual couple often scores over the heterosexual and, in particular, gay couples are more likely to have interests and leisure activities in common.

Questions 8-11 deal with communication.
For many couples, problems arise simply because they do not talk to each other enough, or because they talk without actually communicating. They keep each other at an emotional distance so that real feelings are seldom shared and misunderstandings

inevitably occur. Some people expect from their partner an almost telepathic ability to communicate, because the words they use bear little relation to the message they really want to convey. For example, complaints are directed at easy targets ('You never put the cat out when it's your turn') when the real source of dissatisfaction ('You're not as loving as I'd like you to be') is harder both to recognize and to put into words. If you often have quarrels about trivial things that grow out of all proportion, it usually indicates a much deeper dissatisfaction – about lack of love, or security, or companionship – which you must both confront.

For some couples, feelings of anger cause the most problems. Many people are afraid of showing anger because they feel it will inevitably bring the whole relationship down around their ears. There is at least some foundation for this fear since if you often get very angry it can be enormously destructive of your relationship. Marriage guidance counselors find that anger frequently heads the list of one partner's complaints about the other. However, things are little better if you do not show anger at all, because the problems that caused it may then never be acknowledged or resolved. The tension and resentment that build up within you can be equally destructive. The advice in **Dealing with anger**, p.121, will help you contain and defuse an angry situation before it can do too much damage.

Questions *12-15 concern money.*

Most studies report that between one quarter and one third of all couples quarrel more about money than about anything else. It is not only lack of money that affects a couple's contentment (though it is important, and the less there is, the more fights there are likely to be about it) but also the questions of who should earn it and how it should be spent. Arguments about money are also arguments about trust, about commitment to the relationship, about interdependence and equality. So if money is what you tend to fight about, discover which of these issues are really at stake and deal with them.

Sharing money shows faith in a future together, and indeed almost every couple, heterosexual or homosexual, who have been together for any length of time do this as their commitment grows and the financial strings of their lives become more entwined. But problems can arise if they have different attitudes toward money. If one partner is easy-come, easy-go, while the other is a prudent saver for a rainy day, for example, there may be difficulties; likewise if the higher (or the only) earner wants to exercise greater (or total) control over expenditure.

Questions *16-21 are about privacy and independence.*

However close you are, you will probably feel the need for some privacy from your partner. Couples who live together usually regard private time and personal space as more important than couples who marry. Problems can occur if either partner has an excessive need for privacy or independence because this is likely to affect the time they spend together, which is one of the most important elements binding them. Even so, too much togetherness can be smothering. Life may be equally unsatisfactory for a couple if one partner is so dependent on the other for emotional support and company that he or she allows the other no breathing space.

Arguments about in-laws are often arguments about dependence, about whether a partner has really achieved the necessary emotional break with his or her parents and made a total commitment to the relationship. Such a partner may insist on living close to his or her parents, visiting them unreasonably often, taking their side in an argument against the other partner, and consulting them automatically on every important decision that affects the couple.

Questions *22-25 examine how your work affects the relationship.*

Dissatisfaction here is often about the inroads one partner's job makes on the time they might otherwise spend together. But probably the most serious arguments arise in couples who have not agreed about a woman's right to work or about the extent of her commitment to her work.

Questions *26 and 27 concern your attitudes to parenthood.*

Most studies suggest that children are by no means indispensable to a couple's happiness, even that life together is more fulfilling for the childless couple. The most frequent disagreements are over child-rearing and discipline. If you can develop, or at least present to the children, a united front on the difficult issues, you will improve your chances of avoiding a major source of conflict.

Question *28 concerns the fundamental stability of your relationship.*

Nearly everybody feels like walking out on his or her partner at times, but if you contemplate this frequently then the relationship is clearly not working. Your reasons for planning a separation are almost certainly pinpointed by your answers to the rest of this questionnaire.

ARE YOU SEXUALLY SATISFIED?

Sex is one of the strongest ties that can hold two people together, and it is a bond that you can foster and strengthen by making sure that your sex life is as satisfying as possible for both of you. The questionnaire below deals with some of the most important elements of sexual satisfaction, and it should provide a measure of your contentment with this aspect of your relationship. You can do the questionnaire alone, or better still, with your partner, keeping separate scores. The results will indicate your sexual compatibility and show whether there is a particular problem area.

DO YOU SATISFY EACH OTHER SEXUALLY?

1 Do you have sex:

As often as you want? _____ 2

Not often enough? _____ 0

Too often for your taste? _____ 0

2 How sexually attractive do you find your partner?

Very _____ 2

Fairly _____ 1

Not very _____ 0

3 Who usually initiates sex?

The male partner _____ 2

The female partner _____ 1

Either partner _____ 2

4 Is the 'refusal rate' (when one partner suggests sex):

More or less equal? _____ 2

Very unequal? _____ 0

5 If your partner says no to sex, do you:

Feel rejected, hurt, or angry, and keep a mental note of it? _____ 0

Feel irritated or disappointed but get over it fairly quickly? _____ 1

Accept that he is just not in the mood and settle for a cuddle? _____ 2

6 If you say no to sex, does your partner:

Get angry or upset? _____ 0

Seem briefly disappointed or annoyed? _____ 1

Accept that you are just not in the mood and settle for a cuddle? _____ 2

7 Do you wish your partner was:

Less prudish or inhibited about sex? _____ 0

Less sexually adventurous and eager to experiment? _____ 0

Neither? _____ 2

8 Is your partner as tender and affectionate as you would like during sex?

Always _____ 2

Mostly _____ 1

Never _____ 0

9 Apart from during sex, does your partner show you as much affection as you need?

Mostly _____ 1

Always _____ 2

Never _____ 0

10 How often does your partner persuade you (or attempt to) to try a sexual activity you dislike?

Seldom or never _____ 2

Sometimes _____ 1

Often _____ 0

11 Do you have vaginal problems (or does your partner have erection problems) that make intercourse difficult or impossible?

Seldom or never	2
Sometimes	1
Often	0

12 How often is sex unsatisfactory because you (or your partner) fail to reach orgasm?

Never	2
Sometimes	1
Seldom or never	0

13 How often is sex unsatisfactory because you (or your partner) reach orgasm too quickly?

Seldom or never	2
Sometimes	1
Often	0

14 How often is sex unsatisfactory because your partner just does not seem to be interested?

Seldom or never	2
Often	0
Sometimes	1

15 Has either of you had sex outside the relationship?

Within the last year	0
Since the relationship began	1
Never	2

16 Is sex with your partner as varied as you would like it to be?

Yes	2
Not quite as varied	1
Far less	0

17 How often do you (or does your partner) pick quarrels at bedtime?

Often	0
Occasionally	1
Seldom or never	2

18 How often do you go to bed long before or long after your partner?

Always	0
Sometimes	1
Seldom or never	2

19 Do you suggest sex when it is hard for your partner to respond because of a task that cannot be left?

Often	0
Sometimes	1
Seldom or never	2

20 How often, if sex seems imminent, do you begin to recall past grievances so that you feel resentment toward your partner?

Often	0
Seldom or never	2
Sometimes	1

RATING

High rating (26-40)
This indicates that your present relationship meets your sexual needs very well. You most likely get along well with your partner in other ways, because sexual satisfaction is a good indicator of the quality of your relationship.

Medium rating (16-25)
This shows that you have worked out a sexual relationship that is satisfactory for both partners. However, you will probably both acknowledge that there is considerable scope for improvement in this area. Consult the detailed analysis below about questions for which your score was low.

Low rating (0-15)
This points to a lack of satisfaction with either the quality or the quantity of your sex life, or both. Checking through the detailed analysis below will help you to establish the main causes of dissatisfaction. If you scored low on questions 17-20, and especially if your score on the preceding questionnaire was also low, your lack of sexual contentment may reflect a disharmony in other areas.

ANALYSIS OF THE QUESTIONS

Question 1 deals with sexual frequency.

For most couples, good sex means frequent sex. Couples who have sex infrequently report less overall satisfaction than couples who make love often. It is easy for your sex life to become pared down without either of you fully realizing it. You may, for example, get into a routine of not having sex at a time when one or other of you is tired or busy, and then find that it is not easy to break the habit and establish a new pattern of wanting sex and making time for it. If either of you fails to score on this question, it may be because there is a difference in sex drive between you (see DEALING WITH A SEX-DRIVE DISCREPANCY, p.122). But it may simply be because you have stopped giving sex the priority in your lives that it deserves.

Question 2 concerns sexual attraction.

For this there is no real explanation and certainly no substitute. Finding your partner attractive seems to be one of the most important factors in determining how satisfying your sex life is. You cannot create this sexual chemistry if it does not exist, but you can foster and sustain it when it is present by not taking each other for granted or abandoning all efforts to be attractive to your partner.

Questions 3-6 deal with the sharing of sexual responsibility.

Traditionally, the man suggests sex and the woman either accepts or rejects him, so usually it is the former who determines how much sex the couple have. Couples seem to be happiest, and to have sex most often, when both partners feel equally free to suggest sex or to refuse it, and do so equally often. If you can share control of sex like this you are much less likely to feel angry or rejected if you want sex and your partner does not, or to feel guilty on the occasions when he feels like it and you do not. Inclination rather than obligation will then determine how often you make love.

Questions 7-10, 14 and 16 concern your sexual compatibility.

As in most other areas of your life together, the more similar your sexual likes and dislikes are, the less friction there will be between you. If either of you scores low in this section, turn to ENRICHING YOUR SEX LIFE, p.54, and UNDERSTANDING A MAN'S FEELINGS, p.124.

Questions 11-13 deal with specific sexual problems.

These will inevitably affect the quality of your sexual relationship. If the problem is your own, PAINFUL INTERCOURSE, p.44, OVERCOMING THE FEAR OF PENETRATION, p.98, and HOW TO REACH ORGASM, p.102, will help. If it is your partner who has a sexual problem, you should read UNDERSTANDING A MAN'S FEELINGS, p.124.

Question 15 concerns infidelity.

This is much more likely to be a symptom of dissatisfaction with your relationship than a cause of it. INFIDELITY, p.132, suggests ways of minimizing the damage to your relationship that this situation will almost certainly cause.

Questions 17-20 deal with sexual sabotage.

If your score in this section is low, sex may have become a weapon you use against each other instead of a source of mutual pleasure. You may be withholding it to perpetuate a quarrel or to get even for past grievances. Or you may be using it to make your partner feel inadequate or guilty by always suggesting you make love when it is obviously impossible or inconvenient. If you find that you have reduced your sex life to a minimum by this kind of sabotage, there is sure to be more wrong with your relationship than just sex. Your answers to the preceding questionnaire, on compatibility, may help you discover the underlying problem.

WHAT IS WRONG WITH YOUR RELATIONSHIP?

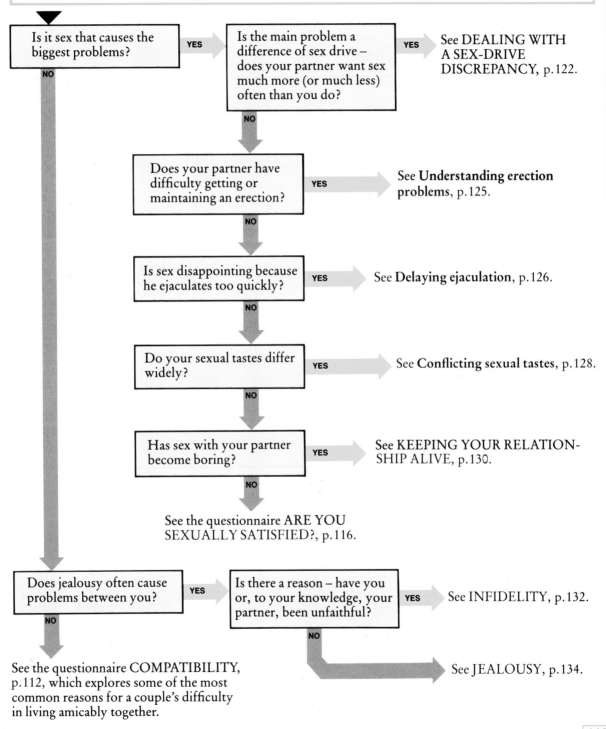

Is it sex that causes the biggest problems? — **YES** → Is the main problem a difference of sex drive – does your partner want sex much more (or much less) often than you do? — **YES** → See DEALING WITH A SEX-DRIVE DISCREPANCY, p.122.

NO

Does your partner have difficulty getting or maintaining an erection? — **YES** → See **Understanding erection problems**, p.125.

NO

Is sex disappointing because he ejaculates too quickly? — **YES** → See **Delaying ejaculation**, p.126.

NO

Do your sexual tastes differ widely? — **YES** → See **Conflicting sexual tastes**, p.128.

NO

Has sex with your partner become boring? — **YES** → See KEEPING YOUR RELATIONSHIP ALIVE, p.130.

NO

See the questionnaire ARE YOU SEXUALLY SATISFIED?, p.116.

Does jealousy often cause problems between you? — **YES** → Is there a reason – have you or, to your knowledge, your partner, been unfaithful? — **YES** → See INFIDELITY, p.132.

NO

NO → See JEALOUSY, p.134.

See the questionnaire COMPATIBILITY, p.112, which explores some of the most common reasons for a couple's difficulty in living amicably together.

LEARNING TO COMMUNICATE

Discussing sex in a general way interests nearly everybody, but fewer find it easy to reveal their personal reactions and sexual preferences. Sharing intimate thoughts and feelings, even with a partner, makes many men and women feel vulnerable. Quite apart from your own inhibitions about speaking out, you may be worried about your partner's reactions if you start to comment on, let alone criticize, any aspect of your shared sex life. Might his feelings be hurt? Even worse, would it make him so angry that he would throw hurtful criticism back at you, or perhaps reject you altogether?

Talking about sex

But, even so, women are generally more ready and more accustomed to talking about their feelings than men. It is usually also very important for women to develop relationships that are as close emotionally as they are physically. And so this is an area in which, if you want things to improve, you may have to take the initiative and shoulder most of the responsibility. Do not expect your partner to be able to read your mind. It is a fallacy to believe that because someone cares for you he will know intuitively exactly what you want. There is no substitute for straight talking if you want to discover what you need from each other.

It is often easier to talk intimately about sex with a new partner; after all, this is what is on both your minds. So take advantage of any new relationship to set up a pattern that can continue as you get to know each other better. At this stage you know little about each other, so there are any number of opportunities to bring up the subject. You need only say something like 'You must tell me if there's anything you'd specially like me to do' or 'I love to be on top sometimes – is that OK by you?'

The right time to talk

For most people the easiest way to start talking about sex is when they are actually making love. Then, it is quite natural to say 'That's nice, I love you to do that'. Some people, however, find it easier to bring up the subject of sexual preferences at other times. This is likely to be the case if you are involved in a long-standing relationship in which you and your partner have not been in the habit of talking about sex.

If you want to set up a new pattern of communication, you will require a lot of tact and patience. It is probably best to introduce the subject when you are on neutral ground – over a drink or a meal, for example, when you should both feel comfortable and relaxed. And broach it indirectly, by means of something you have read or seen on TV, by quoting a friend's experience, or by recounting a dream (fictitious, if necessary).

Reliving pleasurable experiences

It is usually easier, too, to talk in terms of past experience rather than about the present. If you wish you could repeat a certain kind of sexual activity that you once enjoyed together, speak of it reminiscently as a pleasurable experience, as this can lead to a suggestion that you do it again. It may help if you rehearse what you are going to say in advance. Working out the wording and saying it aloud to yourself will increase your confidence when you broach the subject with your partner.

Reassuring your partner

Give reassurance and encouragement whenever you can. It probably works better (at least until you are quite confident of the relationship) to stress what you like rather than complain about what you dislike. So say, 'I love it when you stroke me gently there' rather than 'Why are you always so rough?' Remember that direct criticism is almost always destructive, especially if you give it at an insensitive moment – when your partner is highly aroused, for example. It is better, if you can, to describe to your partner the way you feel rather than find fault with his sexual performance.

Be as explicit as you can in explaining why you feel the way you do. It is important to admit (to yourself first of all, then to your partner) your *real* feelings and convey them as accurately as you can. To say 'I hate the idea of oral sex, it's so animal-like', when what you really mean – and want reassurance about – is 'I'm afraid to try oral sex because you might think I smell bad' is to take the easy way out. Unless you are totally honest, there is no real basis for discussion.

Discover the way he feels by asking direct and very specific questions. Do not just say, 'Was that OK?' Say 'Do you like me to stroke your penis? Is it better when I press harder?' If you try to guess your partner's likes and dislikes and behave as you imagine he would like you to behave, you may guess wrong. And if both of you play this guessing game, neither of you will get what you want. So play it straight, and encourage your partner to do the same. He will probably have as much difficulty (if not more) than you in expressing the way he feels about sex, so be as helpful as you can.

Pick up non-verbal cues by noticing what your partner does to you. You can often assume that if he does something special – spends a long time kissing the small of your back, for example, or fondling your anus – the chances are that he would like you to reciprocate. For many people such cues are the easiest way to let their partner know their sexual preference. But of course they only work to an extent; they are open to misinterpretation and depend on having a partner sensitive enough to recognize them.

Above all, remember that giving or demanding complete self-exposure all at once can make your partner back off if he is not ready for it. Never ask a question you would not be willing to answer yourself or one that you are certain your partner is not willing to respond to at present.

Saying no

For many women, one of the most difficult communication problems is finding a way of telling a partner that you are just not in the mood for sex without making him feel rejected. You yourself undoubtedly know how hurt and rejected you can feel because of a sexual rebuff. It is important to learn how to reject the invitation without rejecting the person.

Many couples who find it difficult to be forthright prefer to adopt a code to convey sexual readiness. You might agree on a 0-10 scale, for example. Then, if either of you says, 'Sorry, but I rate zero tonight', the other knows this means total unwillingness. On the other hand, a 3 or 4 might mean 'I can probably make it if you're really keen.' Or you could choose a code based on appetite, ranging from 'I could eat a horse' down to 'All I need is a cup of black coffee'.

A code system prevents the development of situations fraught with misunderstanding and makes it clear that you are just talking about a temporary mood. The number code allows room for maneuver. If one of you is an 8, for example, while the other shows a flicker of interest with a 3, the person with the lower rating might be prepared to make an extra effort for the sake of the more enthusiastic partner. As long as you agree on the respective values of the code words, the second system might also allow negotiation.

Dealing with anger

For nearly everyone anger and good sex are incompatible. In any relationship, especially a long-term one, quarrels and hurt feelings should be dealt with as they arise, not left to fester. Suppressed resentment contributes to sexual problems and makes them increasingly hard to resolve.

It is important for any couple, particularly those with sexual problems that they are trying to surmount, to be able to deal with anger. Occasional episodes of unpleasantness are bound to arise in nearly every relationship, but they can be resolved without lasting bitterness if the partners can talk over without delay the real cause of the trouble. Below are some guidelines for a sensible approach to such situations.

☐ Tell your partner exactly what has upset you, and do it at the time, not days or weeks later.

☐ Deal with the problem in terms of your own feelings rather than by criticizing your partner's behavior. Say, 'Perhaps I shouldn't get angry when . . . but I do' rather than 'You're so selfish, you don't ever . . .'.

☐ Stick to the particular issue and resolve it. Do not use the present argument as an opportunity to get past resentments off your chest.

☐ Exercise self-control, no matter how irritated you are. Arguments should not be damaging or destructive. So, if you are so angry that you feel like shouting at or hitting your partner, wait until the white heat of your rage dies down before tackling the issue.

☐ Do not make wounding attacks on each other's physical or intellectual shortcomings as these are not easily forgotten or forgiven.

☐ The moment an argument seems to be degenerating into a destructive fight, give it up and suggest that you would rather resolve it later when you both feel calmer.

☐ Make it up before bedtime, or the moment you get into bed. But you probably will not be very responsive if your partner tries to use sex as a way of making up after a fight.

DEALING WITH A SEX-DRIVE DISCREPANCY

One of the commonest, and most frustrating, difficulties that a couple can face is that one partner wants sex much more than the other. In such cases, it is the partner who is less interested who tends to be accused of being abnormal.

Everyone has different sexual needs and, because these vary so widely, there is little point in measuring yourself or each other against any notion of a sexual average, or in regarding such a level of sexual activity as 'normal'. High, medium and low sex drives are all 'normal'; all that matters is whether you can accommodate each other's needs, however limited or great these may be. It certainly does not mean that you are undersexed if you want to make love much less often than your partner, or oversexed if you want to much more frequently.

A temporary sex-drive discrepancy

However well matched you are, there will be times when your sex drives will be out of phase with each other. Like any other appetite, your desire for sex will wax and wane from time to time, and various factors will affect it temporarily. The most crucial of these are your feelings about your partner. Your sex drive is likely to be at its height when you are newly in love or at the beginning of a new relationship. If you are no longer attracted to your partner, or have a relationship that is fraught with anger or resentment, then you can expect your sex drive to be low or even non-existent.

Your psychological and physical health will also have a marked effect on your sex drive. On holiday, when you are relaxed, you will probably have sex much more often, but if you are tired, depressed, or ill, you will have little inclination for it. You will probably notice that your sex drive fluctuates a little throughout your monthly cycle, though the variation seems to be an individual one with no consistent pattern from woman to woman. And you are likely to find that your sexual need increases as you grow more sexually experienced and confident, probably reaching a peak at around 40 before starting to fall off gradually as you enter middle age.

Bridging a sex-drive gap

Nearly every couple can handle, without letting it cause lasting pain or resentment, the temporary waxing and waning of desire that is inevitable in a sexual relationship. But if there is a substantial difference in your appetites you will need to work out some long-term strategy that will prevent the 'high-drive' partner from feeling continually dissatisfied, rejected, or frustrated, and the 'low-drive' partner from feeling under continual pressure to have sex more often than he or she wants. The following notes may help you bridge the gap – at least some of the time.

☐ Remember that sex need not always mean intercourse. Masturbating can help when one partner wants sex and the other does not. Even if you are uninterested or unaroused yourself you can bring your partner to orgasm by hand or orally (see STIMULATION TECHNIQUES, p.58). Alternatively, either of you might prefer to give herself or himself an orgasm while enjoying the closeness of being held by the other.

☐ Do not assume that because you feel unenthusiastic when your partner suggests sex, you cannot be aroused. In the same way that at table the appetite can come in eating, you may discover that all you need is a little stimulation in order to sharpen your desire.

☐ Try to discover a little more about the fluctuations of your sexual feelings over your monthly cycle. There will almost certainly be times when you feel more ready for sex than at others. Whenever you do, seize the opportunity and make the first move. Do not feel that this will only encourage your partner to make even more demands on you. On the contrary, the fact that you are showing more interest may make him feel less need to put pressure on you.

☐ Study the suggestions offered in OVERCOMING INHIBITIONS, p.76. If you have always had a low sex drive, it is possible that something – perhaps the way you were raised or some traumatic sexual experience when you were young – has made you so inhibited that you have always tried to avoid sex. The advice given in that feature may help you to accept your own sexuality more easily, with the result that your desire for your partner increases.

☐ If you are the low-drive partner, when you masturbate alone try to do it to a fantasy image of your partner so that you come to associate him with your feelings of sexual arousal. Start by using your own favorite fantasy, gradually 'shaping' it to include an image of your partner as you become more aroused, and aim to make him eventually the main stimulus.

☐ Do not withhold affection from your partner, especially if your own lack of sexual interest has become an issue between you. You may be tempted to avoid bodily contact for fear that he will interpret a demonstration of affection as a sexual initiative, but if you do hold back he will feel emotionally as well as physically rejected.

☐ Use psychic stimulation: erotic books, magazines, or movies.

☐ Try to feel as positive as you can about your partner. This technique is especially recommended if you no longer feel aroused at all by him. During the initial 'falling in love' stage of sexual attraction, an automatic selection system operates so that although you may realize that your partner has receding hair, protruding ears, is overweight and so on, these shortcomings are mentally filtered out in favor of his more positive characteristics. It is as though, because you have decided to be attracted to this particular man, you can see only his most attractive features. You can deliberately set this process in train by focusing your concentration on these.

☐ Give each other physical pleasure even if you do not want intercourse by practising the exercises **Pleasuring each other**, p.91. Try to do these regularly. You will find that they will help you to maintain a physical and emotional intimacy within which desire is likely to grow.

When to refuse sex

One of the most fundamental differences between men and women is that a woman can have intercourse even though she does not want sex and is unaroused, whereas a man cannot. It is this anomaly that enables a man who wants sex to put unfair pressure on an unwilling partner. It is a popular notion (among men, at least) that a man who is sexually aroused has to have an orgasm, or he will suffer physical pain. But the 'blue balls' myth with which many an adolescent boy has intimidated many a girl, is quite without foundation. It is no more uncomfortable for a man not to have an orgasm once he is aroused than it is for a woman. Both may feel an aching in the groin which is relieved by intercourse to orgasm, but which can equally well be relieved by masturbation, or simply left to disappear.

There will almost certainly be times when love, tenderness, or concern for your partner, or even your own need for physical comfort and closeness, are an adequate reason for saying yes to sex despite the absence of physical desire for your partner. But if you are often persuaded to have sex against your will, because you are afraid to deny your partner it or would feel guilty about doing so, you will get no pleasure from lovemaking and it may eventually come to be repugnant to you.

UNDERSTANDING A MAN'S FEELINGS

Empathy with your partner involves an understanding of the way a man feels about and responds to sex, and an ability to look at sexual problems, whether they are yours or his, from his point of view. Because sex is such a personal and intimate area of our lives we tend to take our partner's view of it very personally. The woman whose partner ogles attractive women or enjoys 'porno' magazines may well find his attitude insulting. And she may assume that any sexual problem he has arises because he does not want her, or that his difficulty is somehow her fault.

A man's sexual needs

Such a lack of empathy between the sexes is often the result of the very different attitudes to sex of men and women. For most men a sexual experience has to achieve the goals of erection and orgasm if it is to be completely satisfying, while women often value intimacy and tenderness as much as intercourse itself. It is therefore quite possible, and indeed common, for a man to reach his goals without meeting his partner's real needs at all. Almost every book about sex (including this one) emphasizes the pleasure to be had from building up to intercourse and the importance of foreplay in arousing a woman so that she has a complete, emotionally fulfilling experience. But men do not always want such an experience themselves. Sometimes all they want is straightforward, no-holds-barred intercourse without preliminaries.

You may find that there are times when you feel like that too, when you come together fully aroused, wanting each other immediately. Do not undervalue this as a physical experience or feel it is inferior to a more prolonged and varied session. It meets a different need – usually, admittedly, a male need – but this may on occasion be yours too.

This difference in attitude helps to explain why women tend to set more value on monogamy than men do. Most men want close and lasting relationships as much as women do, but they seem to be more able to separate emotional from purely physical needs. If, like most women, you have a desire to develop even a casual affair into a relationship, you probably see every potential sexual encounter as a promise of emotional involvement. Therefore an affair which is seen by your partner as simply sexual, and which he perhaps views as casual and uncommitted, may seem to you to pose a serious threat to your relationship.

Taking the initiative

How do men like women to behave in bed? First and foremost, they want them to enjoy it – and to show that they are enjoying it. Sexual responsiveness is one of the things men value most in a partner, and this is why many men like the woman to take the lead occasionally, to demonstrate the importance she attaches to sex. Most men still see themselves as the dominant partner most of the time, but even so, there are few who do not appreciate the value of sharing sexual responsibility occasionally. You need not be 'pushy' or aggressive to share in this way, and in fact these are still negative qualities in women as far as most men are concerned. But it is flattering for a man to feel wanted, and relaxing to have a partner who is prepared to suggest sex and perhaps take over completely and make love to him.

Sexual anxieties of men

Because sex is still so often seen in terms of the hunter and the quarry, it can be hard for a woman to understand how sexually vulnerable men are. A man's fears and anxieties are often far more disabling than those that beset a woman. However sexually insecure or inexperienced a woman is, she can usually conceal her fears, even if it means becoming completely passive. This may inhibit her pleasure, but it seldom precludes sexual activity altogether. A man always labors under the burden of having to achieve and sustain an erection as proof of his feelings and prowess. Without this he may see himself, in terms of sex at least, as nothing.

Perhaps above all else a man needs reassurance that his erection, valuable though it is, is not his only badge of masculinity, and that without it he can still be a desirable partner. So entrenched in many men is the notion that sex without an erection offers nothing that the man who fails in this area is inclined to turn over, in disgruntlement if not despair, and take refuge in a book or sleep. It is often his partner who has to open his eyes to the many other possibilities for sexual pleasure open to a couple.

Many men do need reassurance on a more basic level. Partly because of their natural competitiveness, partly because they have an exaggerated idea of the importance to a woman of penis size, fears of being 'too small' seem to be very common indeed. Through the intimacy of the locker-room and the openness of the public urinal men have a much more thorough knowledge of each other's genitals than women do of theirs. But this does not always provide reassurance, for every man makes comparisons in this matter and many are left with the uneasy feeling that they do not match up to the competition. However, they nearly always see other men's penises in the non-erect state, and although, when flaccid, they can vary quite considerably in size, there is much less difference in size between penises when they are erect. Furthermore, a man's view of his penis from above is a foreshortened one. With this image fixed in his mind, he is very likely to persist in underestimating its length.

So reassure him that it is what he does with his penis that counts, that whatever size it is feels right for you. A certain amount of penis worship will help too. To most women this comes easily because in a close sexual relationship the penis often becomes an object of attention and affection in its own right.

Men's fears about aging

While women see growing old as a threat to their physical desirability, a man's main fear in this area is that he will no longer be able to perform adequately. Anxiety about the loss of potency may make him interpret the small and perfectly normal changes which start to occur in middle age as signs of a serious sexual decline. And while these changes need have little or no adverse effect on his sex life, anxiety about them may inhibit him sexually or even make him switch off altogether so as not to risk failure.

Age can easily become the scapegoat for sexual difficulties, but any really serious problem – a total loss of interest, for example, or persistent erection failure – is unlikely to be a direct result of growing older. Listed below are some effects of aging which may worry your partner, but which are perfectly normal.

☐ It will take him longer to become sexually aroused and his erection may not be as strong. Just thinking about sex is often enough to give a young man an erection, but as your partner grows older he will probably begin to need much more direct manual or oral stimulation of his penis. Another symptom of aging is that he may find it easier to get an erection at some times of the day than at others – in the afternoon, for instance, rather than at night when he is tired.

☐ His erection will not be quite as hard, or its angle as acute, as when he was younger. If this is a problem for you, it may make it easier for him to maintain a firm erection if you raise your buttocks slightly by putting a pillow beneath them, or if you use a woman-on-top position (see SEXUAL POSITIONS, p.63).

☐ It will take him longer to reach orgasm, and he may not have an orgasm every time you have intercourse. If, as is possible, he has always seen orgasm as the inevitable conclusion of intercourse, he may find this very disturbing. But there is the compensation that he is able to sustain his erection much longer. The only danger is that he may feel compelled, when you have sex, to struggle on and on in a desperate attempt to reach a climax. It is best if he can accept that some days this is just not going to happen and stop before you both cease to enjoy it.

☐ Orgasm may be a less intense experience for him than before. Ejaculation generally becomes less powerful with age, so that semen seeps, rather than spurts, out. The feeling of inevitability that formerly preceded orgasm may diminish or disappear too.

☐ His erection will subside more quickly and if he does ejaculate it will take him longer to regain an erection.

Understanding erection problems

An inability to achieve or hold an erection is perhaps the most worrying sexual problem a man can face. 'Impotence', the old-fashioned term for the condition, accurately describes the way it makes him feel. There seems to be nothing he can do either to will an erection or to hide his failure, whatever his feelings for his partner. Moreover the stronger his desire, the greater the problem tends to be.

Erection difficulties have a psychological basis in nearly all cases. However, if a man never has an erection on waking (an erection is part of the body's normal reflex response during dreaming sleep and has nothing to do with his desire for sex) there may be a physical cause and he should seek help. Almost every man has an occasional erection failure, often because he is tired or tense or has drunk too much, or, notoriously, at the beginning of a new relationship when he is anxious not to fail his partner. Erection failure of these kinds is usually temporary, however, and does not mean that your partner has lost interest in you.

Such failures are unimportant in themselves, but they can grow into a more serious problem if a man starts to worry that because he has failed once it may happen again. The more anxious he becomes, the more his erection reflex will be inhibited and the more likely it is that his worst fears about being unable to perform will be realized.

This situation is a vicious circle that can be hard to break. But, perhaps more than any other sexual difficulty, the problem of erection failure is one that you can do a great deal to resolve. The following notes will help you in this.

□ Acknowledge the problem and try to talk about it with him even if he seems reluctant to do so. But do not make it into a big issue. The attitude to take is: 'Don't worry – there's always tomorrow'.

□ Do not behave as if he is rejecting you. This will make him feel even worse.

□ Stroke or suck his penis gently to see if this will help. But if he does not respond quickly, stop. It will make him feel even more tense if he feels that even with this attention he still cannot respond satisfactorily.

□ Take the pressure to perform off him by suggesting that you abandon any idea of intercourse and simply lie together, intimate and relaxed. Once he feels he does not have to get an erection, it may happen spontaneously. If it does, do not be in too much of a hurry to begin intercourse, for this may stir up his performance anxiety so that he loses it once more. Instead, let him set the pace.

Persistent erection failure

If the problem is more serious and erection failure is not merely occasional but happens almost every time, you should reassure him as recommended above, to reduce his anxiety, but you should also make an agreement that for a certain period, say three weeks, you will not attempt intercourse at all.

During this time, make love to each other in any other way you like, three or four times a week. This will be considerably easier if you begin right away to do the exercises described on pp.87-91. He will probably start to get erections again, but stick to your agreement not to have intercourse yet. The aim is that he should recover his confidence in his ability

to have an erection and realize that even if he loses it, it can be regained without difficulty.

When he feels more confident, start to have intercourse again. Take a woman-on-top position (see SEXUAL POSITIONS, p.63) guiding his penis into your vagina and at first just letting him get used to the feeling of being contained. Then start to move gently. Once again, the fewer demands that are made on him, the less anxious he will be. Reassure him that if he does start to feel anxiety or tension build up, he has only to tell you and you will withdraw.

As his confidence grows, he can start to take over more responsibility himself, first of all thrusting while you are on top, slowing down if he feels he is losing his erection, but otherwise gradually increasing the pace. Finally, try other positions. If your partner loses his erection, you may be able to increase his arousal by squeezing his penis with your vaginal muscles or gently stroking his testes. If this does not work, withdraw so that you can stimulate his penis by hand. However, if this course of action does not result in any improvement in your partner's problem, he will do best to seek the help of a qualified sex therapist.

Delaying ejaculation

Many men worry because they believe they do not last long enough when making love, and many women feel that they would enjoy sex more, and perhaps reach orgasm more easily, if only their partner did not ejaculate so quickly. But there is no absolute criterion about how long a man should last. In fact, if you do not reach orgasm even though your partner thrusts for five minutes or more, the problem is not premature ejaculation. More probably it is because you were not fully aroused before penetration. Even if intercourse is fairly brief, adequate foreplay, and in particular clitoral stimulation, should enable you to reach orgasm.

If ejaculatory control is a problem in the early stages of a relationship the simple solution is for the man to wait 15-30 minutes after he has ejaculated and then, if he can regain an erection, repeat intercourse. This time, he will be less excited and so take longer to climax.

As a man grows older he usually acquires more control over ejaculation. But there are a few men who suffer from 'hair-trigger' trouble and ejaculate before, or as soon as, they enter their partner. There are others who can manage to thrust a little but still feel they have virtually no control over when they climax. The two techniques which are described below will help your partner develop better control.

THE STOP-START TECHNIQUE

This exercise teaches the man to recognize the physical sensations leading to orgasm, so that he can learn to hold his arousal just below the point at which ejaculation is inevitable. He is stimulated until he feels orgasm is imminent and stimulation is then stopped until his excitement has subsided. This stop-start process is repeated until he can last 15 minutes without ejaculating.

1 To begin with, stimulate your partner by hand (see **Stimulating the penis manually**, p.57). He should focus all his attention on the sensations, and as soon as he feels a climax is imminent, ask you to stop. When he has calmed down, he should allow you to start again. Repeat this procedure until he has managed to stave off ejaculation for 15 minutes in three consecutive sessions.

2 Repeat the exercise, but this time use a lubricant. This makes control a little more difficult for him because the sensations are more arousing, closer to those he experiences within your vagina.

3 Now try the stop-start technique during intercourse. Use a woman-on-top position (see SEXUAL POSITIONS, p.63) since for most men this produces less intense sensations and so makes it easier for them to maintain control. Move gently up and down, with your partner's hands on your hips to guide you. In this way it is easy for him to indicate when he wants you to stop because ejaculation is imminent. He should try to last 10-15 minutes before thrusting and ejaculating. As he becomes more confident, he should himself be able to thrust, more and more actively, but always stopping when he feels orgasm is imminent.

4 Finally, practise intercourse in a variety of positions (see SEXUAL POSITIONS, p.63). The man-on-top or 'missionary' position is the one in which ejaculatory control tends to be most difficult, so it is best to make this the final stage.

▽ **Using the stop-start technique**
Sit astride your partner, facing him or with your back to him, and move gently up and down on his penis. Be ready to stop immediately he signals to you that he is about to ejaculate.

If, after practising the stop-start method for at least five weeks, your partner feels he has made no progress, you might try an alternative technique. The principle is very much the same, except that instead of simply ceasing stimulation when your partner nears orgasm, you squeeze his penis in the following way, in order to inhibit ejaculation. Grip the penis firmly, but not so hard as to cause pain, using the index finger and the thumb of your preferred hand. Put your thumb on the frenulum (the ridge on the underside where the head and the shaft meet). Bend your index finger around the ridge of the head. Then squeeze, applying firm pressure, for 10-15 seconds. This will make his erection subside and the feeling of imminent ejaculation will disappear.

Now work through all four stages of the stop-start technique, but each time use the squeeze grip as your partner nears a climax. During steps 3 and 4 you will, of course, have to lift yourself gently away from your partner before you can apply the squeeze – and until you are adept at this he may need to give you a slightly earlier warning.

▽ **Using the squeeze technique**
By squeezing the penis just below the head for 10-15 seconds, you can inhibit your partner's urge to ejaculate and cause his erection to subside temporarily. Repeat this procedure two or three times before bringing your partner to orgasm.

Conflicting sexual tastes

Various activities can be incorporated into a couple's sexual routine to provide more excitement or variety, and if you both enjoy them they can strengthen the sexual bond between you. But if one partner actively dislikes something the other enjoys, or if an activity becomes so important to one of you that it takes over completely and becomes a substitute for 'normal' sex rather than just enhancing it, your relationship will suffer. Conflicts often occur in this area because it is here that male and female tastes diverge most widely.

So far as unconventional sex goes, there are three commonsense rules:

☐ Do not do it unless you both enjoy it.

☐ Do not do it if it is harmful.

☐ Do not pressure each other into doing something that one of you finds distasteful.

Oral and anal sex

Far fewer women than men count oral sex as one of their favorite sexual activities. If you hate the idea but your partner loves it, try at least to give it serious thought. If you can resolve any specific anxieties you have (common female fears about it are discussed in **Oral sex**, p.59) you may come to enjoy it. Sucking her partner's penis is one of the best ways in which a woman can become the complete seducer. The intimacy of the act may produce a special response in him which is very emotionally satisfying for both of them. However, if there is any chance that your partner may be infected with the HIV (AIDS) virus, he should wear a condom if he intends to ejaculate during oral sex.

There are probably very few women who suggest anal intercourse on their own initiative, but once they overcome the fear of pain and the idea that it is unhygienic a considerable number of women do enjoy it. Some estimates of the number of couples who have had anal intercourse are as high as 25 per cent. For many of them it is probably a once-only experience, indulged in mostly out of curiosity, rather than a part of their regular sexual repertoire. If you decide to try anal intercourse, there are a few important precautions you should be aware of, particularly those which help to reduce the risk of AIDS (see **Anal Sex**, p.62, and **Guidelines for safer sex**, p. 157).

Sadomasochistic games

Bondage ('tie and tease') is the most widely practised form of sadomasochism (the derivation of pleasure from giving and receiving pain). It is more likely to be the man who suggests it, although many women go along with and enjoy these fantasy-based games. But if you have no real taste for them it is probably because you fear that they will get out of hand. It is best to use loose or token bonds so that the person who is tied can break free if he or she wants to, and never tie the head or neck, or you may cause injury.

A few men need to inflict or receive severe pain in order to be sexually stimulated. Then, sex games cease to be fun and become dangerous. The more involved your partner is in serious sadomasochistic practices, the less likely it is that you will be able to tolerate, far less take part in, them. They are essentially incompatible with a stable, loving relationship, but it can happen that a man with such tendencies finds that they become less important to him if he is in a successful sexual relationship.

Fetishism

A fetish object – an article of clothing or footwear, a particular part of the body, or even something apparently unrelated to sex – produces, or is used to produce, strong sexual arousal. Very many men show a mild degree of fetishism – a preference for large breasts, for example, or for black underwear or stockings. These may enhance a man's arousal, although most men are perfectly able to become excited without them. If your partner has any such strong preference, you can take advantage of it where possible by introducing it occasionally into your sexual routine.

True fetishism, however, puts limits on your sex life rather than enhancing it. For a few men (fetishism seldom occurs in women) the fetish object is so important that they cannot become aroused without it. Such a man cannot, for example, enjoy sex unless his partner is wearing black rubber. In extreme cases an object becomes a complete substitute for a partner, so that a rubber, leather, fur, or plastic garment is all he needs to become aroused or reach orgasm.

You may be happy to go along with your partner's preferences as long as they involve you. In any case, it is reasonable to accept that he finds it exciting to see you dressed in a particular fabric or certain items of clothing. But sometimes, especially if you have had sexual difficulties and sex has ceased to be very satisfying for either of you, the fetish may come to play a larger and larger part in your sex life. The result may well be that your partner can only achieve an erection in certain circumstances – if one of you is wearing a plastic raincoat, say.

What should you do if things reach this stage? You can put pressure on your partner to seek treatment, but unless he himself wholeheartedly wants change, it is unlikely to be very successful. Therapy is most likely to be successful if you go into it as a couple. If more conventional sexual practices can be made more satisfying for you both, fetishism may come to play a less important part in your partner's sex life.

Transvestism

The practice of wearing the clothing of the opposite sex is known as transvestism or cross-dressing. Some men cross-dress because they find that wearing women's clothes excites them sexually, perhaps giving the extra edge to their stimulation that they need. Others simply feel more at ease when dressed as women, preferring to play, if only temporarily, the female role. A few gay men like to cross-dress, but most transvestites are heterosexual and in many cases happily married.

A very small number of men, known as transsexuals, want so much to become women, rather than just dress like them, that they undergo hormone treatment and, in some cases, surgery to produce a sex change.

Coming to terms with transvestism

What should you do if your partner reveals – or if you discover – that he cross-dresses? It depends to a large extent on what he wants and what you are prepared to tolerate. He is unlikely to want to be 'cured', and in any case there is no effective treatment. However, many women find that they can accept their partner's need to cross-dress, especially if it is occasional and discreet. It will probably be easier for you to do this if you were told before becoming fully committed to him than if you discovered it later.

Most countries have supportive organizations for transvestites which provide opportunities for them to meet people with similar interests and to cross-dress in company, but without running the legal risks of doing so in public. Unfortunately, however, membership is likely to reinforce your partner's desire to cross-dress, which may put considerable strain on your relationship.

KEEPING YOUR RELATIONSHIP ALIVE

How do you keep a relationship alive – and not only alive but thriving – year after year? A large part of the answer lies in conquering sexual boredom, which is seen by many couples as the Catch 22 of their relationship. The argument goes thus: a relationship has more chance of lasting if it is monogamous, but sex with the same partner for 30 years – perhaps more – will inevitably be boring, and boredom, if it does not simply erode the joy from a relationship, may well lead to infidelity and so threaten it even more.

But to assume that sex must eventually become boring without an occasional change of partner is to underestimate the consolidating and strengthening role that it can play in a long-term relationship and the capacity of a couple to change and adapt to each other as the years go by.

Growing closer

Even though boredom might be avoidable, change is not. The passion and urgency that characterize the first months of a love affair do, eventually, disappear. But for most people this is more than compensated for by the ease and comfort that come from being with a lover whose body has become familiar and whose sexual rhythms have adapted to and accommodated one's own. Long-term lovers know each other's needs and preferences, have discovered what they most enjoy doing together, and accept and trust each other so that anxieties about sexual performance are unnecessary. Such benefits constitute a large part of the reason why many couples still enjoy sex together after many years and why for some it seems to get even better. These things are not possible in a new relationship, however passionate.

Changing attitudes to sex

So why is it that not all established couples experience a strengthening of their sex life together? The first thing to remember is that sexual sensations remain the same; it is only our attitude to them that changes. The second, if you want to establish the real cause of your boredom, is to look at sex in the wider context of your lives together.

If there is a depressing pall of monotony over everything or if there is so much bad feeling that you do not really enjoy anything you do together, it would be unrealistic to expect sex to be any different. In this case, sexual boredom is only part of a much wider problem. Sex will not flourish, it will not even survive unless the basic elements of attraction and affection remain. If your relationship has grown increasingly monotonous, you need to work out what is wrong between you, with professional assistance if necessary, so that you can regenerate some of your feelings for each other. Then you can start to revive your sex life.

Combatting sexual boredom

If you are basically happy with the quality of your life together, you have all the more reason for examining the causes of sexual tedium. It is possible that you are bored because sex has become too predictable. If you have developed an unvarying routine, or have a very narrow sexual repertoire, then it is not surprising that a sense of sameness has set in.

However, if you are bored in spite of the fact that you have always been sexually innovative and have explored all manner of sexual possibilities, then you probably have a fantasy notion of what sex should be. If so, what you must do is modify your expectations. Reading **Accepting sexual reality**, opposite, will help you to enjoy the sexual relationship you have.

Breaking your sexual routine

Introducing change into a long-established sexual routine is not easy. After year upon year of the missionary position, to announce suddenly that you would like to try being on top may seem too revolutionary, either for you to suggest or for your partner to accept. You will both need, first of all, to accept the idea of change, for as long as you both take it for granted that this is the way things are done, they will go on being done that way. Then you should bring about very small or subtle changes in your routine, simply leaving the light on one day, for example, if you usually make love in the dark. INCREASING YOUR PLEASURE, p.74, suggests various changes of this kind, while SEXUAL POSITIONS, p.63, describes positions that may be unfamiliar but nevertheless rewarding.

When you discuss such changes with your partner, be careful not to make it seem as though you are criticizing him. The rut you have got into is not exclusively the fault of either of you, since even if you have never suggested varying the routine before, nor has your partner. It is, of course, always the easiest option to accept things as they are. But what you need to do now is to find ways of altering that routine so that it will make sex more fun. The following advice should help you.

☐ Do not reject out of hand any suggestion your partner makes without thinking it over and discussing it. This will give you time to get used to the idea and to overcome any inhibitions you may feel, especially if what he is suggesting is very new or seems unconventional to you.

☐ Use fantasies and daydreams to discover the kinds of sexual activity you would like to try. Perhaps, too, there are sexual experiences you have enjoyed in the past that you would like to try and repeat.

☐ Remember that if you find it hard to put your wishes into words, you can indicate what you would like your partner to do to you by doing it, or something similar, to him. (See LEARNING TO COMMUNICATE, p.120).

Accepting sexual reality

For some people disillusionment occurs because the qualities they valued most in the early stages of a relationship – the passion, excitement, and intensity – are the ones that tend to fade fastest. Unless you accept that this happens and learn to value what develops in the place of these qualities, you may well come to regard this calmer, less frenzied phase of the relationship as boring by comparison.

It is possible to feel the same sense of dissatisfaction, not because things are not what they used to be, but because reality has failed to meet your expectations. Almost certainly, this is because those expectations are unattainable and your view of sex is a fantasy one. If you continually hanker after ecstasy, you are bound to find simpler pleasures dull.

Valuing the present

The remedy for entrenched boredom is not to seek new levels of excitement in, for example, fresh sexual activities, an affair, or erotic books or movies. These tactics can add spice when the relationship is a little stale, but only if used in moderation. If they are treated as a last-ditch solution, a fresh process of familiarization will inevitably lead to further disillusionment. Instead, try to feel differently about the way things are right now. It is your outlook on the present that will determine the degree of your future sexual happiness. Below are some guidelines that will help you to get the best from what is available to you right now.

☐ Examine all the good things about sex with your partner. It may not be as exciting as it once was but at least it is reliable. You can probably judge each other's responses well, and you know the kinds of activity you like best. Also, since you are more relaxed with each other, you can prolong lovemaking much more easily that you could in the excitement of a new relationship.

☐ When you are making love, focus strongly on the physical sensations. To feel the location and intensity of pain more clearly, you focus your attention on it. The same principle applies to pleasure.

☐ Live in the here and now: avoid comparisons with past experiences and do not fantasize about those you would like to have in the future.

☐ You should not forget that a two-way process is involved in all fulfilling sexual activity. You will get feedback from the pleasure you give your partner, for the more he enjoys sex with you, the more he will want to please you.

INFIDELITY

A serious affair nearly always involves a conscious decision, no matter how spontaneous or unexpected you have convinced yourself it is. You go into it because your main relationship is not completely satisfying and because you believe the affair will meet some unfulfilled need.

There is some evidence to suggest that while men's extramarital experiences are often a simple search for sexual variety, women are more likely to have affairs if they are unhappy in their marriage or long-term relationship. A woman's infidelity usually has more emotional significance than does a man's. So while women often overestimate the importance of their partner's affairs, there is a strong chance that your partner will underestimate the significance to you of any affair you might have.

If you can understand your own motives it may prevent you from reading more into the affair than is really there. You may also be able to see it in a realistic light as satisfying some of your emotional and physical needs but probably not all of them. If an affair becomes so serious that you begin to think about ending your involvement with your steady partner, it is vital to analyze your reasons for pursuing it if you are not to find yourself in yet another unsatisfactory relationship.

Why do affairs begin?
Here are some of the main reasons why affairs begin:

□ *To feel more valued.* The desire to feel loved and wanted more deeply often provides the impetus for entering into an affair.

□ *Sexual curiosity.* The main variable in sex is the way you feel about the other person. Changing partners just out of curiosity may simply show you that you are gaining very little unless genuine closeness is involved each time. Affairs based mainly on sexual attraction are usually brief and are a poor reason for breaking up your principal relationship.

□ *Excitement.* The idea of an illicit affair can seem much more exciting than a legitimate relationship. Sometimes a successful relationship may seem to present too little challenge, while an affair, with its risks, may make you feel more alive.

□ *Sexual dissatisfaction with a partner.* An affair may show you what is wrong with sex between you and your partner, and even help you to improve things. But there is a risk that the affair may seem an easier option than working on the problem with your partner, so that you will tend to shelve difficulties rather than solve them.

□ *To precipitate a crisis in a relationship that is unsatisfactory.* This does not necessarily mean that you want to turn your affair into another permanent relationship. Wait until the initial passion has died down to see how you really feel.

□ *As a morale booster.* Sometimes an affair is used to boost self-esteem after a career setback, or as tit-for-tat if it is discovered that a partner has been unfaithful.

□ *Looking for the perfect partner.* This is the excuse given by the woman who maintains that she is really monogamous at heart, if only she could find the perfect mate. Almost certainly, she is fooling herself. If you have always had affairs, the chances are that you will find it hard to change completely. It is easy to avoid commitment, to avoid having to work at a relationship, if you always believe something better will turn up.

The effects of an affair
Since an affair is usually embarked upon to meet some unsatisfied need, if it succeeds it may come to be more and more important to you. It will almost certainly force you to examine your commitment to your steady partner. If he discovers what is going on, it is bound to affect, and may even destroy, your relationship. Trust can sometimes be rebuilt, but it takes time and a lot of love and understanding on both sides.

For couples who are living together, without being married, the discovery of an affair may have particularly destructive consequences because the affair will be seen by the injured party as in direct competition with their way of life together and therefore a serious threat. The married couple have a built-in stability, practical, financial and social, that makes dissolution much harder and makes it much more likely that they will ride out the storm.

Making a confession

If, for whatever reason, you confess to an affair (or are found out) your partner's reaction will depend to a large extent on the length and intensity of that involvement. A casual, brief affair is easier to understand and forgive than one of long duration. Do not let guilt about a fleeting liaison tempt you to confess. Provided your infidelity is not symptomatic of real trouble in your relationship, it is your problem, not your partner's. However, in the case of a long affair your partner has to review a substantial section of your life together and accept that the reality of your relationship during this time has been quite different from what he had supposed.

The difficulties of an affair

An affair probably has the best chance of success when it fulfills a simple sexual need for both partners, with no additional demands on either side. But few relationships are as simple as this. Emotional damage to at least one of the parties involved is almost inevitable. Your chances of minimizing this will be improved if you follow a few basic rules:

☐ Learn to compartmentalize your life and your emotions. That is the only way you will be able to give the commitment to each relationship that will enable both to survive.

☐ Do not try to justify what you are doing by focusing on your principal partner's failings.

☐ Do not neglect domestic commitments or let emotional or practical crises build up at home.

☐ Do not spend the necessarily limited time you have with your new lover regretting that it is not more, or bring up when you only have a few more minutes left together tricky issues that cannot easily be resolved. Nearly all affairs have to be managed with one eye on the clock, which may make it difficult to express your feelings spontaneously.

☐ Make sure that the pleasure outweighs the pain brought about by the guilt, the inconvenience, and the often desperate need for secrecy.

☐ If you suspect that your partner is conniving at the affair, making things a little too easy for you, drop it at once if you value him. He may have his own reasons for wanting it to continue, and perhaps you should examine your relationship with him more closely to find out just what they are.

Confronting the situation

Do not seek for confirmation that your partner is having an affair unless you really want to know and you have thoroughly considered all the implications. Most men believe it is possible to have sex without commitment, and tend to view affairs as something intense but short-lived that will eventually fade away, leaving the original relationship intact. If you believe that your relationship is a sound one and that it fulfills most of your and your partner's needs, it is worth fighting for its survival. Remember too that his present involvement may be as ephemeral as such affairs often are.

If it comes to a showdown, remember that the pain of rejection makes the worst possible background against which to conduct a rational discussion that might save your relationship. If you wish to resolve the situation effectively, do not confront your partner until you have gained greater control over your feelings. A bitter and emotional tirade, however justified, precludes any two-way communication and gives your partner no right of reply. There will be details which will seem to you to be of paramount importance at the time: when and where it happened and whether sex was better with the other woman, for example. But be careful what you ask, because often the answers will not help – at least not at this stage, while the wound is open.

Planning a solution

Your partner's affair is symptomatic of a need in him. It may be a need you do not recognize or sympathize with, but you will have a better chance of understanding what went wrong if you acknowledge that need. So the first constructive thing you must do is to set aside time to talk about it together, at length and without interruption.

At first there are only really two points for discussion: why it happened and how your partner feels now. Your own feelings must be so painfully apparent, so inescapable to both of you, that there is really not much point in laboring them. Scarcely anyone is proof against the hurt that discovery of an affair can cause. But if you want to save the relationship, remember that however you feel, it is in your best interests not to say too much that is unforgivable or unforgettable.

It is important to realize that one instance of infidelity does not mean that your partner has embarked on an endless career of affairs. Many couples survive the discovery of an affair and continue a relationship that will undoubtedly be changed, but may nevertheless be strengthened because of increased mutual understanding.

JEALOUSY

Jealousy is one of the most powerful, destructive, and painful emotions. It is often regarded as a measure of the love one person feels for another. Conversely, the absence of jealousy is often taken as a sign of not caring, so that if you or your partner is insecure one may test the other's love by trying to provoke jealousy.

It is more accurate to say that jealousy is a fear of loss rather than a demonstration of love. Unreasonable and frequent jealousy shows not so much that you mistrust your partner but that you cannot trust yourself to hold your relationship together in the face of even the slightest competition. When jealousy runs this deep, the one thing your partner cannot give you is reassurance. Your feelings of insecurity and inferiority are such that you are not prepared to believe anything except the answer that you dread hearing: that there is someone else.

When is jealousy reasonable?

Since jealousy is a fear of losing something you value, there are times, when a relationship is threatened, when only a superhuman would fail to feel it. How much jealousy you show is a matter of both judgment and control. The following notes may help you decide whether your (or your partner's) jealousy is justified.

☐ You are entitled to feel jealous if your partner has been acting suspiciously. If there are sudden significant but unaccountable changes of routine in his hitherto well-organized life, suspicion is probably justified. Suspicion tends to thrive on the accumulation of evidence until it is either substantiated or allayed. It is natural to show flashes of jealousy if your suspicion has been aroused, and to give your partner a warning signal that shows your disquiet.

☐ You are entitled to feel jealous if a partner flirts outrageously with someone else in your presence. This is bad manners on his part and you have a right to complain. He may have had no idea at all that he was hurting you, or he may have been deliberately provoking an outburst because he wanted reassurance that you love him, or because he had a grievance that needed airing. Whatever his motives, you can use jealousy in a positive way; namely, in order to force your respective feelings into the open.

☐ Jealousy is unreasonable when it arises solely from your own feelings of inferiority or insecurity. Questioning your partner endlessly about time he spends apart from you because you find it threatening that he has any life outside your relationship is simply destructive and will make him resentful. Inspecting his belongings for evidence of infidelity is unreasonable, unless you have a solid reason for supposing that he is cheating on you.

☐ It is unreasonable to be jealous of people he knew and loved before you were together. The fact that he is with you now should be enough to reassure you of his love. If you are jealous of the past, keep it to yourself.

If you never show your jealousy you are probably very sensible. But do not be so controlled that you fail to take it up with your partner if he is hurting you or jeopardizing your relationship. If you never feel jealous then you are either lucky in being supremely self-confident and absolutely secure in your relationship or you do not care deeply enough about him to mind losing him.

Rebuilding trust

Jealousy is an especially severe problem for anyone who has discovered that a partner has, in fact, been unfaithful. Even if you know that there is no foundation for your present fears, it is quite natural to worry that what has happened once may happen again, and to be more likely to jump to conclusions than before. Your self-esteem will be at a low ebb, which will make you even more ready to believe that your partner will prefer almost anyone to you.

It takes sensitivity on the part of both of you to build up trust again. You will require enormous determination not to cross-examine him about his every movement, otherwise he will be continually forced onto the defensive. But it is also up to your partner to make sure that you know what he is doing and when he will be home, and to arrange that, as far as possible, you are able to spend your free time together.

CONTRACEPTION

The fear of an unwanted pregnancy can mar even the best sexual relationship. The main contraceptive methods are discussed below, and an indication of their efficiency is also given. Failure rates are given in terms of the percentage of pregnancies that would probably result if 100 healthy young couples used the same method for one year.

The Pill

If it is particularly important for you to have an effective contraceptive method, the Pill is likely to be your choice. It contains synthetic versions of either or both the female hormones estrogen and progesterone. Estrogen prevents ovulation. Progesterone makes the mucus plugging the entrance to the uterus hostile to sperm. Progestogen (synthetic progesterone) affects the uterus lining, making implantation of a fertilized egg unlikely. The combined pill contains both hormones, and is the most effective. This kind of pill is taken for 21 days in every cycle, usually beginning on the fifth day of the period. Everyday combined pills (ED pills) are available for women who find it easier to take a pill daily without a break, but seven in each pack are inactive, so they must be taken in the right order.

Some combined pills are 'phased', the hormone content varying throughout the cycle. The first course is started on the first day of a period and the pills must be taken in the correct order. The combined pill will not work if it is taken more than 12 hours late, or if diarrhea or vomiting occurs.

The progestogen-only pill (also known as the POP or mini-pill) tends to produce fewer side-effects than the combined pill, but, on the other hand, it is marginally less effective. It is started on the first day of the period and then taken daily throughout the cycle, with no pill-free days. The POP must be taken at the same time every day (preferably in the evening) and is not effective if taken more than three hours late. A few women fail to have regular periods when they are using the progestogen-only pill. It does not affect milk production during breast-feeding, unlike the combined pill, which decreases the amount produced and should be discontinued if the user hopes to breast-feed. The recently developed post-coital ('morning after') pill contains progestogen and a high quantity of estrogen and works by expelling the egg, whether fertilized or not. It must be taken within 72 hours of intercourse.

Besides being very effective, the Pill is, for nearly all women, very safe. It gives significant protection against cancer of the ovary and the uterus, and probably offers protection against pelvic inflammatory disease. It gives nearly every woman a regular monthly cycle and reduces the amount of discomfort, bleeding, and premenstrual tension associated with periods.

The Pill is not suitable for women who have a personal or family history of strokes, heart attacks, or raised blood pressure, and a woman may be advised not to take it if she has diabetes. You should seek medical advice immediately if you are taking the Pill and develop any of the following symptoms: pain in the legs or chest, swollen legs or ankles, severe or unusual headaches, or disturbed vision.

Failure rate: less than 1 per cent

The intrauterine device

Commonly known as the IUD or coil, the intrauterine device is a piece of plastic, in some cases containing copper, which is inserted into the uterus. It is second only to the Pill in efficiency, though exactly how it works is still unclear.

An IUD has to be fitted by a doctor or trained nurse, and this will often be carried out during a post-natal visit because insertion is easiest then. Fitting takes only a few minutes and requires no anesthetic. There may be some mild discomfort on insertion and for a few hours afterwards. Threads attached to the end of the IUD are left protruding into the vagina and can be felt with a finger. Their presence should be checked every month, since the device can be expelled without the user being aware of it. (A doctor will, in any case, recommend regular check-ups.) If the user decides she wants to become pregnant (or if, as sometimes happens, pregnancy occurs with the device in place) the doctor will remove it by pulling the protruding threads. This should never be attempted by the user.

The device tends to make a woman's periods longer, heavier and more painful, especially for the first few months after fitting. Because it also seems to render the reproductive system more vulnerable to infection, a woman who has several sexual partners, and so runs an increased risk of contracting a sexually transmitted disease, is probably better off with another form of contraception. The IUD is often not recommended for the woman who has not had children but would like to, because if a pelvic infection should develop, infertility can be the result.

Failure rate: 2 per cent

The cap and the diaphragm

These are rubber or plastic devices that fit, in the case of the cervical cap, over the neck of the uterus, or in the case of the diaphragm, across the vagina, to block the passage of sperm. Initially, they must be fitted by a doctor, or other qualified person, and checked each year and after pregnancy. They must be used with a spermicide to be reasonably reliable, and should be kept in place for at least six hours after intercourse. Caps and diaphragms have no disadvantages, apart from the fact that having to insert them before sex may detract from the spontaneity of lovemaking.

Failure rate: 4 per cent (with spermicide); 15 per cent (alone)

The contraceptive sponge

This device comprises a sponge impregnated with spermicide which is inserted in the vagina before intercourse and left there for a minimum of 24 hours afterward. Like the condom (see below) it is an easily available form of contraception well suited to those with an irregular sex life. However, tests to date on this relatively new product have shown it to be not very competitive with most other contraceptives in terms of efficiency. Therefore it is advisable to use the sponge in conjunction with a condom.

Failure rate: up to 25 per cent

The condom (sheath)

The condom is a fine rubber sheath which is rolled onto the erect penis before insertion into the vagina. Care must be taken to expel all the air from the projection at the end before the condom is put on or, if it is of the plain-ended kind, the tip is pinched to deflate it and left free. The ejaculated semen collects in the end of the condom. The base must be held securely during withdrawal after ejaculation to prevent the condom slipping off and releasing the semen. Use a new condom every time you have intercourse. Put it on as soon as erection occurs.

If the condom is not used as a regular method of contraception, it can nevertheless be useful when a woman has just stopped the Pill but wants to wait a few weeks before becoming pregnant, or during breast-feeding, or if either partner has, or is recovering from, an infection of the reproductive tract. Condoms are a valuable method of contraception because they give some protection against sexually transmitted diseases, including AIDS (see **Guidelines for safer sex**, p.157). Some condoms are lubricated with nonoxynol-9, an ingredient of most spermicides, which kills the HIV virus. It is best to use extra spermicide, partly because this increases the condom's contraceptive efficiency, but also because it gives added protection against AIDS should the condom leak.

Failure rate: 3 per cent (with spermicide); 15 per cent (alone)

Spermicides

These sperm-killing chemicals are obtainable as creams, jellies, foams, pessaries (gel-coated capsules which are slipped into the vagina) or as squares of impregnated film. They are inserted into the vagina before intercourse, and, because they have only limited efficiency on their own, are normally used in conjunction with a condom, cap or diaphragm. Spermicides containing nonoxynol-9 also kill the HIV virus which causes AIDS.

Failure rate: 25 per cent (alone)

Natural (rhythm) method

Some couples, on religious, moral, health, or esthetic grounds, choose not to use artificial contraceptive techniques. The 'natural' methods they prefer attempt to identify those days around the middle of the menstrual cycle when conception is most likely to occur, and intercourse is avoided at those times. Even so, there are very few relatively safe days and a couple have to be willing to abstain from sex for a large part of each month if they are to have a reasonable chance of avoiding pregnancy for any length of time. More importantly, if the couple both have a high sex drive they are likely to find it very restricting.

If it is really important not to become pregnant, natural methods are not recommended. But if conception would not be a real disaster, and if a woman wants to become more attuned to the rhythms of her own body, she may find them worthwhile.

The method that works best is called the sympto-thermal method. It involves making two sets of observations, one of the basal body temperature, and one of the changes in the vaginal mucus discharge. The basal body temperature is the temperature first thing in the morning, on waking. By keeping a chart of her temperature each morning, taken preferably with a purpose-designed thermometer, a woman will notice a monthly pattern. At some point about halfway through the cycle, her temperature will drop by about 0.4°F. Then, 24 hours later, it will rise by about 0.6°F and will remain at this slightly elevated level for the rest of the cycle, until she starts to menstruate again. The drop in temperature occurs at the time she ovulates and the 'safe' days are those between the third day after the temperature rise and the last day of her period.

Observation of the changes that take place throughout the month in the normal vaginal discharge can give additional confirmation of the safe period for sex. At the time of ovulation the volume and consistency of the mucus in the cervix changes. Formerly thick, cloudy, and scant, the discharge becomes thinner, clearer, and much more copious. After about four days it reverts to its original state, when it can be assumed that the fertile days are over.

Unless a woman's cycle is 100 per cent regular every month (and no woman can be absolutely sure of this) it cannot be assumed that it is safe before ovulation has occurred, since there is always the chance that it might occur earlier than usual. The value of these observations lies in enabling a woman to be reasonably sure that ovulation has in fact occurred. She can then relax for the rest of that particular cycle, knowing that she will not conceive.

Failure rate: 20 per cent

Coitus interruptus (withdrawal)

Withdrawal of the penis before orgasm is the oldest contraceptive method and even now is the most widely used on a global scale. It is among the least efficient of methods, and has only the virtues of being free and always available. The aim is for the man to bring his partner to orgasm through intercourse and then to withdraw the penis and ejaculate outside her. The man who is sexually very competent may be able to use it effectively – some of the time.

Failure rate: 10-12 per cent

'Morning after' contraception

Two methods of contraception are available from a doctor for use after unprotected intercourse. Hormone treatment is effective and safe, provided it is started within three days and is not used very often. You will be given two tablets to take immediately and two more to take 12 hours later. There may be brief side-effects of nausea and vomiting. Insertion of an intrauterine device (see above) will also prevent conception, provided this is done within five days – but preferably within three – of intercourse. The next period should start at the usual time, but may be heavier and longer than usual.

Failure rate: 1 per cent

Douching

This method, which involves irrigating the vaginal canal to wash away the sperm, was once practised widely but is a very unreliable means of contraception and is not recommended.

STERILIZATION

Female sterilization is a simple operation which usually requires a general anesthetic. Occasionally, it is done as an out-patient procedure, but usually requires 24-hour hospitalization. The most common method requires a small incision just below the navel, through which a laparoscope is inserted. With this instrument, the fallopian tubes, which lead from the ovary to the uterus, are sealed either electrically (by electrocautery) or by small metal or plastic clips. The operation leaves virtually no scar and causes very little discomfort.

The patient will be sterile immediately after the operation. Although it is possible to rejoin the tubes, this is not always successful and so sterilization should be regarded as irreversible.

Male sterilization, known as vasectomy, is a simpler and slightly safer procedure, not even requiring a general anesthetic. Two small incisions are made in the scrotum and the two vas deferens (sperm-carrying tubes) are cut and their ends tied. Although the tubes can be rejoined, this does not guarantee future fertility, and in most men who have the operation reversed the semen contains sperm once more but far fewer of these are fertile.

The patient is usually advised to wear tight underpants or a jockstrap for a few days after the operation to relieve the dragging feeling in the testes. There may also be some temporary bruising of the scrotum or groin.

Contrary to popular belief vasectomy does not necessarily reduce a man's sexual desire. For about 16 weeks after the operation it is necessary to use additional contraception, since the semen will until then contain sperm.

SEX AND PREGNANCY

There is no medical reason why intercourse should not continue throughout a normal pregnancy, unless you have previously miscarried or have had a threatened miscarriage during a current pregnancy. However, a few men find that the fear of harming the baby during intercourse so inhibits them that they develop erection problems. Your partner may need reassurance that the fetus is well cushioned within the uterus by the fluid that surrounds it, and that the tightly closed neck of the uterus provides a firm barrier between it and the outside world.

Maintaining closeness

Often, simply not having to think about contraception, or the relief that conception has taken place if it has been a problem, makes sex during pregnancy even more enjoyable for a woman. However, particularly during the first three months, you may be less interested in sex than before. The hormonal changes that make you feel nauseous, tired, or emotional may deprive you of the energy and the inclination for sex, and it may be difficult to become aroused. Avoid intercourse for a while if you feel like this, but do not forget physical intimacy altogether. It is especially important for you to keep in touch now, both physically and emotionally, with each other. Even though your desire is at a low ebb, your partner's may not be, and if this is the case you can use the methods recommended in STIMULATION TECHNIQUES, p.57, to satisfy him. Many couples find that pregnancy gives them an impetus to broaden their outlook and discover new ways of pleasing each other that do not depend on intercourse.

Mid-pregnancy

After the discomforts of the first three months have disappeared you will probably feel your desire for sex returning, if indeed it ever diminished. In mid-pregnancy the vaginal tissues become more engorged with blood and lubrication increases, so that you may feel that you are constantly ready for sex.

Choosing a position

As the pregnancy advances, you will find that lovemaking positions that put pressure on your abdomen become increasingly uncomfortable. If your partner uses a man-on-top position, he will need to take more weight than usual on his forearms, and you may find side-by-side, rear-entry, or sitting positions more suitable (see SEXUAL POSITIONS, p.63). A kneeling position may be best if you have backache, and is recommended for the final stage of pregnancy because it puts least pressure on the uterus. Indigestion and heartburn may make it uncomfortable for you to lie flat on your back, even in early pregnancy, and so you may prefer to make love sitting or to prop yourself up on pillows.

Sex after childbirth

For a few weeks – probably at least six after a first pregnancy, but fewer after subsequent births, you are likely to be sore, especially if you have had stitches, so that lovemaking will be uncomfortable. Your skin may feel tight and prickly even if it seems to have healed, and there may be a very tender area, usually at the base of the vagina, near the anus.

A position in which you are on top, or in which you face each other side by side, will avoid putting too much pressure on this sensitive spot. It is probably best to wait until after your post-natal examination, which should reassure you that everything has returned to normal, before having sex again. The first time you have intercourse after the baby is born you will almost certainly feel a little apprehensive and so will tighten up involuntarily to resist penetration. This will increase the likelihood of pain, so try to relax your vaginal muscles, bearing down slightly to prevent yourself tensing up, while your partner penetrates you gently. Because the vagina's natural lubrication does not return for a while after childbirth, you may need to use an artificial lubricant at first.

Even if your lovemaking does not include intercourse for the first few weeks, keep up a pattern of physical affection since it is easy to become baby-oriented to the exclusion of each other.

Remember that, even if you are breastfeeding, you will need contraception, and the means you were using previously may not be suitable now. Some brands of the Pill are unsuitable at this stage, for example, while you will need to be measured for a new diaphragm if you favor this method. (See CONTRACEPTION, p.135.)

A few women lose interest in sex for a while after they have given birth, usually because tiredness and preoccupation with the baby override all other emotions. You may find during this period that you are unable to relax completely and abandon yourself to lovemaking as perhaps you did previously. If this is the case, arrange for the baby to be looked after on occasional evenings, so that you can be alone with your partner without distractions. In a few women loss of interest in sex is prolonged, and may be a sign of the depression which sometimes occurs after childbirth. If so, medical treatment is essential.

Strengthening the pelvic floor muscles

Childbirth does not, as some women and many men fear, stretch the vagina. But it may result in a certain slackness if you have never exercised the vaginal muscles before. You will probably be given special exercises to do after the birth which will tone them up and strengthen your pelvic floor against the risk of a prolapse. (This occurs when the internal organs slip through the weak places in the pelvic floor, which normally supports them.) These Kegel exercises are described on p.85.

Until you have regained your vaginal muscle tone, your partner may prefer to use a position in which your legs are closed, so that his penis is gripped more tightly and the degree of stimulation increased (see SEXUAL POSITIONS, p.63).

CONCEPTION PROBLEMS

A couple of normal fertility with a typically active sex life – having intercourse two or three times a week – can usually conceive a child within a year. But of every 100 couples, ten are unable to have children and fifteen have fewer than they would like. In some cases of infertility the woman alone is at fault, in some the man, and in some both partners.

Tests for infertility

If you have tried for a year and have not been able to conceive, you should visit your doctor together. He will arrange for special tests to be done to establish the cause of infertility, but first he will want confirmation that you have been having sex regularly and that neither of you has a sexual problem (vaginismus or erection difficulties, for example) that makes intercourse difficult. He will then suggest that you concentrate your sexual activity around your most fertile days (two weeks before your period). Probably, he will ask whether your periods are regular, for if they are irregular or infrequent the chances of conception are reduced.

If tests suggest that you seldom ovulate, you may be helped by hormone injections or one of the 'fertility' drugs. Sometimes the problem is a blockage of the fallopian tubes, which carry the egg from ovary to uterus. This can often be cleared by surgery, but if it is not possible, the solution may be *in vitro* fertilization, producing a 'test-tube' baby. In this recently developed and as yet not widely available technique, a ripe egg is taken from the woman's ovary, fertilized with her partner's sperm, and then replaced in the womb, to develop in the normal way.

Male infertility

A man who is able to have intercourse and to ejaculate usually assumes that because he is potent he must also be fertile, but this is not necessarily so. It is only by microscopic examination that a doctor can tell whether a man's semen is fertile. (None of the notions associating baldness or hairy chests with fertility is true.) By far the most common reasons for male infertility are that the semen either contains too few sperm or too many malformed sperm or that they are not sufficiently mobile.

Treatment problems

Male infertility is easier to diagnose than female, but difficult to treat, since the precise cause often remains obscure. Emotional stress, tiredness, and heavy drinking may lower a man's sperm count temporarily, so he should consider his lifestyle if his partner is having difficulty conceiving. Some prescribed drugs also reduce fertility.

Often a few days' abstinence from sex just before a woman's most fertile days – around the middle of her cycle – is recommended, to allow a sufficient build-up of sperm to enhance her partner's fertility. In some cases drug or hormone treatment can boost sperm production, and occasionally it is possible to collect and concentrate sperm by centrifuging the semen and then, by artificial insemination, introduce it into the uterus.

Emotional factors

If you have had sex with your partner for some time and have so far failed to conceive, you may well be experiencing considerable stress, not only because of your own desire to have a child, but also because of family and social pressures that are often insensitively brought to bear on the childless couple. Although there is no scientific proof, emotional factors appear to play a part in governing a couple's ability to start a family.

THE SINGLE WOMAN

Being single may be a way of life you have chosen and are contented with, perhaps because you value your independence and have no particular wish to commit yourself, for the moment at least, to one man. Even so, you may find yourself constantly being pressed to defend your decision in the face of the widespread assumption that every woman wants to marry and have children. It may therefore be difficult to convince other people that you are happy with the life you are leading.

It is in your thirties that these pressures are likely to be most intense. You may be dogged by all sorts of assumptions that have very little basis in the facts of your own life – that women without partners are unhappy, lonely, immature, or sexually frustrated, for example. In your twenties it is normal and acceptable to be unattached, but by your middle or late thirties it is assumed that you have resolved to remain single, or at least have adjusted to a way of life that circumstances have forced upon you.

For many women, of course, being single is a problem. Male-female relationships seem to be programmed to lead, if not to marriage, at least to sex. If friendship is all you want or have to offer, there may well be frequent misunderstandings. Or perhaps, even though you realize that you would be happier if you could establish a close, long-term relationship, this has so far always eluded you.

It is to resolving problems such as these that much of the advice in this part of the book is directed. The first task is to establish why you are single. Is it a conscious, or possibly unconscious, decision on your part? Do you have few opportunities to meet potential partners, or when you do meet men, do you find it hard to develop a relationship? The problem charts that follow analyze these difficulties thoroughly and direct you to other features that will help you to form partnerships more easily or to live the single life more fully, whether you are unattached through choice or circumstance.

WHY ARE YOU SINGLE?

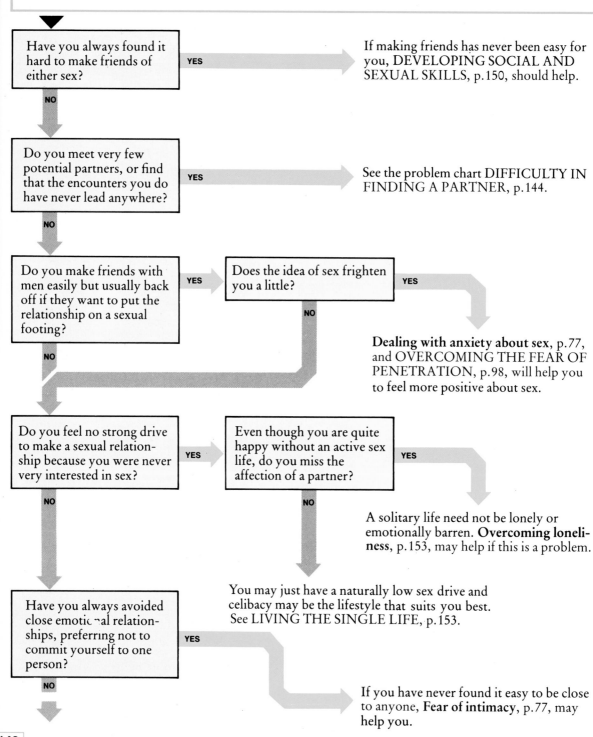

Have you always found it hard to make friends of either sex?

YES → If making friends has never been easy for you, DEVELOPING SOCIAL AND SEXUAL SKILLS, p.150, should help.

NO ↓

Do you meet very few potential partners, or find that the encounters you do have never lead anywhere?

YES → See the problem chart DIFFICULTY IN FINDING A PARTNER, p.144.

NO ↓

Do you make friends with men easily but usually back off if they want to put the relationship on a sexual footing?

YES → **Does the idea of sex frighten you a little?**

YES → **Dealing with anxiety about sex**, p.77, and OVERCOMING THE FEAR OF PENETRATION, p.98, will help you to feel more positive about sex.

NO ↓ (from "Does the idea of sex frighten you")

NO ↓ (from "Do you make friends with men")

Do you feel no strong drive to make a sexual relationship because you were never very interested in sex?

YES → **Even though you are quite happy without an active sex life, do you miss the affection of a partner?**

YES → A solitary life need not be lonely or emotionally barren. **Overcoming loneliness**, p.153, may help if this is a problem.

NO ↓ (from "Even though you are quite happy")

You may just have a naturally low sex drive and celibacy may be the lifestyle that suits you best. See LIVING THE SINGLE LIFE, p.153.

NO ↓ (from "Do you feel no strong drive")

Have you always avoided close emotional relationships, preferring not to commit yourself to one person?

YES → If you have never found it easy to be close to anyone, **Fear of intimacy**, p.77, may help you.

NO ↓

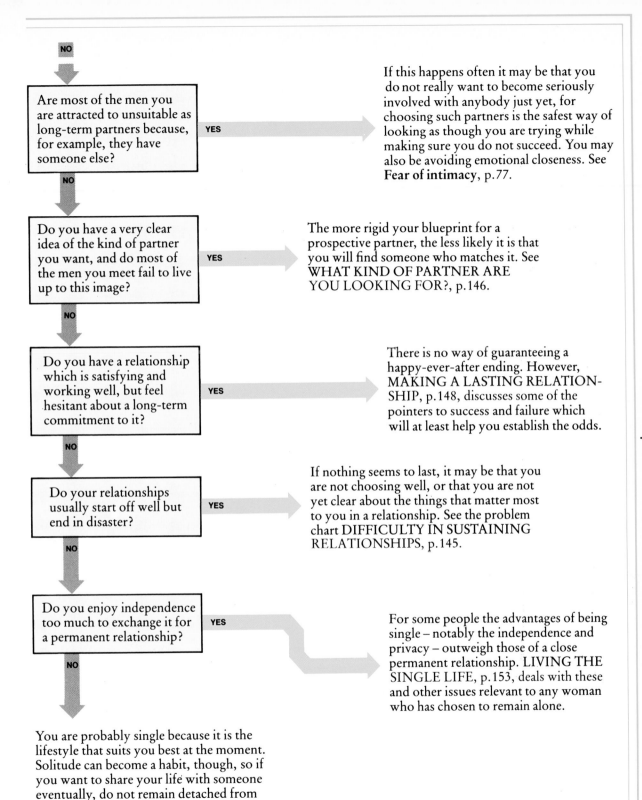

NO

Are most of the men you are attracted to unsuitable as long-term partners because, for example, they have someone else?

YES → If this happens often it may be that you do not really want to become seriously involved with anybody just yet, for choosing such partners is the safest way of looking as though you are trying while making sure you do not succeed. You may also be avoiding emotional closeness. See **Fear of intimacy**, p.77.

NO

Do you have a very clear idea of the kind of partner you want, and do most of the men you meet fail to live up to this image?

YES → The more rigid your blueprint for a prospective partner, the less likely it is that you will find someone who matches it. See WHAT KIND OF PARTNER ARE YOU LOOKING FOR?, p.146.

NO

Do you have a relationship which is satisfying and working well, but feel hesitant about a long-term commitment to it?

YES → There is no way of guaranteeing a happy-ever-after ending. However, MAKING A LASTING RELATIONSHIP, p.148, discusses some of the pointers to success and failure which will at least help you establish the odds.

NO

Do your relationships usually start off well but end in disaster?

YES → If nothing seems to last, it may be that you are not choosing well, or that you are not yet clear about the things that matter most to you in a relationship. See the problem chart DIFFICULTY IN SUSTAINING RELATIONSHIPS, p.145.

NO

Do you enjoy independence too much to exchange it for a permanent relationship?

YES → For some people the advantages of being single – notably the independence and privacy – outweigh those of a close permanent relationship. LIVING THE SINGLE LIFE, p.153, deals with these and other issues relevant to any woman who has chosen to remain alone.

NO

You are probably single because it is the lifestyle that suits you best at the moment. Solitude can become a habit, though, so if you want to share your life with someone eventually, do not remain detached from close relationships for too long. See LIVING THE SINGLE LIFE, p.153.

DIFFICULTY IN FINDING A PARTNER

Are you so shy with men that you find it hard to strike up even casual relationships with them?

YES → Forget about sex for the moment and concentrate on becoming comfortable with men on a friendly basis. **Learning to overcome shyness**, p.81, will help you.

NO ↓

Do you meet a lot of potential partners, but find that they are seldom very interested in you?

YES → Do you pay little attention to how you look or dress?

YES → Take a critical look at yourself in the mirror and, if there is room for any improvement, make it. See **Changing what can be changed**, p.80.

NO ↓

Perhaps you are giving an unfavorable impression without realizing it. See DEVELOPING SOCIAL AND SEXUAL SKILLS, p.150.

NO ↓

Do you often go on one or two dates with a man but find that he very soon seems to lose interest?

YES → Do you perhaps tend to get serious too soon?

YES → It is usually a mistake to try to force the pace. See DEVELOPING SOCIAL AND SEXUAL SKILLS, p.150, and LIVING THE SINGLE LIFE, p.153.

NO ↓

It is often difficult to recognize or acknowledge what makes a relationship fail. The problem chart DIFFICULTY IN SUSTAINING RELATIONSHIPS, p.145 examines some common causes.

NO ↓

Do you have little or no opportunity to meet any potential partners – perhaps because you have moved to a new area or because your job takes up most of your time?

YES → See DEVELOPING SOCIAL AND SEXUAL SKILLS, p.150.

NO → If you have no success in finding a partner although you meet many people, then you may be setting your sights too high by looking for your ideal man. See WHAT KIND OF PARTNER ARE YOU LOOKING FOR?, p.146. Or perhaps you do not really want anyone right now. See LIVING THE SINGLE LIFE, p 153.

DIFFICULTY IN SUSTAINING RELATIONSHIPS

Are most of the men you become involved with very different to you?

YES → It is easier to make a successful relationship with someone with whom you have a lot in common. See MAKING A LASTING RELATIONSHIP, p.148.

NO ↓

Do you get involved with men with problems or who become very dependent?

YES → You are choosing partners who lack emotional stability, perhaps because you need to feel the stronger partner. See MAKING A LASTING RELATIONSHIP, p.148.

NO ↓

Do you find it hard to show love and affection?

YES → If you always hold back emotionally, your partners will feel dissatisfied. See **Fear of intimacy**, p.77.

NO ↓

Do you always look to your parents for support?

YES → Unless you can achieve emotional independence your relationships will always be difficult. See MAKING A LASTING RELATIONSHIP, p.148.

NO ↓

Do you get jealous of anyone your partner shows the slightest interest in?

YES → Your relationships might last longer if you had more confidence. See IMPROVING YOUR SELF-ESTEEM, p.79.

NO ↓

Do you feel that whatever goes wrong is your fault?

YES → Your relationships might last longer if you had more confidence. See IMPROVING YOUR SELF-ESTEEM, p.79.

NO ↓

Are you moody and do you lose your temper easily?

YES → Anger is one of the most destructive factors in any relationship. **Dealing with anger**, p.121, discusses ways of experiencing anger that will not hurt or alienate your partner irretrievably.

NO ↓

Do you often find that although attracted to a partner at first, you lose interest when it gets serious?

YES → See **Fear of intimacy**, p.77, which tells you how to achieve closeness.

NO → If you are still uncertain about why your involvements fail, see MAKING A LASTING RELATIONSHIP, p.148.

WHAT KIND OF PARTNER ARE YOU LOOKING FOR?

One of the greatest illusions you can cherish is to believe that somewhere the man exists who is the perfect partner for you. If adhered to, this belief would condemn nearly everybody to remaining unattached. In fact, there are plenty of men with whom you could fall in love. Some will suit you in some ways, some in others, but it is unlikely that you will get all you want in one man.

The danger of holding out for the perfect partner, quite apart from the fact that he is unlikely to exist, is that it will prevent you from making the most of the relationships you do have. The state of being 'in love' does not last indefinitely. When it happens you will indeed believe you have found perfection. Gradually, though, you will come to realize that he is human – perhaps not quite as strong, or as reliable, or as decisive as you had believed. If these things are very important to you, and if you meet someone else who seems to satisfy you in such respects, you will fall in love with him – until you realize that he too is fallible.

Or it may be that you never feel able to make a proper commitment, to put everything into a relationship, because you are always living in the expectation that something better will come along. You might settle down a little sooner, if this is what you want, if you can settle for a little less. This does not mean in any way that you should be prepared to settle for second-best. However, you will undoubtedly be better off if you can keep a more open mind about what you want.

The dangers of inflexibility

Problems will almost certainly arise if you have such strong ideas about what your partner should be like that you cannot feel attracted to someone who does not conform to them. Obviously, the more rigid your requirements, the less chance there is of finding someone to suit you. Inflexibility is a disadvantage in a long-term relationship too. People change, and your partner will grow older, and possibly fatter, certainly grayer. If such things matter a lot to you, they may endanger the relationship. The personality too is subject to change, and this becomes particularly apparent if you were both young when you met and have matured together.

Probably, like most women, you have your preferences. You may, for example, be irresistibly drawn to anyone who reminds you of your first love, or you may find it impossible to love a man who takes life too seriously. Such preferences matter very much to some women, while for others they are only a marginal influence in their choice of a partner.

ASSESSING YOUR FLEXIBILITY

The following exercises will help you judge whether you are limiting yourself by being too rigid in your requirements of a sexual partner.

1 PHYSICAL PREFERENCES

The aim of the first exercise is to discover which physical characteristics influence your choice of a partner, and how important they are to you.

1 Make a list of ten men you consider physically attractive. They need not be men you know well, or feel a strong sexual attraction to, but simply those whose looks you admire.

2 Next make a list of ten men you do not consider attractive. (Remember, all you are concerned with in these two lists is physical appearance.)

3 Now try to find one quality you really like about each of the men in the first list. List these preferred qualities under the heading 'Positive'.

4 Then, returning to the list of men you find unattractive, compile a list under the heading 'Negative' of ten physical attributes that you see as unattractive in those men. It may occur that you include the opposite of a quality you wrote down in the preceding list: 'fat', for example, in the second list, while you put 'slim' in the list of positive attributes. This does not matter.

5 Work through the lists of positive and negative attributes deciding how important each is. Put a mark beside those which, in either a positive or a negative way, are essential to your sexual interest. If one of your preferences is height, put a mark beside that, while if blond hair is such a turn-off for you that you could never feel attracted to a man who has it, mark that characteristic. Do not mark attributes that you consider important but not crucial.

Now go on to the second exercise, which applies a similar vetting procedure to personality traits.

2 PERSONALITY PREFERENCES

Even when you meet someone you think looks attractive, he does not necessarily excite you sexually. Nearly always it is some personality trait, such as a sense of humor, that tips the balance. You can analyze which of these 'turn-ons' and 'turn-offs' are important to you just as you did before.

1 Think of the men you know reasonably well and consider to be physically attractive.

2 From these select and list ten who arouse you sexually, or have done at some time, and then in a second list, ten who, despite their looks, have never excited any real sexual feelings in you.

3 Next, find ten personality traits among the first ten men that you consider attractive and list these under all the heading 'Positive'. Then list ten unattractive personal characteristics that you find in the second group, listing these under the heading 'Negative'.

4 Decide which of these positive and negative traits are so important as to be indispensable to your sexual interest and put a mark beside them. Ignore those which are not crucial.

Your lists of attractive and unattractive qualities, both physical and personal, constitute your blueprint for sexual attraction. These qualities are what is needed (though not, of course, *all* that is needed) if you are to be sexually attracted to a man. The number of marks you have put down indicates how rigid this blueprint is. Even one or two crucial preferences on each list implies that you are to some extent limiting your choice of potential partners. The fewer marks you have made on your checklist, the more flexible you are and the more men you will find suitable as prospective sexual partners.

You will probably have discovered that the personality preferences matter more than the physical, and that you will be attracted to a man if he meets at least some of your 'turn-on' requirements and as long as these outweigh the 'turn-offs'.

Making yourself more flexible

If your blueprint is very inflexible, it is probably worth trying to change your expectations. The best way to do this is to concentrate your attention on the things about your present partner (or a man you are currently interested in) that appeal most to you. You will probably find that these are qualities that you have listed in the preceding exercises as important but not vital to your sexual interest. You will probably also be able to discover additional qualities that you may not have listed as important but which seem special in this person.

MAKING A LASTING RELATIONSHIP

It is difficult to predict the chances of success of any relationship, for the most unlikely partnerships survive for years, while others collapse which seem to have everything in their favor. Nevertheless, the observations of marriage guidance counselors and studies of the causes of marital breakdown suggest that certain factors predispose a relationship to either success or failure. If you are wondering about your chances of making a lasting partnership, below are some of the most important factors to consider.

☐ *Do not commit yourself too young.* Youthful marriages run the greatest risks of all. Every major study of marriage shows that commitments made before the age of 19 are the least likely to survive (especially if embarked upon because the woman is pregnant). As you mature, you will change, developing different needs and interests from one another. It is possible for two people to move in more or less the same direction, continuing to meet each other's changing needs, but far more likely that you will grow apart.

☐ *Do not commit yourself too soon.* You should not consider making a relationship permanent until you have known each other for at least nine months. It takes most people that long to get to know the best and worst of each other, and living with someone is the best way to discover whether your partnership is likely to stand the test of time.

A stormy involvement is a danger sign. If you have frequent quarrels and, even worse, if one of you has broken off the relationship more than once, it augurs badly for the future, for the pattern is one that is likely to become established. Protracted dating can be suspect too. If you have been talking about, but postponed, a permanent relationship for a couple of years or more, look carefully at your motives. It may be that you are not yet really ready to lose your independence.

☐ *Look for similarity.* Surveys have shown that there is a tendency for like to marry like. While some marriages of opposites do succeed, living together without friction is obviously easier for the couple who have similar interests and attitudes and want much the same things from life. It helps to have at least one or two major interests in common and it is probably best to be similar in age as well. If there is a difference of more than ten years between you, it is likely that there will be differences in outlook that are too great for an easy relationship to develop.

☐ *Look for sexual compatibility.* Sex will not prove the binding force it can be if your feelings about it are very different, or if it plays a much more (or much less) important part in your life than it does in your partner's. Sexual compatibility is not simply a matter of technique, and the mechanics of lovemaking can be learned as you adjust to each other. But it is important that you are truly attracted to and aroused by each other, for it is only on this basis that you will be able to accommodate each other's sexual needs. Given a background of mutual attraction and love, nearly all sexual problems are soluble; without it most are likely to prove insurmountable.

☐ *Look for emotional maturity.* Some personality traits seem to bode particularly ill for the future of a long-term relationship. Anger is probably the most potentially destructive force in relationships. You will have a rough passage with a partner who is domineering, aggressive, or overcritical. And while a relationship may just be able to survive with one immature partner, two will doom it to failure. Low self-esteem also signals trouble, as it produces the insecurity and jealousy that will make a loving and trusting relationship hard to attain.

Overdependence can make an adult and lasting relationship impossible. A partner who is still very reliant on parental support may demand more reassurance from you than you are prepared, or have time, to give. And on the inevitable occasions when you are the one who needs, if only temporarily, to be dependent and supported, he may be quite unable to shoulder the responsibility in an adult fashion.

☐ *Make sure that your partner can provide you with physical closeness and affection.* A person who is emotionally isolated and finds it hard to show affection physically, or to accept it, has poor prospects of sustaining a fulfilling relationship.

□ *Look for flexibility.* The ability to adapt to change is one of the most important attributes to look for in a partner. Neither individuals nor partnerships are static, and a person who is uncompromising may find it hard to meet the changing needs and circumstances of a long-term relationship. Therefore, it is a good sign if, for example, your current or prospective partner is willing to think about new ideas or try new activities.

But, if you have serious doubts about the relationship, do not drift on in the belief that your partner will change. If you find yourself hoping that he will become, under your moderating influence, less moody or extravagant, slower to anger, or less prone to jealousy, you are running a considerable risk. Some people have a great capacity for change, others are the opposite. So if the potential for change matters to you, look for signs of it in a partner before you commit yourself seriously to the relationship, not after.

One ingredient essential for lasting success in a relationship is not listed above because it requires special emphasis. This ingredient is your own certainty about the relationship and the resultant determination to make it work. If you have reservations, they are likely to grow, preventing you from giving the relationship the 100 per cent commitment which more than anything will help it to overcome problems and survive.

Assessing your relationship

Use the checklist below to assess the viability of your relationship. In the column on the left are the bonus factors that are likely to increase your chances of success. These do not guarantee bliss, of course, but they do mean that you are likely to have a more contented life together. In the right-hand column are the risk factors. It seems easier to predict disaster than contentment, partly at least because it attracts more attention: more research has been carried out into the reasons for the break-up of relationships than into the factors which help couples to stay happily together. So it is more a cause for concern if you check several factors on the 'risk' list than if you fail to check many bonus factors.

FACTORS WHICH MAKE A RELATIONSHIP WORK OR FAIL

BONUS FACTORS		RISK FACTORS	
□ Successful cohabitation for at least six months	□ Emotional stability	□ Marrying too young (before 19 years of age)	□ Anger
□ Similar educational and social backgrounds	□ Similar sexual needs	□ Premarital pregnancy	□ Emotional coldness
□ Similar intelligence	□ Flexibility and adaptability	□ Marrying to escape an unhappy home	□ Poor self-image – reflected in low self-confidence
□ Less than ten years difference in age	□ Emotional self-sufficiency	□ Marrying 'on the rebound'	□ Fear of independence
□ Similar attitudes on major issues	□ Ability to give and receive affection	□ Short involvement (under nine months)	□ Possessiveness or extreme jealousy
□ Shared interests and activities	□ Consideration for others	□ Frequent friction or break-ups	□ Selfishness or self-centeredness
□ Similar ambitions and enjoyment of similar lifestyle	□ Similar physical attractiveness of partners	□ Emotional instability	□ Substantial difference in physical attractiveness

DEVELOPING SOCIAL AND SEXUAL SKILLS

The term 'social skill' simply means the art of getting along with people, making them feel by what you say and the way you behave that you value them – and that you are likeable too. Your social skill determines how well you carry off a first meeting, how easy you find it to make friends, and how smoothly you manage to make the transition, where appropriate, from a social to a sexual relationship.

Learning body language

Much of the time, especially at the beginning of a relationship, words are too crude a tool to convey the subtle shades of feeling passing between two people. The messages 'I like you', 'I'd like to get to know you better', 'Let's take this a stage further' are largely conveyed by body language, a system of communication based on the way they stand, move, and look at each other. Both people respond to this, although they may be unaware of doing so.

Everyone uses body language, but not everyone uses it to his or her best advantage. Shy people, for example, often send out the wrong signals without realizing it, producing entirely the wrong response in others. What is simply shyness is often interpreted as boredom, lack of interest, or even hostility. So learning to read, and to use, body language is an important part of being socially adept.

Eye contact

Always look at the person you are talking to, not over his shoulder (which suggests that you are bored or inattentive) or down at the floor (which indicates that you are shy or even shifty). If he drops his eyes you are probably holding your own gaze for rather too long. What most people find comfortable is intermittent eye contact, for about five seconds in every half minute. This shows that you are interested but not putting the other person under uncomfortably close scrutiny.

Eye contact is also one of the simplest and most direct ways of showing that you are sexually interested in someone. For this very reason, if you are shy and meet a man you find attractive, you will probably have difficulty in looking at him directly. Your inclination will be to hide your feelings by dropping your eyes. By making eye contact with him, on the other hand, you are making it easy for him to respond to you if he wants to. Smile as you look into his eyes, and maintain a steady gaze a little longer than you would normally.

Facial expression

If you are often asked if you are feeling OK or are worried about something when in fact you are fine, then your face is not giving the message you want to convey. Smiling is especially important for it is the most direct way of telling a man that you find him attractive, or that you find him pleasant to be with. At the very least, it makes you look friendly and responsive.

Gestures

Use your hands to add emphasis and interest to what you are saying. This is something that is often easiest to learn by watching others. There is no need to be dramatic as quite small movements are usually all that is necessary. Head movements are important when you are listening because they encourage the other person to continue speaking as well as indicating your own interest.

Posture

You will give an impression of self-confidence – however you feel – if you stand straight and hold your head up. When you first meet someone, it is best not to stand either too close or too far away. Many people feel uneasy if a stranger stands right next to them since it seems like an invasion of their personal space. On the other hand, physical proximity is a sign of attraction and it is one of the cues you can give when you want to advance a relationship and put it on a more intimate footing. By contrast, standing much farther away often gives an impression of aloofness or even mistrust.

Physical contact

Touching is another signal you can give when you find someone attractive – but keep it subtle. Watch carefully for the response you get so that you do not overstep the line between showing interest and being pushy or clinging. You will find that it is most often by pointedly prolonged or frequent touching that the pace of a sexual relationship is stepped up.

Most men still prefer to set the sexual pace, but, even so, they want from you a sign that it is safe to increase it a little. So if you want to give 'positive' signals in the early stages of a relationship, stick to safe and subtle ones. Touch his arm as you are talking to him, for example, or if you come up behind him, put a hand on his shoulder in greeting. A touch on the skin is, of course, more intimate than one through clothing. Touching a man's hand lightly with a finger is a more sexual gesture than laying a hand on his arm, for example.

Listen to your voice

Your voice, after your appearance, makes the strongest initial impact on the people you meet. You can get an impression of how others hear you by listening to a tape recording of yourself. Few people like the sound of their own voice at first, but try to pick out the characteristics that might make it difficult or irritating for others to listen to and that you may be able to modify. Does it sound harsh, for example, or too high or too loud? Resolve to speak more softly, if so, but never mumble. Put expression into your speech, but do not overemphasize individual words. Conversation, not oratory, is what you need to become proficient in. Try also to identify and eliminate irritating mannerisms such as frequent hesitation or nervous giggles.

Making conversation

This is one area in which a woman can take the lead as easily as a man. Conversation is the prime ingredient of social success. If you can handle it well, you will make a good first impression on people you meet and it will carry you with confidence through the opening stages of a new relationship. If you find it hard to talk to people, or if they seem unresponsive to you or seldom follow up the first encounter, you may have developed some bad conversational habits. The following notes will help you if this is the case.

☐ Do not be afraid to make the first move, but keep the conversation fairly neutral at first, so that either of you can back off easily if you want to. Talk about things which will not offend or lead to heart-searching – films, books, or leisure activities – for example – before moving on to more personal matters. It is a mistake to tell too much too soon. An immediate outpouring of the intimate details of your personal life will frighten off the other person.

☐ When you meet someone new, do not oversell yourself. It is tempting to try to present yourself in a flattering light, but remember that a false image may be difficult to live up to or, conversely, hard to live down.

☐ Do not wander off the point of conversation, talk too much about yourself, or interrupt the other person continually.

☐ Never answer a question with a flat yes or no. Expand your answer somehow, giving the other person a cue to continue the discussion.

☐ Talk about what really interests you and be positive in what you say. It is even better if you can find something you have in common – a shared interest or a mutual friend perhaps – to keep the conversation flowing.

☐ Try not to let lengthy pauses develop. If you cannot think of a new topic, follow up what the other person last said with a comment, preferably, a question that will sustain the conversation.

☐ When you are listening, remember that this is not a totally passive role. Every now and then make some encouraging response to stress that you are listening. When it is your turn to speak, say something that confirms that you have understood what the other person has said and either agree with it or have a different opinion.

☐ At the end of a conversation, ask yourself how balanced it has been. Have you done all the talking? Or practically none of it? Do you feel you know much more about the other person than he knows about you, or vice versa? Ideally, you should balance your disclosures so that neither of you feels that the other is holding back. Nor should you feel that the other person is disclosing more personal information than you are prepared to give away about yourself.

☐ When you first meet someone, it is not a good idea to prolong the conversation longer than feels comfortable, or, if you are at a party or other social gathering, to cling to him like a limpet. It is better to move on when things are still going well, leaving your new acquaintance free to meet other people. If you like him enough, say something that will make it obvious that you have enjoyed his company and would like to follow up the meeting.

Dating

If you are nervous or unsure of yourself in a social situation, you will feel even more apprehensive when you date someone for the first time. In fact, though, you have a much greater advantage than in a casual social meeting. That you have got this far means that there is something between you, although until you know each other better you will not know how much you want to develop the relationship.

The following guidelines may be helpful if you are worried about how you should behave or what the date might lead to, but they apply equally well to all your relationships with men.

☐ Do not expect every encounter to blossom into a great romance. If you get too serious or seem to expect of the man more than he is prepared to give, you will probably make him retreat.

☐ Do not be on the defensive, assuming every man you date will make a pass at you. This stance can stop you being open and friendly.

☐ When you are with a man, do not boast about former conquests or appear too interested in other men. He is entitled to be the focus of your attention while you are together.

☐ Be flexible about meetings. If a last minute change of plan is unavoidable, or if he has to cancel a meeting, be understanding about it.

☐ Be prepared to pay your way. If you have been out together more than once – and certainly if you are earning more than your partner – you should offer to share the costs.

Handling sexual advances

How you handle a man who makes a pass at you depends almost entirely on how welcome or unwelcome it is. Sexual relationships usually progress by small steps, with each of you giving, and in turn responding to, signs of encouragement. If you pick up and respond to each other's cues correctly it minimizes the risk of either of you being rejected.

When you do have to reject someone, let him down gently. All you need do is decline the offer politely but firmly. You do not have to justify yourself any more than this. If you try to rationalize your refusal on the grounds of morality or fear of pregnancy, you are just presenting him with arguments he will then try to knock down, prolonging the tension. In the end, no one can argue with the fact of how you feel.

Sex is not the inevitable way to round off an evening. Your date has no right to expect it and you are under no obligation to agree to it. There is only one good reason for having sex, and that is because you both want it. Sometimes a man makes a pass automatically because he thinks it is expected of him.

This happens when, for example, the relationship has intensified rather more quickly than either of you really intended, so that it seems as if there is really no other direction in which it can develop.

Most women find sex more satisfying with a partner they know and like, and who feels the same way about them. The danger in stepping up the sexual pace before you have had a chance to get to know each other properly is that you may well wake up the next morning and discover that you do not even like the man you have spent the night with.

YOUR FIRST SEXUAL EXPERIENCE

The driving force behind your first sexual experience may be love, or lust, or curiosity. Whatever the reason, it is an unusual woman who does not feel a little tense or apprehensive. The following advice should help, but do not worry if intercourse is not the ecstatic experience you may have imagined; sex invariably improves with practice.

☐ Choose the right setting. There should be complete privacy, with no fear of interruption, and enough time, so that your lovemaking does not need to be hurried. Having enough time is particularly important, because if you are nervous you will probably take a considerable while to relax and become fully aroused.

☐ Use reliable contraception.

☐ Tell your partner you are a virgin, and ask him to enter slowly and gently, and not to thrust deeply at first. If you have never used tampons, your vagina may be a little tight. Gentle stretching of the entrance by your, or your partner's, fingers beforehand will help.

☐ Your partner will be able to enter you more easily if you spread your thighs wide. A pillow beneath your hips will help too.

☐ A lubricant on your partner's penis will help to supplement your natural vaginal secretions and make penetration easier. Part your vaginal lips with one hand and guide your partner into your vagina with the other. Bear down slightly as his penis enters you to prevent your pelvic-floor muscles tightening against it.

LIVING THE SINGLE LIFE

It is still widely regarded as unusual for a woman to choose to be single, and, consequently, an unattached woman is generally assumed to have tried, but failed, to find a partner.

The benefits of being single

But, for an increasing number of women, being single is a positive option, chosen because it seems to offer more solid rewards than an established relationship or marriage. For them the solitude is valuable: they need the privacy and the physical and emotional space around them that are difficult to secure within an intimate relationship. The exclusivity of marriage, the continual involvement with another person, tend not to suit them as well as the independence and mobility of being alone. These benefits are also felt in the sphere of work, where opportunities for promotion and travel do not present so great a conflict of interests as they do for the married woman.

Overcoming loneliness

Being single brings its problems, however, particularly if you feel you are alone not out of choice but through circumstances. You will have to deal with other people's conviction that you want to be married, even that you ought to be married, which can make you very defensive about your lifestyle. And while privacy is for some women the greatest advantage of being single, for many loneliness and isolation are the worst drawbacks. The woman who has a steady partner is likely to have regular sex and continuity of affection in one relationship. But the single woman whose sex life is spasmodic often has to settle for two quite different sources, seeking warmth and companionship from her friends and meeting her sexual needs on a quite separate basis.

If you are single, you will still want involvement with others and it is important to have a network of people who matter to you and care for you. They can be friends, relatives, even former lovers. It does not matter, as long as you can always call on them when you are feeling low and needing a shoulder to cry on or have something to celebrate.

Your friends should also be people who feel able to turn to you too, so that you can give emotional support as well as receive it. To be able to enjoy the closeness of friends of long standing is the best substitute for the feeling of permanence and caring that a steady sexual relationship can provide.

One of the greatest deprivations for the single person is the lack of physical affection. Masturbation can be a substitute for sex but, perhaps particularly for women, there is no replacement for the comfort of being held. Within a good relationship you can give and receive loving gestures that are accepted just as that, without any obligation to take it further if you are not in the mood. But women often find it hard to obtain non-sexual affection in a casual heterosexual relationship. It is very likely that you will turn to your close female friends if you are single, because true friendship embraces the uncomplicated affection which is a fundamental human need. But with a man who is a genuine friend you may, by being honest about what you want, be able to develop a policy of affection with no strings attached.

Meeting people

You will find that the best ways to meet people, whether as friends or potential partners, are through your work, mutual friends, or through an interest or hobby. These situations all provide some common ground on which to build a relationship, and because such encounters tend to be casual, it is easier for you to develop them at your own pace.

Most single people have married friends who feel compelled to arrange liaisons for them. Accept all such invitations, since at the very least they will broaden your social horizons. But do not expect too much of them; you will probably find it much easier to be yourself when you are not meeting someone who has been selected as a partner for you.

It is often difficult for a woman to make the first social, let alone sexual, move, but when you do meet a man you find attractive and want to see again, take the initiative if he does not do so. A simple ploy will remind him you exist and show him you are interested: a postcard with a flip reference to something you talked about, for example, or offering to lend him a book or record you discussed together, or even the time-honored spare ticket for a concert or the theater. While it is fine to make the first move, do not take over completely. Leave room for him to respond in his own way, by not making all the telephone calls, and, when he does call you, do not make yourself too available.

Relationships at work

The more involved you are with your work, the more likely it is that you will have a special affinity with some of the men you meet through your job. But be cautious about your relationships with married colleagues. Even if you have no intention of disrupting a marriage, you may be regarded by a colleague's wife, as single women often are, as predatory, and however innocuous your friendship, it is open to misinterpretation.

If the relationship develops into a full-blown affair, it can be even more difficult. Should it fail, you may find yourself in an embarrassing position, possibly with your status at work jeopardized. If the affair lasts, a strong alliance of two co-workers, particularly if one or both are in a senior position, may well be seen as threatening by other employees. There will be suspicions, however unjustified, of favoritism or pillow talk which may make your relationships with them difficult. It is also worth bearing in mind that if the management decides that for the sake of peace and efficiency one of you must go, it is nearly always the woman who is asked to move, unless her lover is in a very subordinate position relative to her in the company.

But what options are open to you if you have no circle of friends, perhaps because you have just moved to a new town, or because you meet few congenial people at work? The following alternatives all have their drawbacks but may prove fruitful.

☐ *Computer dating.* The mating game as practised through dating agencies does not have a high success rate, but it is worth trying if you accept that you are more likely to get an improved social life than a perfect love-match. When you first visit an agency, check the membership fees and costs, which vary enormously. Also, ask about the number of clients on the books, since the bigger the 'pool' the agency draws from, the greater are your chances of meeting someone suitable.

☐ *Singles clubs and bars.* Members of singles clubs are often lonely and shy and you may find that all you have in common with them is the fact that you are unattached. But they do provide social activities that will give you as many evenings in the company of others as you want, and the chance of friendship or more. If you are new to the area, such clubs will provide the easiest way of meeting the largest number of people in the shortest time. Singles bars, on the other hand, are often simply a pick-up place with no pretense of offering anything else. If all that you really want is a steady supply of sexual partners, singles bars, like many discos and clubs, will meet your needs.

☐ *Advertisements and contact magazines.* Unfortunately, there is no foolproof way of screening dangerous or weird advertisers or respondents. Nor can there be any guarantee of common interests or compatibility on any level. Remember, too, that such advertisements are very often placed by men with only sex in mind and you risk disappointment, or worse, in responding.

Dealing with sexual relationships

Being single need not mean being celibate, of course, but you may go through periods when, for various reasons, you need time to be alone or free from sexual involvement. Sexual abstinence can be beneficial, giving you a chance to take stock of your life, and masturbation will relieve your sexual tension.

A woman's sex drive is usually closely related to the way she feels about a particular person. When there is no one you feel especially attracted to, you will probably find that your interest in sex lies dormant and that you do not miss it greatly.

However, two factors often complicate sex if you are single. First, for most women a sexual relationship must entail some emotional involvement if it is to mean much, and if you are looking for more than just physical pleasure you can be particularly vulnerable. Secondly, there is a common assumption that if you are getting no sex at the moment, you must want it, expecially if you have recently lost a partner. A man may even imply that by suggesting sex he is somehow doing you a favor.

Deciding what you want

Women often agree to have sex when they do not want to. Sometimes it is in order to hold a man's interest or to keep a relationship going. Often, it is because they are made to feel there is something wrong with them if they do not want it. Frequently, too, they want love, affection, or approval and having sex seems to be the easiest, or only, way of getting these. Finally, there is the common but illogical notion that a man's sexual desire is somehow a woman's responsibility – that she has caused his arousal and is therefore duty-bound to satisfy him.

At times, any of these can be sufficient reason to have sex – if you are happy about it. But sometimes you will encounter sexual pressure that amounts to blackmail. It is your right to decide whether, with whom, and when you have sex, but the following guidelines should help you if you do find yourself in a difficult situation with a date.

- Forestall trouble, if it seems imminent, by being explicit. Make it clear that any friendly gesture you make is not a sexual one. If this fails, take your leave without further delay.

- Never allow yourself to be forced into 'proving' that you love someone by having sex with him. Love is given willingly, not under threat.

- Never feel obliged to have sex because your date has spent money entertaining you. A man who has taken you out to dinner, for example, is not automatically entitled to spend the rest of the night with you. If it makes you feel better, pay your own way so that you need feel no such pressure. Even simply offering to buy him a drink during the evening will immediately put the relationship on a more equal footing so that sex is not so easily regarded by your partner as a quid pro quo for his expenditure.

- Not wanting to have sex with someone does not mean that you are frigid. However, it can mean that the man you are with does not interest you in that way. If you are accused of 'frigidity' when you refuse a man it might be worth pointing this out to him. Some men habitually blame women in this way for their own failure.

- You will gain approval, even prestige, in being part of a couple, and it may be tempting to start a liaison for just that reason. But you will be happier if you resist social pressure to enter a sexual relationship with a man who means little to you. Let your feelings, not other people's, guide you.

Making the most of your sex life

A single woman cannot, or rather normally does not, seek sex in the way that men do, often because such sexual freedom simply does not appeal to her. And yet if you have the conventional female view of sex as only truly satisfying within the context of a permanent and loving relationship, you are limiting your own options unfairly. Sex can be good in many different sorts of relationship. Because such involvements do not have the social strictures of marriage or parenthood on them, they may be able to change and develop more freely. But you need to be armed with a realistic outlook on the following lines if you are to pursue sexual independence.

- Do not expect every relationship to provide all you need. Very few can do this (although it is often unreasonably expected of a marriage).

- Do not try to justify every affair or sexual experience you have by persuading yourself that you have fallen in love. There may be times when you will meet and respond to someone entirely on the basis of physical attraction. Do not feel guilty about it (why should you if you are free?) but do not try to see more in it than is really there. By persuading yourself that you are in love you will make yourself much more emotionally vulnerable if the affair ends.

- Do not get into the habit of regarding every relationship that ends as a terrible mistake, still less as your own personal failure. If it was good but is no longer, regard it as a worthwhile relationship that has simply run its course.

◁ **Choosing the single life**
The decision to remain unattached can be a rewarding one. The benefits include independence and privacy, while the absence of a steady partner need not mean a sexless existence.

It is difficult for anyone to enjoy sex if they are feeling ill or off-color. Any chronic or painful illness, for example, will almost always tend to decrease your desire for sex, and if you are taking drugs for any illness, these too may decrease your desire for sex or your sexual responsiveness. Your general life-style can also affect your sex life. Heavy drinking can dull sexual feelings and arousal. A serious weight problem, besides being a turn-off for your partner, means that in all probability you will be breathless, less mobile and therefore less sexually vigorous. If pain or discomfort during intercourse becomes a problem at the menopause, hormone replacement therapy (see p.43) will usually help. Your mental state is important too. A depressive illness can affect your self-esteem and lower your sexual confidence, and will nearly always lead to loss of interest in sex.

Some medical problems cause specific sexual difficulties – but often these are remediable. Advice on some of the most common medical conditions that affect sexual functioning is given below. Your doctor may be able to give you further practical help.

Arthritis (and stiff or painful joints)

Reduced mobility and a consequent restriction of sexual activity are usually associated with these conditions. Hip disease, in particular, is often a problem for women.

What you should do

Choose the time of day when you have least pain to make love and, if you use painkillers, take them half an hour beforehand. Before making love, rest and take a warm bath. Experiment to discover the most comfortable position. A rear-entry position is likely to be best if you have hip disease. Use pillows for support and greater comfort.

Multiple sclerosis

Difficulty in achieving orgasm, loss of sexual appetite, and reduced genital sensation may be caused by this condition.

What you should do

Multiple sclerosis runs a fluctuating course, and if problems develop you should try to maintain the habit of having sex, in the knowledge that there will be times when the disease is less severe and sex can be enjoyed.

Diabetes mellitus

There is little evidence to suggest that diabetes has any marked effect on sexual functioning in women. The main problem that diabetic women face is a tendency to develop yeast infections (see VAGINAL DISCHARGE, p.48).

COPING WITH PHYSICAL DISABILITY

Often the main sexual problem for the physically disabled woman is that she has no sex life at all. She has to overcome not only her physical disability and the problem of finding a partner, but must also cope with the widespread attitude of others that a handicapped person should not want or need sex.

Remember that you have as much right as anybody to a sex life and, if your condition prevents you from living independently, to privacy to enjoy it. Even if your sex life is diminished, you will still need the warmth and affection of a close relationship. So aim to develop new friendships, because it is in this way that you will most easily find lovers.

Try not to cut yourself off from other people, or to think of your disability as the most important thing about you. In any relationship you make, a period of trial and error will be inevitable before you discover how best to meet each other's sexual needs. Therefore it is particularly important that you are able to talk to each other freely. If you have no sexual partner at present, masturbation will relieve tension, and also keep your sexual feelings alive, so that if a prospective sexual partner comes along, you will be ready to take advantage of the opportunity.

Ileostomy/colostomy

Embarrassment and fears that you may have become less attractive to your partner are the main barriers to sexual enjoyment after such operations.

What you should do
Make sure you have a well-fitting bag and that it is securely fastened to your body. Always empty your bag before you have sex, and learn to predict when it is likely to be full, so that you can time your lovemaking accordingly. You will probably find that it is best, for example, not to make love for an hour or two after you have eaten. If the bag seems to get in the way, try a different lovemaking position (see SEXUAL POSITIONS, P.63). Until you are used to your condition, you may feel more comfortable if you wear a nightdress. Tell a new partner about it and reassure him that sex will not be harmful.

Mastectomy

Loss of a breast often has a profound effect on a woman's self-esteem. It may affect your relationship and even cause you to avoid sex altogether.

What you should do
Your partner's assurance that you are still desirable is the best therapy you can have, and it is important that you do not distance yourself so that he is unable to offer it. Provided no pressure is put on the wound, you can begin to have sex as soon as you like, and this will help you to regain your sexual confidence. You may prefer to make the loss of your breast less obvious, perhaps by choosing a side-by-side position in which you lie on the affected side.

Respiratory and heart disease

Any condition that causes breathlessness or angina on exertion may limit your sexual activity, but it certainly need not preclude it completely.

What you should do
Choose a position for intercourse that is comfortable and does not involve strenuous movement, and let your partner play the more active role. If you have been prescribed drugs to take before exercise (bronchodilators for asthma or nitroglycerines for angina, for example) take these before you have intercourse. Avoid heavy meals before making love. If you have recently had a heart attack, you may be worried that sex might precipitate another. However, if your doctor tells you that moderate exercise is safe, sexual intercourse will be safe too. If you are still in doubt, ask him if there is any danger in having sex.

Chronic kidney failure

Kidney failure often causes a woman to lose interest in sex and become less responsive. These problems may, however, be as much due to the general feeling of malaise, or even depression, that often affects sufferers from kidney failure.

Thyroid disorders

Most people suffering from hypothyroidism report some loss of interest in sex. Hyperthyroidism may occasionally cause this too, although in about 10 per cent of people sexual appetite is actually increased. These effects usually disappear once the disorder has been treated.

GUIDELINES FOR SAFER SEX

Sex does not cause AIDS, and 'safer sex' does not mean no sex, or no physical contact. It is safe to live with someone who has AIDS, to sleep in the same bed, share the same household utensils, and hug them. The danger lies in allowing an infected person's body fluids – blood, semen, vaginal fluids and (to a much lesser extent) saliva to enter your own body through a cut or abrasion. The table below puts various sexual activities into categories according to the risk of this happening. Using a condom (which the HIV virus cannot penetrate) as a barrier during intercourse will greatly reduce this risk, especially if you also use a spermicide (see CONTRACEPTION, p.135).

The best guarantee of a safe sex life is to stay with one regular partner. If you change partners often, or if your regular partner has other sexual contacts, the only sensible policy is always to use condoms and spermicides.

NO RISK
Solo and mutual masturbation; massage (excluding the genital area); using unshared sex toys.

LOW RISK
Intercourse (anal or vaginal) with a condom and spermicide; fellatio ("sucking") without ejaculation, or wearing a condom.

HIGH RISK
Intercourse (anal or vaginal) without using a condom; using shared sex toys; any sex act which draws blood.

SEXUALLY TRANSMITTED DISEASES

A sexually transmitted disease (STD) is nearly always transferred by vaginal or anal intercourse, or oral-genital contact. Most of the organisms that cause these diseases thrive only in warm, moist conditions and cannot survive outside the body for more than a few minutes. It is virtually impossible to contract an STD through contact with, say, a lavatory seat, although infection may spread via a towel handled immediately after use by an infected person.

It is essential to seek medical help promptly if you think you have a sexually transmitted disease. Treatment is simple and effective, provided it is started early enough. You should avoid sex altogether until you are cured. Your recent sexual partners should also contact a doctor as soon as possible.

Non-specific urethritis (NSU)

An infection of the urinary passage, which in women usually produces no symptoms except, occasionally, a slight increase in vaginal discharge. If your partner has NSU, you will be given antibiotics, even if you are symptom-free, as you can carry the organism which causes NSU and reinfect him. NSU can spread to the fallopian tubes and cause infertility.

Genital herpes

Not everyone who comes into contact with this viral disease develops it, and many people have symptomless attacks and acquire immunity. The first bout may last 2-3 weeks. About half of all sufferers have subsequent attacks, but these tend to be shorter and less severe. Attacks often recur when the sufferer is run down or under stress. If the infection is active at the end of a pregnancy, a Caesarean section may be recommended, to prevent infection of the baby on its passage through the birth canal.

Symptoms Genital itching, followed by a rash on the vulva of red patches with white, itchy blisters. These may burst to form shallow, very painful ulcers. There may be tenderness and swelling in the groin, pain on urination, fever, and general discomfort. Symptoms appear 2-20 days after contact.

Treatment At present there is no effective treatment, although a drug is available that accelerates healing and so reduces the length of time you are infectious and uncomfortable. An analgesic such as aspirin or a local anesthetic will relieve pain. Abstain from sex while you still have symptoms. Because there is an association between genital herpes and cervical cancer, once you have had the infection you should have a cervical smear annually thereafter.

Gonorrhea

A bacterial infection, more common in men than women.

Symptoms Women may show no symptoms. However, there may be an increase in vaginal discharge, or, if the infection is in the rectum, moistness, and pus on the faeces. Infection may spread to the uterus and fallopian tubes and there is an approximately 10 per cent chance that one such attack may cause blockage of the tubes, resulting in infertility.

Treatment By antibiotics. You should avoid all sexual contact until you are cured.

Syphilis

A rare disease which affects women less than men. The first sign is a hard, painless but highly infectious sore (chancre) at the site of the infection, which disappears spontaneously. The disease can be successfully treated with antibiotics: if untreated, more serious symptoms, leading eventually to death, may develop several years later.

Genital warts

Warts on the vulva are fairly common and mildly contagious. They spread more easily in moist conditions, and so may develop when there is an increased vaginal discharge, for example during an attack of vaginal yeast infection, or during pregnancy.

Because there is an association between genital warts and cancer of the cervix, it is important, if you have ever been infected with vaginal warts, to have regular cervical smears.

Pubic lice ('crabs')

Minute blood-sucking insects which appear in the pubic or anal hair. The lice appear several weeks after the infection and may cause severe itching, especially at night.

Treatment Application of a special cream or lotion.

AIDS

Acquired Immune Deficiency Syndrome (AIDS) is caused by the human immunodeficiency virus (HIV). The virus is present in body fluids – blood, semen, and sometimes saliva, though in saliva the quantities are probably too small to cause infection. AIDS is primarily a sexually transmitted disease, but it can also be passed on by transfusion with infected blood, or by the shared use of a hypodermic needle or syringe amongst intravenous drug users.

Once inside the body, the virus penetrates and multiplies inside the T4 white blood cells which play a vital part in the body's defences against some infections and cancers. Eventually the cells burst, releasing HIV particles into the blood which can then infect more T4 blood cells. As cells are gradually destroyed, the person becomes more prone to infections of the lungs, gut, or brain, or to various forms of cancer, such as Kaposi's sarcoma, a rare form of skin cancer. At the moment it seems probable that between 1 in 10 and 1 in 3 of those infected with the virus will eventually develop AIDS, but the exact figure is not known.

AIDS cannot be transmitted by casual social contact; to cause infection, the virus must actually enter the body through a cut or abrasion in the skin or the mucous membranes which line the rectum, vagina or mouth. The rectum is especially vulnerable because its lining is thin and delicate, so anal intercourse carries a higher risk than most other forms of sexual activity. The disease can also be spread by vaginal intercourse. Use of a condom helps to prevent infection (see **Guidelines for safer sex**, p.157). Most doctors believe that the chances of catching AIDS from a single sexual encounter with an infected person are very small. It is repeated sexual contact with an infected person or persons that is likely to lead to infection.

Symptoms Some people infected with the HIV virus do not develop symptoms, though they can still infect others. A few people develop a glandular fever-like illness soon after infection, which clears up without treatment, but most feel perfectly well. People who have had the infection for some months or years may develop permanently swollen lymph glands, and tend to develop common skin infections. Some people then develop a variety of symptoms, including fever, weight loss, diarrhea and oral thrush, which are known as the AIDS-related complex, or ARC. ARC is not itself fatal, but people who develop it are more likely to develop full-blown AIDS. This usually has a pattern of repeated infections, weight loss, weakness and eventual death. On average, about 3-4 years elapse between infection and the development of AIDS.

Treatment Although there is no vaccine or cure for AIDS at present, the conditions associated with it can often be treated. Early trials suggest that in a few cases the drug Retrovir (AZT) may 'buy time' by slowing down the progress of the disease, though the drug has very unpleasant side-effects.

TESTING FOR AIDS

When someone is infected with the HIV virus that causes AIDS, their body develops antibodies against the virus. A blood test for the presence of HIV antibodies provides a fairly reliable indication as to whether or not the person is infected with the virus. If you are in a 'high risk' group (that is, if your partner is an active homosexual, if you or your partner have many casual sexual relationships, or are intravenous drug users), you may wonder whether to take the antibody test. It may seem easier to know, so you can face the fact that you are antibody positive (if that is what the test indicates), rather than have to cope with the uncertainty of not knowing.

However, testing does not always provide conclusive proof that you either will or will not develop AIDS. Although the test is reliable, it is not 100 per cent reliable; a second, different type of test is usually carried out on any positive sample to confirm the result. Moreover, the HIV antibodies take a few weeks (or even months) to develop, so a test carried out shortly after you have been infected will give a negative result. Finally, although a positive antibody test shows that you have been exposed to the virus, it does not mean that you will inevitably develop AIDS.

A positive test result has important implications, so counselling is advisable for anyone who is considering having the test. People who are antibody positive are usually advised only to tell those who actually need to know – their doctor, dentist, close friends, and of course their sexual partner. Sadly, there are still many misconceptions about AIDS, and there is unnecessary discrimination against people who have the disease or are antibody positive.

RESOURCE GUIDE

RECOMMENDED READING

General

Barbach, L. *For yourself: The fulfillment of female sexuality.* New York, NY, Signet, 1976

The Boston Women's Health Book Collective. *The new Our bodies, ourselves.* New York, NY, Simon & Schuster, Inc., 1984

Comfort, A. *The joy of sex.* New York, NY, Simon and Schuster, 1974

Fettner, A. Guidici and Check, W. A. *The truth about AIDS* (revised and updated edition). New York, NY, Holt, Rinehart and Winston, 1985

Friday, Nancy. *My secret garden: Women's Sexual Fantasies.* New York, NY, Trident Press, 1973

Heiman, J., LoPiccolo, L. and LoPiccolo, J. *Becoming orgasmic: A sexual growth program for women.* Englewood Cliffs, New Jersey, Prentice-Hall, 1976

Kline-Graber, G. and Graber, B. *Woman's orgasm: A guide to sexual satisfaction.* New York, NY, Fawcett Library, 1975

Kubler-Ross, E. *AIDS: The ultimate challenge.* New York, NY, Macmillan, 1988

Penney, A. *How to make love to a man.* New York, NY, Dell, 1982

Westheimer, W. *Dr Ruth's guide to good sex.* New York, NY, Warner, 1984

For couples

Barbach, L. *For each other: Sharing sexual intimacy.* New York, NY, Doubleday, 1982

Gochros, H.L. and Fischer, J. *Treat yourself to a better sex life.* Englewood Cliffs, New Jersey, Prentice-Hall, 1980

McCarthy, B. and McCarthy, E. *Sexual awareness: Enhancing sexual pleasure.* New York, NY, Carroll & Graf Publishers, 1984

Phillips, D. and Judd, R. *Sexual confidence.* New York, NY, Bantam Books, 1982

For older readers

Butler, R.N. & Lewis, M.I. *Love and sex after sixty: A guide for men and women in their later years.* New York, NY, Harper & Row, 1976

For disabled or handicapped readers

Bullard, D.G. & Knight, S.E. (editors) *Sexuality and physical disability: Personal perspectives.* St. Louis, Mo., C.V. Mosby, 1981

Kempton, W. *Sex education for persons with disabilities that hinder learning.* N. Scituate, Mass. Duxbury Press, 1975

ORGANIZATIONS

Sex therapy and education

For information on sex therapy clinics and sex education programs, contact:

American Association of Sex Educators, Counselors, and Therapists (AASECT) 600 Maryland Avenue SW, Washington, DC 20024.

Information services for homosexuals

The following organizations provide information and advice for homosexual men and women:

Div. 44, Gay and Lesbian Concerns, American Psychological Association, 1200 17th Street NW, Washington, DC 20036.

Institute for Human Identity, 490 West End Avenue, New York, NY 10024.

Los Angeles Gay and Lesbian Community Services Center, 1213, N. Highland Avenue, Los Angeles, CA 90038.

Your Sexual Profile Chart

Use the chart below to create your own sexual profile. See p.24 for instructions.

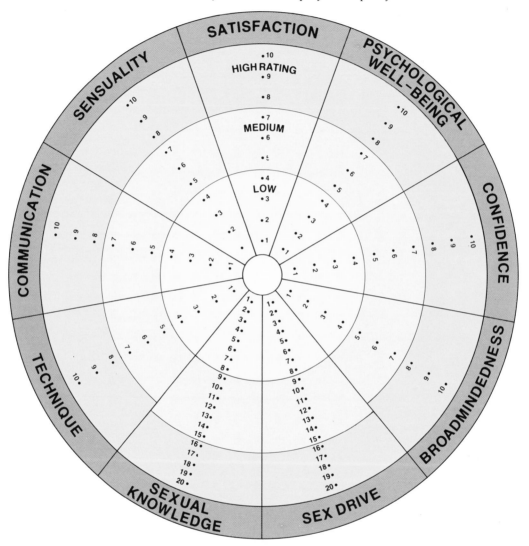

KEY TO ORIENTATION QUESTIONNAIRE (p.23)

☐ **A** You are exclusively heterosexual.

☐ **B** You are predominantly heterosexual, but under some conditions you may show a flicker of lesbian interest.

☐ **C** You are predominantly heterosexual, but have a strong lesbian element.

☐ **D** You are bisexual.

☐ **E** You are predominantly lesbian, but with an element of heterosexuality.

☐ **F** You are predominantly lesbian.

☐ **G** You are exclusively lesbian.

SEXUAL
HAPPINESS
A Practical Approach

PART TWO
MEN

YOUR SEXUAL PROFILE

Your answers to the following questionnaires together
form your sexual profile, a complete picture of the
attitudes and behavior that shape your relationships and
determine how much enjoyment you get and give in sex.
By collating your scores for the questionnaires in the form
of a chart, you can create your sexual profile. Instructions
on how to do this are given on pp. 176-7.
The answer to each question in the questionnaires on
pp. 166-74 carries a score. By checking your total score for a
questionnaire against the **What you should do** box that
follows it, you will obtain an assessment of where you
stand in the particular area of your sex life under
examination. The questionnaire on p. 175 is not rated in this
way, and serves simply to determine your orientation.
A low or medium score for a questionnaire indicates that a
particular aspect of your sexual experience is limiting your
happiness. An appropriate remedy is suggested where
necessary, the first step of which is usually to refer to other
sections of the book. Often the situation is indeed
remediable. You can change almost any aspect of your sex
life that is a problem and this book will help you do so.

SEXUAL KNOWLEDGE

How much do you know about sex and sexual physiology?

Indicate by a T or F in the box whether each of the statements below is true or false. Compare your total score with the ratings following the questionnaire.

1 Circumcision makes the penis less sensitive. □

2 Masturbation is bad because it leads to a loss of interest in sex with a partner. □

3 A condom gives some protection against AIDS. □

4 Vasectomy (male sterilization) cannot usually be reversed. □

5 Vasectomy usually reduces a man's desire for sex. □

6 The withdrawal method is an effective form of contraception. □

7 Conception is most likely around the middle of your partner's menstrual cycle. □

8 Sexually transmitted diseases can be caught from a lavatory seat. □

9 Sexual abstinence is bad for you. □

10 A hairy chest is an indication of virility. □

11 If a man is potent (able to have intercourse) he is therefore fertile. □

12 A woman's urinary passage is separate from her vagina. □

13 Simultaneous orgasm is necessary for satisfactory sex. □

14 The clitoris is a small, sensitive organ situated within the inner vaginal lips. □

15 The outer vaginal lips are the same in every woman. □

16 Most women need clitoral stimulation as well as intercourse to reach orgasm. □

17 Sportsmen can conserve their strength by abstaining from sex before a big event. □

18 Sexual intercourse during menstruation does no physical harm to either partner. □

19 Women who have passed the menopause have little interest in sex. □

20 A 'frigid' woman cannot be aroused. □

For key to answers see p.175.

Give yourself a point for each correct answer.

WHAT YOU SHOULD DO

High rating (16-20) Now try the questionnaire TECHNIQUE, p.173, to make sure that your skill matches your grasp of theory.

Medium rating (9-15) Check wrong answers (see below) and try TECHNIQUE, p.173.

Low rating (0-8) Besides checking your wrong answers (see below) and trying the questionnaire TECHNIQUE, p.173, see the problem charts

NEGATIVE FEELINGS, p.182, UNFULFILLED EXPECTATIONS, p.186, and MASTURBATION ANXIETY, p.190.

You will find full answers to the questions as follows:

Question **1** – p.233; **2** – p.190; **3** – p.284; **4,5** – p.285; **6** – p.284; **7** – p.286; **8** – p.309; **9** – p.291; **10,11** – p.286; **12** – p.206; **13** – p.213; **14,15** – p.206; **16** – p.275; **17** – p.272; **18** – p.273; **19** – p.276; **20** – p.273.

SEX DRIVE

How strong is your appetite for sex?

For each of the following questions, circle the score to the right of your answer.
Compare your total score with the ratings following the questionnaire.

1 If you are under 55, do you have sex:

More than three times a week? ———— 2
Once or twice a week? ———— 1
Less than once a week? ———— 0

If you are 55 or over, do you have sex:

More than once a week? ———— 2
Once or twice every couple of weeks? ———— 1
Seldom or never? ———— 0

2 How often do you masturbate?

At least 4-6 times a week ———— 2
Once a week or less ———— 0
Two or three times a week ———— 1

3 Did you first have sexual intercourse:

Earlier than most of your friends? ———— 2
Around the time that most of your friends ————
were starting to have sex? ———— 1
At a later age than most of your friends? ———— 0

4 Do you have genital stirrings when not consciously thinking of sex:

Once or twice a week? ———— 1
Most days? ———— 2
Seldom or never? ———— 0

5 Do you have erection problems?

Not very often ———— 1
Seldom or never ———— 2
Often ———— 0

6 Do you fantasize about sex (apart from when masturbating or making love):

Very often? ———— 2
Sometimes? ———— 1
Seldom or never? ———— 0

7 Do you think about sex:

Several times a day? ———— 2
Most days? ———— 1
Seldom or never? ———— 0

8 Have you been sexually involved with more than one person at a time:

Several times? ———— 2
Seldom? ———— 1
Never? ———— 0

9 Do erotic magazines:

Always excite you? ———— 2
Not turn you on at all? ———— 0
Sometimes excite you? ———— 1

10 Are your close relationships mainly:

Sexual? ———— 2
Tinged with a strong sexual element? ———— 1
Just friendly without sexual overtones? ———— 0

WHAT YOU SHOULD DO

High rating (16-20) You have a strong sex drive, which is fine if you have a partner who satisfies you.

Medium rating (9-15) Your sex drive should be no bar to sexual satisfaction. You can confirm this by doing the questionnaire ARE YOU SEXUALLY SATISFIED?, p.265.

Low rating (0-8) Consult the problem chart LACK OF INTEREST, p.180. In many cases a lack of sex drive presents no problems, but check if it is a symptom of illness. See SEX AND HEALTH, p.307.

PSYCHOLOGICAL WELL-BEING

Can you enjoy sex without anxiety or guilt?

For each question, circle the appropriate score. Compare your
total score with the ratings following the questionnaire.

	YES	NO		YES	NO
1 Do you feel sex is unimportant and has never played a large part in your life?	0	1	**6** Do you worry about catching AIDS, though you are not in a high risk group?	0	1
2 Are you a solitary person, unable or unwilling to get emotionally close to others?	0	1	**7** Are you usually confident of your ability to perform sexually?	1	0
3 Would you describe yourself as a jealous person?	0	1	**8** Are you completely sure about your preference for heterosexual relationships to homosexual ones, or vice versa?	1	0
4 Do you feel that unless you control yourself, sex might dominate your life?	0	1	**9** Do you often feel difficulty in living up to the masculine role expected of you?	0	1
5 Do you find sex messy? Are you repelled by the sight, odor, and feel of seminal or vaginal fluid, for example, or do you feel uneasy unless you can take a bath or shower right after intercourse?	0	1	**10** Does the idea of unusual sexual practices (involving violence or underage partners, for example) excite you more than the thought of conventional sex?	0	1

WHAT YOU SHOULD DO

High rating (8-10)

You are able to relax and respond naturally in a sexual situation. However, sexual functioning is very easily thrown off balance, so where you scored 0 on a question, consult the appropriate problem chart (see **Low rating**). This will help you to increase your sexual enjoyment even more.

Medium rating (5-7)

This suggests that fear or guilt about sex probably makes it hard for you to enjoy a sexual relationship fully. Consult the appropriate problem chart on the questions for which you scored 0 (see **Low rating**).

Low rating (0-4)

Your capacity for, and interest in, sex are needlessly limited. The problem charts listed below deal with factors which commonly influence psychological health and attitudes to sex. Consult them as follows on questions for which you scored 0:

Question 1 – LACK OF INTEREST, p.180; **2** – LACK OF EMOTIONAL INVOLVEMENT, p.184; **3** – LOW SELF-ESTEEM, p.188; **4-7** – NEGATIVE FEELINGS, p.182; **8,9** – HETEROSEXUALITY/HOMOSEXUALITY CONFLICTS, p.198; **10** – UNUSUAL SEXUAL PRACTICES, p.201.

SATISFACTION

Are you satisfied with your sex life?

For each question, circle the appropriate score. Compare your
total score with the ratings following the questionnaire.

	YES	NO		YES	NO
1 Are you getting as much sex as you would like?	1	0	**6** Is sex usually as good as you had imagined it would be?	1	0
2 Are you getting the kind of sex you like, so that you usually do the things you most enjoy?	1	0	**7** Is sex always or frequently disappointing?	0	1
3 Does your usual sexual partner still arouse you?	1	0	**8** Do you usually feel relaxed, happy, and comfortable after sex?	1	0
4 Do you believe that most people get more excitement from sex than you do?	0	1	**9** Do you feel that your partner usually enjoys sex as much as you do?	1	0
5 Do you normally anticipate sex with great pleasure?	1	0	**10** Is your usual partner too sexually demanding?	0	1

WHAT YOU SHOULD DO

High rating (8-10)
You seem happy with both the quality and quantity of your sex life. If you have a regular sexual partner, do the questionnaire ARE YOU SEXUALLY SATISFIED?, p.265, together. This will give a measure of your sexual compatibility and show you whether your partner's satisfaction equals yours.

Medium rating (5-7)
Ask yourself whether the main source of dissatisfaction is your relationship with a particular person or whether you perhaps have an unrealistic idea of how great sex ought to be. The questionnaires COMPATIBILITY, p.260, and ARE YOU SEXUALLY SATISFIED?, p.265, will be helpful in the former case. In the latter case, the problem chart UNFULFILLED EXPECTATIONS, p.186, will help you develop a more realistic view of sex.

Low rating (0-4)
Besides consulting the questionnaires and problem chart referred to above, it is especially important to complete the other questionnaires in the first part of the book. Further low ratings may enable you to identify causes of your low level of satisfaction.

SENSUALITY

How important is bodily contact to you in a loving relationship?

For each question, circle the appropriate score. Compare your total score with the ratings following the questionnaire.

	YES	NO		YES	NO
1 Do you know the erogenous zones of your own body (those areas that particularly arouse you when they are touched)?	1	0	**6** Do you often hug or kiss a lover simply to show affection, or just when you feel like sex?	1	0
2 Do you feel self-conscious or uncomfortable when your partner touches or caresses you after your orgasm?	0	1	**7** Do you like to hold hands or link arms when walking with a lover?	1	0
3 Are you physically demonstrative with people you are fond of, regardless of their sex?	1	0	**8** Do you prefer to make love in the nude?	1	0
4 Do you think it unmasculine to be physically demonstrative?	0	1	**9** After sex, do you dislike caressing your partner?	0	1
5 If you cannot sleep or are depressed, does it help to be held or to hold someone?	1	0	**10** Do you enjoy sleeping with your partner, whether or not you have had sex?	1	0

WHAT YOU SHOULD DO

High rating (8-10)
Sensuality and physical closeness, both vital in making rewarding sexual relationships, come easily to you. EXPANDING YOUR SEXUAL REPERTOIRE, P.204, will help you make the most of this ability.

Medium rating (5-7)
This suggests that you have the capacity for enjoying physical closeness but have not developed it sufficiently. If your sex life is not as fulfilling as you believe it could be, turn to the problem chart UNFULFILLED EXPECTATIONS, p.186, which will give you advice on how to improve the situation.

Low rating (0-4)
Your lack of physical demonstrativeness probably reflects an emotional coolness which could seriously affect your capacity to make close relationships. The problem chart LACK OF EMOTIONAL INVOLVEMENT, p.184, will help you to develop a greater capacity for closeness.

COMMUNICATION

How well can you communicate – both verbally and non-verbally – with your sexual partner?

For each question, circle the appropriate score. Compare your
total score with the ratings following the questionnaire.

	YES	NO		YES	NO
1 Do you usually talk with a partner about her and your own likes and dislikes in lovemaking?	1	0	**6** Do you find it difficult to make up after a quarrel?	0	1
2 Have you ever told a partner about your sexual fantasies?	1	0	**7** Are you capable of telling your partner that you love her?	1	0
3 If a partner wants sex but you are not in the mood, can you indicate this without making her feel rejected?	1	0	**8** Would you be embarrassed to tell a new partner you prefer to use a condom to reduce the risk of AIDS?	0	1
4 If you have a temporary sexual difficulty – an inability to get an erection, for example – can you discuss it freely with your partner?	1	0	**9** If your partner is hurt or angry, do you often react by becoming angry yourself?	0	1
5 Are you reluctant to express anger or hurt because you fear that it might harm your relationship?	0	1	**10** Do you always discuss contraception with a new partner?	1	0

WHAT YOU SHOULD DO

High rating (8-10)
You obviously communicate well with your partner, but EXPANDING YOUR SEXUAL REPERTOIRE, p.204, may help you to make even more of this ability.

Medium rating (5-7)
You are slightly inhibited when it comes to communication with a partner. The problem chart NEGATIVE FEELINGS, p.182, examines some of the reasons for this and directs you to helpful features.

Low rating (0-4)
Because you lack the ability to express yourself, you are missing out on a vital element in successful sexual relationships. Turn to problem chart LACK OF EMOTIONAL INVOLVEMENT, p.184.

CONFIDENCE

How do you rate your sex appeal and ability as a lover?

For each question, circle the appropriate score. Compare your
total score with the ratings following the questionnaire.

	YES	NO		YES	NO
1 Do you often avoid asking for a date because you are afraid that you will be turned down?	0	1	**6** Do you think it is more important to please your partner than to achieve satisfaction for yourself?	0	1
2 Do you feel that your penis is smaller than other men's?	0	1	**7** If your partner suggested that you change your sexual routine, would you be likely to take it as a criticism of your ability as a lover?	0	1
3 Are you uncomfortable about being naked in front of your partner?	0	1	**8** Are you frightened of being rejected if you suggest a change in your sexual routine?	0	1
4 Do you sometimes avoid intercourse because you doubt your competence?	0	1	**9** When things go wrong with your relationship, do you always, or most often, assume it is your fault?	0	1
5 Do you believe you are as good a lover as most other men?	1	0	**10** Do you seldom feel jealous?	1	0

WHAT YOU SHOULD DO

High rating (8-10)
You are obviously confident in your sexual relationships. Sometimes, though, too much self-confidence can make you rather unaware of others' feelings. If your relationships seldom last long, see the problem chart DIFFICULTY IN SUSTAINING RELATIONSHIPS, p.296, which may help you pinpoint the reasons for this.

Medium rating (5-7)
Your slight lack of self-confidence may make you shy and even cause you to seem unfriendly to others. If so, consult the problem chart LOW SELF-ESTEEM, p.188, which will direct you toward helpful features. If you feel that your diffidence limits your sexual experience, see the section on DIFFICULTY IN FORMING SEXUAL RELATIONSHIPS, p.294.

Low rating (0-4)
A poor self-image may be limiting your social as well as your sexual enjoyment. Begin by consulting the problem chart LOW SELF-ESTEEM, p.188. But if your problem is so severe that it prevents you forming relationships, you should read DIFFICULTY IN FINDING A PARTNER, p.292.

TECHNIQUE

How capable are you of arousing and satisfying a partner?

For each question, circle the appropriate score. Compare your
total score with the ratings following the questionnaire.

	YES	NO		YES	NO
1 Are you able to delay your orgasm in order to prolong intercourse?	1	0	**6** Do you find leisurely foreplay a waste of time or frustrating?	0	1
2 Does it trouble you if your partner tries to initiate sex?	0	1	**7** After sex, do you always cuddle your partner affectionately?	1	0
3 Do you often find it difficult to achieve or sustain an erection?	0	1	**8** Do you genuinely like women and enjoy their company?	1	0
4 Have you varied your lovemaking technique over the last six months by, for example, trying a new position or simply having sex in a different place or at an unusual time?	1	0	**9** When you have an orgasm during intercourse and your partner does not, do you usually try to satisfy her by other means?	1	0
5 Do you always make sure a woman is fully aroused before you penetrate her?	1	0	**10** Do you normally take the trouble to create a romantic setting or mood as a prelude to sex?	1	0

WHAT YOU SHOULD DO

High rating (8-10)
You are obviously a competent lover. But love-making is a subtle skill. Therefore, if your scores for the questionnaires SENSUALITY, p.170, and COMMUNICATION, p.171, are considerably lower than your score here, you probably need to develop your ability to make your partner feel emotionally, as well as physically, fulfilled. Follow the advice given in the ratings guides to these questionnaires.

Medium rating (5-7)
You may well have inhibitions which affect your sexual skill. Consult the problem chart NEGATIVE FEELINGS, p.182. It may be, though, that your real problem is simply inexperience. The problem chart UNFULFILLED EXPECTATIONS, p.186, will direct you to helpful features.

Low rating (0-4)
Do not be discouraged by your low score. Sexual technique can be learned and it is never too late. It is also important to examine your feelings about sex (see NEGATIVE FEELINGS, p.182, and UNFULFILLED EXPECTATIONS, p.186). However, if it seems that your problems are predominantly a matter of technique rather than attitude, they are most likely dealt with in ERECTION PROBLEMS, p.192, and PREMATURE EJACULATION, P.194.

BROADMINDEDNESS

How tolerant of sexual freedom and experimentation are you?

For each question, circle the appropriate score. Compare your
total score with the ratings following the questionnaire.

	YES	NO		YES	NO
1 Do you prefer to make love with the light on?	1	0	**6** Do you enjoy oral sex?	1	0
2 Do you think a partner's infidelity is a good enough reason to end an otherwise happy relationship?	0	1	**7** Do sexually explicit movies, magazines, or books embarrass you?	0	1
3 Does anything other than the male-on-top position seem wrong to you?	0	1	**8** Have you tried anal sex?	1	0
4 Would you think less of a friend if you discovered he was homosexual?	0	1	**9** Have you tried group sex?	1	0
5 Have you ever used a mirror to watch yourself making love?	1	0	**10** Have you ever acted out any of your sexual fantasies with a partner?	1	0

WHAT YOU SHOULD DO

High rating (8-10)

You have a very tolerant attitude toward sexual
self-expression. However, are you quite sure your
interest in novelty does not suggest a degree of
boredom with your present sex life? If your rating for
the questionnaire SATISFACTION, p.169, is not
equally high, turn to the problem chart UNFUL-
FILLED EXPECTATIONS, p.186, which suggests
possible reasons for dissatisfaction and features
which will help you overcome it. If you answered
"Yes" to questions eight or nine you might be a little
more cautious in your approach to sex. Both of these
are 'high risk' activities as far as AIDS is concerned.
The use of a condom and spermicide can reduce the
dangers, but the safest sexual relationships are those
in which neither partner has any other sexual
contacts. Resist pressure to be 'broadminded' if it
involves doing anything you feel is dangerous or
anything that simply does not appeal to you.

Medium rating (5-7)

You are probably reasonably happy with your
cautious attitude toward sex. But if you find you have
lost some of your enthusiasm, turn to the problem
chart LACK OF INTEREST, p.180. Perhaps you
have never found sex very exciting, in which case the
problem chart UNFULFILLED EXPEC-
TATIONS, p.186, will help you.

Low rating (0-4)

You are undoubtedly too cautious about sex, and
perhaps even find it sinful or shameful. Such attitudes
are almost certainly limiting your sexual happiness.
The problem chart NEGATIVE FEELINGS, p.182,
will direct you to features that will help you develop a
more balanced outlook. See also the questionnaire
PSYCHOLOGICAL WELL-BEING, p.168.

ORIENTATION

Are your sexual inclinations heterosexual, homosexual, or somewhere between the two?

Read through the statements and choose the one that most accurately describes you.
If you have no sexual experience, try to imagine what your inclinations might be.

	RATING		RATING
I am sexually aroused only by, and have sex only with, women.	A	I have sex with both men and women, but my sexual fantasies are more often about men.	E
I am sexually aroused by women, but have occasional fantasies of sex with men.	B	I prefer men and have little interest in women as sexual partners.	F
I prefer sex with women, but have occasional homosexual encounters that mean little to me.	C	I am sexually aroused only by, and have sex only with, men.	G
I am equally aroused by men and women and enjoy sex with both.	D		

WHAT YOU SHOULD DO

Your choice among the above statements gives you a rating on a scale of sexual orientation adapted from the one devised by the sexologist Alfred Kinsey. To check your rating, turn to p.314. The ratings are not value judgments; if you are comfortable with your orientation, you need do nothing about it. But if you find it hard to reconcile your sexual inclinations with other areas of your life, study the problem chart HETEROSEXUALITY/HOMOSEXUALITY CONFLICTS, p.198.

KEY TO SEXUAL KNOWLEDGE QUESTIONNAIRE (p.166)

TRUE: Questions 3, 4, 7, 12, 14, 16, 18
FALSE: Questions 1, 2, 5, 6, 8, 9, 10, 11, 13, 15, 17, 19, 20

THE SEXUAL PROFILE CHART

Using the blank chart on p.160 (or a photocopy), indicate your score for each of the questionnaires by marking the appropriate point on the rating scale. Join the points to create your sexual profile.

Your rating for sexual satisfaction is the touchstone of this exercise. What you will probably find is that alongside factors that contribute to your satisfaction there are others that are clearly limiting it.

Your scores for the four questionnaires on the right-hand side of the chart – **Psychological well-being**, **Confidence**, **Broadmindedness**, and **Sex drive** – reflect your fundamental attitudes to sex. High scores here indicate that you are sexually confident, while low scores suggest that you are perhaps inhibited in this area or have little interest in sex. (These factors are often linked, since a consistent lack of enthusiasm can conceal powerful inhibitions.) The questionnaires on the left-hand side of the graph – **Sensuality**, **Communication**, **Technique**, and **Sexual knowledge** – deal with those aspects of your sexual identity that are likely to affect your technique and your ability to be close to a partner.

Low scores in any part of your profile chart indicate problems, and advice is given in the ratings guides following the questionnaires. A serious imbalance in your scores is also a cause for concern. For example, it is possible to enjoy high confidence which conceals from you a poor grasp of sexual technique or an inability to understand another person's feelings. Similarly, your sexual knowledge may be extensive but you may lack confidence so that it is rarely, or never, put into practice.

It is possible for you to score low in one area without your being aware of the need – or simply the scope – for improvement in another. In this connection, it is particularly important to realize that while you may score low on the right-hand side and nevertheless feel sexually satisfied, your partner may remain unfulfilled. Accordingly, a lack of sexual confidence or a narrow-minded outlook may well underlie an inability to express warmth to your partner or may create difficulties in the practical aspects of lovemaking. Such problems will be reflected in low scores in the relevant areas on the left of the chart.

In a similar way you may be untroubled by a low score low on communication or on sensuality, since many men find it hard to talk about their feelings or to express physical (but not necessarily sexual) tenderness.

SAMPLE PROFILE CHARTS

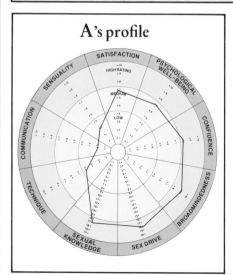

A's profile

A sees himself as very 'macho'. He has a strong sex drive, plenty of confidence, and is both experienced and knowledgeable. Yet his satisfaction rating is medium. He has never married and his relationships with women tend to be passionate but brief. Understandably, he has begun to wonder why they do not last.

There is a distinct imbalance in *A*'s profile. While the right side betrays no obvious sexual hang-ups, the low ratings on the left indicate that, although he is by no means ignorant or a slow starter in matters of sex, he cannot easily communicate his feelings. In fact, it seldom occurs to *A* to show affection to his partner, or to acknowledge hers, except during sex.

A needs to learn to become more emotionally close to a partner. The problem chart LACK OF EMOTIONAL INVOLVEMENT, p.184, and the feature UNDERSTANDING A WOMAN'S FEELINGS, p.273, will help him understand that a sexual relationship is a two-way affair. By allowing himself to be more open with a woman and by appreciating her feelings, he will increase his pleasure and the chances of a stable relationship.

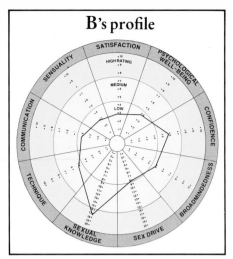

B's profile

B's satisfaction rating is low, and the uniformly poor ratings on the left side of his profile reinforce the suggestion that his relationship is very inadequate. The right side, however, shows low ratings for psychological well-being and broadmindedness, which together point to a problem in his feelings about sex.

In fact, B has strong homosexual leanings (indicated by an E rating on the Orientation questionnaire) which he finds it hard to acknowledge. He married partly to demonstrate his 'normality' and, sexually, the relationship has never been satisfactory.

The problem chart HETEROSEXUALITY/HOMOSEXUALITY CONFLICTS, p.198, and the feature COMING TO TERMS WITH HOMOSEXUALITY, p.253, will help B gauge the strength of his homosexual feelings and discover what kind of lifestyle he wants. His generally ambivalent attitude to sex will need to be resolved, however, if he is to make a success of any sexual relationship. The problem chart NEGATIVE FEELINGS, p.182, will help him to do this.

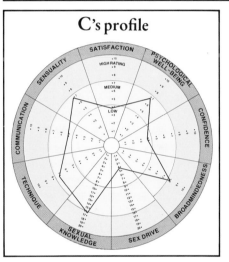

C's profile

C has an unexpectedly low satisfaction rating. The medium ratings on the left side of his profile suggest that he is a competent lover and able to make and sustain sexual relationships. But the right side shows a surprising lack of confidence and drive. C's relationship has deteriorated since, during a period of overwork and worry, he was several times unable to gain an erection. Each failure increased his anxiety about becoming impotent and eventually his fears became so intense that he avoided sex altogether. Because C found it hard to talk about the problem, his partner began to believe that he no longer loved or trusted her, and her own distress has driven a further wedge between them.

The problem chart ERECTION PROBLEMS, p.192 will reassure C that his temporary difficulty is unlikely to develop into a permanent problem unless he continues to worry about it. He would also do well to study LEARNING TO COMMUNICATE, p.270, which will help him overcome his inhibitions about speaking frankly about his feelings.

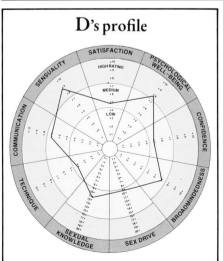

D's profile

D is in his teens and having his first sexual relationship. The right side of his profile points to a positive and enthusiastic attitude to sex. The absence of hang-ups, combined with high ratings for sensuality and communication, mean that he will probably find future sexual relationships easy. But, on the left, his relatively low ratings for knowledge and technique suggest that he experiences 'technical' difficulties when making love.

The fact is that D's eagerness and inexperience lead him to ejaculate prematurely. Understandably, this is affecting his self-confidence and explains why he does not find sex particularly satisfying at present.'

Nevertheless, D's profile should reassure him that, sexually, he has good prospects and no reason to lack confidence. The problem chart PREMATURE EJACULATION, p.194 will confirm that his difficulty is one that will almost certainly disappear as his experience grows, whether the present relationship lasts or not. The chart also directs him to advice that will help him start dealing with the problem right away.

2

PROBLEM CHARTS

Each of the following self-diagnostic problem charts will
help you track down the reasons for a particular sexual
difficulty and offer you advice on resolving it. By means of
a logically constructed network of questions to be
answered either with a YES or a NO, the fourteen charts
will lead you to conclusions based on authoritative
research and expert opinion. Always begin at the first
question and follow through to the correct endpoint for
your special set of circumstances. The endpoint that you
reach will either provide brief advice or, more often, refer
you to other parts of the book where the problem is
discussed in greater detail and self-help programs are
given. Follow up cross-references in every case, so as not
to miss further advice. In a few instances you may be
advised to make use of a related problem chart or,
occasionally, to seek professional help.

LACK OF INTEREST

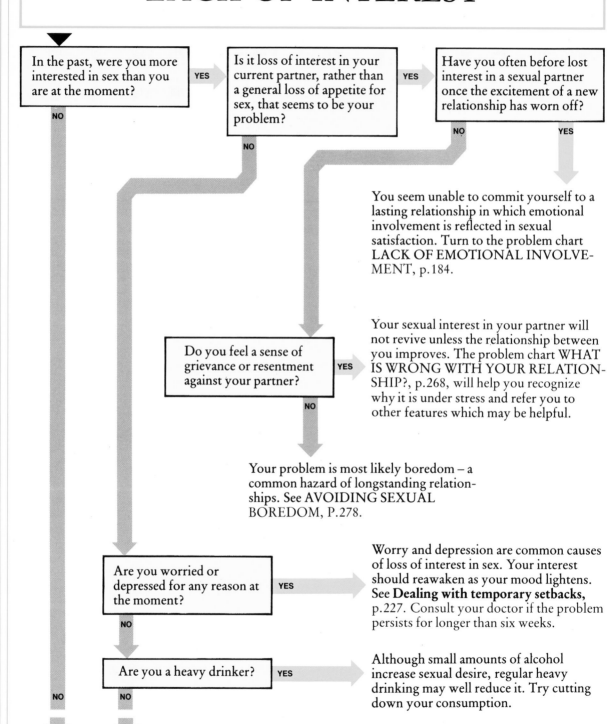

In the past, were you more interested in sex than you are at the moment?

YES → Is it loss of interest in your current partner, rather than a general loss of appetite for sex, that seems to be your problem?

YES → Have you often before lost interest in a sexual partner once the excitement of a new relationship has worn off?

YES → You seem unable to commit yourself to a lasting relationship in which emotional involvement is reflected in sexual satisfaction. Turn to the problem chart LACK OF EMOTIONAL INVOLVEMENT, p.184.

Do you feel a sense of grievance or resentment against your partner?

YES → Your sexual interest in your partner will not revive unless the relationship between you improves. The problem chart WHAT IS WRONG WITH YOUR RELATIONSHIP?, p.268, will help you recognize why it is under stress and refer you to other features which may be helpful.

Your problem is most likely boredom – a common hazard of longstanding relationships. See AVOIDING SEXUAL BOREDOM, P.278.

Are you worried or depressed for any reason at the moment?

YES → Worry and depression are common causes of loss of interest in sex. Your interest should reawaken as your mood lightens. See **Dealing with temporary setbacks,** p.227. Consult your doctor if the problem persists for longer than six weeks.

Are you a heavy drinker?

YES → Although small amounts of alcohol increase sexual desire, regular heavy drinking may well reduce it. Try cutting down your consumption.

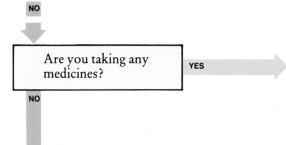

Are you taking any medicines?

YES → A few drugs, notably tranquilizers and some of those taken for high blood pressure, can affect your sexual desire. Talk to your doctor; he may be able to change your drug to one with less severe side-effects. See **The sexual side-effects of drugs**, p.308.

NO ↓

Do you have any specific sexual problem – inability to maintain an erection, for example?

YES → Loss of interest in sex is a natural reaction to a persistent sexual problem. Consult the chart in this part of the book that deals with your particular difficulty. If you have a steady sexual partner, you should discuss your problem with her so that she understands she is not to blame for your lack of desire.

NO ↓

Do you have more than two of the following symptoms: dry, thinning hair; dry, thickened skin; loss of energy and appetite; increased susceptibility to cold air?

YES → You may be suffering from underactivity of the thyroid gland, a condition that reduces the sex drive and both mental and physical energy. Consult your doctor; treatment is easy and effective.

NO ↓

Are you over 60?

YES → Unless you are well into your sixties, it is unlikely that age has seriously affected your sex drive, although some of the doubts and fears associated with the aging process may have done so. See the problem chart SEX AND AGING, p.196.

NO ↓

Does your lack of interest trouble you because, for example, your partner's sex drive is greater than yours or you feel you are missing out on something that most people enjoy?

YES → It is quite normal for partners to have sex drives of different intensity. DEALING WITH A SEX-DRIVE DISCREPANCY, p.272, should help to dispel your anxieties.

NO ↓

The intensity of your sex drive is not a gauge for measuring sexual satisfaction. Everyone has different sexual needs, and if your needs are met by your partner and if you meet hers, you have a good sex life.

NEGATIVE FEELINGS

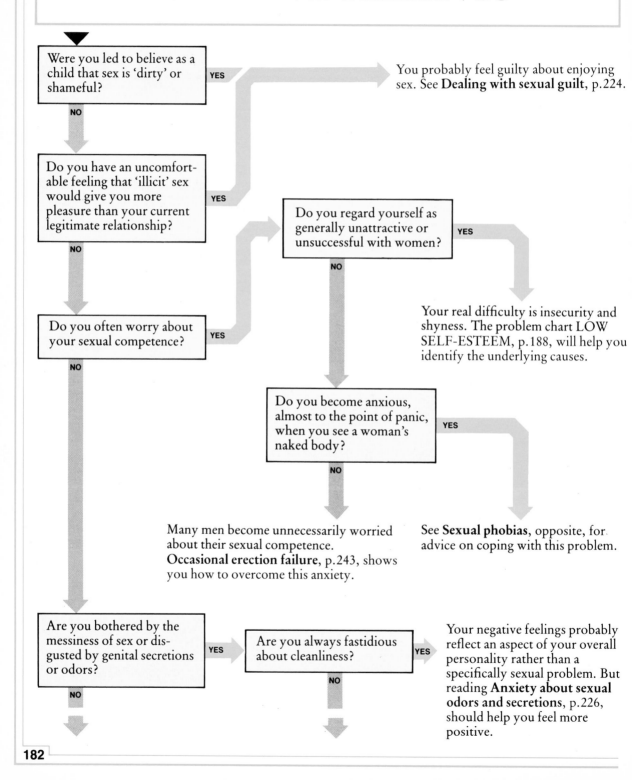

Were you led to believe as a child that sex is 'dirty' or shameful?

YES → You probably feel guilty about enjoying sex. See **Dealing with sexual guilt**, p.224.

NO ↓

Do you have an uncomfortable feeling that 'illicit' sex would give you more pleasure than your current legitimate relationship?

YES →

Do you regard yourself as generally unattractive or unsuccessful with women?

YES → Your real difficulty is insecurity and shyness. The problem chart LOW SELF-ESTEEM, p.188, will help you identify the underlying causes.

NO ↓

NO ↓

Do you often worry about your sexual competence?

YES →

Do you become anxious, almost to the point of panic, when you see a woman's naked body?

YES → See **Sexual phobias**, opposite, for advice on coping with this problem.

NO ↓

Many men become unnecessarily worried about their sexual competence. **Occasional erection failure**, p.243, shows you how to overcome this anxiety.

NO ↓

Are you bothered by the messiness of sex or disgusted by genital secretions or odors?

YES →

Are you always fastidious about cleanliness?

YES → Your negative feelings probably reflect an aspect of your overall personality rather than a specifically sexual problem. But reading **Anxiety about sexual odors and secretions**, p.226, should help you feel more positive.

NO ↓

NO ↓

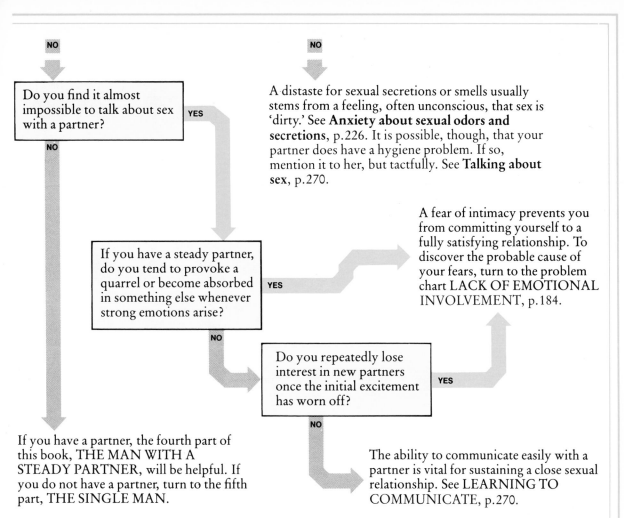

NO

Do you find it almost impossible to talk about sex with a partner?

YES

A distaste for sexual secretions or smells usually stems from a feeling, often unconscious, that sex is 'dirty.' See **Anxiety about sexual odors and secretions**, p.226. It is possible, though, that your partner does have a hygiene problem. If so, mention it to her, but tactfully. See **Talking about sex**, p.270.

NO

NO

If you have a steady partner, do you tend to provoke a quarrel or become absorbed in something else whenever strong emotions arise?

YES

A fear of intimacy prevents you from committing yourself to a fully satisfying relationship. To discover the probable cause of your fears, turn to the problem chart LACK OF EMOTIONAL INVOLVEMENT, p.184.

NO

Do you repeatedly lose interest in new partners once the initial excitement has worn off?

YES

NO

If you have a partner, the fourth part of this book, THE MAN WITH A STEADY PARTNER, will be helpful. If you do not have a partner, turn to the fifth part, THE SINGLE MAN.

The ability to communicate easily with a partner is vital for sustaining a close sexual relationship. See LEARNING TO COMMUNICATE, p.270.

SEXUAL PHOBIAS

A few men suffer anxiety so intense that it amounts to a phobia about part of the female body – usually the breasts or genitals – or about vaginal secretions. These feelings are nearly always part of a general view of sex as unclean or shameful, but this kind of phobia may indicate a general obsession with cleanliness.

However, genital phobia that arises from guilt or anxiety about sex can be overcome by a technique known as desensitization. This involves exposing yourself gradually to whatever it is that makes you feel uncomfortable, usually through visual images or your own fantasy. When your anxiety level has decreased you can start to face what you fear in reality.

Start by glancing through sexually explicit magazines. Then look at the pictures in more

detail, gradually focusing more and more on the breasts and genitals but stopping to relax whenever your tension rises unbearably. Eventually (though it may take some weeks) you should be able to look at these and similar pictures without feeling uncomfortable and they may even start to make you feel sexually aroused. When you have reached this point, it will help your progress if you can masturbate, using the pictures as a stimulus to fantasy.

Likewise, take sex with a partner by stages, first caressing her clothed body, then, with her cooperation, doing the **Sensate-focusing exercises**, p.235. Remember that you have to push yourself a little to make your anxiety dissolve, but allow yourself to stop when you want to.

LACK OF EMOTIONAL INVOLVEMENT

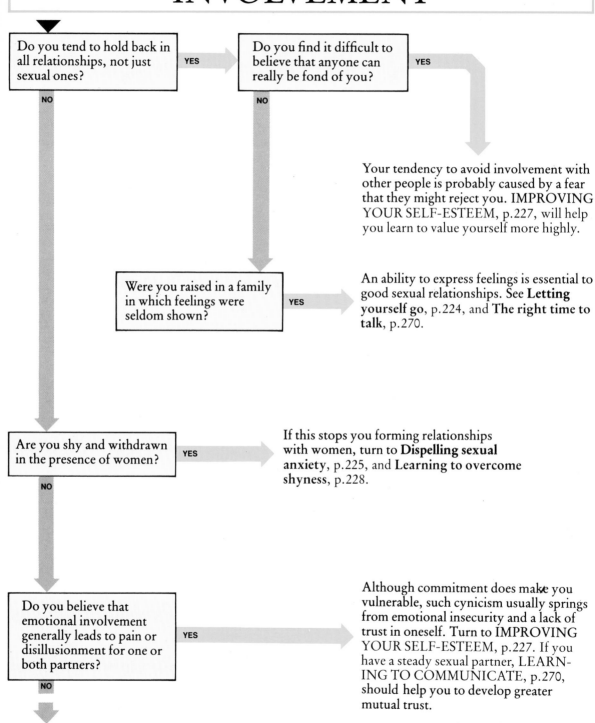

Do you tend to hold back in all relationships, not just sexual ones?

YES →

Do you find it difficult to believe that anyone can really be fond of you?

YES →

Your tendency to avoid involvement with other people is probably caused by a fear that they might reject you. IMPROVING YOUR SELF-ESTEEM, p.227, will help you learn to value yourself more highly.

NO ↓

Were you raised in a family in which feelings were seldom shown?

YES →

An ability to express feelings is essential to good sexual relationships. See **Letting yourself go**, p.224, and **The right time to talk**, p.270.

NO ↓

Are you shy and withdrawn in the presence of women?

YES →

If this stops you forming relationships with women, turn to **Dispelling sexual anxiety**, p.225, and **Learning to overcome shyness**, p.228.

NO ↓

Do you believe that emotional involvement generally leads to pain or disillusionment for one or both partners?

YES →

Although commitment does make you vulnerable, such cynicism usually springs from emotional insecurity and a lack of trust in oneself. Turn to IMPROVING YOUR SELF-ESTEEM, p.227. If you have a steady sexual partner, LEARNING TO COMMUNICATE, p.270, should help you to develop greater mutual trust.

NO ↓

Are you reluctant to express tenderness or talk about love because it is 'unmanly' to show such feelings?

YES → **What makes a good lover?**, p.204, explains why the 'macho' image is not necessarily the most sexually successful one.

NO

Are there times when you refrain from caressing your partner because you think it will lead to sexual intercourse, which you may not want at the time?

YES → Touching need not lead inevitably to sexual activity. The feature LEARNING TO SHARE PLEASURE, p.235, explains the value of non-sexual caresses.

NO

Do you feel that sexual intercourse is the only way to express love?

YES → **Assessing your sexual repertoire**, p.204, will show you that you are taking an unnecessarily narrow view. And, as STIMULATION TECHNIQUES, p.206, illustrates, intercourse is only one way among many to demonstrate affection and desire.

NO

If you do not or cannot feel warmth and affection for your partner, there may be something basically wrong with the partnership itself. The questionnaire COMPATIBILITY, p.260, should help you analyze your relationship and perhaps become closer to your partner.

MEN ♂ 2 PROBLEM CHARTS

185

UNFULFILLED EXPECTATIONS

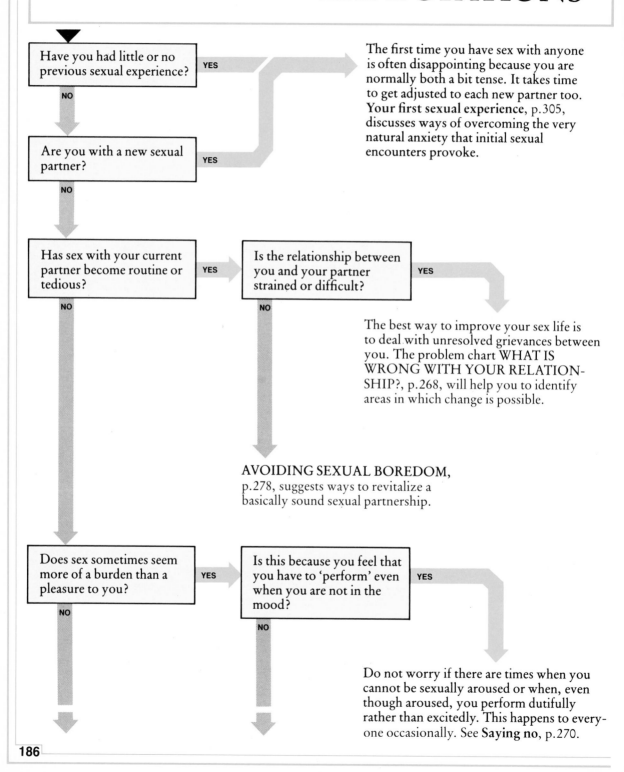

Have you had little or no previous sexual experience?

YES → The first time you have sex with anyone is often disappointing because you are normally both a bit tense. It takes time to get adjusted to each new partner too. **Your first sexual experience,** p.305, discusses ways of overcoming the very natural anxiety that initial sexual encounters provoke.

NO ↓

Are you with a new sexual partner?

YES →

NO ↓

Has sex with your current partner become routine or tedious?

YES → Is the relationship between you and your partner strained or difficult?

YES → The best way to improve your sex life is to deal with unresolved grievances between you. The problem chart WHAT IS WRONG WITH YOUR RELATION-SHIP?, p.268, will help you to identify areas in which change is possible.

NO ↓

AVOIDING SEXUAL BOREDOM, p.278, suggests ways to revitalize a basically sound sexual partnership.

NO ↓

Does sex sometimes seem more of a burden than a pleasure to you?

YES → Is this because you feel that you have to 'perform' even when you are not in the mood?

YES → Do not worry if there are times when you cannot be sexually aroused or when, even though aroused, you perform dutifully rather than excitedly. This happens to everyone occasionally. See **Saying no,** p.270.

NO ↓

NO ↓

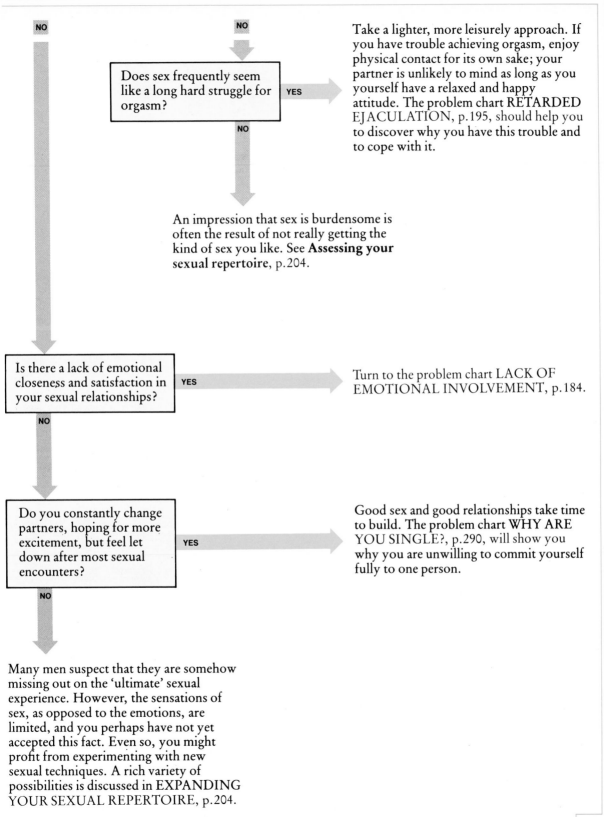

Does sex frequently seem like a long hard struggle for orgasm?

YES

Take a lighter, more leisurely approach. If you have trouble achieving orgasm, enjoy physical contact for its own sake; your partner is unlikely to mind as long as you yourself have a relaxed and happy attitude. The problem chart RETARDED EJACULATION, p.195, should help you to discover why you have this trouble and to cope with it.

NO

An impression that sex is burdensome is often the result of not really getting the kind of sex you like. See **Assessing your sexual repertoire**, p.204.

Is there a lack of emotional closeness and satisfaction in your sexual relationships?

YES

Turn to the problem chart LACK OF EMOTIONAL INVOLVEMENT, p.184.

NO

Do you constantly change partners, hoping for more excitement, but feel let down after most sexual encounters?

YES

Good sex and good relationships take time to build. The problem chart WHY ARE YOU SINGLE?, p.290, will show you why you are unwilling to commit yourself fully to one person.

NO

Many men suspect that they are somehow missing out on the 'ultimate' sexual experience. However, the sensations of sex, as opposed to the emotions, are limited, and you perhaps have not yet accepted this fact. Even so, you might profit from experimenting with new sexual techniques. A rich variety of possibilities is discussed in EXPANDING YOUR SEXUAL REPERTOIRE, p.204.

LOW SELF-ESTEEM

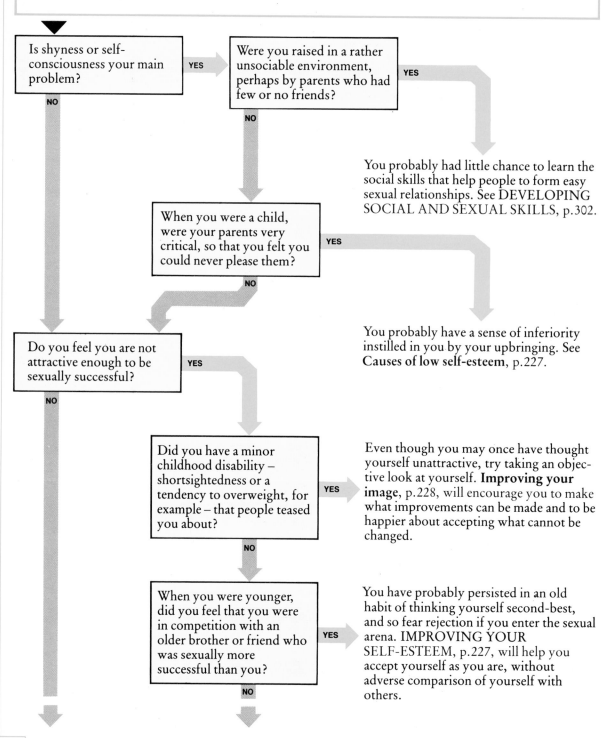

Is shyness or self-consciousness your main problem?

YES → Were you raised in a rather unsociable environment, perhaps by parents who had few or no friends?

YES → You probably had little chance to learn the social skills that help people to form easy sexual relationships. See DEVELOPING SOCIAL AND SEXUAL SKILLS, p.302.

NO ↓

When you were a child, were your parents very critical, so that you felt you could never please them?

YES → You probably have a sense of inferiority instilled in you by your upbringing. See **Causes of low self-esteem**, p.227.

NO ↓

NO ↓ (from first question)

Do you feel you are not attractive enough to be sexually successful?

YES → Did you have a minor childhood disability – shortsightedness or a tendency to overweight, for example – that people teased you about?

YES → Even though you may once have thought yourself unattractive, try taking an objective look at yourself. **Improving your image**, p.228, will encourage you to make what improvements can be made and to be happier about accepting what cannot be changed.

NO ↓

When you were younger, did you feel that you were in competition with an older brother or friend who was sexually more successful than you?

YES → You have probably persisted in an old habit of thinking yourself second-best, and so fear rejection if you enter the sexual arena. IMPROVING YOUR SELF-ESTEEM, p.227, will help you accept yourself as you are, without adverse comparison of yourself with others.

NO ↓

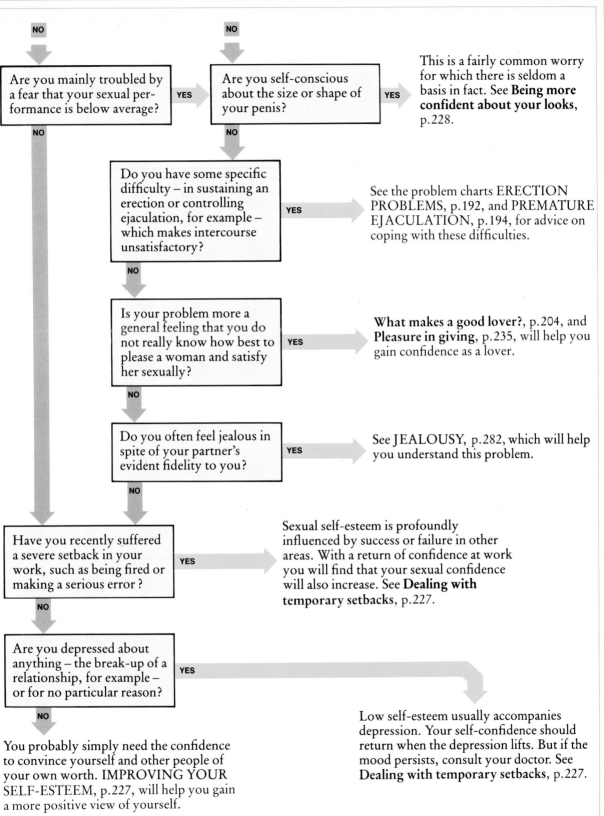

NO

Are you mainly troubled by a fear that your sexual performance is below average?

NO

YES →

NO

Are you self-conscious about the size or shape of your penis?

NO

YES →

This is a fairly common worry for which there is seldom a basis in fact. See **Being more confident about your looks**, p.228.

Do you have some specific difficulty – in sustaining an erection or controlling ejaculation, for example – which makes intercourse unsatisfactory?

NO

YES →

See the problem charts ERECTION PROBLEMS, p.192, and PREMATURE EJACULATION, p.194, for advice on coping with these difficulties.

Is your problem more a general feeling that you do not really know how best to please a woman and satisfy her sexually?

NO

YES →

What makes a good lover?, p.204, and **Pleasure in giving**, p.235, will help you gain confidence as a lover.

Do you often feel jealous in spite of your partner's evident fidelity to you?

NO

YES →

See JEALOUSY, p.282, which will help you understand this problem.

Have you recently suffered a severe setback in your work, such as being fired or making a serious error?

NO

YES →

Sexual self-esteem is profoundly influenced by success or failure in other areas. With a return of confidence at work you will find that your sexual confidence will also increase. See **Dealing with temporary setbacks**, p.227.

Are you depressed about anything – the break-up of a relationship, for example – or for no particular reason?

NO

YES →

You probably simply need the confidence to convince yourself and other people of your own worth. IMPROVING YOUR SELF-ESTEEM, p.227, will help you gain a more positive view of yourself.

Low self-esteem usually accompanies depression. Your self-confidence should return when the depression lifts. But if the mood persists, consult your doctor. See **Dealing with temporary setbacks**, p.227.

MASTURBATION ANXIETY

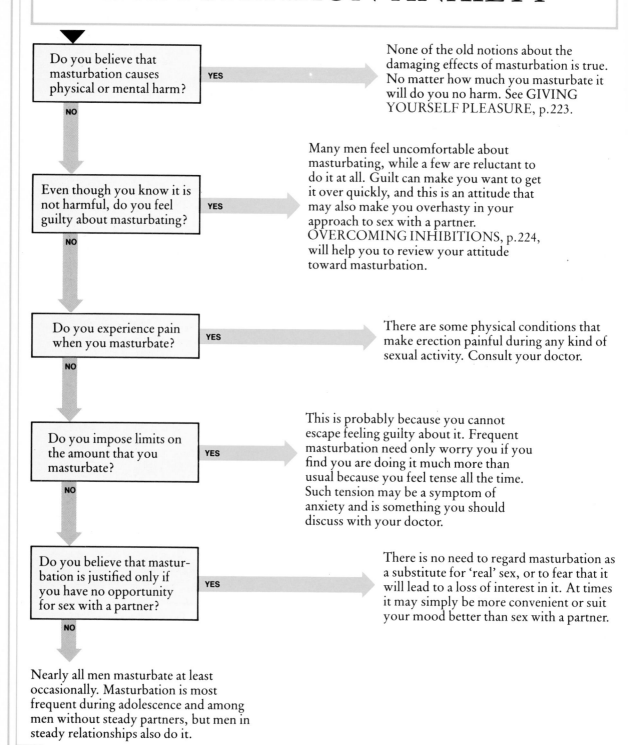

Do you believe that masturbation causes physical or mental harm?

YES — None of the old notions about the damaging effects of masturbation is true. No matter how much you masturbate it will do you no harm. See GIVING YOURSELF PLEASURE, p.223.

NO

Even though you know it is not harmful, do you feel guilty about masturbating?

YES — Many men feel uncomfortable about masturbating, while a few are reluctant to do it at all. Guilt can make you want to get it over quickly, and this is an attitude that may also make you overhasty in your approach to sex with a partner. OVERCOMING INHIBITIONS, p.224, will help you to review your attitude toward masturbation.

NO

Do you experience pain when you masturbate?

YES — There are some physical conditions that make erection painful during any kind of sexual activity. Consult your doctor.

NO

Do you impose limits on the amount that you masturbate?

YES — This is probably because you cannot escape feeling guilty about it. Frequent masturbation need only worry you if you find you are doing it much more than usual because you feel tense all the time. Such tension may be a symptom of anxiety and is something you should discuss with your doctor.

NO

Do you believe that masturbation is justified only if you have no opportunity for sex with a partner?

YES — There is no need to regard masturbation as a substitute for 'real' sex, or to fear that it will lead to a loss of interest in it. At times it may simply be more convenient or suit your mood better than sex with a partner.

NO

Nearly all men masturbate at least occasionally. Masturbation is most frequent during adolescence and among men without steady partners, but men in steady relationships also do it.

PAINFUL INTERCOURSE

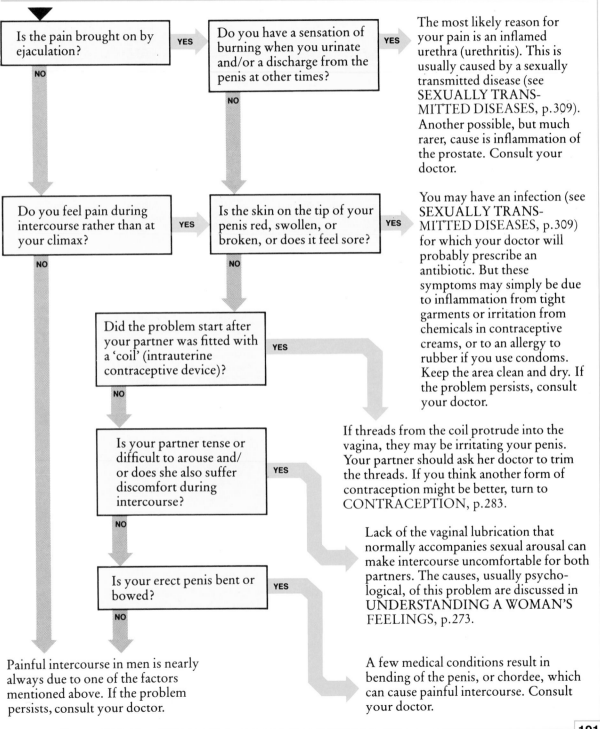

Is the pain brought on by ejaculation?

YES → **Do you have a sensation of burning when you urinate and/or a discharge from the penis at other times?**

YES → The most likely reason for your pain is an inflamed urethra (urethritis). This is usually caused by a sexually transmitted disease (see SEXUALLY TRANSMITTED DISEASES, p.309). Another possible, but much rarer, cause is inflammation of the prostate. Consult your doctor.

NO ↓ (from ejaculation)

NO ↓ (from burning sensation)

Do you feel pain during intercourse rather than at your climax?

YES → **Is the skin on the tip of your penis red, swollen, or broken, or does it feel sore?**

YES → You may have an infection (see SEXUALLY TRANSMITTED DISEASES, p.309) for which your doctor will probably prescribe an antibiotic. But these symptoms may simply be due to inflammation from tight garments or irritation from chemicals in contraceptive creams, or to an allergy to rubber if you use condoms. Keep the area clean and dry. If the problem persists, consult your doctor.

NO ↓

NO ↓

Did the problem start after your partner was fitted with a 'coil' (intrauterine contraceptive device)?

YES → If threads from the coil protrude into the vagina, they may be irritating your penis. Your partner should ask her doctor to trim the threads. If you think another form of contraception might be better, turn to CONTRACEPTION, p.283.

NO ↓

Is your partner tense or difficult to arouse and/or does she also suffer discomfort during intercourse?

YES → Lack of the vaginal lubrication that normally accompanies sexual arousal can make intercourse uncomfortable for both partners. The causes, usually psychological, of this problem are discussed in UNDERSTANDING A WOMAN'S FEELINGS, p.273.

NO ↓

Is your erect penis bent or bowed?

YES → A few medical conditions result in bending of the penis, or chordee, which can cause painful intercourse. Consult your doctor.

NO ↓

Painful intercourse in men is nearly always due to one of the factors mentioned above. If the problem persists, consult your doctor.

ERECTION PROBLEMS

Have you ever been able to get an erection and have intercourse? — **YES** → **Does your erection fail only occasionally?** — **YES** → **Does this usually happen at the start of a new relationship?**

NO (from "Have you ever been able...")

NO (from "Does your erection fail only occasionally?")

NO (from "Does this usually happen at the start of a new relationship?")

YES (from "Does this usually happen at the start of a new relationship?")

Is your problem that the thought of sex or the proximity of your partner is no longer enough to produce an erection?

NO / **YES**

'Performance anxiety' is a common cause of erection failure, especially in a new relationship, and is nearly always a temporary problem. See **Occasional erection failure**, p.243.

Most men, as they grow older, and particularly if they are in a longstanding relationship, need an increasing amount of direct stimulation of the penis to become aroused. Your partner may not realize that she needs to give you this kind of stimulation unless you tell her. See **Talking about sex**, p.270.

Are you concerned because your erection is not as hard as it used to be? — **YES** →

This usually happens as you grow older, but it need not affect your sex life as long as your penis remains erect enough for penetration. See the problem chart SEX AND AGING, p.196.

NO

All men have occasional erection failure, and many worry needlessly. It becomes a problem only if you constantly fear that it might happen whenever you want to make love. See **Preventing erection failure**, p.87.

In the past, have you had difficulty in intercourse because you have usually ejaculated too soon? — **YES** →

Erection problems often start because of repeated attempts to 'block' sexual excitement in order to prevent premature ejaculation. This difficulty responds well to treatment. See DELAYING EJACULATION, p.246.

NO **NO**

NO   NO

Do you drink heavily?   YES

Alcohol may affect your ability to achieve an erection and continual heavy drinking may cause permanent erection problems. See SEX AND HEALTH, p.307.

NO

Have you ever had an erection in a sexual relationship with a man?

Sexual anxiety is the root cause of most erection difficulties. If it happens so often that it is severely affecting your sex life, see **Treatment program for erection problems**, p.244.

NO   YES

Have you always avoided sexual contact because you feared rejection or felt you were unattractive or even somehow abnormal?   YES

If you have erection problems only with women, you obviously prefer male partners, whether or not you admit it to yourself. Consult the questionnaire ORIENTATION, p.175, which will help you decide the extent of your homosexuality. The problem chart HETERO-SEXUALITY/HOMOSEXUALITY CONFLICTS, p.198, explores the difficulties you may have in accepting your homosexuality. See also COMING TO TERMS WITH HOMOSEXUALITY, p.253.

NO

These feelings of inadequacy are examined in greater detail in the problem chart LOW SELF-ESTEEM, p.188.

Was your upbringing puritanical and sex a taboo subject in your family?   YES

NO

Sexual inhibitions resulting from an extremely straitlaced upbringing can lead to erection problems. See **Dealing with sexual guilt**, p.224

Erection failure is sometimes due to a hormonal or physical condition. Your doctor can arrange for tests to determine whether this is the cause of your problem.

OTHER CAUSES OF ERECTION PROBLEMS

Many medical conditions, surgical operations, and drugs can cause temporary erection problems. See SEX AND HEALTH, p.307.

Whatever the cause of your problem, do not resort to either aphrodisiacs or mechanical devices to achieve or maintain an erection. These methods do not work and can be harmful. A very small number of men have a physical condition that completely prevents erection and some can be helped by special penile implants that stiffen the penis for insertion into the vagina. Some types have the drawback of producing a permanent erection, but all make intercourse (but not ejaculation, if there is a difficulty in this area) possible. For most men, however, the problem of erection failure is a product of the mind not the body.

PREMATURE EJACULATION

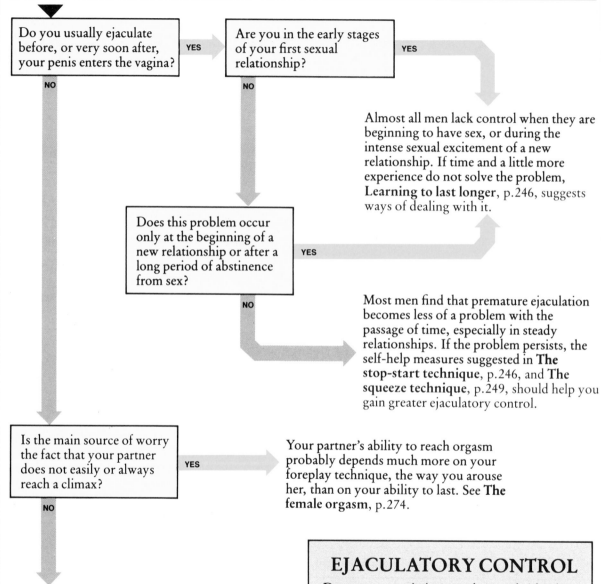

Do you usually ejaculate before, or very soon after, your penis enters the vagina?

YES → Are you in the early stages of your first sexual relationship?

YES → Almost all men lack control when they are beginning to have sex, or during the intense sexual excitement of a new relationship. If time and a little more experience do not solve the problem, **Learning to last longer**, p.246, suggests ways of dealing with it.

NO ↓ Does this problem occur only at the beginning of a new relationship or after a long period of abstinence from sex?

YES → (to the box above)

NO → Most men find that premature ejaculation becomes less of a problem with the passage of time, especially in steady relationships. If the problem persists, the self-help measures suggested in **The stop-start technique**, p.246, and **The squeeze technique**, p.249, should help you gain greater ejaculatory control.

NO ↓ Is the main source of worry the fact that your partner does not easily or always reach a climax?

YES → Your partner's ability to reach orgasm probably depends much more on your foreplay technique, the way you arouse her, than on your ability to last. See **The female orgasm**, p.274.

NO ↓ You may be expecting too much of yourself. There is no absolute criterion for how long you should last; perhaps you are regarding a quite normal performance as too short. It may help to know, though, that many men take longer to reach orgasm with their partner on top. See SEXUAL POSITIONS, p.211.

EJACULATORY CONTROL

Do not try to gain increased control either by 'switching off' sexually (thinking about something else during intercourse) or by using ointments that claim to make the penis less sensitive. It is better to gain control by learning to recognize the sensations that build up to orgasm than by trying to ignore or suppress them. See **The stop-start technique**, p.246.

RETARDED EJACULATION

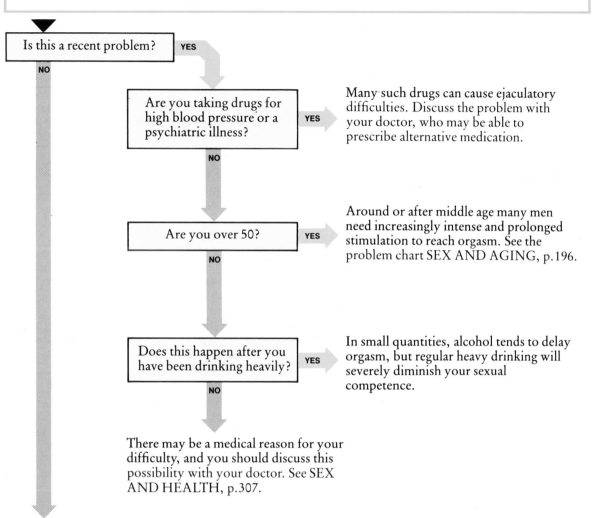

Is this a recent problem? — **YES** →

Are you taking drugs for high blood pressure or a psychiatric illness? — **YES** →

Many such drugs can cause ejaculatory difficulties. Discuss the problem with your doctor, who may be able to prescribe alternative medication.

NO ↓

Are you over 50? — **YES** →

Around or after middle age many men need increasingly intense and prolonged stimulation to reach orgasm. See the problem chart SEX AND AGING, p.196.

NO ↓

Does this happen after you have been drinking heavily? — **YES** →

In small quantities, alcohol tends to delay orgasm, but regular heavy drinking will severely diminish your sexual competence.

NO ↓

There may be a medical reason for your difficulty, and you should discuss this possibility with your doctor. See SEX AND HEALTH, p.307.

NO (from first question) ↓

Your problem most likely stems from an inability to relax sexually. This tension often results from a sense of guilt or anxiety with its roots in childhood. See **Dealing with sexual guilt**, p.224. SPEEDING EJACULATION, p.251, suggests self-help measures for the physical aspects of the problem. It could be, however, that hostility to your partner, or to women in general, underlies your difficulty. See OVERCOMING THE FEAR OF INTIMACY, p.226, and DIFFICULTY IN SUSTAINING RELATIONSHIPS, p.296.

PROSTATECTOMY

Sometimes a man may be worried by an apparent absence of ejaculation after having a prostatectomy (surgical removal of the prostate gland). Without the prostate, seminal fluid may flow backward into the bladder instead of being ejaculated normally. When this, which is known as retrograde ejaculation, happens, the urine will look cloudy, but the backward flow is not harmful and the ability to experience orgasm is not affected.

SEX AND AGING

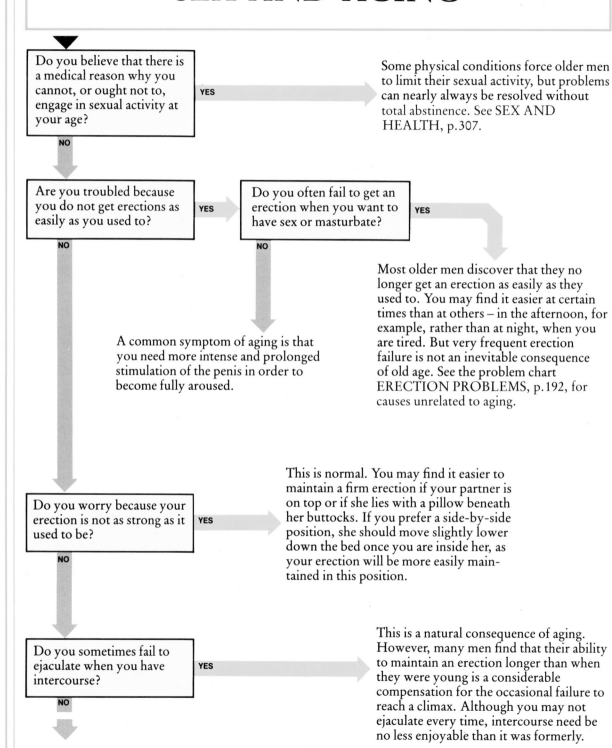

Do you believe that there is a medical reason why you cannot, or ought not to, engage in sexual activity at your age?

YES → Some physical conditions force older men to limit their sexual activity, but problems can nearly always be resolved without total abstinence. See SEX AND HEALTH, p.307.

NO

Are you troubled because you do not get erections as easily as you used to?

YES → Do you often fail to get an erection when you want to have sex or masturbate?

YES → Most older men discover that they no longer get an erection as easily as they used to. You may find it easier at certain times than at others – in the afternoon, for example, rather than at night, when you are tired. But very frequent erection failure is not an inevitable consequence of old age. See the problem chart ERECTION PROBLEMS, p.192, for causes unrelated to aging.

NO → A common symptom of aging is that you need more intense and prolonged stimulation of the penis in order to become fully aroused.

NO

Do you worry because your erection is not as strong as it used to be?

YES → This is normal. You may find it easier to maintain a firm erection if your partner is on top or if she lies with a pillow beneath her buttocks. If you prefer a side-by-side position, she should move slightly lower down the bed once you are inside her, as your erection will be more easily maintained in this position.

NO

Do you sometimes fail to ejaculate when you have intercourse?

YES → This is a natural consequence of aging. However, many men find that their ability to maintain an erection longer than when they were young is a considerable compensation for the occasional failure to reach a climax. Although you may not ejaculate every time, intercourse need be no less enjoyable than it was formerly.

NO

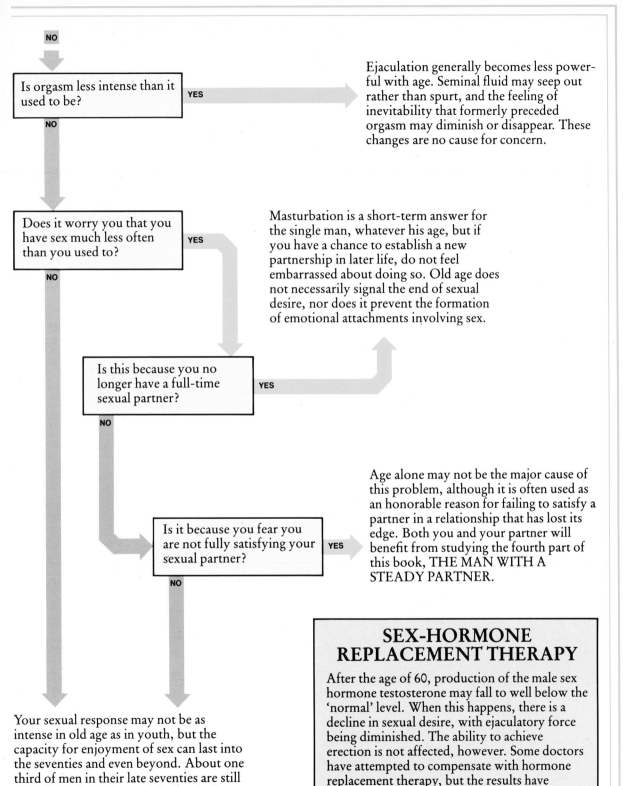

NO

Is orgasm less intense than it used to be?

YES → Ejaculation generally becomes less powerful with age. Seminal fluid may seep out rather than spurt, and the feeling of inevitability that formerly preceded orgasm may diminish or disappear. These changes are no cause for concern.

NO

Does it worry you that you have sex much less often than you used to?

YES → Masturbation is a short-term answer for the single man, whatever his age, but if you have a chance to establish a new partnership in later life, do not feel embarrassed about doing so. Old age does not necessarily signal the end of sexual desire, nor does it prevent the formation of emotional attachments involving sex.

NO

Is this because you no longer have a full-time sexual partner?

YES →

NO

Is it because you fear you are not fully satisfying your sexual partner?

YES → Age alone may not be the major cause of this problem, although it is often used as an honorable reason for failing to satisfy a partner in a relationship that has lost its edge. Both you and your partner will benefit from studying the fourth part of this book, THE MAN WITH A STEADY PARTNER.

NO

Your sexual response may not be as intense in old age as in youth, but the capacity for enjoyment of sex can last into the seventies and even beyond. About one third of men in their late seventies are still sexually active and sexual decline is slower in those who have always had a full sex life.

SEX-HORMONE REPLACEMENT THERAPY

After the age of 60, production of the male sex hormone testosterone may fall to well below the 'normal' level. When this happens, there is a decline in sexual desire, with ejaculatory force being diminished. The ability to achieve erection is not affected, however. Some doctors have attempted to compensate with hormone replacement therapy, but the results have usually been disappointing.

197

HETEROSEXUALITY/ HOMOSEXUALITY CONFLICTS

Is your main problem the stigma attached to being homosexual and the fear that your homosexuality may be revealed to your family and friends?

YES → The pros and cons of 'coming out' are discussed in **The problems of being gay**, p.253. This will help you gain confidence in your right to choose the sexual lifestyle that contributes most of your happiness.

NO ↓

Is this because you have a specific sexual problem – erection difficulties, for example?

YES → Such problems are essentially the same for gay men as for heterosexual men. Consult the problem charts on pp.192-5, which, with the appropriate modifications, are applicable to you.

NO ↓

Are homosexual relation-ships difficult for you to make or for some reason unsatisfactory?

YES →

NO ↓

Are you troubled because you seem unable to form a stable relationship with a man?

YES → Although homosexual relationships tend to be shorter than those of heterosexuals, many homosexuals do become long-term partners. **How to safeguard your relationship**, p.254, suggests ways of increasing a partner's stability.

NO ↓

Are you unsure about your sexual preferences and attracted to both men and women?

NO ↓   **YES** ↓

Are you married or involved in a heterosexual relationship and finding this stressful?

YES → You may need to try out sexual relation-ships with partners of both sexes before you can decide what suits you best. Until then, keep your options open and do not be pressured either into either 'coming out' or conforming to a heterosexual lifestyle. See **Making the choice**, p.253.

NO ↓

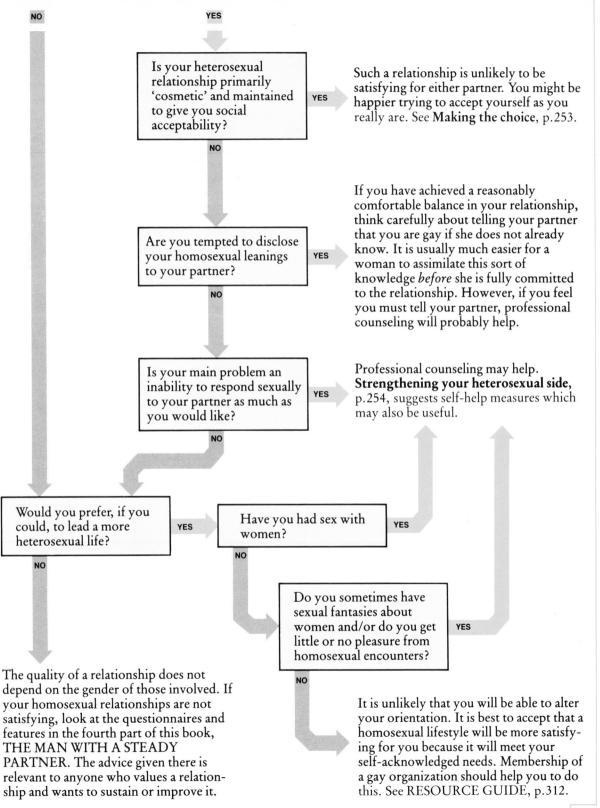

NO   **YES**

Is your heterosexual relationship primarily 'cosmetic' and maintained to give you social acceptability?

YES → Such a relationship is unlikely to be satisfying for either partner. You might be happier trying to accept yourself as you really are. See **Making the choice**, p.253.

NO

Are you tempted to disclose your homosexual leanings to your partner?

YES → If you have achieved a reasonably comfortable balance in your relationship, think carefully about telling your partner that you are gay if she does not already know. It is usually much easier for a woman to assimilate this sort of knowledge *before* she is fully committed to the relationship. However, if you feel you must tell your partner, professional counseling will probably help.

NO

Is your main problem an inability to respond sexually to your partner as much as you would like?

YES → Professional counseling may help. **Strengthening your heterosexual side**, p.254, suggests self-help measures which may also be useful.

NO

Would you prefer, if you could, to lead a more heterosexual life?

YES → Have you had sex with women?

YES →

NO

Do you sometimes have sexual fantasies about women and/or do you get little or no pleasure from homosexual encounters?

YES →

NO

The quality of a relationship does not depend on the gender of those involved. If your homosexual relationships are not satisfying, look at the questionnaires and features in the fourth part of this book, THE MAN WITH A STEADY PARTNER. The advice given there is relevant to anyone who values a relationship and wants to sustain or improve it.

It is unlikely that you will be able to alter your orientation. It is best to accept that a homosexual lifestyle will be more satisfying for you because it will meet your self-acknowledged needs. Membership of a gay organization should help you to do this. See RESOURCE GUIDE, p.312.

GENDER PROBLEMS

Is your only problem that you sometimes find it difficult to live up to the traditional male role, or feel you would like to develop your feminine side a little?

YES → The 'macho' image is not one that many women find particularly attractive. In fact they often value the traditionally feminine qualities – tenderness, warmth, the ability to show feelings – much more. See **What makes a good lover?**, p.204.

NO

Do you occasionally enjoy dressing as a woman?

YES → At such times do you wear make-up and behave as much like a woman as possible?

YES → Is this because you find it sexually arousing to wear women's clothes?

NO → Is it because you feel more relaxed and comfortable dressed as a woman?

YES

NO (clothes question) → There are indications of transvestism, which is discussed on p.256.

NO

Do you sometimes have homosexual relationships simply because they seem easier and less threatening than heterosexual ones?

YES → This does not mean that you are homosexual, but that you do not yet have the confidence in your own masculinity to make relationships with women. See **Dispelling sexual anxiety**, p.225.

NO (relaxed question) → Is it because you feel you really *are* a woman, despite a male body and genitals?

YES

NO (really a woman question) → Do men attract you sexually more than women?

NO

You probably just enjoy cross-dressing for fun or as a defiant gesture because it is taboo. It does not necessarily follow that you have a gender problem.

YES (men attract you) → This tendency, transsexualism, is discussed on p.257.

Your ability to feel masculine depends in part on your sexual self-esteem. If this is low, you are sure to have doubts about yourself. IMPROVING YOUR SELF-ESTEEM, p.227, should help you feel more confident of your masculinity.

If you have recently 'come out' as a homosexual you may enjoy being exaggeratedly effeminate for a while. Once you feel at home in your new role, however, this tendency and the urge to cross-dress will probably disappear.

UNUSUAL SEXUAL PRACTICES

Do you like playing sex games involving force?
YES → **Do these involve only mild beatings or tying each other?**
YES → **Does your partner enjoy them?**

Few women enjoy rough treatment and you may have to resort to prostitutes. If you have an overwhelming urge to hurt or humiliate a sexual partner, consult a doctor or sex therapist immediately. See RESOURCE GUIDE, p.312.

Slight physical force in lovemaking is harmless. See **Sadomasochism**, p.277.

You will harm your relationship if you force your partner into these games. See **Conflicting sexual tastes**, p.276.

Do you like to wear women's clothes?
YES → See the problem chart GENDER PROBLEMS, p.200.

Do inanimate objects such as shoes, or rubber or leather garments, play an important part in your sex life?
YES → **Is it only by using these that you become sexually aroused or achieve orgasm?**
NO → **Does your partner (if you have one) object to your use of these sexual aids?**

Treatment for this tendency (known as fetishism) is available if you want to develop a more conventional approach to sex, but it is unlikely to be successful unless you are very determined to change. See **Fetishism**, p.277.

An element of fetishism is common in many men and is quite harmless.

Do you get sexual excitement from surreptitiously rubbing yourself against strangers (frottage), spying on their private life (voyeurism), or exposing your genitals to them (exhibitionism)?

These acts are usually performed in order to avoid real sexual contact out of a fear of rejection. They are harmless, but illegal. Consult a doctor.

Are you sexually attracted to children?

Sexual contact between an adult and a minor – pedophilia – is illegal and can cause serious psychological harm to the child. Consult a doctor if you feel you might give way to this desire.

Unconventional sex (providing you are not breaking the law) concerns only you and your partner.

3

IMPROVING YOUR SEX LIFE

The aim of this part of the book is to help you develop
your full sexual potential, discover ways of enhancing and
sustaining a good sex life, and derive more enjoyment if it
is currently unsatisfying. The advice given is relevant to
any man, married or single, regardless of age or experience.
However good your sex life, it can be fun to try something
new, to experiment a little. This helps to keep your interest
in each other alive, and ensures that your relationship will
continue to be as sensual as it ever was. There is never a
need to feel too old, or that you have been together too
long, to make any changes. It is even possible that you may
get more pleasure from the activities suggested than you
would have done when you were younger and less sure of
yourself and your partner.

This section also deals with some of the difficulties that
take the edge off sexual enjoyment. However longstanding
a sexual problem is, do not feel that it is too late to try to
resolve it. You will experience a marked improvement in
your sex life, or overcome your problems altogether, if you
follow the self-help programs.

EXPANDING YOUR SEXUAL REPERTOIRE

In recent years, many surveys have revealed that women are largely in accord as to their sexual likes and dislikes. What has emerged most clearly is that many no longer want the strong, silent, 'macho' male. Instead, they value the man who can make them feel good emotionally as well as physically.

What makes a good lover?

While a large part of being a good lover lies in the ability to satisfy your partner's emotional needs, you also need to keep the relationship exciting by exploring a range of sexual activities. Below you will discover techniques to make your sex life less routine. But first, some pointers to becoming a more sensitive lover.

☐ Be sensual as well as sexual. For most women, the caresses of foreplay, which you may see simply as a way of 'priming' your partner for sex, can be as enjoyable as intercourse itself.

☐ Use touch to show affection, as well as to ask for sex. A hug or a kiss need not just be a prelude to bed but can show simply that you care for her.

☐ Do not be afraid to let your arousal wane during sex and to relax and talk a while.

☐ Remember that afterplay matters as much as foreplay. You need not do much, but a cuddle and a few loving words are essential. Never roll over and go straight to sleep, or leap out of bed and get dressed.

☐ Do not approach a new sexual activity as a challenge – something designed to test you – but as a possible source of pleasure. The only real failure is not enjoying what you are doing. But be guided by instinct. An experience is not necessarily good because it is new. If you are not drawn to something, do not try it. If you do it and dislike it, do not repeat it.

☐ If sex has always seemed something of a disappointment, it probably will not help much just to widen your repertoire. Sex can provide only a limited range of sensations, and what takes it beyond the predictable for most people is the quality of the relationship involved.

☐ Women can accept an occasional failure, and it may even make you more human, vulnerable, and easy to love. If you feel obliged to be constantly ready for sex, you will take the inevitable occasional failure too hard.

ASSESSING YOUR SEXUAL REPERTOIRE

The checklist on the right will help you determine the scope of your sexual experience and, because it may include possibilities that you think would be fun but have never tried, will widen your horizons. It also gives you a chance to judge the degree of pleasure you are currently getting from sex and to test the balance of giving and receiving between you and your steady partner (if you have one). If your preferences include things you enjoy doing for a partner as well as things you like to have done for you, you are more likely than not to be able to maintain a satisfactory relationship.

On a 0–4 scale, indicate in the columns provided: first, how much you enjoy the activity, and, secondly, how often you do it. The list is highly selective, so feel free to add other activities you perform that are not included.

Checking your ratings

Ideally you should find that activities to which you have assigned a high enjoyment rating also have a high frequency rating. If not, ask yourself why not. On the other hand, if there are any activities to which you have assigned a higher rating for frequency for than for enjoyment, give some serious thought to the question of why this is so. Are you doing something you do not particularly like chiefly to please your partner? If so, this is a healthy attitude – but only up to a point. The frequent practice of any activity that you dislike may not only cause resentment but could lead to erection difficulties.

A balanced relationship

Why not study the above list together so as to consider how well your responses match each other?

Items 2, 6, 8, 10, 12, 14, 22, and 24 are things you can do to arouse and please your partner. Items 3, 7, 9, 11, 13, 15, 23, and 25 are things your partner can do to you. Your frequency ratings and levels of enjoyment for each of these two sets of activities should be similar, if not exactly the same.

If they are not, what is the reason? Does one of you tend to be the giver, the other the recipient of pleasure? If this is the case, you will probably both find a better balance between your roles more fulfilling. You might also consider activities which you feel you would enjoy very much, but which, for some reason, you have never tried. These, of course, would attract a high enjoyment rating but nil for frequency. Having acknowledged your lack of fulfilment in these areas, you need to share your problems with your partner, particularly if it is her reluctance that has prevented experimentation.

ENJOYMENT RATING				FREQUENCY RATING			
Very high	4	Low	1	Regularly	4	Seldom	1
High	3	Nil	0	Often	3	Never	0
Medium	2			Sometimes	2		

	ENJOY-MENT	FRE-QUENCY		ENJOY-MENT	FRE-QUENCY
1 'French kissing' (tongues in each other's mouths).			**14** Giving your partner an orgasm by manual stimulation.		
2 'Petting' (fondling your partner's clothed body).			**15** Being manually stimulated to orgasm by your partner.		
3 Having your partner fondle your clothed body.			**16** Having intercourse in a man-on-top position.		
4 Seeing your partner naked.			**17** Or with your partner on top.		
5 Being seen naked.			**18** Or in a side-by-side position.		
6 Caressing your partner's naked body.			**19** Having intercourse in a rear-entry position.		
7 Having yours caressed.			**20** Or in a sitting position.		
8 Kissing your partner's breasts and sucking the nipples.			**21** Having intercourse in a standing position.		
9 Having your partner kiss and suck your nipples.			**22** Fondling or kissing your partner's buttocks and anus.		
10 Exploring and stroking your partner's genitals.			**23** Having your buttocks and anus fondled or kissed.		
11 Having your partner explore and stroke your genitals.			**24** Using oral stimulation to bring your partner to orgasm.		
12 Licking and kissing your partner's genitals.			**25** Being brought to orgasm by oral stimulation.		
13 Having yours kissed.					

STIMULATION TECHNIQUES

The stimulation techniques or foreplay described here are used by most couples to arouse each other, but they need not always lead to intercourse. They are in themselves valuable as a source of pleasure.

Clitoral stimulation

Stimulation of the clitoris, the method most women use for masturbation, is probably the most effective way of arousing a woman and the easiest way for many women to reach orgasm. It is, however, a technique at which, according to surveys of American women, most men are not very skilful.

Your partner, knowing her own body and its reactions, can show you the precise spot, the pressure, and the rhythm that excite her most. So ask her to guide your hand at first if you have not tried clitoral stimulation before. If she is too inexperienced or inhibited to help you in this way, you will have to experiment. The following guidelines should help

you, but you will certainly get further more quickly if you can talk freely to each other.

☐ Be gentle when you touch the clitoris as it is a delicate and sensitive organ. A lubricant – for example, your partner's vaginal fluid, your own saliva, or a commercial preparation – will minimize irritation.

☐ Do not use direct or sustained pressure on the clitoris unless you are sure your partner likes it; many women find it irritating or even painful. Indirect pressure through the folds of flesh around the clitoris is generally both more comfortable and more stimulating. Use your whole hand, all the fingers, the palm, or the heel of the hand, rather than just one or two fingers. This spreads a subtle but highly satisfying pressure over the entire highly responsive clitoral area.

◁ **The female genitals**
The external female genitals are known as the vulva. On arousal the vaginal lips fill with blood and cushion the orifice. The outer lips, the labia majora, vary in shape and color, while the inner pair, the labia minora, are generally pinker and moister.

◁ **The clitoris**
This small, highly sensitive organ is situated within the inner vaginal lips.

— LABIA MAJORA
— CLITORIS
— URETHRAL ORIFICE
— LABIA MINORA
— VAGINAL ORIFICE

CLITORAL STIMULATION TECHNIQUES

Individual preferences vary enormously, but at least one of the methods described below should work for your partner.

1 CIRCULAR MOVEMENTS

1 Place your hand over the clitoral area, applying light pressure with your fingers or palm, and move it gently round and round.

2 Move it up so that the heel is at the top of the vulva, right over the clitoris. Your hand should be resting partly on the pubic bone on either side. In this position you can press quite firmly as you rub.

3 Alternatively, you can put your hand, palm downward, over the pubic mound so that your fingers overhang the clitoral area. Pressing gently, make firm, circular movements.

◁ **Using the heel of the hand**
With the heel of your hand on the clitoris and the pubic bone either side of it, apply firm pressure while making a circular rubbing movement.

Rotating the palm ▷
You can give firm but gentle circular stimulation to the whole clitoral area when the palm of your hand covers the pubic mound and the fingers hang down.

2 VIBRATORY MOVEMENTS

1 Cup your hand over the whole area and vibrate it rapidly.

2 Brush your fingers rapidly to and fro across the clitoris.

3 With your hand resting on the pubic mound, put a finger each side of the vaginal lips and vibrate them from side to side.

4 Rub on each side of the inner vaginal lips at the base of the clitoris. Because you are applying pressure through the fleshy folds rather than directly to the clitoris, you can press quite firmly.

5 An effective alternative is a combination of clitoral stimulation with digital penetration of the vagina (make sure that your fingernail has no jagged edges). Using your right hand, palm upward, slip your middle finger into the vagina. Your other fingers should be bent forward so that the knuckles press against the clitoral area.

6 Move the finger gently in and out, pressing on the front wall of the vagina, so stimulating an especially sensitive area (known as the G spot). This internal vaginal pressure, combined with friction on the clitoris, is intensely pleasurable.

7 Rubbing the tip of the penis against the clitoris is perhaps the best means of arousal.

◁ **Brushing with the fingers**
The simplest method of stimulating the clitoris with a vibratory action is to brush your fingers rapidly back and forth against it.

Stimulating the G spot ▷
While you use your middle finger to explore the front wall of the vagina, with its highly sensitive G spot, your knuckles can stimulate the clitoris indirectly by pressing on the surrounding area.

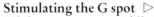

MEN ♂ 3 IMPROVING YOUR SEX LIFE

ORAL SEX

Stimulation of the male genitals with the mouth is known as fellatio, corresponding stimulation of the female genitals as cunnilingus. Both are fairly safe activities as far as the transmission of AIDS is concerned (see **Guidelines for safer sex,** p.310).

Most men enjoy both giving and receiving oral sex. Some, however, would like to try it but hesitate to mention it to their partner, feeling that it is abnormal or something to be ashamed of. Others avoid it because they dislike genital odors and secretions (see **Anxiety about sexual odors and secretions,** p.226.

When such inhibitions are overcome, oral sex is usually highly enjoyable for both partners.

You can use oral stimulation to arouse each other before intercourse, or as an alternative means of reaching orgasm. But you should avoid it if either of you has an infection of the mouth or the genitals.

Oral stimulation ▷
The '69' position allows mutual oral-genital contact and can be intensely exciting. Many couples, however, prefer to take turns in giving each other oral stimulation, as it is easier to concentrate on either giving or receiving pleasure than to do both simultaneously.

Fellatio

Many women, even if they are happy to try oral sex, are unsure of exactly what to do. Try to be as explicit as you can when you tell your partner what you would like. At first it is probably best just to suggest that she kisses your penis until she feels more comfortable with the idea of taking it into her mouth.

She will probably soon want to take the whole head inside her mouth and suck it, using her tongue to play on the sensitive underside ridge, or frenulum. She will need to open her mouth wide and close her lips (but not her teeth) firmly around the head.

Then she can move her mouth up and down on your penis, just as you would move it in her vagina. She can make an extension of her mouth by encircling your penis with her thumb and forefinger, moving mouth and hand up and down on it in the same rhythm. You can guide her head with your hands to indicate the pace you prefer but be careful not to force her movements.

As she becomes more confident she will probably take more of the shaft into her mouth, and you will want to thrust lightly. Remember, though, that she may not be able to let your penis touch the back of her throat without gagging, and so you should allow her to control the depth of your thrusts.

△ **Taking it slowly**
If your partner has never sucked your penis before, she will probably prefer just to kiss or lick it at first.

Current evidence suggests that the HIV (AIDS) virus is probably not transmitted during oral sex, possibly because saliva contains a substance which inactivates the virus. However, someone who has mouth sores, a mouth infection or bleeding gums (which are all quite common) may be at risk if an infected partner ejaculates in their mouth. Use of a condom during oral sex will prevent infection (see **Guidelines for safer sex**, p.310).

Cunnilingus

Since the tongue is softer than the fingers, it can be used to provide gentler stimulation of the clitoris. Your partner will probably find cunnilingus extremely satisfying, as long as she feels you too are enjoying it. Nothing detracts from a woman's pleasure in oral sex as much as a suspicion that it is being done dutifully, out of consideration for her. The following advice should help you give your partner maximum pleasure.

Begin by kissing and licking the pubic mound, the inner side of the thighs, and the lower belly. Now move your tongue over the genital area, flicking it along the fleshy folds up to the clitoris. Note your partner's responses, and act accordingly.

Gently probe the clitoris with your tongue. Again, discover from her reactions the kind of stimulation that your partner most enjoys. Begin by simply nuzzling and sucking. You may also find it exciting to vibrate your tongue rapidly against the clitoris.

Use your hands, too – to caress her breasts, stroke her thighs, or hold her buttocks firmly. Such gestures bring an additional closeness that is easily overlooked during cunnilingus.

△ **Fear of choking**
Your partner can allay any anxiety she might have about choking by encircling the penis with one or more fingers to limit penetration. Remind her to keep her teeth clear of the particularly sensitive head of your penis (left).

△ **Arousing your partner**
Kissing the area around your partner's vaginal entrance will sharpen her anticipation as well as providing indirect but intense stimulation of the clitoris.

△ **Penetration with the tongue**
Thrusting your tongue in and out of the entrance to the vagina may prove highly arousing for your partner. But some women prefer attention to the clitoris.

△ **Using the tip of the tongue**
By separating the vaginal lips and holding them open gently with both hands, you can flick the tip of your tongue over the exposed clitoris.

ANAL SEX

The most basic form of anal stimulation is known as postillionage, which means touching the partner's anus during intercourse or oral sex. The anal area is very sensitive, and postillionage can intensify erotic sensations greatly.

Penetration of the rectum by a section or all of the finger is a more advanced version of the technique. If you and your partner want to do this, use some lubrication on the finger, and make sure there are no jagged fingernails. If she slips her finger a couple of inches inside your rectum and exerts pressure forward on your prostate gland, you will experience intense excitement.

Anal intercourse – penis in rectum – is primarily a homosexual activity, but a substantial minority of heterosexual couples occasionally practice it. However, because the lining of the rectum is thin, delicate and easily damaged, the HIV (AIDS) virus is more easily transmitted during anal intercourse than during any other form of sexual activity. The inserter should always wear a strong condom and use plenty of a spermicide or lubricant containing nonoxynol-9, which has been shown to kill the HIV virus. Penetration can be painful, so make

it slow and gentle. Stop immediately if your partner asks you to. If your partner is on top, she can control entry and depth of penetration.

△ **Hygienic precautions**
Never have vaginal intercourse after anal without washing your penis well, or you both risk genital infection.

SEXUAL POSITIONS

There are six basic groups of positions for intercourse, within which there are innumerable variations that differ only in minor details such as the relative position of your limbs or the angle of your bodies to one another. Many of the examples selected for the following pages combine a high degree of stimulation with comfort.

Some of the positions are especially appropriate for particular situations – during pregnancy, for example. Others are strictly for fun, with no special value except that of novelty, but you may find them worth trying on occasion.

The value of experimentation

Do not feel you have to go entirely by the book when you try a new position. If it feels awkward, make small adjustments until it is right for both of you. You will probably find that, no matter how many of them you try, you will keep coming back to the few that give you and your partner the most mutual pleasure.

If you prefer this approach, it does not mean that you are unadventurous, but that you have experimented enough to know what you like. (The obvious time for experimentation is at the beginning of a new relationship when you want to explore each other's bodies and search out each other's preferences. It is also useful after you have been together a long time and want to enliven your lovemaking by trying something new.)

Remember that:

☐ Penetration is easiest if your partner's thighs are widely spread.

☐ Positions in which your partner's knees are bent up to her chest allow for deepest penetration.

☐ A position in which your partner's legs are held together provides maximum stimulation for the penis.

MAN-ON-TOP POSITIONS

The man-on-top positions, and in particular the 'missionary', in which the man lies between the woman's slightly parted legs, are probably the most widely used group of positions. They give you almost total control over intercourse, but allow your partner very little freedom of movement. These positions are, for most men, the easiest in which to reach orgasm.

Deep penetration with intense stimulation of clitoris and penis ▷
In this position, the vulva faces downward to a greater degree than in the more common knees-flexed postures, providing extra stimulation for the clitoris. Penetration is deep and the entrance to the vagina is narrowed, so that the penis also receives considerable stimulation.

Compensating for a short penis ▷
This deep-penetration position is useful if the penis is short. The vaginal opening is slack, but the clitoris receives good stimulation and the woman is able to move in rhythm with her partner.

▽ **'Split-level' position**
In this 'split-level' position the woman lies on the bed and the man stands or kneels beside it. By lifting her, he can alter the angle of penetration.

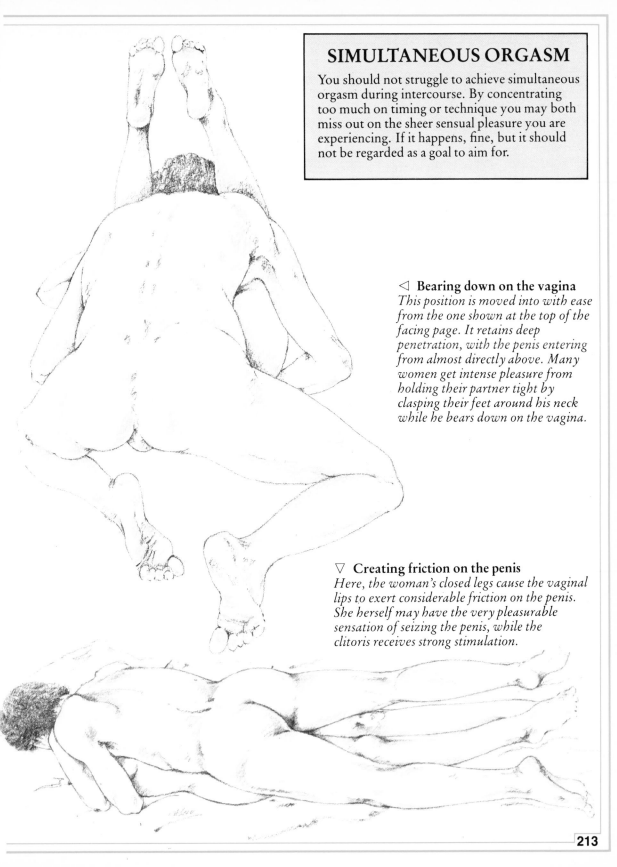

SIMULTANEOUS ORGASM

You should not struggle to achieve simultaneous orgasm during intercourse. By concentrating too much on timing or technique you may both miss out on the sheer sensual pleasure you are experiencing. If it happens, fine, but it should not be regarded as a goal to aim for.

◁ **Bearing down on the vagina**
This position is moved into with ease from the one shown at the top of the facing page. It retains deep penetration, with the penis entering from almost directly above. Many women get intense pleasure from holding their partner tight by clasping their feet around his neck while he bears down on the vagina.

▽ **Creating friction on the penis**
Here, the woman's closed legs cause the vaginal lips to exert considerable friction on the penis. She herself may have the very pleasurable sensation of seizing the penis, while the clitoris receives strong stimulation.

WOMAN-ON-TOP POSITIONS

Many couples find the woman-on-top positions particularly satisfying. They give your partner a chance to make love to you, allowing her to control both depth of penetration, which can be helpful if she is apprehensive through lack of experience, and the tempo of lovemaking. These positions are good if you are much heavier or if she is pregnant.

Stimulating the penis ▷
Of all the woman-on-top positions this probably offers the best combination of intense stimulation of the penis with ease of movement for the woman. Her up-and-down, rather than horizontal, motion is less tiring than in positions in which her body is extended.

◁ **Astride, face-to-face**
This position, which can be very exciting for both partners, allows the man to fondle the breasts and clitoris and lets them enjoy each other's face. The woman can make side-to-side or back-and-forth movements, or can rotate on the penis. To intensify genital sensations for both partners she has only to lean back slightly.

◁ **Astride, face-to-back**
Positions in which the man lies on his back are generally relaxing for him. In this position, both penetration and stimulation of the penis are moderate, so that it is easier for him to delay ejaculation. The woman's posture allows her to make vigorous and highly stimulating movements without discomfort.

Genital friction ▷
Physical intimacy is guaranteed in this position, but movement for both partners demands considerable exertion in the trunk and thighs. This effort in itself, though, can be very exciting as it gives a strong sense of striving together for orgasm. The woman's tightly closed legs heighten friction between the vagina and the penis.

REAR-ENTRY POSITIONS

This group of positions allows penetration while lying, standing, sitting, kneeling, or with the woman on top. In most of these positions the woman does not bear the man's weight and so has considerable freedom to move during intercourse. Most offer the advantage that you can fondle your partner's breasts and clitoris at the same time and nearly all are comfortable when she is in late pregnancy.

◁ **Pushing and pulling**
Here, the man can thrust vigorously by gripping the woman's waist (in itself exciting for both) and pushing and pulling her up and down. Alternatively, his partner can provide the stimulation by moving in any direction. The farther forward she leans, the greater the friction; the farther back, the deeper the penetration.

◁ Rear entry with man kneeling

Most rear-entry positions are physiologically natural in that the vagina is well aligned with the erect penis. However, many women feel that to kneel, especially with the head lowered, is too submissive or too animal-like. The man can compensate for the closeness his partner may miss by fondling her breasts or clitoris.

Rear entry with man standing ▷

With the woman kneeling on the bed, penetration is deep and the slightly upturned vagina creates strong friction.

G-SPOT STIMULATION

The vagina is not overall a very sensitive organ, but it does have two particularly sensitive spots: the entrance, and a small area, known as the Graffenburg or G spot, about halfway up the front wall. Many women find that pressure on this area produces orgasm.

The G spot is stimulated in any position in which the penis presses against the front vaginal wall. The ones that are best will depend on the particular 'fit' of you and your partner(see SEXUAL POSITIONS, p.211). G-spot stimulation in man-on-top positions is increased by putting a pillow under your partner's hips.

SIDE-BY-SIDE POSITIONS

For relaxed, unhurried lovemaking, side-by-side positions are ideal, and couples often fall comfortably asleep locked together after making love this way. Side-by-side intercourse works well in pregnancy too, or if either of you is very heavy. A drawback for the woman is that her clitoris gets little stimulation from the pressure of your body, but in some variants it can be stimulated manually.

△ **Clitoral stimulation with leg**
This intimate and relaxed position can be achieved by rolling over from a straightforward man-on-top position. However, to begin intercourse in this way, the woman should raise her uppermost leg so that her partner can enter her from the side. By placing his thigh between hers, he can increase clitoral stimulation.

△ **Comfortable prolonged intercourse**
With both partners on their sides, rear entry is easy. This position is comfortable, so that it is suitable for prolonged intercourse. To gain deeper penetration the man should hold the upper half of his body away from his partner.

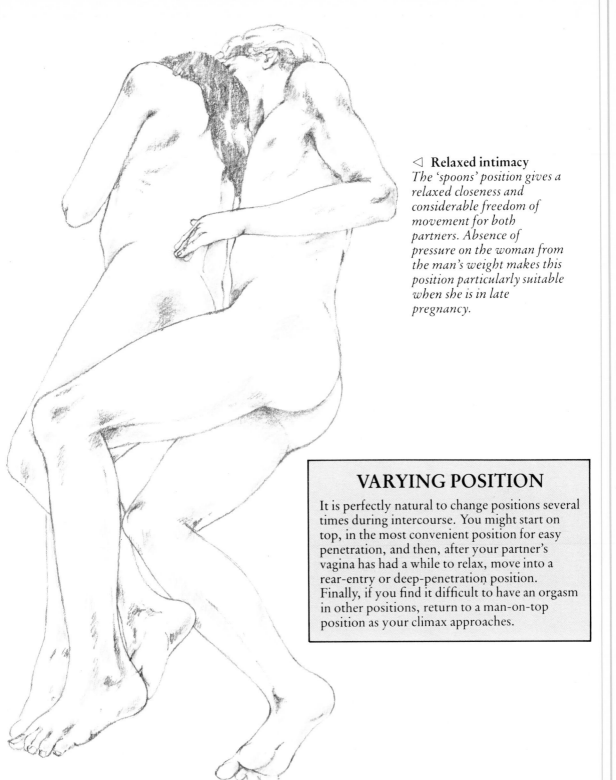

◁ **Relaxed intimacy**
The 'spoons' position gives a relaxed closeness and considerable freedom of movement for both partners. Absence of pressure on the woman from the man's weight makes this position particularly suitable when she is in late pregnancy.

VARYING POSITION

It is perfectly natural to change positions several times during intercourse. You might start on top, in the most convenient position for easy penetration, and then, after your partner's vagina has had a while to relax, move into a rear-entry or deep-penetration position. Finally, if you find it difficult to have an orgasm in other positions, return to a man-on-top position as your climax approaches.

SITTING POSITIONS

Although few of the sitting positions allow you much movement or direct genital stimulation, many couples find them erotic, partly because of their novelty and partly because they provide a strong sense of intimacy. They are also restful positions that can be used when you want intercourse again after a tiring first bout.

Sitting, woman astride ▷
Sitting positions in which the couple face each other are psychologically stimulating and strong on novelty, if somewhat restrictive of movement. But, by stretching his arms out behind him to support himself, the man can thrust or at least make it easier for the woman to move on his penis.

◁ **Using a chair**
A chair gives support for the man's back, allowing him to embrace his partner and to caress her breasts and clitoris. The position is intimate but little movement is possible, so that orgasm is unlikely for either partner unless the woman is adept in the use of her vaginal muscles.

STANDING POSITIONS

As with the sitting positions, the main benefit here is novelty. However, penetration is often difficult, especially if you are much taller than your partner, and she may need to stand on something in order to effect it.

△ **Supporting the woman**
Considerable agility and strength are required in this position and it is likely to be no more than a brief variant of the position shown on the right. The man can support his partner as shown here, if she is light, or by placing one or both hands under her buttocks.

△ **Basic standing position**
This is the simplest standing position, often used when a couple want to dispense with the preliminaries. In order to keep the penis from slipping out, the woman usually needs to close her legs. If the man wants to thrust vigorously his partner can use a wall for support.

INCREASING YOUR PLEASURE

The following checklist suggests activities you and your partner might try if you want to introduce some novelty into a relationship which has become slightly stale. These are not necessarily things you will want to do often, however much you enjoy them. They are meant to introduce variety into a sexual routine, not simply to become part of that routine, for used too often they easily lose their stimulus.

You may not like all the ideas suggested. For example, although some men find it very exciting to share their sexual fantasies with their partner, others would consider this an intolerable invasion of privacy. Use your own judgement, and regard this list as merely a starting point to stimulate your imagination. As with any form of sexual activity, all that really matters is that you should both enjoy what you do.

☐ Take a bath or shower together.

☐ Make love in the dark (if you usually prefer some light) and vice versa.

☐ Make love somewhere other than the bed – on a chair, sofa, or rug, perhaps.

☐ Make love at an unusual time. Come home from work at lunchtime, for example.

☐ Use a mirror to watch yourselves making love.

☐ Make love outdoors, but be careful to choose a place where you will not be interrupted.

☐ Create a sensual atmosphere with music and candlelight.

☐ Combine lovemaking with a snack and a bottle of wine in bed.

☐ Read an erotic novel or poetry to each other in bed, or watch a sexy video together.

☐ Give each other a sensual and relaxing overall massage with scented body oils. Also, use feathers, velvet, fur, and other textures to give a variety of sensations to the skin.

☐ Tell your partner your favorite fantasy. If your own fantasy life does not seem to give you the right degree of excitement, read Nancy Friday's book *Men in Love*. This describes a wide variety of male erotic fantasies and may stimulate your imagination.

☐ Use a vibrator (see below).

Planning your lovemaking

Perhaps the most valuable boost you can give to your lovemaking is to give it enough time, so that it can be as leisurely, sensuous, and prolonged as you like. Plan for it as you would plan for any other worthwhile activity. It is no compliment to your partner, and will almost certainly limit your enjoyment, if sex is usually a last-minute activity, squeezed in after the late movie when you are both almost too tired to stay awake.

VIBRATORS

As a sex aid, vibrators are generally more rewarding for women than for men. They operate at different frequencies, but the most effective frequency is about 80 Hz and, since battery-operated vibrators usually work at a lower frequency, an electric model is probably best. For the most intense sensations, place the head of the vibrator against the highly sensitive underside of the head of your penis – the area known as the frenulum (see p.231).

You can also use the vibrator to stimulate your partner's clitoris directly, and most women can reach orgasm this way, even if they have difficulty doing so during intercourse or through manual stimulation. Some models have a head that is designed to apply particularly intense stimulation to the clitoris and are for use exclusively in this way. Others can be strapped to the back of your hand so that vibrations are transmitted indirectly to the clitoris as you caress it. You can also use this second type of vibrator to give your lover a pleasantly different overall massage. Vibrators will teach you both more about your bodies' responses.

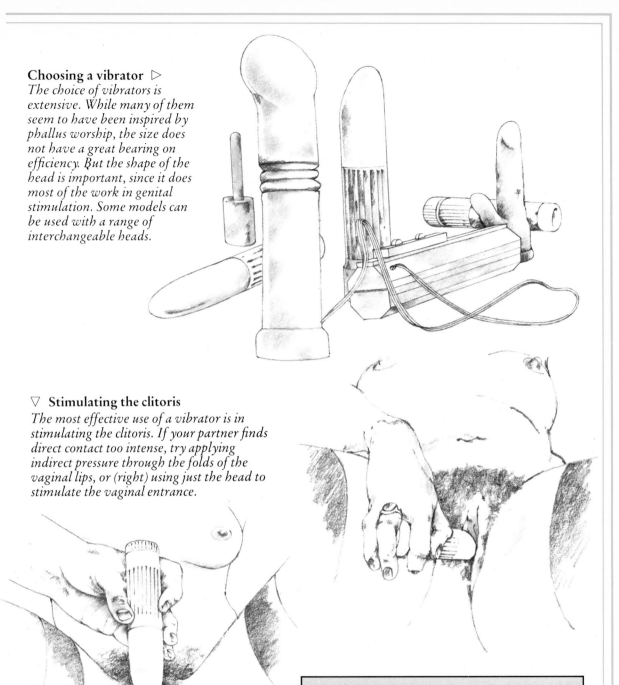

Choosing a vibrator ▷
The choice of vibrators is extensive. While many of them seem to have been inspired by phallus worship, the size does not have a great bearing on efficiency. But the shape of the head is important, since it does most of the work in genital stimulation. Some models can be used with a range of interchangeable heads.

▽ **Stimulating the clitoris**
The most effective use of a vibrator is in stimulating the clitoris. If your partner finds direct contact too intense, try applying indirect pressure through the folds of the vaginal lips, or (right) using just the head to stimulate the vaginal entrance.

AIDS PRECAUTIONS

To avoid the risk of AIDS, vibrators – and any other sex toys that you use – should never be shared unless they are cleaned thoroughly after use. The HIV virus is destroyed by ordinary household disinfectant or bleach, and also by dish-detergent diluted in hot water.

OVERCOMING INHIBITIONS

Inhibitions are feelings that interfere with your natural sexual response and so prevent you from enjoying sex or even becoming aroused. Nearly always they are the result of experiences that have made you feel guilty or anxious about sex; a puritanical upbringing, for example, or a disastrous episode in adolescence.

Few of us are entirely free from such hang-ups, but they are seldom so severe that they limit our sex lives significantly. Usually we can avoid the particular circumstances or activities that make us feel uncomfortable, but in extreme cases inhibitions may seriously disrupt the whole of your sex life, making you suppress your feelings or even avoid sex completely. The aim of the self-help programs described below is to enable you to modify old attitudes and patterns of behavior or to replace them with new and more flexible ones.

Dealing with sexual guilt

If you feel guilty about sex, you need to give yourself 'permission' to be sexual and to believe that sexual pleasure is something that everyone has a right to. The aim of the following advice is to increase your sexuality, which you may have so consistently and successfully repressed that you think of yourself as someone who has little interest in or desire for sex.

☐ *Develop your fantasy life.* This is a good place to start, because it is safer to let go of your inhibitions in your imagination than in reality. If you find it hard to conjure up fantasies, use sexually explicit magazines or books to stimulate your imagination. Do not worry if your fantasies include people other than your partner or practices that would normally horrify you. Fantasy is used here simply as a way of examining long-suppressed feelings, and it does not necessarily indicate your true preferences. Nor does it follow that you would ever act out your fantasies in reality.

☐ *Learn to like your body.* The exercises in GETTING IN TOUCH WITH YOUR BODY, p.230, and GIVING YOURSELF PLEASURE, p.233, are an important part of this program. They will help you to feel comfortable with your body and sexual feelings.

☐ *Reassess your attitudes.* Take a fresh look, in the light of adult experience, at the sexual views and attitudes you acquired as a child. Rigorously examine any preconceptions as though you were considering them for the first time. Are they based largely on an emotion that is hard to justify rationally? If so, try to jettison them.

☐ *Become a hedonist.* A common characteristic of men who carry a heavy load of sexual guilt is that they cannot help believing that all pleasure for its own sake is wrong. If you are the kind of person who feels guilty about, say, relaxing instead of working constantly, or about spending money on occasional luxuries, you most likely feel uneasy about enjoying life too much. Make yourself more receptive to pleasure by creating space in your life for sensual enjoyment – of food, music, pictures, or erotic literature, for example. This should make it easier to view sex as another source of legitimate pleasure.

☐ *Learn not to be a spectator.* If you have always had difficulty in accepting your own sexual feelings you probably tend to stand back mentally when you are having sex, disassociating yourself by thinking about other things or watching rather than feeling your own performance. When you have sex, try to concentrate on what you feel, tune in to the sensations you experience, and be aware all the time of your partner's body as you touch her and yours as she touches you. The sensate-focusing exercises in LEARNING TO SHARE PLEASURE, p.235, are one way of practising this concentration on pleasure.

☐ *Letting yourself go.* If you feel inhibited in your sex life, you may be disturbed by the idea of losing control when you make love, of appearing vulnerable, ridiculous, or simply undignified. Maybe you have always made love in silence because it seems to draw less attention to what you are doing, or because you were made to feel as a child that it was somehow animal-like to let go or to show enjoyment. One of the ways to overcome this is to practise a deliberate loss of self-control in sex. For example, respond to your feelings by moving more, breathing more heavily, or yelling, expressing the pleasure you feel in any way you like. You will probably find it easier to do this first when you masturbate.

Dispelling sexual anxiety

Many men think that sexual difficulties begin only in bed and exclusively concern their ability to perform successfully. This 'performance anxiety' is discussed in detail in OVERCOMING ERECTION PROBLEMS, p.243. For a large number of men, though, anxiety about sex is not limited to worries about performance, but extends to their ability to make any kind of close or sexual relationship with women. If you are in this position, use the minimal dating program below to take gradual steps toward a normal social and sexual life. If you have been anxious about sex for so long that you have avoided contact with women for some time, start at the beginning of the program. If you feel comfortable about being on friendly terms with women, but have difficulty turning a social, platonic relationship into a sexual one, start at step 3.

MINIMAL DATING PROGRAM

You will find it easier to use this program if you also read DEVELOPING SOCIAL AND SEXUAL SKILLS, p.302.

1 Your first goal is to make a 'neutral' date that will provoke as little anxiety in you as possible. It should be with a woman you like but not one you find especially attractive. Choose a place or activity without strong romantic overtones: lunch in a popular restaurant, a drink at lunchtime or after work, or a visit to an art gallery or concert, for example. Repeat this undemanding kind of dating a few times until your anxiety has decreased to more manageable proportions.

2 The next step is to make a date with a woman to whom you *are* attracted and, if possible, one who you think might find you attractive. You will feel much more tense about this but, once again, keep the activity neutral and the relationship platonic.

3 Now place your friendship on a more sexual footing. Resolve, though, that you are not yet going to have sex with your date, even if she indicates that she would like to. But you should let her know you are attracted and find out if she feels the same way. You can show as much physical affection as you choose, provided you do not end up in bed. Dine at home by candlelight, or in a frankly romantic restaurant, or choose a sexy movie and hold her hand, in order to step up the sexual pace. You will probably need to push yourself a little, but not so much that you become unbearably anxious again. Some increase in tension is natural if you are (as you should be) genuinely interested in the woman you are with. If you make no progress at all, something is lacking: either courage on your part or the necessary sexual spark between you. If you are holding back because of a fear of rejection, this is the moment to take a few risks. By continuing to try, you increase your chances of success as well as failure.

4 Once you have achieved a little closeness with someone you are attracted to and who seems to feel the same way about you, you will need to confront the underlying problem: anxiety about your sexual performance. There are two very different approaches you can take:

(i) If you feel you know the woman well enough to be to some extent confident of a sympathetic reaction, simply tell her. Explain that you have had problems in the past and, although you very much want her, you are worried they might recur. You may well find that your openness improves your standing with her and allows you to become more trusting of each other. If so, your anxiety will probably decrease. However, if she is unsophisticated, inexperienced, or easily embarrassed, your revelations may make her so uncomfortable that she will be unable to help you. A further difficulty is that for many men the thought of disclosing their problem is even more anxiety-provoking than the problem itself. In both cases the second approach may be better.

(ii) Trust to luck. Go right ahead without preparing your partner for the possibility of failure. There may be no failure, especially if, having made contact with a woman again, you have managed to become slightly less self-critical and anxious about your performance. And even if things do not go as well as you had hoped, you will at least have achieved greater intimacy, which will make it easier for you to talk about your problem.

OVERCOMING THE FEAR OF INTIMACY

Within the framework of a close relationship, sex is safe: you can communicate your needs and show your feelings without fear of rejection or ridicule. But many men, even though they may acknowledge a need for more closeness in their relationships, find it hard to achieve. Indeed, they often fear it and fight shy of it.

If you want to feel closer to your partner, the following suggestions will help. Because you are attempting to change a very fundamental part of your nature you will need a high degree of commitment, but the rewards, in your sexual and your emotional life, will be correspondingly great.

☐ Choose the right partner, or at least minimize your chances of choosing a totally unsuitable one. See MAKING A LASTING RELATIONSHIP, p.300, which shows how you sabotage your own chances of success by becoming involved in a relationship that is very likely to fail.

☐ Set aside some time when you can talk daily to your partner about what has happened to you during the day and discuss problems. Make a special effort to talk about what matters most to you and do not avoid emotional or sexual issues. LEARNING TO COMMUNICATE, p.270, will help you here.

☐ Let your partner see the 'bad' side of you. It is easy to let anyone know the good things about you, but much more difficult to expose aspects of yourself about which you feel worried, guilty or ashamed. However, it is revealing these problem areas that makes for true intimacy.

☐ Show your feelings. Affectionate touching is the most straightforward way of demonstrating a need to be close. Show anger, too, if you feel it, but not in a destructive way. See **Dealing with anger**, p.271.

☐ Give your partner the opportunity to do things for you, letting go of your emotional independence a little. It is particularly important to be able to ask for things sometimes. In doing this you will be acknowledging that you have needs and allowing your partner to meet them.

☐ Spend time together on leisure activities. Do not use excuses such as the pressure of work to avoid spending time alone with your partner.

☐ Do not distance yourself, by provoking a quarrel, for example, whenever you sense that your partner is getting too close to you.

☐ Do not focus on your partner's shortcomings or least attractive features so that you lose sexual interest in her as soon as you feel you are becoming more involved than you want to be.

☐ The sensate-focusing exercises in LEARNING TO SHARE PLEASURE, p.235, are designed to foster intimacy. However, it is important to realize that these exercises provide you with an excellent opportunity for employing all the tactics to avoid intimacy which contribute to your problem. Do not allow yourself to be too tired or too busy to do them, or to remember past injustices and notice physical imperfections as soon as you begin to feel emotional and physical satisfaction.

ANXIETY ABOUT SEXUAL ODORS AND SECRETIONS

If you are bothered by the inevitable smells and messiness of sex, it may be because you have come to associate sex with excretion. The two functions are, in fact, quite separate and if the genitals are kept clean by daily washing they do not normally smell. When you are sexually aroused though, your genitals do have a characteristic odor, and so do your partner's. Most people find this not only pleasant, but exciting. Furthermore, the sexual secretions – vaginal fluid and semen – are harmless, and almost odorless and tasteless too.

If you are uncircumcized, draw your foreskin back when you wash your penis, otherwise a strong-smelling secretion (smegma) can build up under the foreskin. (See **Talking about sex**, p.270.)

IMPROVING YOUR SELF-ESTEEM

To have self-esteem is to feel that you are worth something. A poor self-image affects not only the way you behave toward other people – shyness and jealousy are nearly always the result of low self-esteem, to take prime examples – but also the way they behave toward you, because people tend to accept you at your own self-evaluation. A lack of self-esteem puts you at a disadvantage in social situations, because fear of being rejected usually makes you overeager to please others and very reluctant to risk giving offense. And, naturally, your self-esteem has a direct bearing on your confidence about attracting and retaining sexual partners.

Causes of low self-esteem

Timidity and a sense of the inevitability of failure may be built into a man's personality as the result of an upbringing by parents who were too strict, over-critical, or even unloving. A child will accept his parents' view of him; if they do not make him feel good, lovable and successful, it it not surprising that he grows up believing he is of little worth. Often, too, a man's self-image is colored by childhood teasing that made him believe he was unattractive, or by unsuccessful adolescent experiences of sex that made him feel inadequate.

Even a normally self-confident man may suffer a temporary loss of self-esteem if he fails in an area that is important to him. A setback at work or the break-up of a relationship that means a lot to him will diminish his sexual confidence as well as affecting his general outlook.

Dealing with temporary setbacks

When you have suffered a major blow to your self-esteem it is important first of all to try to see your failure in perspective, as only part of you and your life, not the whole of it. Focus on other areas in which you have had more success. For the time being, concentrate your energies on something at which you are unlikely to fail and which will restore your self-image. For example, after the break-up of an affair, you may find it helps to immerse yourself in your work more than usual, or to start on a new and adventurous project.

Remember that after any loss of prestige or self-esteem, whether at work or in a relationship, you may be tempted to embark on an affair simply because it seems to be the easiest and quickest way to soothe your bruised ego. Such rebound affairs are a risky way to deal with the problem because they are likely to lead to another failure. It is probably better to wait until you have regained your emotional equilibrium.

If, in two or three months, you still feel at a disadvantage sexually, your problem may be more deep-seated. The program that follows is designed to help you overcome such difficulties.

PROGRAM FOR IMPROVING YOUR SELF-ESTEEM

This program, divided into an assessment section and a self-improvement section, will help you to build up your self-esteem and begin to accept yourself as a sexually desirable male. Other parts of the book form essential complements to the program, and you will be directed to these at certain points.

1 ASSESSMENT

Assess your strengths and weaknesses by compiling two lists. First, list your good points, intellectual and emotional as well as physical; secondly, list your faults – the things about yourself that you wish were different or could be improved. Bear in mind the following suggestions:

☐ Try to be specific. Do not simply put down 'good-natured' or 'ugly,' for example. Work out how you are positively good-natured (you like kids, you are a free spender, etc) or negatively ugly (you are pimply, fat, bald, etc).

☐ Do not be tempted to overlook or minimize your strengths. Nearly everyone remembers to write down 'acne' if he has it; far fewer will remember to give themselves credit for a clear skin.

☐ Include among your strong points attributes or skills not directly related to sexual competence. Are you a handyman, for example, or do you play a sport reasonably well? Similarly, if someone else has a talent you admire and believe would give you more self-confidence if you had it – an ability to play the guitar, or skill with computers, for example – list it among your weaknesses.

Now analyze your lists, beginning by comparing them. Are the weaknesses far more numerous than the strengths? If so, why? Perhaps you are being unfair to yourself. A poor self-image may be making you so self-critical that you have dismissed some of your good points as unworthy of mention.

Examine your list of strengths. Are you making good use of those you do have? If there are situations in which you shine, how often do you find yourself in them? If you have a good eye for a ball and enjoy tennis, for example, have you joined a club? Do you even play regularly? And what about your best features? If you are tall, inspect your posture, for a round-shouldered slouch negates the positive aspects of height. If your eyes are one of your most attractive features, learn how to use them to your best advantage. (See **Eye contact**, p.302.)

Finally, examine your list of faults. Delete the ones you can do nothing about. For example, you cannot make yourself six inches taller. The list will still contain a number of things you can change if you are willing to invest time and energy.

2 SELF IMPROVEMENT

The second element of the program will enable you to improve your physical appearance and develop greater self-assurance.

Improving your image

Start with your physical appearance. It is in this area that changes are most easily made and most readily appreciated by others. Would you look better with a different hairstyle or, if you wear spectacles, with contact lenses? Grow a moustache if you think it will suit you; shave off a beard if you suspect it does not.

Look at your clothes. When buying new ones, do not just play safe. Study magazines, advertisements, and store windows, and choose clothes in which you would really feel good. If you have always dressed conservatively, try a more casual approach; if you have been a sloppy dresser, neaten up. Try to buy at stores that suit the image you would like to present. And get good aftershave. This will soon become a pleasantly recognizable part of that image.

Whatever changes you make, introduce them gradually, one at a time, over about six months. This will give you and everyone else time to adjust to them. You will also find it necessary to accustom yourself to other people's changed impression of you. Although this will ultimately boost your self-esteem, it may embarrass you at first if you have always avoided drawing attention to yourself.

Being more confident about your looks

Get to know and like your face and physique as they really are. Too many men feel dissatisfied with their looks not because of gross or obvious abnormalities but simply because they do not add up to their ideal image of a good-looking man. But there is hardly a man who is physically perfect and few women expect physical perfection in their lovers. The exercises in GETTING IN TOUCH WITH YOUR BODY, p.230, should help you gain a more positive view of yourself.

If you have felt sexually inadequate over the size or shape of your genitals, remember that you probably underestimate the size of your penis. The fore-shortened view that you get from above makes it look smaller than it is. Remember, if other men's penises look a lot bigger than yours, that you have probably seen theirs in a resting, flaccid state, and while there is a wide variation in the size of non-erect penises, size differences tend to disappear with erection since small penises swell more than large ones. And remember too that the vagina will mold itself to a penis of any size. The penis you perhaps regard as too small need not lessen your partner's enjoyment, for what you do with it is more important than its size.

Learning to overcome shyness

Over 80 per cent of people questioned in a recent survey said they had felt shy at some time or in some situations, and of these over 40 per cent admitted that shyness was a constant problem for them. So the chances are strong that the person you are too timid to talk to feels much the same as you.

Do not automatically label yourself 'shy'. Instead, regard yourself only as feeling shy in certain situations – in large groups, for example, or with attractive strangers. Giving up the label is the first step toward overcoming the problem itself.

Have faith in your likeability. Shy people usually lack the social skill to make others believe that they are worth knowing. Believe it yourself, and you will communicate your belief without even trying. For this very important part of the program, turn to DEVELOPING SOCIAL AND SEXUAL SKILLS, p.302.

Try not to concentrate on your own feelings of self-consciousness, or to brood about what people think of you. Instead, give your entire attention to anyone you talk to or to any situation, whether sexual or not, that you find yourself in. Some psychologists suggest that an excellent way to overcome shyness is to become involved in a social or political cause. Involvement of this sort provides an opportunity to make a fresh start as an unshy person in a non-sexual situation. A sense of sexual ease should soon follow. You may also find it helpful to read **Dispelling sexual anxiety**, p.225.

Finally, make sure you pick the right sexual partner. Many men seem deliberately to sabotage their self-esteem by choosing partners who lower it even more. Not many men can function well with a lover who is critical or rejecting. A partnership based on love and support is essential for anyone whose self-esteem is fragile or for whom self-consciousness is a problem.

Learning to be more assertive

Practise saying no to suggestions you normally, though unwillingly, say yes to. If you have fallen into a pattern of habitually doing something you dislike just because you think it is expected of you – seeing too much of your partner's, or even your own, relatives when you have little in common, for example – break the habit. If your partner regularly pressures you into watching her favorite TV program, invite her to watch yours next time. Assertiveness should not be equated with aggressiveness. It simply means expressing the way you feel and implies no criticism of your partner or others for feeling or wanting something different.

Do not be afraid to ask for things you want. Start by requesting small favors of friends. You might ask if you can borrow something, for example. Or ask someone to pick up the occasional item for you if he or she is going shopping. Sometimes even these small requests will not be granted (other people are assertive too) but part of learning assertiveness is being able to accept an occasional rebuff without interpreting it as a serious rejection.

Practise making decisions and, if they are minor, do not spend time worrying about whether they are right or wrong. A good starting point is to resolve never to say, 'I don't really mind' when you are asked whether you prefer one thing to another. If you have

a preference, make it known. Even if you really do not care, make a firm, immediate decision.

Take deliberate risks by acting out of character sometimes. It helps if you can think of it as 'acting'. Allow yourself to seem to lose your temper, for example, if the occasion is right and everyone knows you are a man who never loses his temper. Their impression to date may well be that you do not dare to lose your temper, and their realization that you can show anger, when appropriate, may do wonders for your reputation and consequently for your self-confidence.

Make a deliberate effort to do something you find especially difficult, such as striking up a conversation with strangers or making a justified complaint. Sometimes you may get the snub or even the hostile reaction you dread, but most often you will receive a satisfactory response and a large boost to your self-esteem.

When you have gained confidence and feel more comfortable about asking for what you want among acquaintances and friends, introduce a little more assertiveness into your sexual relationships. You may find this difficult if it involves discussions about sex and your sexual feelings, but LEARNING TO COMMUNICATE, p.270, will help you overcome the problem.

Assessing your progress

After you have worked on the above program for three months, check your progress by answering once again the questionnaire CONFIDENCE, p.172 Compare your result with your previous rating. Has there been any improvement? Check whether your answers pinpoint any specific area you can work on. If your rating is still low, concentrate on **Learning to be more assertive**, above.

Remember that you are trying to change ideas about yourself that you have probably held for most of your life. Do not be discouraged if, like most old habits, they die hard. If you are determined to change and to give up an outdated view of yourself, and if you are willing to take a few risks and expose yourself to a few minor disappointments, you will almost certainly win through.

GETTING IN TOUCH WITH YOUR BODY

The sight and feel of each other's bodies is one of the special joys of lovemaking and, particularly in the early stages of a relationship, a couple can derive almost as much pleasure from exploring each other as from intercourse itself. Naturally, your enjoyment of sex will be diminished, or even prevented altogether, if you are embarrassed about being naked in front of your partner, or if you are at all self-conscious about the way your body looks.

The chemistry of attraction

Self-consciousness usually springs from the belief that you are unattractive on account of physical imperfections. And yet bodily perfection is, as far as the majority of women are concerned, irrelevant to whether or not they find a partner sexually attractive. The chemistry of sexual attraction is so subtle, unpredictable and idiosyncratic that it is often incomprehensible to anyone but those involved.

Your partner's view of you will be quite different from your own or that of anyone else, and she may even find especially endearing the characteristics that you regard as flaws.

Learning to accept your body

The following exercises should help to lessen your self-consciousness, and make you more comfortable with yourself and more aware of your body as a resource for sexual pleasure. The exercises might seem narcissistic at first, and it is quite probable that you will dislike the idea of doing them, especially if, like many men, you seldom use a mirror except to shave or straighten your tie. However, it is important to understand that the aim of the program is not to encourage self-love but to boost self-confidence. In order to feel as relaxed as possible when doing the exercises, you should also ensure that you have privacy and plenty of time.

△ **The non-erect penis**
At rest, the penis is about half as long as it is during arousal, when the spongy tissue becomes engorged with blood to produce an erection.

△ **Circumcision**
This surgical operation, which is usually carried out for religious or or medical reasons, removes the foreskin that covers the head of the penis.

1 Study your naked body in a full-length mirror. Look long and hard at your face and then let your eyes travel slowly down to your toes. Imagine that you are seeing yourself for the first time. Look from every angle, and watch yourself kneeling, bending, sitting, moving around. Look over your shoulder to examine your back and the set of your buttocks.

2 Note what is special about you; not perfect, but special. These are the features that make you unique, the qualities that appeal to any woman who finds you sexually attractive.

3 Like everyone else, you have a mix of good and not-so-good features. Look at your body again, but this time focus your attention on your best points. Gloss over the ones you dislike, regarding them as part of the whole, but not a part that matters all that much. They are there, so accept them, but do not dwell on them to the exclusion of everything else.

4 Now study your genitals. Feel your testes. One, usually the left, hangs slightly below the other. This is normal. Look at your penis. When not erect, it is probably between two and four inches long. As you know, it lengthens considerably when erect. This is because its three cylinders of spongy tissue become engorged with blood when you are sexually aroused. These cylinders are enclosed in a fibrous sheath, and as the spongy tissues fill and press against the sheath, the penis hardens. Let your fingers play on the surface of your penis. You will probably find that the most sensitive area is the head and, in particular, the ridge on the underside where the head joins the shaft. This is known as the frenulum.

5 Finish the exercise by taking a warm bath. Soap your hands and explore your body with them. Notice the different sensations you experience by varying your touch and pressure, and identify the changes in skin sensitivity from area to area. Explore your genitals again too, but do not spend much time on them. The aim of this part of the exercise is to become aware of sensations in the whole body.

6 Dry yourself. Again, focus on sensations and do not be in too much of a hurry.

7 If you like the idea, try using a body lotion and enjoy the feeling as you rub it into your skin.

The frenulum
The head of the penis is more sensitive than the shaft, and the ridge of skin on the underside is particularly well provided with nerve-endings. This is known as the frenulum.

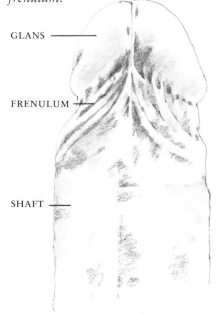

GLANS ———

FRENULUM ——

SHAFT ——

Varying angles of erection
The angle of erection varies from man to man and tends to become less acute with age.

Assessing your progress

By repeating the exercise several times over the course of three or four weeks you can develop a positive image of yourself as you really are, without making adverse comparisons with the body you formerly wished you possessed. Do you feel reasonably comfortable doing the exercise? And do you feel you would now be equally at ease with your sexual partner? If so you can increase your body awareness still more by practising with her the sensate-focusing exercises on p.235.

If, however, you feel you have made little progress it might be helpful to take a different approach. Try a sauna or massage, for example. Both experiences will help you focus your attention on your body as a source of pleasure. Other sections of the book may be helpful too, particularly IMPROVING YOUR SELF-ESTEEM, p.227, and OVERCOMING IN-HIBITIONS, p.224. These are both aimed at helping you feel more relaxed about yourself as a sexually active person, so that you will be more at ease in a sexual relationship.

▽ **Getting to know your body**
The ultimate aim of the preceding self-examination exercises is to feel unself-conscious about your body when with a sexual partner. But first you must become familiar and relaxed with it when alone. Your progress will be faster if you ensure that you have adequate time and complete privacy for the exercises.

GIVING YOURSELF PLEASURE

It is not so long ago that the term 'self-abuse' was a popular synonym for masturbation. This attitude began to change rapidly after 1948, when the Kinsey Report (*Sexual Behavior in the Human Male*) revealed not only that over 90 per cent of American men had masturbated, but that its only harmful effect was to give many of them a groundless sense of anxiety and guilt. Modern physicians and psychologists agree that masturbation is a matter of self-pleasuring rather than self-abuse; nor is it regarded simply as a means of relieving sexual tension for the man without a partner, but as an acceptable way for almost every man to learn how best to satisfy his sexual needs.

But even though you may accept rationally that masturbation is both harmless and widely practised, you may still have some reservations about it. It is worthwhile making the effort to overcome these inhibitions, and you will find that the exercise program which follows will help you in this and promote your sexual self-discovery.

Giving yourself maximum pleasure

This program will also help any man who feels reluctant to touch his penis, but prefers to masturbate by rubbing his genitals against something. If you dislike touching your penis you are likely to feel uncomfortable when a woman caresses it, which will make it difficult for you to enjoy sex.

You will want privacy for the exercises and you should also set aside plenty of time for them. This second consideration is particularly important if you have always regarded masturbation as something to be done furtively and hurriedly. Your only objective is to discover the sensations that are most pleasurable and to enjoy them in a relaxed, comfortable way. It does not matter if you do not reach orgasm, or even fail to get an erection, for you will still have learned a good deal about the kind of stimulation you get most pleasure from.

1 Try to discover which areas of your penis are most sensitive, touching each area in turn, varying the degree of pressure you apply. Whether or not you are circumsized makes no difference to the sensitivity of your penis.

2 If you are uncircumcized, draw the foreskin back and forth over the head repeatedly until your penis is erect.

△ **Exploring your penis**
Stimulate your penis by hand in different ways in order to discover which parts, and what kinds of touch, give you the most pleasure.

▽ **Sensitivity of the penis**
There is no difference in sensitivity between the exposed head of the circumcized penis and the head of the uncircumcized penis, shown here. In both cases the underside of the head is the area most susceptible to pressure.

Masturbating

When you have a firm erection, start to rub the skin on the shaft up and down, varying the rhythm and the length of the strokes in order to experience as wide a range of sensations as possible.

3 If you are circumcized, try alternately squeezing and releasing your penis. You should soon develop an erection.

4 Now stroke the shaft of the penis, varying the pressure you use. Experiment to see whether you prefer a rapid downward movement followed by a slow upward one, or vice versa. Do not rush it.

5 If you feel you are about to reach orgasm before 15 minutes have passed, stop. When the urge to ejaculate has subsided, start stroking again.

6 When you have grown so excited that you can no longer hold back, let yourself go thoroughly, focusing your mind only on the sensations involved.

Assessing your progress

If you enjoy the exercise program and find you can keep going without reaching a climax too soon then you are doing well. If the sensations are less intense than you think they should be, try using a lubricant such as KY jelly or a massage lotion. Often this enhances sensations and makes it easier to focus on them. You can also employ fantasy, or erotic magazines or books, to increase your arousal. If you

find, after doing it a few times, that the exercise still makes you feel very tense, relax for a few minutes beforehand.

ANTICIPATING EJACULATION

Are you unable to stop yourself reaching a rapid climax? If so, you have not yet learned to 'read' the body signals which indicate that ejaculation is inevitable. If this remains a problem after you have been doing the exercise for two to three weeks, you will do best to study DELAYING EJACULATION, p.246.

It is possible that you may find the exercise difficult if you do not normally use your hands to masturbate. If this is the case, masturbate next time in your usual way, but touch your penis just before you ejaculate. From then on, each time you masturbate, stroke and caress it a little earlier each time. Eventually, you will find that you can ejaculate easily by means of manual stimulation.

LEARNING TO SHARE PLEASURE

The following exercises are known as 'sensate focusing' exercises because they help you and your partner focus on the sensations that are produced by exploring each other's bodies. They involve a program of intimate stroking and stimulation that stops short of intercourse.

SENSATE-FOCUSING EXERCISES

Learning to concentrate on your body's sensations can help to freshen any partnership, but it is particularly important for a man who has trouble relaxing and enjoying sex because of qualms about intercourse or physical intimacy in general. Men sometimes fear that something is expected of them by their sexual partner that they may not be able to deliver, and the anxiety that this causes leads to tension. This is why these exercises do *not* involve intercourse (or even, initially, genital contact). Their purpose is to guide you toward enjoyment of physical contact as an end in itself, without the demands of performance. You cannot fail, because you are not being asked to succeed – only to experience. All you need is a willing partner, privacy, and enough time to approach the exercises in an unhurried manner. Both of you should be naked, of course, and for many couples a bath or shower together can be a relaxing preliminary.

Regular practice

The exercises are done in a three-stage series. In order to derive the maximum benefit from them, you should try to practise each stage three times a week for two or three weeks before advancing to the next. It is a good idea to make a point of alternating your activities so that the partner who is the first to give pleasure at one session is the first to receive it the next time. Although these exercises are an important part of several self-help therapy programs, any couple can benefit from occasional tender and imaginative sex play in which they try to rediscover all the sensations of which their bodies are capable without setting themselves the usual goals of intercourse and orgasm.

1 PLEASURE IN GIVING

Caressing another person's body is a very special source of pleasure. It need not have any overt sexual content, which is why, during this first stage of the exercises, your attentions do not extend to the genital area. You may find that the pleasure for both of you is increased if the active partner lubricates his or her hands with body lotion.

1 Start the session with your partner lying face down while you kneel either beside or astride her. Gently fondle and stroke her whole body, working your way down from her head to her toes.

2 During this part of the exercise, you are in complete control. Explore your partner's body with your hands and kiss it in any way that feels good to you. She can gently push your hand away if you do something she does not enjoy.

3 After 10 minutes (or longer if you like) change places. Now just relax and enjoy the sensations while your partner caresses and massages you. Feel what is happening to you and focus your attention on each spot she touches. Try not to stand back mentally and watch her.

4 Now you should change position so that your partner can lie on her back while you gently stroke her face and body. (You should avoid touching her breasts or genitals at this stage.)

5 Now lie back while, avoiding your penis and testes, she pleasures you. Do not try to direct or guide her, but if she does something you find uncomfortable, gently move her hand.

6 If you begin to feel at all tense or anxious, ask her to stop for a while but to resume caressing you as soon as you are relaxed again.

7 If you feel sexually aroused at the end of the session, try masturbating. (Your partner should not do this for you at this stage.) However, you might feel so relaxed that you simply fall asleep straight after the session.

▽ Relaxing your partner

Massage sessions usually begin with the back, because attention to this area rarely fails to produce a sense of ease. You may choose simply to stroke your partner's back or to brush the skin lightly with your fingertips rather than massage it. But, whatever your preference, the face-down position will help your partner to relax. In this stage of the program you should concentrate totally on giving pleasure.

△ **Stroking the legs and feet**
Do not use too light a touch on the sensitive inside of the leg and the sole of the foot, as your partner may find it irritating. However, as you develop a definite rhythm she will find the sensations very soothing.

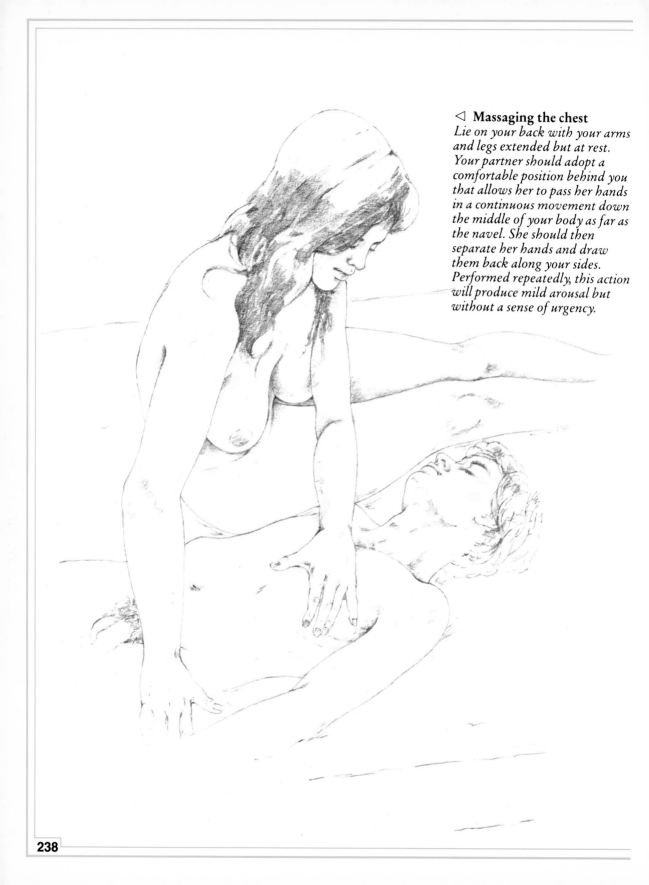

◁ **Massaging the chest**
*Lie on your back with your arms
and legs extended but at rest.
Your partner should adopt a
comfortable position behind you
that allows her to pass her hands
in a continuous movement down
the middle of your body as far as
the navel. She should then
separate her hands and draw
them back along your sides.
Performed repeatedly, this action
will produce mild arousal but
without a sense of urgency.*

Caressing the lower back ▷
To enjoy another very pleasurable form of caress you lie face down while your partner sits astride you and explores the lower part of your back with her hands. Concentrate solely on the pleasure she is giving you and put aside any feeling of selfishness. If you carry out the exercises conscientiously, both of you will learn to give and enjoy pleasure fully.

◁ **Changing roles**
*By taking it in turn
to receive pleasure,
you will be more able
to focus on the
sensations.*

2 PLEASURE IN RECEIVING

After practising the preceding exercises for a couple of weeks, move on to the second stage, below. This is a similar set of exercises, except that here the emphasis is on the reactions of the person being caressed rather than on those of the active partner. Instead of simply accepting the attention, the passive partner gives positive feedback to his or her lover about what feels particularly enjoyable. The ban on intercourse and genital touching is still in force.

1 Caress your partner, face-down, then face-up, as before, but try to discover the most sensitive areas of her body and the kind of stimulation she enjoys most. She may, for example, prefer a gentler touch, or perhaps a rougher one, than you yourself would enjoy.

2 Now take your turn, letting her know, in words or gestures, what feels especially good. Guide her hand with yours if you want, and if she kisses you in a certain spot in a way that is highly pleasurable, tell her. Concentrate on your own feelings and do not waste time worrying about whether she might be getting tired or bored. Her turn will come again after 10 minutes or so.

3 At the end of the session, tell each other how you both felt and discuss what most pleased each of you.

Assessing your progress

If, after practising for two to three weeks, you both feel at ease and relaxed with each other during the exercises, you are ready to progress to the third stage. This teaches you how to touch each others' genitals to give maximum pleasure. But do not worry if either of you still feels mildly anxious while doing the exercises. Carry on for another week or so and then, when you feel more comfortable, go on to stage three, which is described below.

Barriers to enjoyment

If you found it was much easier and more enjoyable to caress your partner than to be caressed, it is possible that guilt about sex is inhibiting your enjoyment. Or it may be that you are afraid your partner does not find you attractive, or that the exercise bores her. In each of these cases you cannot concentrate on your own feelings. Try, over the next four sessions, asking your partner for exactly what you want, letting her do only what you ask for. Some men find it easier to lie back and be caressed than to take the active role. If you feel this way, it is worth examining your feelings closely to see whether you have some hostility toward your partner or ambivalence about the relationship which makes it difficult for you to show tenderness and affection. The questionnaires COMPATIBILITY, p.260, and ARE YOU SEXUALLY SATISFIED?, p.265, and the problem chart WHAT IS WRONG WITH YOUR RELATIONSHIP?, p.268, may help you to confront this possibility.

These exercises are designed to promote closeness. If you have encountered within yourself an almost insurmountable resistance to doing them, it is probably because you feel very threatened by the idea of a close relationship. In this case (and likewise if you felt very detached, with no feelings except, perhaps, boredom) you may need professional help to lower your defenses so as to allow yourself to become more emotionally involved.

3 TOUCHING THE GENITALS

You and your partner are now ready to take turns arousing each other by fondling the genitals as well as the rest of the body. Once again, though, stop short of intercourse. The aim of the exercises is simply to fully enjoy this form of contact.

1 With your partner lying on her back, move your hands to her breasts and cup each one so that you can kiss and gently suck the nipples. If your partner is responsive, you will feel the nipples stiffen.

2 Brush your hands across her belly and genital area. Run your fingers through her pubic hair. Be ready to pause for a while if she becomes obviously tense or anxious, but continue these intimate caresses for several minutes.

3 Using a lubricant such as KY jelly, move your fingers lightly around the entrance to the vagina (but not into it) gently stroking it. Then touch the clitoris, which you will feel as a firm spot covered by a hood of skin, at the point where the inner vaginal lips meet at the front. Do not rub hard or use direct pressure, but stroke it softly. The clitoris is a highly sensitive organ with a wealth of nerve endings.

4 Now it is your turn to be fondled. Your partner should stroke your chest and belly, run her fingers through your pubic hair, and caress your inner thighs, moving gradually up to your testes, which she should caress and squeeze gently.

5 Concentrate on your body and the way it responds to her touch. Tell her the sort of pressure you enjoy most, and if you begin to feel tense, ask her to stop for a while. It does not matter whether or not you have an erection. Just experience the pleasure of a tender touch on your genitals.

6 Next, sit down in a comfortable position on the bed. Use a pillow or other support if you like. Your

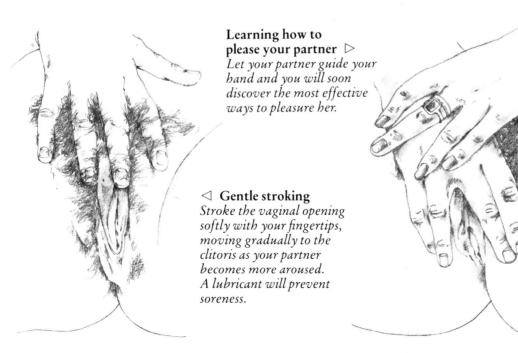

Learning how to please your partner ▷
Let your partner guide your hand and you will soon discover the most effective ways to pleasure her.

◁ **Gentle stroking**
Stroke the vaginal opening softly with your fingertips, moving gradually to the clitoris as your partner becomes more aroused. A lubricant will prevent soreness.

partner should lean back between your thighs, and guide your fingers so that they stimulate her clitoris in the way she likes best. Remember that the clitoris extends much farther than can be seen. Instead of concentrating on the visible tip, you can probably pleasure her most by exerting light pressure on the side of the clitoris through the vaginal lips. Apply saliva or an artificial lubricant and experiment by varying both pressure and tempo. Do not neglect the rest of her body; caress it with your free hand.

7 Change places so that she is sitting and you are lying between her legs. Show her by guiding her hand how to stimulate your penis to produce maximum pleasure, and tell her precisely how you like it. You will almost certainly get an erection, but it does not matter if you do not as you will still feel pleasure.

8 If you have an erection, your partner should play with your penis for a little while, then move her hand to another part of your body and let the erection subside before caressing it again.

9 Orgasm is not the object of this exercise. But if either of you becomes highly aroused you can continue manual stimulation until you climax.

10 Once you both feel quite comfortable doing the exercise you can, if you want, use your lips and tongue to arouse each other (see **Oral sex**, p.208). Your partner will tell you, or push you away gently, if she is not yet ready to try this.

Assessing your progress

If you have both been able to enjoy the preceding exercises without feeling tense or anxious, you can incorporate them into your repertoire of sex play. There will probably be times when, although you do not feel like intercourse, you can enjoy the gentle stimulation of genital pleasuring.

If doing the exercises makes you feel tense or anxious, or if you find yourself switching off by thinking of something quite irrelevant instead of focusing on your feelings, try to relax for a while before starting. Some mild anxiety is natural when you begin to do the exercise. It is possible that you will only feel anxious when it is your turn to be caressed. If so, next time you do the exercise continue to caress your partner, forgoing your own turn. In this way you should gradually become more confident. If you found that you were concerned about genital secretions, odors or appearance – either yours or your partner's – **Anxiety about sexual odors and secretions**, p.226, may be reassuring.

If, after practising the exercises for 4-6 weeks, you have seen no real improvement and still find them difficult, you will probably find professional help valuable (see RESOURCE GUIDE, p.312).

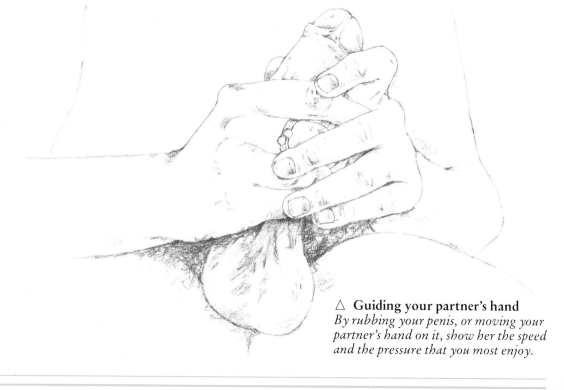

△ **Guiding your partner's hand**
By rubbing your penis, or moving your partner's hand on it, show her the speed and the pressure that you most enjoy.

OVERCOMING ERECTION PROBLEMS

Inability to achieve or maintain an erection is probably the most worrying sexual problem a man can face. The old-fashioned term for the condition – impotence – accurately describes the feelings that such failure produces in a man. In terms of sexual functioning, however, the word is almost useless because it is made to describe every degree of erection failure, from the occasional occurrence, for some trivial reason, to the failure to ever achieve, under any circumstances, an erection.

Difficulty in getting an erection

You may sometimes find you can neither get nor hold an erection, particularly after a heavy drinking session or when you are tired and unenergetic. This is not a serious problem and most men experience such moments. On the other hand, if such episodes have become the rule rather than the exception, consult your doctor as there may be a medical basis for the problem. Similarly, you should see your doctor if you have *never* at any time had an erection: the problem may well have a physical cause.

Physical and hormonal reasons for erection difficulties are relatively rare, however. In most cases there is a psychological reason for persistent failure. The problem can arise as a result of guilt instilled during childhood or adolescence, or it may stem from boredom with a long-standing partnership (see AVOIDING SEXUAL BOREDOM, p.278). Or – and this is probably the most common cause – it can arise because one or two minor episodes become magnified into a major worry about the ability to perform. This state of mind, referred to as 'performance anxiety', inhibits the capacity to achieve and/or maintain an erection.

Occasional erection failure

Almost certainly, at one time or another, you have failed to get an erection when you wanted to, or achieved only a partial erection, or lost it at a critical moment. This can happen if you have sex when you are not really in the mood, or are not fully attracted to the person you are with but have allowed yourself to be drawn into a sexual situation. Sometimes, too, a natural anxiety interferes with your erection. Nervousness in a new relationship or guilt in an illicit one, for example, can do this. Occasional failures of this type are significant only if you immediately label yourself 'impotent' or allow yourself to dwell on the possibility of further failure.

Preventing erection failure

If you find such failures becoming more frequent, it is probably because you expect too much of yourself, or because you are trying to perform under the wrong conditions. The self-help measures suggested below are designed to keep episodes of failure to a minimum. But, what is even more important, they will help you to avoid the anxiety that can lead to a serious long-term problem.

☐ Have sex only when you are in the mood for it.

☐ Accept that you are a man, not a machine. There is no reason why your feelings or your sexual performance should always be the same. You feel more turned-on at some times than at others, and occasionally you will need extra stimulation. If you have a steady partner, she may not realize this unless you tell her.

☐ Avoid casual encounters – at least until your sexual confidence improves. You will be less anxious and more able to function if you can form a stable relationship with a partner whose reactions you know and trust.

☐ Do not judge your performance in terms of your penis. Mutual satisfaction is often achievable without intercourse, although in a physically close situation an erection may develop without a conscious effort on your part.

☐ If you fail to get an erection, or lose it just before or during intercourse, do not overreact. Simply explain what has happened: 'I guess I'm too tired (I've drunk too much) tonight. Let's try again tomorrow', and do not feel guilty. But do reassure your partner that it is not her fault. Most important, do not withdraw physically or mentally just because intercourse is for the time being out of the question. Stay intimate with your partner in any way you like that does not involve intercourse. If you enjoy being together, erection or not, you will have less anxiety about the possibility of failing next time.

TREATMENT FOR ERECTION PROBLEMS

If erection failure occurs so often that it severely affects your sex life, and if the measures recommended above have not helped, try the following set of exercises. Their aim is to dispel your anxiety by helping you accept the fact that even if an erection subsides, gentle stimulation can usually bring it back. In doing these exercises you will be free from worries about your sexual performance because you are not required – in fact, you are not allowed – to have intercourse until you feel confident enough to do so.

The first stage of the exercise can be practised without a partner. Thereafter, though, you need the cooperation of a sympathetic woman who is fond enough of you to undertake with patience and, ideally, pleasure, the gradual steps that comprise the treatment. If you lack such a partner at the moment, or if anxiety about 'impotence' has made you avoid all sexual relationships, the **Minimal dating program**, p.225, may help you establish a relationship with the kind of congenial partner you need.

Try to do the following exercises at a time when you feel most in the mood for sex.

1 Begin to stimulate your penis by hand, using whatever fantasy most arouses you, until it is fully erect. (If you cannot get an erection in this way, simply repeat the procedure each day until it works.) Now stop the stimulation and let the erection subside completely. Switching your concentration to some non-sexual subject will hasten this.

2 When your penis is soft, begin to masturbate once more, and when you have a full erection, deliberately lose it again. Then stimulate yourself a third time and carry on until you ejaculate if you feel like it. If you find it difficult to regain an erection after deliberately losing it (or if you cannot get one at the beginning of the exercise) you will find that a lubricant will enhance the sensations considerably.

Repeat this exercise until you are confident that, in solitude at least, you can achieve an erection, lose it voluntarily, and regain it. Confidence should come after the third or fourth successful repetition of the full exercise.

You now need a cooperative partner, with whom you should read through the next stage of the program and discuss it. It is important for you both to realize that you have to be selfish, and put your own needs first, if the treatment is to be effective. Your partner must be prepared for some frustration because at this stage you cannot have full intercourse, even though you may both be highly excited. But you can, of course, give her an orgasm either manually or orally at the end of each session.

1 Do together the sensate-focusing exercises described in LEARNING TO SHARE PLEASURE, p.235. Simply relax and enjoy being caressed by your partner. Do not worry about whether or not you get an erection.

2 Now your partner tries to stimulate you manually to erection, but not to orgasm. A lubricant enhances the sensations, making it easier to gain an erection. It is best to do this step of the exercise at the time of day when you usually feel most responsive.

3 When you have achieved an erection, your partner stops, letting it die away completely, and then begins to stimulate you again. If she is willing to stimulate you orally, you will find this an infallible way of regaining an erection (or of gaining one at the beginning of the exercise if it proves difficult). This step will reassure you that although an erection is lost it can be regained at will. Once you are confident that you can gain, lose, and regain an erection in your partner's presence, have her bring you to orgasm.

Practise these exercises three or four times a week for three or four weeks before you progress to the next stage, below, in which you will learn to relax while in your partner's vagina.

1 Sitting astride you, but without attempting penetration, your partner caresses your penis until you have a full erection.

2 Your partner now guides your penis into her vagina. Concentrate on how this feels for a few moments, and then ask her to move gently. You can thrust if you like, but if you feel you are reaching orgasm, ask her to withdraw from you. Do not ejaculate inside her at this stage. If you lose your erection through anxiety, do not attempt full penetration next time you do the exercise, but just rub your penis between your partner's vaginal lips instead.

3 When you feel comfortable about vaginal containment, thrust more vigorously, setting a pace that feels right for you. Your partner can increase

◁ Producing an erection

Having adopted an astride position that is comfortable for both of you, your partner should then caress your penis until it is fully erect.

▽ Enjoying vaginal containment

When your partner has guided your penis into her, concentrate on the feeling of being contained before beginning to thrust.

▽ Caressing the testes

As you develop a rhythm of thrusting, your partner can increase your excitement by reaching down and fondling your testes.

your arousal by stroking your testes or by using her vaginal muscles to squeeze your penis and, if necessary, you can withdraw so that she can stimulate you manually. You can ejaculate inside her if you like, but withdraw if you feel at all anxious.

4 If you find it hard to ejaculate with your partner on top, adopt a man-on-top position at your next session. As your confidence grows, experiment with new positions and more vigorous thrusting. But always slow down and simply enjoy being contained if you feel you are losing your erection.

Assessing your progress

Provided you take the program one step at a time, without feeling you must hurry on to the next stage before you are ready, your sexual performance should become far more reliable within a few months. There may still be times – in a new sexual relationship, for example – when you will feel anxious. But you will have no reason to think of yourself as even slightly 'impotent'. To prevent a real problem from developing again, however, follow the guidelines suggested in **Preventing erection failure**, p.243, in all future sexual encounters.

DELAYING EJACULATION

Ejaculation is a reflex muscular contraction and there comes a point in a man's sexual arousal when it is inevitable. Many men worry because they feel that they reach this point too soon. They often imagine that they and their partner would enjoy intercourse much more, and it would be much easier for the woman to reach orgasm, if they could only hold off ejaculation for just a few minutes longer than normal.

There is, however, no absolute criterion for how long you should last. It is possible that you have unrealistic expectations, so, before deciding you have a 'problem' needing treatment by the 'stop-start' or 'squeeze' techniques described below, try the following approach.

Learning to last longer

Make sure your partner is fully aroused before you start to have intercourse. Foreplay should last 20 minutes at least, so that even if intercourse is brief, lovemaking is not. When you do start to have intercourse, try at first making movements less stimulating than thrusting; a circular movement of the hips to move the penis in the vagina, for example. An even simpler method is to wait 15-30 minutes after you have ejaculated and then, if you can regain an erection, have intercourse again. This time the edge will be off your arousal, so you will probably be able to last longer. This method is especially effective if you are young and sexually inexperienced (as you grow older you will automatically develop a degree of control). Some beginners find that increasing the frequency of masturbation also reduces their sexual tension and enables them to delay ejaculation during intercourse.

However, there are a few men who suffer from a 'hair-trigger' problem: some can manage to thrust a little but still feel they have virtually no control over when they reach a climax, while others ejaculate before they even touch their partner. If you fit into either of these categories, the exercises described here will probably be very successful in helping you to develop greater control.

THE STOP-START TECHNIQUE

The following series of exercises, which was originally developed by Dr James Semans, is aimed at teaching you how to hold your level of arousal just below the point at which ejaculation is inevitable. You do this by gradually learning to recognize the physical sensations leading up to your climax and by modifying accordingly the movements you make during intercourse. Semans discovered that the stop-start technique is of enormous assistance to many of the large number of men who ejaculate so quickly that sex tends to prove disappointing to both themselves and their partners.

Most men who practise these exercises gain good control in 2-10 weeks. You may find, however, that a somewhat different approach, using the 'squeeze' technique developed by Masters and Johnson (see p.249) is more effective for you. In either case you will need the cooperation of a sympathetic partner. Single men, whether heterosexual or homosexual, will find they can gain a good measure of control by practising just the first three steps of the stop-start method. These involve only manual stimulation and do not require the assistance of another person.

1 Masturbate with a dry hand, focusing your attention only on the pleasurable sensations you experience in your penis, not on the sexual fantasies normally associated with masturbation. When you feel you are about to ejaculate, stop and relax. Start again when you no longer feel close to orgasm. Repeat the stop-start procedure, making a conscious effort to stave off an ejaculation, for fully 15 minutes. You may not succeed at first, but continue this preliminary exercise until you have had three consecutive 15-minute sessions without premature ejaculation. The first few times you do the exercise, you will probably have to stop and start quite often, but you will gradually learn to read your body signals more accurately and will need to pause less frequently.

2 The next step is to do the same exercise using a lubricant such as KY jelly. Because this produces much more intense sensations, the timing of your orgasm will be more difficult to control. Again your goal should be to delay ejaculation during three consecutive 15-minute sessions.

△ **Heightening the sensations**
When you have gained ejaculatory control during masturbation with a dry hand, try to delay orgasm while using a lubricant, which intensifies the sensations. Your excitement will be greater but the stop-start routine will make it possible.

3 You have now developed enough control to try to keep down your arousal without stopping stroking your penis. Masturbate with a dry hand, but whenever you become very excited alter the strokes so that the excitement is eased. To do this, you can either slow down the tempo, use a different type of stroke or degree of pressure, or concentrate on less sensitive areas of the penis. Do not stop altogether, as you did in steps 1 and 2. Experiment in order to find out which method works best for you. The aim is to last 15 minutes – at this stage without stopping – for three consecutive sessions.

4 At this point your partner becomes involved. First, explain to her the procedure you have gone through.

Then stimulate your penis with a dry hand while you lie back with your eyes closed and concentrate, as you did in the first step of the exercises, on the sensations. As soon as you feel ejaculation is imminent, ask her to stop for a few moments to let the arousal subside. As before, try to last for 15 minutes before ejaculating and take the next step only after three successful sessions.

5 Repeat step 4, but this time with a lubricant. You will find this extremely exciting. Just enjoy the feelings of mounting excitement and let nothing distract you. If you feel close to orgasm too soon, however, ask your partner to stop until the excitement dies down.

△ Woman on top
With your partner uppermost, it will probably be easier to keep your excitement within bounds than if you are on top. Once again, your aim should be to hold off ejaculation for fifteen minutes on three consecutive occasions.

▽ Adopting a range of positions
It is best to gain control in a variety of positions before trying the man-on-top position, which tends to present the greatest difficulty for men with premature ejaculation problems.

6 Three consecutive successes in step 5 indicate that you now have enough control to try the stop-start technique during intercourse. The best position at first is with your partner lying comfortably on top of you (see SEXUAL POSITIONS, p.211). When your penis has been inserted, put your hands on her hips to guide her and ask her to move gently up and down. Stop her as soon as you feel you are about to ejaculate, and start again when the urge has gone. Do not thrust; just feel the movement and concentrate on the sensations. Try to last 15 minutes before thrusting and ejaculating. Repeat this type of relaxed intercourse three or four times, permitting yourself each time to thrust more often and more actively, but always stopping if you approach orgasm before the end of 15 minutes. If you ejaculate too soon do not regard this as the end of the exercise: simply relax for at least 15 minutes and then begin intercourse once again.

7 Practice intercourse in different positions such as side-by-side or rear-entry before you finally move to the man-on-top position, which is the one in which delaying ejaculation is most difficult.

Assessing your progress

If, after practising the stop-start exercises for at least five weeks, your control is no better, try changing to the squeeze technique described below. Some men find this exercise more effective, but problems sometimes arise because it can seem boring, or because your partner feels frustrated or neglected. However, it is essential for you to concentrate on your own feelings during this period. And because it is an exercise that usually produces good results, the eventual improvement in your sex life should make temporary boredom worth enduring. Your partner need not be frustrated at the end of the session, since after ejaculation you can bring her to orgasm, manually or orally. (see STIMULATION TECHNIQUES, p.206).

It is possible, if it worries you unduly to have to rely on your partner's help during these exercises, that you feel insecure, either about yourself or your relationship. It will help to talk things over with her, but if doing this has always proved difficult for you, you should turn to LEARNING TO COMMUNICATE, p.270, which suggests ways of making it easier to discuss sex.

THE SQUEEZE TECHNIQUE

This is a somewhat more complex technique than the stop-start method for treating premature ejaculation. It requires your partner to squeeze your penis in a way that inhibits ejaculation when you feel it is imminent. Let her grip it firmly, using two fingers and the thumb of one hand. Her thumb should be placed on the frenulum, which is the area on the underside of the penis where the head and the shaft meet. Her first finger should be opposite the thumb and the others around the shaft. She should apply fairly firm pressure, without moving her fingers, since too light a touch can arouse you instead of inhibiting ejaculation.

1 Your partner masturbates you as in steps 4 (dry hand) and 5 (with lubrication) of the stop-start technique. But instead of removing her hand when you signal to her that you are about to ejaculate, she squeezes your penis for 15-20 seconds, which causes your erection to subside. She then begins to stimulate you again. Repeat the procedure two to three times before allowing ejaculation to occur.

2 When you have gained a degree of control in this way, you are ready for intercourse; but of a particular kind. Your partner sits astride you and guides your erect penis into her vagina, where it remains with neither of you moving until you warn her (in good time) that you are near orgasm. She immediately lifts herself gently away and applies the squeeze grip. Repeat the exercise two or three times before you let yourself climax.

3 When you are quite sure that your control has improved (this will probably be after you have practised step 2 three or four times) you should try gentle movement during intercourse. Using the same woman-on-top position, begin to thrust a little, and encourage your partner to move her hips slightly. But she should be prepared to withdraw and squeeze whenever you give her the signal. Within a few weeks you should be able to maintain this pause-and-squeeze kind of intercourse for 15-20 minutes without ejaculating.

4 Now attempt intercourse in other positions. You may find that control remains difficult in the traditional male-on-top position. But if you practise step 1 of the squeeze technique at least once a week for the next three months, you should, by the end of that period, have gained ejaculatory control that will be useful in all types of sexual activity.

The squeeze ▷
By squeezing the penis just below the head for 15-20 seconds, your partner inhibits your urge to ejaculate and causes your erection to subside temporarily. Repeat this procedure two or three times before ejaculating.

PRESSURE

PRESSURE

◁ **Applying the squeeze during intercourse**
When some control has been gained over ejaculation outside the vagina, you should try the squeeze technique during intercourse. At your signal that ejaculation is near, your partner should immediately raise herself off your penis and grasp it firmly.

SPEEDING EJACULATION

Most men have a degree of control over when they ejaculate. They learn, through practice, how to hold their excitement below the critical level at which orgasm occurs, delaying it until they feel completely ready to let go and climax.

The problem of overcontrol

However, a few men tend to have too much control. Although they feel sexually aroused and have firm erections, they cannot 'let go', so that the normal ejaculatory reflex is inhibited. Sometimes there is a physical basis for the problem: a few drugs inhibit ejaculation (see **The sexual side-effects of drugs**, p.309) and, similarly, some medical and surgical conditions (see SEX AND HEALTH, p.307). Therefore, it is a good idea to see your doctor and tell him about the problem if it is one that has developed only recently.

As you grow older, you will probably find that you need longer and stronger stimulation before you ejaculate, and you may not reach a climax every time you have sex. This is not a problem, rather a boon for your partner, since the ability to last longer is one of the advantages of middle and later life. However, you may need to make some mental adjustments if you are to accept the fact that intercourse will not always end in ejaculation.

True ejaculatory overcontrol may be so severe that the man cannot ejaculate at all, even when he masturbates. But this is a rare problem and one which will almost certainly need the help of a professional sex therapist. If overcontrol seems to be your problem, the chances are that you have it to a much milder degree: perhaps you can ejaculate if your partner stimulates you by hand, but you cannot climax in her vagina, for example.

TREATMENT PROGRAM FOR SPEEDING EJACULATION

The aim of the exercises that follow is to give you intense physical stimulation with progressively closer contact with your partner, but at the same time to distract you so that you cannot easily hold back and exercise too much control over ejaculation. Practise each step of the treatment as often as is necessary to gain complete confidence, and at every stage use fantasy or the memory of past sexual pleasure to increase your excitement.

You may find the first two or three steps of the program easy, but work through them all quickly until you reach your 'sticking point'. Your partner's help will be an essential part of the treatment, so it is important for her to read through the exercises with you beforehand so that she understands what she has to do.

1 The first step is to ejaculate comfortably in your partner's presence. Sit close together but with your backs to each other. Masturbate until you ejaculate, using KY jelly or another lubricant. Repeat this step several times until you feel at ease doing it.

2 Now involve your partner. Hold her against you as you masturbate. Practise as often as you need to until you can ejaculate easily while she watches you.

3 Your partner now helps you ejaculate, using manual or – if you both prefer – oral stimulation. Guide her hand to show her the kind of vigorous stimulation you need as she will probably be too gentle. She should use plenty of lubricant.

4 At your next session, start to learn to ejaculate progressively closer to your partner's vagina, though not yet inside. She should try to use less vigorous stimulation now, to prepare you for the gentler sensations of vaginal containment.

5 When you are confident you can ejaculate with your partner stimulating you, you are ready to progress to intercourse with ejaculation. Your partner stimulates you until you are close to ejaculation and then you enter her, adopting a position in which she can reach your penis and continue to stimulate it with her hand as you thrust. Ask her to stop when your orgasm is imminent so that you ejaculate through thrusting alone.

6 The final step is to climax through intercourse alone, without additional manual stimulation. However, your partner should stimulate you by hand first, so that you are highly aroused before you

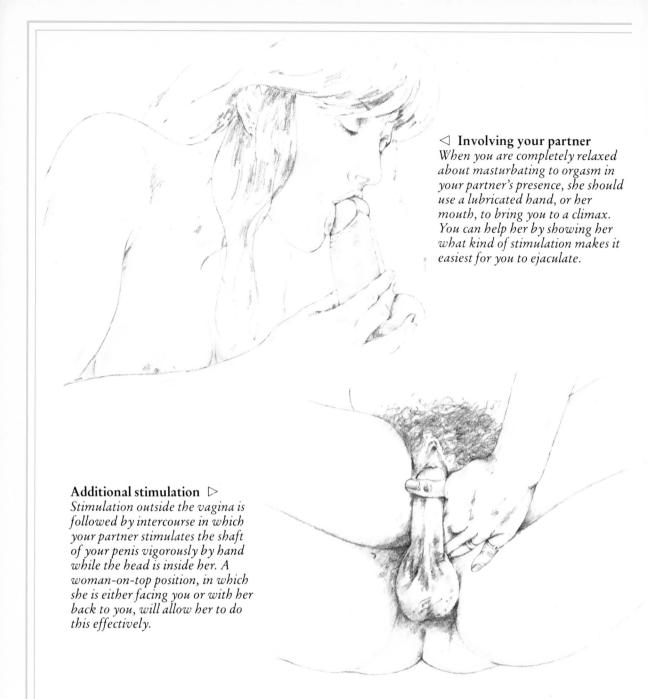

◁ Involving your partner
When you are completely relaxed about masturbating to orgasm in your partner's presence, she should use a lubricated hand, or her mouth, to bring you to a climax. You can help her by showing her what kind of stimulation makes it easiest for you to ejaculate.

Additional stimulation ▷
Stimulation outside the vagina is followed by intercourse in which your partner stimulates the shaft of your penis vigorously by hand while the head is inside her. A woman-on-top position, in which she is either facing you or with her back to you, will allow her to do this effectively.

enter her. A man-on-top position in which her legs are closed is particularly effective because it increases the friction on the penis.

Assessing your progress

If you find that you 'block' at any stage of this program so that further progress seems impossible, it is probable that for some reason you are 'holding back' mentally as well as physically from your partner. The most common reason for this is a fear of close involvement with women, although there may be a particular conflict in your relationship which needs to be resolved before self-help therapy can be effective. Also, see OVERCOMING THE FEAR OF INTIMACY, p.226, and the problem charts in the fifth part, THE SINGLE MAN, which examine some of the difficulties involved in forming and sustaining relationships.

COMING TO TERMS WITH HOMOSEXUALITY

Life for the sexual minorities has always been difficult, as it has for most minorities. Homosexual men may find that the life they lead is at odds with the life their family and friends believe they are leading. They may want to 'come out', though they are apprehensive about other people's reactions. They may find it hard to accept the fact of their own sexual orientation, or even wish they could modify their sexual preferences to conform with other people's expectations.

Many of the problems gays have arise from the social discrimination, based on prejudice, against them. Sadly, the public's present awareness of the dangers of AIDS, often coupled with a lack of factual knowledge about the disease, has meant that gays are facing yet another rising tide of intolerance. They also have to deal with their own fears about the disease (see **Testing for AIDS**, p.311), and perhaps modify their sex lives to minimize the risks they run with regard to the virus.

Making the choice

The heterosexual male seldom questions his sexual preferences and he is fortunate in that his inclinations fit in with what is expected of him. But if you suspect that your sexual preference is for other men, you are likely to question your own feelings, or sometimes even to go through the motions of a normal heterosexual life, before you can accept that preference. The questionnaire ORIENTATION, p.174, should help you decide where your true inclinations lie, but if you still find it hard to decide, consider the following points:

☐ If you are under 21, do not assume, because you have had some homosexual feelings or experiences, that these have necessarily set the pattern for your adult life. Most men have homosexual encounters at some time in their lives, usually in adolescence. As you have more opportunity to meet women and gain more confidence with them you will probably find that you grow more attracted to them.

☐ You may need to try out a variety of relationships with people of both sexes to discover what suits you best. Do not let yourself be pressured by either gay or straight friends into committing yourself one way or the other until you are really sure about what you really want.

☐ What matters most in deciding on your sexual preference is what arouses you. If you have no sexual interest at all in women, or if you have a strong aversion to heterosexual activity, the situation will not change. However intellectually appealing, however much simpler a heterosexual life might seem, you will do better to accept your homosexual orientation.

☐ If you continue to be troubled by uncertainty about your inclinations, or if you have difficulty in accepting the fact that you are gay, ask your doctor to refer you to a counselor or clinical psychologist.

If there is a quite definite heterosexual element in your make-up (your rating for ORIENTATION will be C-E) you may be able, if you wish, to strengthen the heterosexual side of your personality (see p.254). A homosexual life is not an easy one, and about 20 per cent of gay men marry in an attempt to conceal their true orientation, to deny it to themselves, or to rid themselves of their homosexual impulses. But such relationships are usually troubled and short-lived unless they are based on a core of genuine heterosexual feeling. If women do not arouse you at all, your best policy is to try to accept the fact and adopt a homosexual way of life rather than make yourself and a woman unhappy.

The problems of being gay

If you are homosexual you will encounter the same sexual problems (erection difficulties or premature ejaculation, for example) as other men, but there are a few which are of special concern to gay men. Foremost among these are the social problems of deciding whether, and to what extent, to 'come out'. Probably more than half of all homosexuals decide to tell their families, though no more than a third tell their employers, fellow-workers or friends.

Coming out can obviously make life easier in that there is no longer a need for secrecy or concealment, and yet more difficult in that it may restrict your job options and incur the disapproval of family or friends. This is a decision only you can make, but the chances are that if you do decide to tell the people who matter most to you, they will understand and you will feel, eventually, much more at ease both with yourself and them.

Whether or not you decide to come out completely, you will find it very helpful to have the support of a gay organization through which you can meet homosexual friends. (See RESOURCE GUIDE, p.312). Once you have adopted a homosexual lifestyle, you may feel less need to conceal it from those close to you. Even so, you do not have to make any statements about it if you do not want to.

Sexually transmitted diseases

If you are homosexual you are more likely to catch a sexually transmitted disease (STD) and, in particular, your chances of contracting AIDS (Acquired Immune Deficiency Syndrome) are higher than those of heterosexual men (see SEXUALLY TRANS-MITTED DISEASES, p.309). Single homosexual men are not necessarily more promiscuous than single heterosexual men, but the homosexual lifestyle usually provides partners more readily and so there is a greater risk of infection. The straight male's sexual ambitions are curtailed to some extent by the more monogamous attitude of women. Because of the danger of AIDS and other STDs, many gay men are reducing the number of their sexual partners, and opting for 'safer sex' activities (see **Guidelines for safer sex**, p.310).

The search for a stable relationship

The happiest homosexuals are the ones who have a steady partner and draw most of their emotional and sexual satisfaction from that person. The evidence suggests that gay men are just as dependent for their happiness as heterosexuals on having a close, loving and stable relationship.

Unfortunately, though, homosexual affairs tend to be more numerous, casual, and fleeting than heterosexual ones. Because men usually understand each other's need for sexual variety, such opportunistic liaisons seldom break up a good relationship. But the more casual partners a man has, the more chance there is that one such meeting may develop into a serious relationship. When this happens, the stability of the homosexual couple is just as vulnerable as that of a heterosexual pair.

How to safeguard your relationship

Many gay men do manage, in spite of the difficulties, to make strong and lasting commitments to each other, and, being of the same sex, they are often more companionable and sympathetic to each other's needs and interests than many mixed-sex couples. What can *you* do if you want to increase your chances of a lasting relationship? Here are some tips:

☐ Choose your partner for the right reasons, so that you have more in common than just sex. The advice that is given in MAKING A LASTING RELATIONSHIP, p.300, applies to anyone, whatever their sexual orientation, who is looking for security.

☐ Decide how 'open' you want your relationship to be. However much freedom you intend to give each other, in practice it will work better if you establish certain rules. For example, you may feel more able to take a partner's infidelity if he tells you exactly what is going on, or on the other hand, you may prefer to know absolutely nothing about it. You may agree that there will be no sex with friends and that you will never give your telephone number to casual partners. You may also promise that you will not abandon the other at a party so that he has to come home alone or that, whatever happens, you will always spend the night together.

☐ Stay away from the unattached gay scene as much as you can. Spend your leisure time together and base your social life as much as possible on home and mutual friends, gay or straight.

☐ Remember that the quality of a relationship does not depend on the gender of the people involved. If your relationship is not bringing you much happiness, turn to COMPATIBILITY, p.260. This questionnaire may be used, with appropriate modification, by any gay couple who want to analyze the reasons for their dissatisfaction.

☐ Try to feel positive about your homosexuality. If you see it as wrong, you will find it hard to make good relationships and, at worst, you may tend to sabotage them because you believe you do not deserve to be happy.

Strengthening your heterosexual side

You may, however, want to develop the heterosexual side of your personality but feel that it is impossible to make a successful straight relationship unless you overcome your homosexual feelings altogether. This is not necessarily true, and anyway it is unlikely that your gay inclinations will vanish altogether. But you may be able to make them less important to you. If you can do this, there is no reason why they should threaten a heterosexual relationship. It may help you to consider that while a completely heterosexual man is likely to occasionally fancy women other than his partner, he does not necessarily act on his desires. The following advice will also help you reinforce your heterosexual inclinations.

☐ Masturbate using heterosexual fantasies to heighten your responsiveness to women. At first you may need to keep yourself at a distance in your fantasy, perhaps by simply being an onlooker – imagining another man making love to a woman, for example. You may find yourself concentrating on the man at first, but gradually shape the fantasy so that you pay more attention to the woman, until finally you yourself are playing the male role in your imagination. Monitor your reaction to your fantasies. They should show you what most easily arouses you, and they may help you to focus on any specific

fears you have about heterosexuality – anxiety about being rejected, for example, or an aversion that you have to female genitals. You may find **Sexual phobias**, p.183, helpful if you have the latter problem.

☐ If you have difficulty becoming aroused in your first sexual encounters with women, fantasize about men for the time being.

☐ When you start to (re)discover heterosexual relationships, do not be discouraged if you have some failures. It is important not to give up or to imagine that if you do not succeed immediately you have set yourself an impossible target. Give yourself time and remember that if you do not manage to strengthen your heterosexual side so much that you could fully commit yourself to a woman, you still have your homosexual feelings on which to base relationships. You are therefore losing nothing.

△ **Finding a steady partner**
Sensation-seekers have fostered the erroneous notion that all gay men are promiscuous. In fact, most gay men develop steady relationships after passing through a period of sexual experimentation, just as heterosexual males do.

ORIENTATION PROBLEMS

Most men have a strong sense of their own maleness, and find it easy to conform to the stereotype of masculinity. But this view of the male as the active, aggressive, dominant partner in any relationship is falling out of favor with both men and women. For both sexes there is great satisfaction in a merging of sexual roles so that however confident they are in their own masculinity, men are free to develop the 'feminine' qualities of caring and tenderness rather than cling to a restrictive 'macho' image.

Gender conflicts

A few men have problems because they lack an innate sense of being male. This makes it difficult for them to play a masculine role. There is a conflict between their 'core' gender – the sex they feel themselves to be – and their evident maleness. They may feel real only when they dress or behave as women.

Transvestism

The practice of dressing as a member of the opposite sex is known as transvestism. It is probably not rare but, because of the secrecy it involves, there can be no authoritative estimate of the number of men who practise it. Some men, known as fetishistic transvestites, cross-dress because they find wearing women's clothes sexually arousing. It may provide the special stimulation they need or it may be an end in itself, providing sexual satisfaction whether or not a partner is involved.

In many cases, though, the transvestite cross-dresses simply because he feels more at ease, more wholly himself, when dressed as a woman. It may be that he cross-dresses only in the privacy of his own home. Alternatively, he may try to pass as a woman in public, and, if so, much of his satisfaction will come from the success with which he does this. Often a transvestite can maintain a double life, with distinct male and female personalities, for years. But occasionally a transvestite's desire to play a female role becomes so intense that he decides he wants to *be* a woman rather than simply dress as one (see **Transsexualism**, opposite).

Homosexual transvestism

Most transvestites are heterosexual and about three quarters marry and have children. A small group of homosexuals, however, are effeminate in appearance and behavior and may cross-dress to reinforce these traits. But while the true transvestite will go to a great deal of trouble to look as much like a real woman as possible, the homosexual 'queen' will go over the top in his impersonation, creating a caricature rather than a realistic image of womanhood.

Coming to terms with transvestism

Very few male transvestites see their desire to cross-dress as an 'illness' or seek medical treatment unless there is marital or family pressure on them to do so. There is, in any case, no specific treatment to 'cure' the condition (though if you are determined that this is what you want, some kinds of behavior therapy may help, especially with fetishistic transvestism). But, as a general rule, if you consult a doctor you will be offered help with specific problems such as the effect on your marriage.

Marriage and transvestism

Many women can accept their partner's need to cross-dress, especially if it is occasional and discreet. But the more determined you are to develop and enhance your feminine side, the more strain you are likely to put on your relationship. If you value your partner, you will try to make cross-dressing a less important part of your life.

If you have not yet established what you hope will be a long-lasting relationship, but want to do so, you should think about the impact your cross-dressing is likely to have on your life with a partner. The following course of action is recommended once you have decided to confront the problem. Tell your partner about your cross-dressing before you are both fully committed to the relationship. If you do not tell her in advance she will feel even more cheated if she discovers at a later date and will then find it much harder to accept, having become used to you as a 'normal' male.

If your partner can accept what you have told her, try to agree on limits to your future cross-dressing, and you may in time be able to reduce the habit still further. Alternatively, your partner may feel able to cope provided she is not involved and you keep that part of your life separate. Or you may agree to cross-dress at home but never in public or in company. If you are very fortunate, your partner may be prepared to give you advice on clothes and make-up and let you play the feminine role at least some of the time.

Most countries have organizations (see RE-SOURCE GUIDE, p.312) which not only give support and counseling to transvestites, but provide opportunities for them to meet others and cross-dress in company without running the risks involved in doing so in public.

Transsexualism

For a very small number of men cross-dressing is not enough. This kind of man does not simply want to look and act like a woman, but to *be* one. The transsexual, as he is known, is convinced, despite possessing male genitals, that he is in fact a woman. Sometimes he will manage to lead a reasonably contented double life, but often he will seek surgery to become as nearly female as possible. Unlike transvestites, transsexuals seldom marry.

Treatment for the transsexual

The ultimate goal for the transsexual man is a sex-change operation. However, when he first consults a doctor, the latter will almost certainly suggest other solutions before allowing him to undergo irreversible surgery. He may recommend that his patient tries to carry on living the dual-life of the transvestite, for example. Or, if he has a male partner already, in anticipation of a sex change, the patient may be advised to test whether both he and his partner can accept and feel as comfortable with this kind of relationship as with a homosexual one.

Preparing for a sex change

If you feel strongly that a sex change is the only answer for you, you will be expected to spend at least 18 months living and supporting yourself as a woman before surgery is considered. You are likely to meet many problems that cannot be solved by surgery and this period will give you a chance to decide whether you will be able to cope with them. Meanwhile,

practical steps will be suggested to prepare the ground and make it easier for you to pass as a woman. It is possible that you may find that these are enough and that you will put aside the idea of surgery. If you should wish to develop the feminine side of your personality prior to making a decision about surgery, you might find the following advice useful.

☐ Avoid the temptation to be over-feminine in your dress and make-up. Padding and corseting, for example, may produce a figure that seems feminine to you, but will look like a caricature to others. You will do better to be more unobtrusive. Remember too that by day most women dress casually and wear little make-up. The sort of effect you may be striving for would probably look out of place except on a film set.

☐ Hormonal treatment may be given, but it will not work miracles. It will make your hips and thighs more feminine and rounded, your face fuller, and your skin softer. But it will not enlarge the breasts very much, or alter your voice or the male pattern of hair distribution on the face and body.

☐ Electrolysis will remove facial hair permanently, but it takes very many treatments over a period of about five years.

☐ Training with a therapist will help you learn the social skills involved in being a woman.

Sex-change operations

In a male-to-female sex change, a vagina is modeled from the skin of the penis and scrotum. Complications are quite common, but if the operation is successful the subject is able to have intercourse as a woman, and may enjoy pleasurable sensations and even orgasm. A sex-change operation does not, of course, enable the recipient to have children, nor to be legally married as a woman.

BISEXUALITY

Gay men sometimes develop heterosexual relationships at the same time as having homosexual ones, and some marry. A substantial number of straight men have homosexual experiences in adolescence, particularly if living in an all-male environment, and a few have similar encounters when their marriage is under stress or their partner is pregnant. But there are very few men who are always equally responsive to either sex and can, or would care to, be described as bisexual. A true bisexual may be tempted to present his more acceptable heterosexual side in the face of society's disapproval. He also has to contend with the viewpoint of many homosexuals that bisexuality is a refusal to choose.

4

THE MAN WITH A STEADY PARTNER

Being part of a couple implies emotional commitment as well as sexual attachment and most couples prefer their relationship to be sexually exclusive. Monogamy is still the ideal most people strive for, even if it is not always achieved, and they expect of it both emotional security and physical satisfaction. Many of the problems you will face as a couple and which are discussed in this part of the book will arise simply because you have made this commitment to each other. They seem to be the most inescapable facts of a shared life. Few long-term partners will not experience, at some time or other, the overfamiliarity that can lead to boredom, or at least to a sexual wistfulness. Many will experience jealousy, or have to deal with the threat of infidelity.

The final section of this part of the book deals with contraception, with the problems of the couple who want to have a child but have so far been unable to, and offers guidance to the man whose partner is pregnant or has recently given birth.

COMPATIBILITY

Being compatible as a couple means being able to live together in a pleasurable and satisfying way. This is possible when your personalities and viewpoints are reasonably similar or complement each other so well that there is seldom serious conflict between you. The qualities that make for compatibility in a relationship are discussed more fully in MAKING A LASTING RELATIONSHIP, p.300.

Yet it is quite possible to live together happily even though you may not seem, in theory, altogether compatible. Indeed no couple who live together for any length of time will see eye to eye on every issue, or always have the same needs at the same time. As important and valuable as compatibility of temperament is being able to deal with issues as they arise and to resolve them by making the necessary shifts of attitude before the whole relationship is jeopardized.

If you can do this, it will benefit your sex life as well as your overall happiness. The couple who get along well in other ways and who are loving and committed to each other will not normally allow sexual differences or difficulties to sour their whole relationship. Sex therapists have found, too, that while most sexual problems can be resolved successfully if a couple's general relationship is close and loving, therapy is less likely to succeed if there is hostility between the people involved.

Certain areas of a shared life are especially vital to the wellbeing of a relationship, while others are abundant sources of discontent. The questionnaire that follows explores these crucial areas, allowing you to see how well you have adjusted to each other's needs. You can answer on your own, but it is better to both do it, each keeping your own score.

HOW WELL DO YOU SUIT EACH OTHER?

1 How much of your leisure time do you spend with your partner?

Most	2
Some	1
Little or none	0

2 How many of your friends are mutual friends whose company you both enjoy?

Few or none	0
Most	2
Some	1

3 If your partner wants to spend a quiet evening at home together do you usually:

Welcome and enjoy it?	2
Not mind?	1
Feel bored?	0

4 If you have dinner in a restaurant with just your partner do you find:

It is a good opportunity to talk?	2
You have got very little to say to each other?	0
It is quite pleasant but not stimulating?	1

5 If your work (or your partner's) began to limit your time together would you:

Try to alter your timetable?	2
Decide there was little you could do?	1
Welcome it?	0

6 Of your three main interests how many does your partner share?

One or two	1
All three	2
None	0

7 How often do you vacation together?

Always	2
Usually	1
Rarely	0

8 If your partner is clearly worried about something, does she usually:

Refuse to talk about it?	0
Discuss it with you?	2
Talk about it if you press her?	1

9 When you talk about what you have been doing, thinking, or feeling, how often does your partner seem interested?

Sometimes	1
Always	2
Seldom	0

10 Do disagreements with your partner most often lead to:

Discussion?	2
A spirited argument?	1
Serious or prolonged hostility?	0

11 How often do you quarrel fiercely over trivial issues?

Often	0
Seldom or never	2
Occasionally	1

12 Are you ever concerned because your partner is much more of a spendthrift (or more careful with money) than you are?

Never	2
Sometimes	1
Continually	0

13 If an expensive item is needed for use by both of you (a car or furniture, for example) how often do you have what you consider a fair say in choosing it?

Sometimes	1
Always	2
Seldom or never	0

14 Do you feel you have less say than you would like in deciding how unallocated money is spent?

No, I am happy with the situation	2
Yes, I would like more say	1
What I would like is seldom considered	0

15 Do you agree with your partner on domestic expenditure?

Not at all	0
Completely	2
The situation could be better	1

16 Do you ever feel lonely or resentful because your partner seems to have a greater need for solitude than you do?

Seldom or never	2
Sometimes	1
Often	0

17 Does your partner 'crowd' you so that you have little or no time for yourself?

Most of the time	0
Seldom or never	2
Sometimes	1

18 Would you like to spend more time doing things without your partner?

Not at all	2
A little more	1
Much more	0

19 How often do problems arise because your partner resents you seeing other people or doing things without her?

Occasionally	1
Seldom or never	2
Often	0

20 How often does jealousy cause problems between you?

Seldom or never	2
Occasionally	1
Often	0

21 Do you feel that your partner's parents loom too large in your life, that you spend too much time with them, or that her views about things that only concern the two of you are too much influenced by theirs?

Not at all	2
A little	1
Very much	0

22 Do you wish that your partner's approach to work was:

More ambitious?	0
Less ambitious?	0
Neither	2

23 Does your job ever disrupt your time together?

Seldom	2
Often	0
Sometimes	1

24 Does your partner's job ever disrupt your time together?

Sometimes	1
Often	0
Seldom	2

25 Do you and your partner agree about a woman's right to work if she wants to?

Completely	2
With reservations	1
Not at all	0

26 If you have no children, do you and your partner agree about whether or when to start a family?

With reservations	1
Not at all	0
Completely	2

27 If you have children, do you feel that your partner's attitude toward their rearing is:

About right?	2
Too strict?	0
Too easygoing?	0

28 Have you ever seriously considered ending your relationship?

Often	0
Never	2
Once or twice	1

RATING

High rating (36-56)

This suggests that you are content in your relationship, and that it meets most, if not all, of your emotional needs. You probably feel you have room to grow within it too, even though it gives you the support and security you currently need.

Medium rating (25-35)

This indicates that you probably get on well enough for your relationship to have a good chance of permanence. However, if you scored low in a particular group of questions, consult the detailed analysis of the questions, below.

Low rating (0-24)

This suggests that dissatisfaction with your day-to-day life is likely to spill over into your sex life. Couples who argue a lot tend to have a less active and less satisfying sex life. Look through your answers to discover where the major difficulties lie. Does your partner score low on the same questions? If so, you probably both need to make adjustments in those areas. If there is a discrepancy between your scores, it may be that one partner is making *all* the adjustments. In this case the low-scoring partner may need to be a little more assertive if you are to achieve a more balanced and satisfying relationship.

ANALYSIS OF THE QUESTIONS

Questions 1-7 deal with companionship.
Companionship is one of the most important things you can give each other. A 1983 survey of American couples indicated that couples who spend little of their time together are less satisfied and therefore more liable to break up than more companionable couples.

You are more likely to be happy and to develop a more intimate relationship if you have mutual friends and interests. If you spend too much time away from each other you risk loosening the bonds of intimacy. The main danger for the couple who spend little of their free time together is that they may come to find that most of the time they do spend together is concerned largely with resolving domestic problems, particularly those involving money. Since these are certainly the least appealing aspects of a shared life, their relationship will grow less and less rewarding and there may seem to be little reason to make strenuous efforts to sustain it.

Companionship seems to be an area in which the homosexual couple often scores over the heterosexual. Gay couples are more likely to have interests and leisure activities in common than are heterosexual couples. It is usually worthwhile for the heterosexual couple to seek activities that interest them both and to make an attempt to enjoy more leisure time together.

Questions 8-11 deal with communication.

For many couples, problems arise simply because they do not talk to each other enough, or because they talk without actually communicating much, keeping each other at an emotional distance so that real feelings are seldom shared and misunderstandings inevitably occur. Some people expect from their partner an almost telepathic ability to communicate, because the words they use bear little relation to the message they really want to convey. For example, complaints are directed at easy targets ('You never put the cat out when it's your turn') when the real source of dissatisfaction ('You're not as loving as I'd like you to be') is harder both to recognize and to put into words. If you often have quarrels about trivial things that grow out of all proportion, it usually indicates a much deeper dissatisfaction – about lack of love, or security, or companionship – which you must both confront.

For some couples, feelings of anger cause the most problems. Many people are afraid of showing anger because they feel it will inevitably bring the whole relationship down around their ears. There is at least some foundation for this fear since if you often get very angry it can be enormously destructive of your relationship. Marriage guidance counselors find that anger frequently heads the list of one partner's complaints about the other. However, things are little better if you do not show anger at all, because the problems that caused it may then never be acknowledged or resolved. The tension and resentment that build up within you can be equally destructive. The advice in **Dealing with anger**, p.271, will help you contain and defuse an angry situation before it can do too much damage.

Questions 12-15 concern money.

Most studies report that between one quarter and one third of all couples quarrel more about money than about anything else. It is not only lack of money that affects a couple's contentment (though it is important, and the less there is, the more fights there are likely to be about it) but also the questions of who should earn it and how it should be spent. Arguments about money are also arguments about trust, about commitment to the relationship, about interdependence or equality. So if money is what you tend to fight about, discover which of these issues are really at stake and deal with them.

Married couples usually pool their resources, often sharing a bank account, to show their trust in and commitment to each other. Couples who live together often try, at least to begin with, to maintain separate finances, which certainly gives them one less issue to quarrel about. By doing this they are also, perhaps unconsciously, ensuring that the ties between them will be easier to dissolve if necessary.

Sharing money shows faith in a future together, and indeed almost every couple, heterosexual or homosexual, who have been together for any length of time do this as their commitment grows and the financial strings of their lives become more entwined. But problems can arise if they have different attitudes toward money. If one partner is easy-come, easy-go, while the other is a prudent saver for a rainy day, for example, there may be difficulties; likewise if the partner who is the higher (or the only) earner feels he or she should exercise far greater or even total control over expenditure.

Questions 16-21 are about privacy and independence.

However close you are, you will probably feel the need for some privacy from your partner. This is a need that seems to be more pressing for women than for men. Couples who live together usually regard private time and personal space as more important than couples who marry, because they feel that independence within the relationship is essential. Every couple has to find the balance between independence and separateness that suits them best. Problems can occur if either partner has an excessive need for privacy or independence because this is likely to affect the time they spend together, which is one of the most important elements binding them. Even so, too much togetherness can be smothering. Life may be equally unsatisfactory for a couple if one partner is so dependent on the other for emotional support and company that he or she allows the other no breathing space.

Arguments about in-laws are often arguments about dependence, about whether a partner has really achieved the necessary emotional break with his or her parents and made a total commitment to the relationship. Such a partner may insist on living close to his or her parents, visiting them unreasonably often, taking their side in an argument against the other partner, and consulting them automatically on every important decision that affects the couple.

Questions 22-25 examine how your work affects the relationship.

Dissatisfaction here is often about the inroads one partner's job makes on the time you might otherwise spend together. But probably the most serious arguments arise in couples who have not agreed about a woman's right to work or about the extent of her commitment to her work. This problem is among those most likely to break up a relationship.

Ambition affects significantly the way you feel about each other. While women like their partners to be ambitious and successful, men – unless they are very confident and successful themselves – are usually less happy about having an ambitious partner.

Questions 26 and 27 concern your attitudes toward parenthood.

Most studies suggest that children are by no means indispensable to a couple's happiness, even that life together is more fulfilling for the childless couple. Where there are children, the most frequent disagreements in the sphere of parenthood concern, as might be expected, the basics of their rearing and the particularly difficult question of discipline. However, if you can genuinely develop, or at least present to the children, a united front on these issues, you will avoid a major source of potential conflict.

Question 28 concerns the fundamental stability of your relationship.

Nearly everybody feels like walking out on his or her partner at times. But if you have frequently taken this course of action, only to return, or even if you merely contemplate if often, then the relationship is clearly not working. Your reasons for planning a separation are almost certainly pinpointed by your answers to the rest of this questionnaire. Study the detailed analysis of the other questions.

Lasting compatibility ▷
The willingness to confront problems in a relationship and to be flexible about their resolution is indispensable to long-term compatibility.

ARE YOU SEXUALLY SATISFIED?

Sex is one of the strongest ties that can hold two people together, and it is a bond that you can foster and strengthen by making sure that your sex life is as satisfying as possible for both of you. The questionnaire below deals with some of the most important elements of sexual satisfaction, and it should provide a measure of your contentment with this aspect of your relationship. You can do the questionnaire alone, or better still, with your partner, keeping separate scores. The results will indicate your sexual compatibility and show whether there is a particularly problematic area.

DO YOU SATISFY EACH OTHER SEXUALLY?

1 Do you have sex:

As often as you want? — 2
Not often enough? — 0
Too often for your taste? — 0

2 Do you find your partner attractive?

Very — 2
Fairly — 1
Not very — 0

3 Who usually initiates sex?

The male partner — 1
The female partner — 0
Either partner — 2

4 Is the 'refusal rate' (when one partner suggests sex):

More or less equal? — 2
Very unequal? — 0

5 If your partner says no to sex, do you:

Feel rejected, hurt, or angry, and keep a mental note of it? — 0
Feel briefly irritated or disappointed? — 1
Accept that she or he is not in the mood? — 2

6 If you say no to sex, does your partner:

Get angry or upset? — 0
Seem briefly disappointed or annoyed? — 1
Understand that you are just not in the mood? — 2

7 Do you wish your partner was:

Less prudish or inhibited about sex? — 0
Less fond of sexual experimentation? — 0
Neither — 2

8 Do you get enough affection during sex?

Always — 2
Mostly — 1
Never — 0

9 Do you get affection outside of sex?

Always — 2
Never — 0
Mostly — 1

10 How often does your partner want you to try a sexual activity you dislike?

Seldom or never — 2
Sometimes — 1
Often — 0

11 Do you have erection problems (or does your partner have vaginal problems) that make sex difficult or impossible?

Seldom or never — 2
Sometimes — 1
Often — 0

12 Is sex unsatisfactory because you (or your partner) fail to reach orgasm:

Sometimes? — 1
Never? — 0
Seldom or never? — 2

13 How often is sex unsatisfactory for you because you (or your partner) reach orgasm too quickly?

Seldom or never ————————— 2
Sometimes ————————————— 1
Often ——————————————— 0

14 How often is sex unsatisfactory for you because your partner just does not seem interested?

Seldom or never ————————— 2
Sometimes ————————————— 1
Often ——————————————— 0

15 Has either of you had sex outside the relationship?

Within the last year ——————— 0
Since the relationship began ———— 1
Never ——————————————— 2

16 Is sex with your partner as varied as you would like it to be?

Yes ———————————————— 2
Not quite as varied ——————— 1
Not at all —————————————— 0

17 How often do you (or does your partner) pick quarrels at bedtime?

Often ——————————————— 0
Occasionally —————————— 1
Seldom or never ————————— 2

18 How often do you go to bed long before or long after your partner?

Always ——————————————— 0
Sometimes ————————————— 1
Seldom or never ————————— 2

19 Do you suggest sex when it is hard for your partner to respond because of a task that cannot be left?

Often ——————————————— 0
Sometimes ————————————— 1
Seldom or never ————————— 2

20 How often, if sex seems imminent, do you begin to recall past grievances so that you feel resentment toward your partner?

Often ——————————————— 0
Seldom or never ————————— 2
Sometimes ————————————— 1

RATING

High rating (26-40)

This shows that your present relationship meets your sexual needs very well. You most likely get along well with your partner in other ways, because sexual satisfaction is a good indicator of the quality of your relationship.

Medium rating (16-25)

This indicates that you have worked out a sexual relationship that suits both partners. However, you will probably both acknowledge that there is scope for improvement. Consult the detailed analysis below about questions for which your score was low.

Low rating (0-15)

This suggests a lack of satisfaction with either the quality or the quantity of your sex life, or both. However, checking through the detailed analysis below will help you to establish, and then set about dispelling, the principal causes of dissatisfaction. If you scored low on questions 17-20, and especially if your score on the preceding questionnaire was also low, your lack of sexual contentment may reflect a disharmony in other areas of your relationship. Clearing up difficulties which may be marring your everyday life together will almost certainly lead to greater enjoyment of sex for both of you.

ANALYSIS OF THE QUESTIONS

Question 1 deals with sexual frequency.

For most couples, good sex means frequent sex. Couples who have sex infrequently report less overall satisfaction than couples who make love often. It is easy for your sex life to become pared down without either of you fully realizing it. You may, for example, get into a routine of not having sex at a time when one or other of you is tired or busy, and then find that it is not easy to break the habit and establish a new pattern of wanting sex and making time for it. If either of you fails to score on this question, it may be because there is a sex-drive discrepancy between you (see DEALING WITH A SEX-DRIVE DISCREPANCY, p.272). But it may simply be because you have stopped giving sex the priority in your lives that it deserves.

Question 2 concerns sexual attraction.

For this there is no real explanation and certainly no substitute. Finding your partner attractive seems to be one of the most important factors in determining how satisfying your sex life is. You cannot create this sexual chemistry if it does not exist, but you can foster and sustain it when it is present by not taking each other for granted or abandoning all efforts to be attractive to your partner.

Questions 3-6 deal with the sharing of sexual responsibility.

Traditionally, the man suggests sex and the woman either accepts or rejects him, so usually it is the former who determines how much sex the couple have. Couples seem to be happiest, and to have sex most often, when both partners feel equally free to suggest sex or to refuse it, and do so equally often. If you can share control of sex like this you are much less likely to feel angry or rejected if you want sex and your partner does not, or to feel guilty on the occasions when she feels like it and you do not. Inclination rather than obligation will then determine how often you have sex.

Questions 7-10, 14 and 16 concern your sexual compatibility.

As in most other areas of your life together, the more similar your sexual likes and dislikes are, the less friction there will be between you. If either of you scores low in this section, you will find EXPANDING YOUR SEXUAL REPERTOIRE, p.204 and UNDERSTANDING a WOMAN'S FEELINGS, p.273, helpful.

Questions 11-13 deal with specific sexual problems.

Such problems will inevitably affect the quality of your sexual relationship. If the problem is your own, the relevant features will help. If it is your partner who has a sexual problem, reading **The female orgasm**, p.274, together will probably be helpful to both of you.

Question 15 concerns infidelity.

This is much more likely to be a symptom of dissatisfaction with your relationship than a cause of it. INFIDELITY, p.280, suggests ways of minimizing the damage to your relationship that this situation will almost certainly cause.

Questions 17-20 deal with sexual sabotage.

If your score in this section is low, sex may be unsatisfying because it has become a weapon you use against each other instead of a source of mutual pleasure. You may be using it as a punishment, withholding it to perpetuate a quarrel or to get even for past grievances. Or you may be using it to make your partner feel inadequate or guilty by always suggesting you make love when it is obviously impossible or inconvenient. If you find that you have reduced your sex life to a minimum by this kind of sabotage, there is sure to be more wrong with your relationship than just sex. Your answers to the preceding questionnaire, on compatibility, may help you discover the underlying problem.

WHAT IS WRONG WITH YOUR RELATIONSHIP?

Is it sex that causes the biggest problems between you?

YES →

Is the main problem a difference of sex drive, so that you want sex much more (or less) often than your partner?

YES →

See DEALING WITH A SEX-DRIVE DISCREPANCY, p.272.

NO ↓

Does your partner seem uninterested in sex, making it hard for you to arouse her?

YES →

See **Women and sexual satisfaction**, p.273.

NO ↓

See **The female orgasm**, p.274.

Are you concerned because your partner does not easily or often reach orgasm?

YES →

NO ↓

Is your sex life temporarily unsatisfactory because sex is painful for your partner?

YES →

See **Painful intercourse**, p.276.

NO ↓

Does your partner seem to have a strong dislike or fear of sex?

YES →

Does she feel that she is 'too small', so that her vagina tightens and intercourse becomes difficult or impossible?

NO / **YES**

NO ↓

Your partner's inhibitions about sex may stem from an upbringing which made her feel it was 'dirty' or wrong. If you can encourage her to talk about her feelings, you will probably be better able to understand how she feels and perhaps even help her develop a more positive attitude toward sex.

See **Fear of penetration**, p.275.

NO

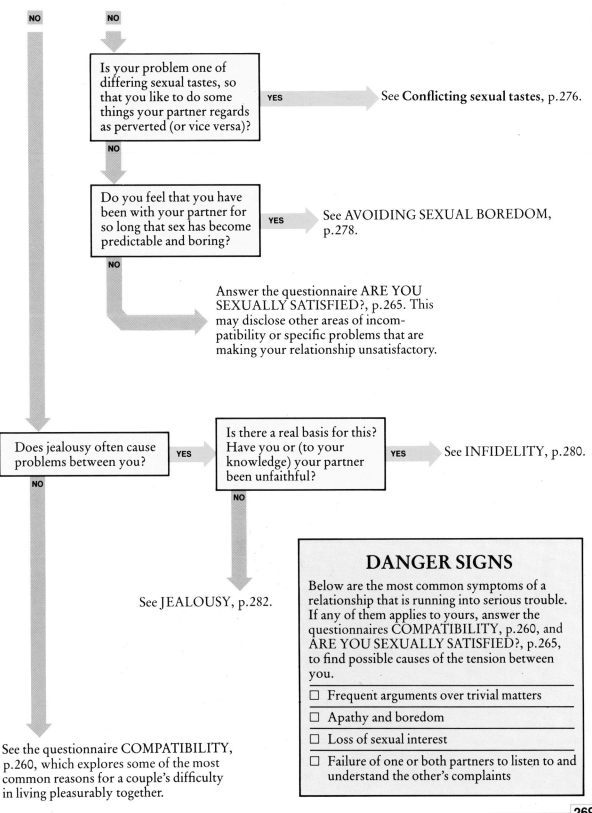

NO   **NO**

Is your problem one of differing sexual tastes, so that you like to do some things your partner regards as perverted (or vice versa)?

YES → See **Conflicting sexual tastes**, p.276.

NO

Do you feel that you have been with your partner for so long that sex has become predictable and boring?

YES → See AVOIDING SEXUAL BOREDOM, p.278.

NO

Answer the questionnaire ARE YOU SEXUALLY SATISFIED?, p.265. This may disclose other areas of incompatibility or specific problems that are making your relationship unsatisfactory.

Does jealousy often cause problems between you?

YES → Is there a real basis for this? Have you or (to your knowledge) your partner been unfaithful?

YES → See INFIDELITY, p.280.

NO

See JEALOUSY, p.282.

NO

See the questionnaire COMPATIBILITY, p.260, which explores some of the most common reasons for a couple's difficulty in living pleasurably together.

DANGER SIGNS

Below are the most common symptoms of a relationship that is running into serious trouble. If any of them applies to yours, answer the questionnaires COMPATIBILITY, p.260, and ARE YOU SEXUALLY SATISFIED?, p.265, to find possible causes of the tension between you.

☐ Frequent arguments over trivial matters

☐ Apathy and boredom

☐ Loss of sexual interest

☐ Failure of one or both partners to listen to and understand the other's complaints

LEARNING TO COMMUNICATE

Talking about sex in a general way interests nearly everybody, but few find it easy to discuss personal reactions and sexual preferences. Sharing intimate thoughts and feelings with a partner means revealing private areas of oneself, and this makes many men needlessly uncomfortable.

Talking about sex

Gestures – a hug in the right place at the right time, for example – can say a lot, but without words they can be misunderstood. Do not expect your partner to be able to read your mind, for it is a fallacy to believe that if she cares for you she will know what you want. There is no substitute for straight talking if you want to discover what you both need.

Take advantage of a new relationship by starting to discuss your preferences, and encouraging your partner to discuss hers, as soon as you begin to have sex. It is often much easier to talk intimately to someone you do not know well than to break an established routine and start talking to a long-term lover with whom you have always found it difficult to talk about sex.

Communicate directly, and be as specific as you can. Do not just say, 'How was that?' Say, 'Did I get the pressure right?' or 'Was I touching you in the right place?' or 'Was it too fast for you?' And say straight out what *you* would like to do or not do, what *you* want or do not want. If you try to guess your partner's likes and dislikes and behave as you believe she prefers, you may guess wrong. And if both of you play this game, neither of you is likely to get what you want. So be direct and encourage your partner to be the same.

Reassuring your partner

Give reassurance and encouragement whenever you can. It probably works better (at least until you are quite confident of the relationship) to stress what you like rather than complain about what you dislike. So say, 'That feels great,' rather than 'I don't much like what you're doing now'. Comments beginning 'You never ....' or 'You always ....' convey criticism of a partner's ability in bed and usually make for tension.

You should be particularly tactful if you want to introduce a topic that is clearly sensitive, such as personal hygiene. One approach is to suggest that the problem may be one you share. Ask her to check your breath, for example, and to tell you if it is bad. It is then reasonable for you to do the same. Or tell her you have not taken a bath for a couple of days and suggest you shower together before bed.

Giving or demanding complete self-exposure all at once can make your partner back off if she is not ready for it. Never ask a question you would not be willing to answer yourself or one that you are sure will deeply embarrass your partner.

The right time to talk

For most men the best time to start talking about sex is during lovemaking. Try to be appreciative, letting your partner know what you like while you are enjoying it. Try also to be discreetly inquisitive. Ask your partner, 'Do you like that?' or 'Shall I go on with it?' Let her feel that you will respond to whatever hints she might like to make. At the same time, casually mention your own preferences.

Some men, though, find it easier to bring up the subject of sexual preferences at other times. This is likely to be the case if you are involved in a long-standing relationship in which you and your partner have not been in the habit of talking about sex. Try introducing the subject when you are on neutral ground – over a drink or a meal, for example, when you should both feel comfortable and relaxed. And broach it indirectly, by means of something you have read or seen on TV, or even by quoting a friend's experience.

Reliving pleasurable experiences

It is usually easier, too, to talk in terms of past experience rather than about the present. If you wish you could repeat a certain kind of sexual activity that you once enjoyed together, speak of it reminiscently as a pleasurable experience, as this can lead to a suggestion that you do it again. It may help if you rehearse what you are going to say in advance. Working out the wording and saying it aloud to yourself will increase your confidence when you broach the subject with your partner.

Saying no

For many men, one of the most difficult communication problems is finding a way of telling a partner that you are just not in the mood for sex without making her feel rejected. You yourself undoubtedly know how hurt and rejected you can feel because of a sexual rebuff. It is important to learn how to reject the invitation without rejecting the person. You could, for example, say, 'I'd love to sit and talk for a while but I'm just not in the mood for sex tonight'. Or you might decline gently and say, 'Why don't we just have a cuddle?'

Many couples who find it difficult to be forthright prefer to adopt a code to convey sexual readiness. You might agree on a 0-10 scale, for example. Then, if either of you says, 'Sorry, but I rate zero tonight', the other knows this means total unwillingness. On the other hand, a 3 or 4 might mean 'I can probably make it if you're really keen.' Or you could choose a code based on appetite, ranging from 'I could eat a horse' down to 'All I need is a cup of black coffee'.

A code system prevents the development of 'heavy' situations fraught with misunderstanding. It makes it clear that you are just talking about a temporary mood. The number code, in particular, allows for maneuver. If one of you is an 8, for example, while the other shows a flicker of interest with a 3, the person with the lower rating might be prepared to make an extra effort for the sake of the more highly aroused partner. As long as you agree on the respective values of the code words, the second system might also be used in this way.

Picking up non-verbal cues
Pay particular attention to what your partner does to you during sexual encounters. You can usually assume that when she emphasizes a gesture she wants to enjoy the same thing. Such non-verbal cues are the easiest way for some people to let their partners know their sexual preferences. So if she should suck your nipples or fondle your genitals or anus, the chances are strong that reciprocation would be very welcome.

Dealing with anger
For nearly everyone anger and good sex are incompatible. In any relationship, especially a long-term one, quarrels and hurt feelings should be dealt with as they arise, not left to fester. Suppressed resentment contributes to sexual problems and makes them increasingly hard to resolve.

It is important for any couple, particularly those with sexual problems that they are trying to surmount, to be able to deal with anger. Occasional episodes of unpleasantness are bound to arise in nearly every relationship, but they can be resolved without lasting bitterness if the partners can talk over without delay the real cause of the trouble. Here are some guidelines for a sensible approach to such situations:

☐ Tell your partner exactly what has upset you, and do it at the time, not a week later.

☐ Deal with the problem in terms of your own feelings rather than your partner's behavior. Say, 'Perhaps I shouldn't get angry when . . . but I do' rather than 'You're so selfish, you don't ever . . .'.

☐ Stick to the particular issue and resolve it. Do not use the present argument as an opportunity to get past resentments off your chest.

☐ Exercise self-control, no matter how irritated you are. Arguments should not be damaging or destructive. So, if you are so angry that you feel like shouting at or hitting your partner, wait until the white heat of your rage dies down before tackling the issue.

☐ Do not make wounding attacks on each other's physical or intellectual shortcomings as these are not easily forgotten or forgiven.

☐ The moment an argument seems to be degenerating into a destructive fight, give it up and suggest that you would rather resolve it later when you both feel calmer.

☐ Make it up before bedtime, or as soon as you get into bed, but never try to use sex to make up after a fight. Most women are very turned off by this and the rift then takes even longer to heal.

DEALING WITH A SEX-DRIVE DISCREPANCY

Couples often wonder about how often they should be having sex, as though they are somehow failing if they fall behind the probable average of about 2.5 times a week. But quoting averages is pointless, since all that matters is that you should make love as much, or as little, as you both want.

It is part of the widespread 'macho' ideal that a man should always be interested in and ready for sex. Consequently, if sex has never been important to you, or if you suddenly find you have less drive than usual, you may start to harbor doubts about your masculinity.

A few men even believe the old myth, perpetuated by sports coaches who feel that sexual abstinence will magically put an edge on a sportsman's performance, that 'too much' sex weakens a man. It does not. Never be influenced by the notion that sex is a competitive sport.

Fluctuating sexual appetite

Like any other appetite, your sexual needs will wax and wane, and various factors make it perfectly natural to lack desire. The most crucial of these is your feeling toward your partner. If you are no longer attracted to her, or have a relationship that is fraught with anger or resentment, then your sex drive is likely to be low, or even non-existent.

Again, if you are depressed, for example, you will probably have little interest in sex. And it is natural for your sex drive to decrease when you are physically ill and to subside a little in later life too.

Inhibitions and your sex drive

If you have always had a low sex drive, it is possible that the way you were raised, or a traumatic experience with sex when you were young, has so inhibited you that you have always suppressed that part of your feelings, perhaps even avoiding sex altogether. If this is the case you should find OVERCOMING INHIBITIONS, p.224, helpful.

A high or low sex drive becomes a problem only when it differs very greatly from your partner's. This is a difficulty which is likely to be more serious if your own drive is much lower than your partner's, partly because of the general assumption that men should initiate sex, and partly because it is easier, physically, for a woman to have intercourse when not aroused than it is for a man.

Bridging a sex-drive gap

However, a sex-drive discrepancy need not mean that one of you is continually frustrated. Listed below are some of the most effective ways in which you can sustain a close and loving sexual relationship when intercourse is not as frequent as the more highly sexed partner would wish.

☐ Remember that sex need not involve intercourse. Even if you are not aroused yourself, you can use manual and oral stimulation to satisfy your partner (see STIMULATION TECHNIQUES, p.206) or give each other the relaxing pleasure of skillful caresses (see LEARNING TO SHARE PLEASURE, p.235).

☐ Many men feel that desire should be spontaneous, that they should not need direct stimulation in order to become aroused. This is not the case and is even less so as you grow older. So let your partner arouse you.

☐ Use psychic stimulation: erotic books, magazines, or videos, or fantasy.

☐ If masturbation by one partner, while being held by the other, suits you both it can prove a good way of achieving both satisfaction and closeness when the 'low-drive' partner does not want intercourse. However, it will not provide a solution on every occasion.

☐ If you are the 'low-drive' partner, when you masturbate alone try to do it to a fantasy image of your partner so that you come to associate her with your feelings of sexual arousal. Start by using your own favorite fantasy, whatever it is, gradually 'shaping' it to include an image of your partner as you become more aroused, so that she eventually becomes the main stimulus.

☐ Do not withhold affection from your partner, especially if your own lack of sexual interest has become an issue between you. You may be tempted to avoid bodily contact for fear that she will interpret a demonstration of affection as a sexual initiative, but if you do she will feel emotionally as well as physically rejected.

UNDERSTANDING A WOMAN'S FEELINGS

Among the most important contributions a man can make to his relationship with a woman are to understand how she feels about and responds to sex, and to look at sexual problems from her point of view. Because sex is such an intimate area of our lives we tend to take our partner's problems very personally. For example, if you have a temporary erection problem because you are tired or preoccupied, your partner, unless she understands you very well, may need reassurance that your body's lack of reaction is not her fault nor indeed anything to do with your feelings for her. The reverse is also true: you will be able to sympathize and perhaps help her with any problem she has if you can understand that it does not arise from her feelings about you. (Occasionally a problem will arise from her feelings about you, and it is important that you understand when this is the case.)

Women and sexual satisfaction

Lack of empathy between the sexes is often the result of the very different attitudes toward sex of men and women. For most men sex has to achieve the goals of erection and orgasm if it is to be fully satisfying, while women often value the feelings of closeness and tenderness as much as sexual excitement. Therefore, it is very easy (and very common) for a man to achieve his sexual goals without meeting his partner's real needs at all. This difference of outlook has great bearing on other aspects of your relationship and is explored more fully in **What makes a good lover?**, p.204. It explains why, for example, monogamy matters so much more to women than to men. To a woman, a sexual encounter may well represent a potential emotional involvement and therefore a threat to her principal relationship. When she has 'outside' sex, she is more likely to be looking for a special relationship than simply seeking variety. You may have difficulty convincing your partner that a casual sexual affair was just that and no more, because, for her, emotional commitment is such an important component of sex.

What is frigidity?

The term 'frigidity' has come to be used pejoratively, to imply not only that a 'frigid' woman does not like sex, but often that she does not like men. It is an easy defense for a man who has failed to interest or arouse

a woman to decide that she is 'frigid' and so neatly transfer the blame to her.

Quite apart from being an unfair description, the term 'frigid' is an imprecise one, making no distinction between the different sexual problems that women can face. A woman may have a temporary lack of interest in sex, so that she does not easily become aroused, for example. She may enjoy sex but seldom reach orgasm, or she may have such an intense fear of penetration that intercourse is impossible. Very rarely does the problem stem from a total aversion to sex – the emotional coldness that is implicit in the word 'frigid'. But often, if a woman does have this type of problem, it may be exacerbated, or will at least remain unresolved, because her partner knows little about how a woman's sexuality differs from his own.

A woman's need of arousal

The major difference between a woman who is not sexually aroused and a man with an erection problem is that a woman can allow a man to make love to her without being excited herself, while a man cannot perform without the excitement that produces an erection. But having sex when she is not properly aroused will not be pleasurable for her and it may even be painful, because her vagina will fail to become adequately lubricated. And, if intercourse is forced upon her, she will almost certainly feel used.

Often, even if your partner does not seem to be interested in sex at first, you will be able to arouse her, but there may be times when she is particularly uninterested. A woman's sexual responsiveness (like a man's) varies from time to time. Many women find that their sexual desire is at its peak during menstruation, for example. Intercourse at this time is, despite a widespread belief to the contrary, harmless. Your partner may like to wear a diaphragm (if she uses one) when the flow is heavy, and a towel on the bed will take care of any leakage. Many of the things which affect your own level of interest or ability to get an erection will affect your partner too. These include physical and emotional illness, alcohol, and drugs (see problem charts LACK OF INTEREST, p.180, and ERECTION PROBLEMS, p.192). Listed on the following page are further factors that influence a woman's sexual arousal which both you and your partner should be aware of.

☐ Inadequate stimulation is the most obvious reason for a woman's failure to become aroused. If you are in too great a hurry for intercourse you may not be giving your partner the stimulation of her body, breasts, and genitals that she needs to arouse her. When she is excited her nipples will become erect, the vaginal lips and 'hood' of her clitoris will swell, her vagina will become wet and, when she is fully aroused, its lower part will swell and widen.

☐ The fear of pregnancy can lessen a woman's desire for sex. You can allay this fear by ensuring that you use a contraceptive technique that you both feel confident about (see CONTRACEPTION, p.283).

☐ Negative feelings about a partner have a profound effect on a woman's sexual response. Most women need to feel emotionally close to a partner to become aroused, and anger, hurt, or an unresolved quarrel normally make a woman far less responsive.

☐ Exhaustion frequently leads to a loss of sexual interest. The woman who faces the demands of the home, children, and perhaps a job as well, may simply not have the time and energy needed for good sex.

☐ Pain during intercourse inevitably makes it difficult for a woman to anticipate sex with pleasure (see **Painful intercourse**, p.276).

☐ Do not overlook the possibility that your partner's lack of interest, especially if it is longstanding, may be a reflection of a problem you yourself have. If sex has never been truly satisfying for her, perhaps because you reach orgasm too soon and then fall asleep, her disappointment may have gradually turned into a lack of interest.

The female orgasm

Both men and women are sometimes confused about the female orgasm. Your partner may worry about whether she has orgasms at all, and whether what she experiences is what she is supposed to feel. If she is not sure, you may feel it is your responsibility, while she may feel it is her failure. What ought to be simply a source of pleasure easily, and often unnecessarily, becomes a cause for concern. The following facts about the female orgasm may help both you and your partner if you have problems or gaps in your understanding in this area.

☐ The female orgasm is a series of intense pulsations within the vagina. Few women can reach orgasm through penetration alone. Unless a woman has been fully aroused by clitoral stimulation, she will have difficulty in reaching a climax during intercourse.

☐ The strength of the orgasm and the ease with which it is reached vary from woman to woman and in the same woman from time to time. Your partner may find she has sensations that are much more intense than usual at certain times of her menstrual cycle or in particular positions.

☐ Orgasm is not indispensable for a woman's sexual satisfaction. Sometimes, or even always, your partner may feel happy and relaxed after sex without having had one. If this is truly the case, then you need not worry.

☐ If your partner has had little sex she may not have had an orgasm before. Most women need to learn to experience orgasm as they become more relaxed and confident of their own sexuality.

☐ Your partner needs continuous stimulation to achieve a climax, and no matter how near she is to it, the pleasurable sensations will die away if you cease to stimulate her.

☐ Women usually find orgasm easiest to achieve, and often most intense, through masturbation. But many of the women interviewed for the influential Hite report on female sexuality said that even though the intensity of the climax reached this way was greater, they felt a 'vaginal emptiness', a desire to be filled by a penis, which intercourse was better able to satisfy.

☐ While a man has a 'refractory' period after ejaculation, during which he cannot achieve another erection however much he is stimulated, many women are capable of having another orgasm, and sometimes several more in quick succession, if they are stimulated again shortly after reaching a climax. However, this does not mean that they necessarily want multiple orgasms. Nor does it mean that you have to be a sexual athlete to satisfy your partner. If she wants to have more than one orgasm, you can bring her to her first climax by using your hand or your tongue, and then have intercourse, with or without simultaneous manual stimulation of the clitoris, depending on how aroused she is.

Helping your partner reach orgasm

Clitoral stimulation is the key to orgasm for a woman. If your partner has never experienced a climax, encourage her to masturbate. Almost all women can achieve orgasm through masturbation, and in this way she will learn the most effective methods of stimulating her clitoris. You can then apply these when you make love to her. What is much more likely, however, is that she can climax during masturbation but finds it harder, perhaps even impossible, to do so during intercourse. You will probably find that at least one of the following techniques will make it possible for her. Whichever method you use, make sure that she is highly aroused before you enter her.

Minimum entry

In a man-on-top position, raise yourself on your hands and move just the tip of your penis in and out of her vaginal lips, so that there is a distinct pull on them. This technique will probably not give you the stimulation you seek, but if you employ it between periods of deeper thrusting, it can be very arousing for your partner.

Maximum withdrawal

Withdraw your penis as far as you can after each thrust. This feels very good for most women because it creates the same sensations as the technique described above, pulling the vaginal lips and stimulating the highly sensitive entrance.

Imitating a favorite masturbation method

If your partner usually keeps her legs together when she masturbates, adopt an intercourse position that allows her to do this. If she parts her legs, take up an appropriate position to make her feel equally relaxed (see SEXUAL POSITIONS, p.211).

Dual-stimulation

Choose a position for intercourse in which you can easily reach your partner's clitoris with your hand (see SEXUAL POSITIONS, p.211) so that you can give her additional manual stimulation. Alternatively, suggest that she stimulate herself manually while your penis is inside her.

Alleviating 'performance anxiety'

Like men, women sometimes find that their sexual performance is inhibited by anxiety. It may be that your partner concentrates so much on whether she is pleasing you or is making you impatient because of her failure to come as quickly as she would like to, that she fails to focus on and fully experience her own sensations. Encourage her to forget performance goals and to simply enjoy whatever she feels.

Fear of penetration

Sometimes a woman has such an intense fear of being penetrated or even having her genitals touched that she reacts to every sexual advance by an automatic tightening that is quite beyond her control, of the muscles surrounding her vaginal entrance. This, of course, makes penetration impossible. Often the problem starts after a painful or traumatic experience of intercourse, although it may be the result of a restrictive upbringing that has left her with an irrational fear of sex. Exceptionally, there is a physical reason for this condition, which is known as vaginismus, and so it is always advisable for a woman suffering from it to be examined by a doctor. The condition almost always responds well to loving and patient treatment, so that you can probably help her to overcome it. The following exercise program enlists your help in tackling the problem.

1 Reassure your partner that her fears about her vagina being too small, which is almost certainly how she thinks of it, are the product of her imagination and not based on fact. Explain to her that the vaginal walls are enormously distensible, and that since they can accommodate the passage of a baby, she can take your penis with ease.

2 Encourage her to examine her vaginal area with a mirror, so that she knows exactly how it is formed.

3 This stage will probably be the hardest for her, but once she has managed it, everything else will proceed more smoothly. She should insert just the tip of a well-lubricated finger, as far as the first joint, into her vagina. At first she will probably only feel able to touch the entrance, but it is important that at each attempt she inserts the finger just a little more. When she feels her vaginal muscles tightening, she should pause, deliberately tighten them still more around her finger, and then relax them. After repeating this exercise several times she will begin to feel she has control over her vaginal muscles.

4 When she can fairly comfortably insert one finger as far as it will go into her vagina, she should try using two fingers.

5 She should now feel confident enough to let you insert your finger (after you have checked that you have no jagged fingernails) in the same way. Ask her to relax and tighten her muscles around it.

6 After a few weeks of this exploratory treatment, first with her fingers, then with yours, she should be ready to try intercourse. When you do so, it is important, first, that she is thoroughly aroused (use extra lubrication if necessary) and, secondly, that you let her adopt a woman-on-top position so that she can lower herself onto your penis as slowly and gently as she likes. Do not thrust to begin with, but just let her get used to the sensations caused by the presence of your penis in her vagina.

Throughout this treatment, remember that she is working at overcoming a very profound fear and that it is not to do with her feelings about you but with those about intercourse. Understand that she will be as upset as you are by the reaction of her body, which is completely at odds with the way she wants to react.

Painful intercourse

Sex is rarely painful for a man (see PAINFUL INTERCOURSE, p.191) but there are several conditions, some fairly common, which can cause a woman pain during intercourse. If your partner has such a problem suggest that she see a doctor and wait until the condition has righted itself before you attempt intercourse again.

Painful intercourse is normally due to one or more of the following factors:

☐ Vaginal or bladder infection (by far the most common cause)

☐ An allergy reaction to deodorants, douches, or bath additives

☐ Deep thrusting by the male that aggravates endometriosis (pelvic infection)

☐ Pressure on an ovary owing to retroverted uterus (rare, and painful only in certain positions)

Pain is also common after childbirth, especially if there are episiotomy scars. It may also be the result of a lack of vaginal lubrication, usually either because the woman is insufficiently aroused or because of changes in the vagina due to aging (see below).

Sex and aging

Many women find that their sex drive intensifies in their late thirties and forties. And while the menopause (which usually occurs some time between the ages of 45 and 55) marks the end of a woman's reproductive life, it need not, and seldom does, signal the end of her sexual activity. Sometimes, after the menopause, there is a thinning of the lining of the vagina and a decrease in its lubrication that can make intercourse painful.

If your partner has this problem her doctor may suggest hormone replacement therapy, but lubrication with water or saliva may be all that is needed. It helps too, to keep up an active sex life because this increases the flow of blood to the vagina and helps to retard the effects of aging. Like you, your partner will probably take longer to become aroused as she grows older. Therefore sex is likely to become a more leisurely and relaxed affair, with greater emphasis on the intimacy and comfort of a loving relationship and less on the goal of orgasm.

Conflicting sexual tastes

There are various activities which can be incorporated into an unadventurous sexual routine to provide greater stimulation or variety. If you both enjoy them, they can increase your pleasure as well as strengthening the sexual bond between you. But if one partner dislikes something the other enjoys, or if an activity becomes so important to one of you that it becomes a substitute for your usual sexual activities rather than just enhancing them, you will encounter a conflict of interests. This situation is common, since male and female tastes often diverge widely.

In matters of unconventional or unfamiliar sexual practices there are three cardinal rules:

☐ Do not do it unless you both enjoy it.

☐ Do not do it if it is harmful to either partner.

☐ Do not put pressure on your partner to do it if she clearly does not want to.

Oral and anal sex

Most surveys suggest that fewer women than men include oral sex among their favorite sexual activities. If it is new to your partner, she may be apprehensive when you first suggest it, in part at least because she does not know what is expected of her. You will therefore have to be prepared to give her explicit instructions. Do not expect her to give you oral stimulation unless you are happy to do the same for her. She may or may not want to swallow your semen, and this should be entirely her decision. Do not act as though she is somehow failing you if she prefers not to.

Few women suggest anal sex. Most are convinced that it will hurt or that it is unhygienic, and unless you are very gentle, and wash your penis thoroughly if you are going to have vaginal intercourse afterwards they would be right in each case. There is, in addition, the very real danger that this is an activity which carries a high risk of AIDS. If you are reluctant to give it up because it is something that you and your partner both enjoy very much, wearing a strong condom lubricated with nonoxynol-9 (a substance which destroys the HIV virus) makes it safer. (See **Oral sex**, p.208, **Anal sex**, p.210, and **Guidelines for safer sex**, p.310).

Sadomasochism

The practice of sadomasochism is based on the derivation of sexual pleasure from inflicting and receiving pain. Most sadomasochistic relationships have one dominant and one submissive partner and these roles are often adopted to an extreme degree.

The mildest form of sadomasochism is bondage, in which, in order to heighten the sexual excitement of both, the 'dom' ties or chains the 'sub'. Beating is also a common sadomasochistic practice. Many women go along with mild forms of bondage – if your partner agrees to try it, never tie the neck or head, or subject each other to more pain than the recipient wants – and enjoy gentle fantasy-based games. But if your woman has no real taste for them it is probably because she feels that the situation will get out of hand. She may also find it hard to understand, unless she feels the same way, how loving feelings can be translated into painful or humiliating actions.

Sadomasochistic games are something your partner is more likely to tolerate because you enjoy them rather than because she enjoys them herself. The serious sadomasochist is nearly always male, and the man who has not got a steady partner willing to engage in bondage, flagellation, or similarly motivated practices must turn to prostitutes specializing in these areas.

Fetishism

A mild degree of fetishism – the taste for women in fishnet stockings or fancy underwear, for example – is a feature of most men's sex lives. Fetish objects such as these garments may enhance their sexual excitement but most men are not dependent on them for arousal. However, if you are a true fetishist you will need a special item or set of circumstances in order to become aroused. For example, you will not enjoy sex unless you are wearing rubber. For the extreme fetishist, just wearing rubber, leather, plastic, or fur is all that is needed to produce arousal and orgasm. In such cases the fetish takes over completely and becomes a substitute for a partner.

Fetishism seldom, if ever, occurs in women, so it is unlikely that you will find a partner who truly shares your tastes. You may well find a woman sympathetic to your preferences in this area if they involve her, and she will probably accept that you find it exciting to see her dressed in whatever clothing arouses you. However, it is likely to seriously disturb her if you can only achieve an erection when wearing a particular garment and your sex life will undoubtedly suffer if your fetishism threatens to replace rather than enhance the sex between you.

A few men have a special fetish: they become aroused by dressing in women's clothes. This practice, known as fetishistic transvestism, and the way if may affect your relationship, are examined in more detail in **Transvestism**, p.256.

◁ **Power games**
Most people think about, and occasionally practise, adopting a sexual role different from their customary one. A few, however, need to act out their fantasy in the form of an elaborate ritual of submission.

AVOIDING SEXUAL BOREDOM

Boredom is seen by many couples as the Catch 22 of their relationship. The argument goes thus: a relationship has more chance of lasting if it is monogamous, but sex with the same partner for 30 years – perhaps more – will inevitably be boring, and boredom, if it does not simply erode the joy from a relationship, may well lead to infidelity and so threaten it even more.

But to assume that sex must eventually become boring without an occasional change of partner, is to underestimate the consolidating and strengthening role that it can play in a long-term relationship and the capacity of a couple to change and adapt to each other as the years go by.

The inevitability of change

Even though boredom might be avoidable, change is not. The passion and urgency that characterize the first months of a love affair do, eventually, disappear. But for most people this is more than compensated for by the ease and comfort that come from being with a lover whose body has become familiar and whose sexual rhythms have adapted to and accommodated one's own. Long-term lovers know each other's needs and preferences, have discovered what they most enjoy doing together, and accept and trust each other so that anxieties about sexual performance are unnecessary. Such benefits constitute a large part of the reason why many couples still enjoy sex together after many years and why for some it seems to get even better. These things are not possible in a new relationship, however passionate.

Changing attitudes to sex

So why is it that not all established couples experience a strengthening of their sex life together? The first thing to remember is that sexual sensations remain the same; it is only our attitude toward them that changes. The second, if you want to establish the real cause of your boredom, is to look at sex in the wider context of your lives together.

If there is a depressing pall of monotony over everything or if there is so much bad feeling that you do not really enjoy anything you do together, it would be unrealistic to expect sex to be any different. In this case, sexual boredom is only part of a much wider problem. Sex will not flourish, it will not even survive unless the basic elements of attraction and affection remain. If your relationship has grown increasingly monotonous, you need to work out what is wrong between you, with the help of professional counseling if necessary, so that you can regenerate some of your feelings for each other. Then you can start to revive your sex life.

Combatting sexual boredom

If you are basically happy with the quality of your life together, you have all the more reason for examining the causes of sexual tedium. It is possible that you are bored because sex has become too predictable. If you have developed an unvarying routine, or have a very narrow sexual repertoire, then it is not surprising that a sense of sameness has set in.

However, if you are bored in spite of the fact that you have always been sexually innovative and have explored all manner of sexual possibilities, then you probably have a fantasy notion of what sex should be. If so, what you must do is modify your expectations. Reading **Accepting sexual reality**, p.279, will help you to get the most from the sexual relationship you have at present.

Breaking your sexual routine

Introducing change into a long-established sexual routine is not easy. After year upon year of the missionary position, to suggest that your partner might like to see what it is like on top may seem to be too revolutionary, either for you to suggest or for your partner to accept. You will both need, first of all, to accept the idea of change, for as long as you both take it for granted that this is the way things are done, they will go on being done that way. Then you should bring about very small or subtle changes in your routine, simply leaving the light on one day, for example, if you usually make love in the dark. EXPANDING YOUR SEXUAL REPERTOIRE, p.204, suggests various changes of this kind and describes positions for intercourse that may be unfamiliar but nevertheless rewarding.

When you discuss such changes with your partner, be careful not to make it seem as though you are criticizing her. The rut you have got into is not exclusively the fault of either of you, since even if you have never suggested varying the routine before, nor has your partner. It is, of course, always the easiest option to accept things as they are. But what you need to do now is to find ways of altering that routine so that it will make sex more fun.

Expressing your needs

Your own fantasies and daydreams are a good way of finding out the kinds of sexual activity you would really like to try. So, too, are past sexual experiences you have particularly enjoyed. It is a good idea to talk to your partner about something in theory before you put it into practice, so that she has time to get used to the idea and perhaps to overcome any inhibitions. This is especially important if what you suggest is unconventional to her.

If you would like your partner to do something for you, one way of indicating this is to do it, or something similar, for her. This kind of non-verbal communication can be very useful if you find it hard to put your sexual wishes into words. But most important of all, if your partner is very resistant to the idea of change, do not press it, at least for the moment. Reassure her that it is because you enjoy sex with her and value the relationship that you want to keep the former as exciting as you can.

Accepting sexual reality

For some people disillusionment occurs because the qualities they valued most in the early stages of a relationship – the passion, excitement, and intensity – tend to fade fastest. Unless you are realistic enough to acknowledge that this is bound to happen, and to learn to value what develops in their place, you may come to regard this calmer, less frenzied phase of the relationship as boring.

It is possible to feel the same sense of dissatisfaction, not because things are not what they used to be, but because reality has failed to meet your expectations. Almost certainly, this is because those expectations are unattainable and your view of sex is a fantasy one. If you continually hanker after ecstasy, you are bound to find simpler pleasures rather run-of-the-mill.

Valuing the present

The remedy for entrenched boredom is not to seek new levels of excitement in, for example, fresh sexual activities, an affair, or erotic books or movies. These tactics can add spice when the relationship is a little stale, but only if used in moderation. If they are treated as a last-ditch solution, a fresh process of familiarization will inevitably lead to further disillusionment. Instead, try to feel differently about the way things are right now. It is your attitude toward the present that will determine the degree of your future sexual happiness. Below are some guidelines to getting the best from what is available to you right now.

□ Examine all the good things about sex with your partner. It may not be as exciting as it once was but at least it is reliable. You can probably judge each other's responses well, and you know the kinds of activity you like best. Also, since you are more relaxed with each other, you can prolong lovemaking much more easily that you could in the excitement of a new relationship.

□ When you are making love, focus strongly on the physical sensations. These are the same as ever, and if they feel less intense it is probably because you have come to pay less attention to them. To feel the location and intensity of pain more clearly you focus your attention on it. The same principle applies to pleasure.

□ Live in the here and now: avoid comparisons with past experiences and do not fantasize about those you would like to have in the future.

□ You should not forget that a two-way process is involved. You will get feedback from the pleasure you give your partner, for the more she enjoys sex with you, the more she will want to please you, and so on.

INFIDELITY

A serious affair nearly always involves a conscious decision, no matter how spontaneous or unexpected you have convinced yourself it is. You go into it because your main relationship is not completely satisfying and because you believe the affair will meet some unfulfilled need.

Casual affairs, on the other hand, are often opportunistic, perhaps starting just because you are away from your partner and happen to meet someone attractive. Never let guilt about this sort of liaison tempt you into confession. Provided your infidelity is not symptomatic of any real trouble in your relationship, it is your problem, not your partner's.

Why do affairs begin?

If an affair becomes so serious that you begin to think about breaking with your steady partner, it is vital to analyze your reasons for continuing with it if you are not to find yourself in yet another unsatisfactory relationship. Here are some of the main reasons why affairs begin:

☐ *A need for sexual variety or to satisfy curiosity.* Such motivations are especially likely if you have had very few partners. Affairs based mainly on sexual attraction are usually brief and are a poor reason for breaking up your relationship.

☐ *Excitement.* This is the prime reason for some men. The idea of an illicit affair is much more exciting than a legitimate relationship and often a man will ruin a valued relationship through one or more affairs. Sometimes a successful relationship may seem to present too little challenge, while an affair, with the risks it involves, may make you feel more alive.

☐ *Sexual dissatisfaction with a partner.* An affair may show you what is wrong with sex between you and your partner, and even help you to improve things. But there is a risk that the affair may seem an easier option than working on the problem with your partner, so that you will tend to shelve difficulties rather than solve them.

☐ *To satisfy an emotional need.* The desire to feel loved and wanted in a new way often provides the impetus for entering into an affair.

☐ *To precipitate a crisis in a relationship that is unsatisfactory.* This does not necessarily mean that you want to turn your affair into another permanent relationship. Wait until the heat has died down to see how you really feel.

☐ *As a morale booster.* Sometimes an affair is used to boost self-esteem after a career setback, or as tit-for-tat if it is discovered that a partner has been unfaithful.

☐ *Looking for the perfect lover.* This is the excuse given by the man who maintains that he is really monogamous at heart, if only he could find the perfect mate. Almost certainly, he is fooling himself. If you have always had affairs, the chances are that you will find it hard to change completely. It is easy to avoid commitment, to avoid having to work at a relationship, if you always believe something better will turn up.

The effect on your relationship

Most men believe it is possible to have sex without commitment, and tend to view affairs as something intense but fleeting, that will eventually fade away, leaving their main relationship intact. But however much you want to keep an affair on a casual or friendly basis, emotions can, and often do, get out of hand. An affair is usually embarked upon to meet some unsatisfied need. If it succeeds, it may come to be more and more important to you, affecting your wholehearted commitment to your steady partner, however little you want it to. If she discovers what is going on, it is bound to affect, and may even destroy, your relationship.

For couples who are living together, without being married, the discovery of an affair may be particularly destructive because it will be seen by the injured party as a feasible alternative to their way of life together. The married couple have a built-in stability, practical, financial and social, that makes dissolution much harder and makes it much more likely that they will ride out the storm.

If for whatever reason, you confess to an affair (or are found out) your partner's reaction will depend to a large extent on the length and intensity of that involvement. A casual, brief affair is easier to understand and forgive than one of long duration. In the latter case your partner has to review a substantial section of your life together and come to terms with the fact that the reality of your relationship during this time has been quite different from what she had supposed.

The difficulties of an affair
An affair probably has the best chance of success when it fulfills a simple sexual need for both partners, with no additional demands on either side. But few relationships are as simple as this. Emotional damage to at least one of the parties involved is almost inevitable. Your chances of minimizing this will be improved if you follow a few basic rules:

☐ Learn to compartmentalize your life and your emotions. That is the only way you will be able to give the commitment to each relationship that will enable both to survive.

☐ Do not try to justify what you are doing by focusing on your principal partner's failings.

☐ Do not neglect domestic commitments or let emotional or practical crises build up at home.

☐ Do not spend the necessarily limited time you have with your new lover regretting that it is not more, or bring up when you only have a few more minutes left together tricky issues that cannot easily be resolved. Nearly all affairs have to be managed with one eye on the clock, which may make it difficult to express your feelings spontaneously.

☐ Make sure that the pleasure outweighs the pain brought about by the guilt, the inconvenience, and the often desperate need for secrecy.

☐ If you suspect that your partner is conniving at the affair, making things a little too easy for you, drop it at once if you value her. She may have her own reasons for wanting it to continue, and perhaps you should reexamine your relationship with her more closely to find out just what they are.

Discovering an affair
A woman's infidelity is less likely to be casual than a man's, and more likely to have some emotional significance. So while women often overestimate the importance of their partner's infidelity, there is a chance that men may underestimate the importance an affair holds for a woman.

Do not seek for confirmation that your partner is having an affair unless you really want to know and you have thoroughly considered all the implications. If it comes to a showdown, remember that the pain of rejection makes the worst possible background against which to conduct a rational discussion that might save your relationship. A bitter and emotional tirade, however justified, precludes any two-way communication and gives your partner no right of reply. There will be details which will seem to you to be of paramount importance at the time: when and where it happened and whether sex was better with the other man, for example.

Planning a solution
Your partner's affair is symptomatic of a need in her. It may be a need you do not recognize or sympathize with, but you will have a better chance of understanding what went wrong if you acknowledge that need. So the first constructive thing you must do is to set aside time to talk about it together, at length and without interruption. At first there are only really two points for discussion: why it happened and how your partner feels now. Your own feelings must be so painfully apparent, so inescapable to both of you, that there is really not much point in laboring them. Scarcely anyone is proof against the hurt that discovery of an affair can cause. But if you want to save the relationship, remember that however you feel, it is in your best interests not to say too much that is unforgivable or unforgettable.

It is important to realize that one instance of infidelity does not mean that your partner has embarked on an endless career of affairs. Many couples survive the discovery of an affair and continue a relationship that will undoubtedly be changed, but may nevertheless be strengthened because of increased mutual understanding.

JEALOUSY

Jealousy is one of the most powerful, destructive, and painful emotions. It is often regarded as a measure of the love one person feels for another. Conversely, the absence of jealousy is often taken as a sign of not caring and an insecure partner may test the other's love by trying to provoke jealousy.

It is more accurate to say that jealousy is a fear of loss rather than a demonstration of love. Unreasonable and frequent jealousy shows not so much that you mistrust your partner but that you cannot trust yourself to hold your relationship together in the face of even the slightest competition. When jealousy runs this deep, the one thing your partner cannot give you is reassurance. Your feelings of insecurity and inferiority are such that you are not prepared to believe anything except the answer that you dread hearing: that there is someone else.

When is jealousy reasonable?

Jealousy is a fear of losing something you value and there are times, when a relationship is threatened, when only a superhuman would fail to feel it. How much jealousy you show is a matter of both judgment and control. The following notes will help you decide whether your (or your partner's) jealousy is justified and will help you handle it.

☐ You are entitled to feel jealous if your partner has been acting suspiciously. If there are sudden significant but unaccountable changes of routine in a partner's hitherto well-organized life, suspicion is probably justified. Suspicion tends to thrive on the accumulation of evidence until it is either substantiated or allayed. It is natural to show flashes of jealousy if your suspicion has been aroused, and to give your partner a warning signal that shows your disquiet.

☐ You are entitled to feel jealous if a partner flirts outrageously with someone else in your presence. This is bad manners on her part and you have a right to complain. She may have had no idea at all that she was hurting you, or she may have been deliberately provoking an outburst because she needs reassurance that you love her, or because she has a grievance that needs airing. Whatever her motives, you can use jealousy positively to force your respective feelings into the open.

☐ Jealousy is unreasonable when it arises solely from your own feelings of inferiority or insecurity. Questioning your partner endlessly about time she spends apart from you because you find it frightening that she has any life outside your relationship is simply destructive and will make her resentful. Searching her handbag or inspecting her belongings for evidence of infidelity is unreasonable, unless you have a solid reason for supposing that she is cheating on you.

☐ Jealousy is unreasonable when it is retrospective. You should not be jealous of people she knew and loved before you were together. The fact that she is with you now should be enough to reassure you of her love. If you are jealous of the past, keep it to yourself.

If you never show your jealousy you are probably very sensible. But do not be so controlled that you fail to take it up with your partner if she is hurting you or jeopardizing your relationship. If you never feel jealous then you are either lucky in being supremely self-confident and absolutely secure in your relationship or you do not care deeply enough about her to mind losing her.

CONTRACEPTION

The fear of an unwanted pregnancy can mar even the best sexual relationship. The pros and cons of the various contraceptive methods available are discussed below, and an indication of their efficiency is also given. Failure rates are given in terms of the percentage of pregnancies that would probably result if 100 healthy young couples used the same method for one year.

It is important to choose a method you are both happy with, and this in itself will help to ensure its success.

The Pill

The contraceptive pill, usually referred to as the Pill, contains synthetic versions of either or both the female hormones estrogen and progesterone. The former prevents ovulation. The latter makes the mucus plugging the entrance to the uterus hostile to sperm and affects the uterus lining, making implantation of a fertilized egg unlikely. The combined pill contains both hormones, and is the most effective. The progesterone-only pill has the fewest side-effects, but is slightly less effective. The 'morning after' pill must be taken within 72 hours of intercourse. Higher in estrogen, it works by expelling the egg, whether fertilized or not.

The side-effects of the Pill vary and a woman may find one brand suits her better than another. But there is unlikely to be a serious risk in taking it, except for women who suffer from, or have a family history of, deep-vein or coronary thrombosis, stroke, or other circulatory disorders, particularly high blood pressure. Doctors also advise women who have diabetes or who are over 35, to change to some other method. Overweight women and smokers are also discouraged from taking the Pill.

Failure rate: less than 1 per cent

The intrauterine device (IUD)

Commonly referred to as an IUD, the intrauterine device is a piece of molded plastic, in some cases containing copper, which is inserted into the uterus. It is second only to the Pill in efficiency, though exactly how it works is still unknown.

An IUD has to be fitted by a doctor or trained nurse, and this will often be carried out during a post-natal visit after pregnancy because insertion is easiest then. The device tends to make a woman's periods longer, heavier and more painful, especially for the first few months after fitting. Because it also seems to render the reproductive system more vulnerable to infection, a woman who has several sexual partners, and so runs an increased risk of contracting a sexually transmitted disease, is probably better off with another form of contraception. The IUD will probably not be recommended for a woman who has not had children but would like to, because if a pelvic infection should develop, infertility can be the result.

Failure rate: 2 per cent

The cap and the diaphragm

These are rubber or plastic devices that fit, in the case of the cervical cap, over the neck of the uterus, or in the case of the diaphragm, across the vagina, to block the passage of sperm. Initially, they must be fitted by a doctor, or other qualified person, and checked each year and after pregnancy. They must be used with a spermicide to be reasonably reliable, and should be kept in place for at least six hours after intercourse. Caps and diaphragms have no disadvantages, apart from the fact that having to insert them before sex may seem to detract from the spontaneity of lovemaking. A very few people are allergic to the rubber of which they are made.

Failure rate: 4 per cent (with spermicide); 15 per cent (alone)

The contraceptive sponge

This device comprises a sponge impregnated with spermicide which is inserted in the vagina before intercourse and left there for a minimum of 24 hours afterward. Like the condom (see below) it is an easily available form of contraception well suited to those with an irregular sex life. However, tests to date on this relatively new product have shown it to be not very competitive with most other contraceptives in terms of efficiency. Therefore it is advisable to use it in conjunction with a condom for greater protection.

Failure rate: up to 25 per cent

The condom (sheath)

The condom is a fine rubber sheath which is rolled onto the erect penis before insertion into the vagina. Care must be taken to expel all the air from the projection at the end before the condom is put on or, if it is of the plain-ended kind, the tip is pinched to deflate it and left free. The ejaculated semen collects in the end of the condom. The base must be held securely during withdrawal after ejaculation to prevent the condom slipping off and releasing the semen. Use a new condom every time you have intercourse. Put it on as soon as erection occurs.

Condoms have always been a valuable method of contraception: they are becoming more popular because they give some protection against AIDS and other sexually transmitted diseases. Some condoms are lubricated with nonoxynol-9, an ingredient of most spermicides, which kills the HIV (AIDS) virus. Use extra spermicide to increase the condom's contraceptive efficiency and give added protection against AIDS if the condom leaks.

Check the date label when you buy condoms (they begin to deteriorate after about two and a half years), and don't expose them to heat or strong light. You will probably need to use additional lubricant, even on those which are ready-lubricated; choose one which is water-soluble, because oil or petroleum-based lubricants will make latex condoms brittle and break easily.

One brand on the market (Mentor contraceptives) has an adhesive inside which seals the condom to the skin, enabling it to stay firmly in place if the penis becomes softer or harder during sex. Scented condoms (to which a few people are allergic) are also available, as are 'ribbed' or textured condoms with a roughened exterior. Some women like the extra stimulation these provide, others find it irritating.

Failure rate: 3 per cent (with spermicide);
15 per cent (alone)

Spermicides

These sperm-killing chemicals are obtainable as creams, jellies, foams, pessaries (gel-coated capsules which are slipped into the vagina) or as squares of impregnated film. They are inserted into the vagina before intercourse, and, because they have only limited efficiency on their own, are normally used in conjunction with a condom, cap or diaphragm. Spermicides containing nonoxynol-9 also kill the HIV virus which causes AIDS.

Failure rate: 25 per cent (alone)

Coitus interruptus (withdrawal)

Withdrawal of the penis before orgasm is the oldest contraceptive method and even now is the most widely used on a global scale. It is among the least efficient of methods, and has only the virtues of being free and always available. The aim of the method is for the man to bring his partner to orgasm through intercourse and then to withdraw the penis and ejaculate outside her. The man who is sexually very competent may be able to use it effectively – some of the time. It is not a good method for someone who lacks good ejaculatory control, or who suffers from 'performance anxiety' (see **Dispelling sexual anxiety**, p.225). Unless you are reasonably relaxed and sexually confident it will be yet another source of worry. Remember that if you have been drinking alcohol or taking drugs, you will have less control than usual. Finally, don't use the method if you have intercourse a second time within a few hours – sperm from the first ejaculation can remain in the pre-ejaculatory fluid.

Failure rate: 10-12 per cent

Natural (rhythm) method

Some couples, on religious, moral, health, or esthetic grounds, choose not to use artificial contraceptive techniques. The 'natural' methods they prefer attempt to identify those days around the middle of the menstrual cycle when conception is most likely to occur, and intercourse is avoided at those times. Even so, there are very few absolutely safe days and a couple have to be willing to abstain from sex for a large part of each month if they are to have a reasonable chance of avoiding pregnancy for any length of time.

Natural methods should be practised under the guidance of a doctor or a suitably qualified person. The technique that works best is called the sympto-thermal method. This involves keeping a chart of the woman's early-morning body temperature (which rises slightly just after ovulation) and inspecting the mucus discharge of her vagina (which undergoes certain changes at ovulation). The method has the drawback that it requires a great deal of accurate observation and meticulous record-keeping by the woman. More importantly, if the couple both have a high sex drive they are likely to find it very restricting.

Failure rate: 20 per cent

▽ Choosing a method of contraception

Discuss contraception with your partner and do not assume that it is her sole responsibility. Most methods do in fact demand more of the woman, but this is no reason for her to make the decision alone.

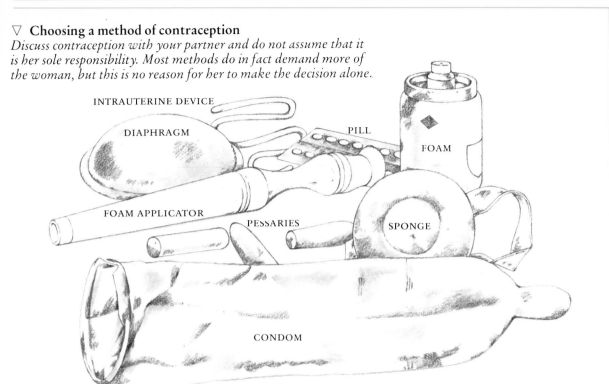

INTRAUTERINE DEVICE

DIAPHRAGM

PILL

FOAM

FOAM APPLICATOR

PESSARIES

SPONGE

CONDOM

VASECTOMY

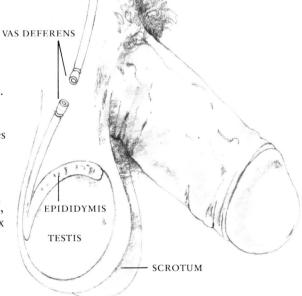

Both male and female sterilization are totally effective contraceptive techniques and do not affect sex drive. The male operation, known as vasectomy, is a simpler and slightly safer procedure, not even requring a general anesthetic. Two small incisions are made in the scrotum and the two vas deferens (sperm-carrying tubes) are cut and their ends tied. The whole procedure takes about 20 minutes. Although the tubes can be rejoined, this does not guarantee future fertility, since the semen contains fewer sperm. The operation should therefore be considered irreversible. However, contrary to popular belief, vasectomy does not necessarily reduce a man's sex drive.

The patient is usually advised to wear tight underpants or a jockstrap for a few days after the operation to relieve the dragging feeling in the testes. There may also be some temporary bruising of the scrotum or groin. For about 16 weeks after the operation it is necessary to use additional contraception, since the semen will not be sperm-free until all the sperm present in the vas deferens have been ejaculated.

VAS DEFERENS

EPIDIDYMIS

TESTIS

SCROTUM

△ The purpose of vasectomy
Severing and tying the ends of the sperm-carrying tubes prevents sperm from entering the urethra. Consequently, after vasectomy the ejaculate comprises only seminal fluid.

CONCEPTION PROBLEMS

A couple of normal fertility with a typically active sex life – having intercourse two or three times a week – can usually conceive a child within a year. But of every 100 couples, ten are unable to have children and fifteen have fewer than they would like.

A man who is able to have intercourse and to ejaculate usually assumes that because he is potent he must also be fertile, but this is not necessarily so. In some cases of infertility the woman alone is at fault, in some the man, and in some both partners. It is only by microscopic examination that a doctor can tell whether a man's semen is fertile. (None of the notions associating baldness or hairy chests with fertility is true.)

If you have tried for a year and your partner has not been able to conceive, you should visit your doctor together. He will arrange for special tests to be done to establish the cause of infertility, but first he will want confirmation that you have been having sex regularly and that neither of you has a sexual problem (erection difficulties or vaginismus, for example) that makes intercourse difficult. He will then suggest that you concentrate your sexual activity around your partner's most fertile days (two weeks before her period is due). Probably, he will ask whether your partner's periods are regular, for if they are irregular or infrequent the chances of conception are reduced.

Male infertility

By far the most common reasons for male infertility are that the semen either contains too few sperm or too many malformed sperm or that they are not sufficiently mobile. Usually between two and five millilitres of semen are ejaculated at a time, and in order to make conception likely, the concentration of sperm in the semen should probably be more than 60 million per millilitre. If the concentration falls below 20 million per millilitre, the man may well be described as sub-fertile, although conception may still be possible.

Semen infertility is easy to diagnose but difficult to treat, since the precise cause often remains obscure.

Emotional stress, tiredness, and heavy drinking may lower your sperm count temporarily, so it is worth altering your lifestyle if your partner is having difficulty conceiving. Some prescribed drugs also reduce fertility. Your doctor will advise you on this.

Often a few days' abstinence from sex just before your partner's most fertile days may allow a sufficient build-up of sperm to boost your fertility. In some cases drug or hormone treatment can boost sperm production, and occasionally it is possible to collect and concentrate sperm by centrifuging the semen and then, by artificial insemination, introducing it into the woman's uterus. If the problem is a blockage in the sperm ducts, it can be remedied by surgery, but if the semen contains very few sperm or very many abnormal sperm there is little that can be done.

Female infertility

This is more difficult to diagnose, but easier to treat, than male infertility. If tests suggest that your partner seldom ovulates, she may be helped by hormone injections or one of the 'fertility' drugs. Sometimes the problem is a blockage of the fallopian tubes, which carry the egg from ovary to uterus. This can often be cleared by surgery, but if it is not possible, the solution may be *in vitro* fertilization, producing a 'test-tube' baby. In this recently developed and as yet not widely available technique, a ripe egg is taken from the woman's ovary, fertilized with her partner's sperm, and then replaced in the uterus, where it continues normal development.

If you have had sex with your partner for some time and she has not conceived, you may be under considerable stress, not only because of your own desire to have a child, but also because of family and social pressures that are often insensitively brought to bear on the childless couple. Although there is no scientific proof, emotional factors appear to play a part in governing a couple's ability to start a family. Therefore it is worth remembering that the more relaxed you are about the possibility of conception, the greater your chances of success.

SEX AND PREGNANCY

There is no medical reason why intercourse should not continue throughout a normal pregnancy, unless your partner has had a previous miscarriage or she has had a threatened miscarriage during this pregnancy. However, a few men find that the fear of harming the baby during intercourse so inhibits them that they develop erection problems. In fact, the foetus is well cushioned by the uterine fluid and the tightly closed neck of the uterus provides a firm barrier against the outside world.

Maintaining closeness

Often, simply not having to think about contraception, or the relief that conception has taken place if it has been a problem, makes sex during pregnancy even more enjoyable. However, particularly during the first three months, your partner may be less interested in sex than before. The hormonal changes that often make her feel nauseous, tired, or emotional may deprive her of the energy and the inclination for sex, and it may be difficult to arouse her. Avoid intercourse for a while if she feels like this, but do not forget physical intimacy altogether. If she does want to make love, remember that her breasts will be very tender, even in early pregnancy.

Choosing a position

As the pregnancy advances, your partner will find that lovemaking positions that put pressure on her abdomen become increasingly uncomfortable. If you use the man-on-top position, you will need to take more weight than usual on your forearms, and you may find side-by-side, rear-entry, or sitting positions more suitable (see SEXUAL POSITIONS, p.211). A kneeling position may be best if your partner has backache, and is recommended for the final stage of pregnancy because it puts least pressure on the uterus. Indigestion and heartburn may make it uncomfortable for your partner to lie flat on her back, even in early pregnancy, and so she may prefer to make love in a sitting position or at least to prop herself up on pillows.

Sex after childbirth

For a few weeks – usually at least six after a first pregnancy – your partner is likely to feel discomfort, especially if she has had stitches. Her skin may feel tight and prickly even if it seems to have healed, and there may be a very tender area, usually at the base of the vagina, near the anus.

A position in which your partner is on top, or in which you face each other side by side, will avoid putting too much pressure on this sensitive spot. It is best to wait until after her post-natal examination, which should reassure her that everything has returned to normal, before having sex again.

Even if your lovemaking does not include intercourse for the first few weeks, keep up a pattern of loving contact, stimulating each other manually or orally to maintain the flow of physical affection between you, since it is easy to become baby-oriented to the exclusion of each other.

Remember that, even if your partner is breastfeeding, you will need contraception, and the means you were using previously may not be suitable now. Some brands of the Pill are unsuitable at this stage, for example, while your partner will need to be measured for a new diaphragm if you favor this method. (See CONTRACEPTION, p.283.)

Vaginal toning exercises

Childbirth does not, as many men fear, permanently stretch the vagina. The entrance may not be as tight as before, and the muscles may be a little lax, but the postnatal exercises your partner will be advised to do will tone these up. At first it may help to use a position in which your partner's legs are closed, so that your penis is gripped more tightly.

A few women lose interest in sex for a while after they have given birth, usually because tiredness and preoccupation with the baby override all other emotions. Very occasionally this loss of interest is prolonged, and may be a sign of the depression which sometimes occurs after childbirth. In such cases medical treatment is essential.

5

THE SINGLE MAN

Some men are single by choice, usually because they do not want to be tied down to a single partner or have not yet found a woman to whom they want to commit themselves fully. Being single is a stage they pass through and enjoy, not a problem requiring immediate solution. However, for many men, being single *is* a problem. While realizing that they would be happier if they could establish a close long-term relationship, they regard commitment and permanence as beyond their grasp.

Among the aims of this part of the book is to widen the single man's options so that if he remains unattached he does so because he wants to, not because he is unable to find a partner or develop a close bond with one woman.

The intention is to make it easier for him to form worthwhile relationships, even if these do not involve a long-term commitment, and to broaden and strengthen the social life on which his sexual contacts will largely depend. The following pages also include advice for the man who is unhappy about being unattached. You may be single because you never seem to meet anyone who might be a potential partner, or because, even when you do meet a woman, you find it hard to start any sort of relationship with her. These difficulties are discussed in the problem chart WHY ARE YOU SINGLE?, p.290. Or your difficulty may lie not in an inability to meet people or to make friends, but in putting a friendly or casual relationship onto a sexual footing. The problem chart DIFFICULTY IN FORMING SEXUAL RELATION-SHIPS, p.294, analyzes some of the reasons for this failure. There are a few men who find that although they have an active sex life, their affairs are always short-lived. Stable relationships elude them and they experience dis-appointment time after time in their search for permanence. If this is your situation, the problem chart DIFFICULTY IN SUSTAINING RELATIONSHIPS, p.296, will be helpful.

WHY ARE YOU SINGLE?

Have you always found it difficult to find friends of either sex?

YES → The skills involved in forming friendships can be learned if they do not come naturally to you. IMPROVING YOUR SELF-ESTEEM, p.227, should convince you that you are worth knowing, while DEVELOPING SOCIAL AND SEXUAL SKILLS, p.302, tells you how to 'promote' yourself successfully.

NO ↓

Do you meet very few potential partners or have little success in developing the opportunities that you do have?

YES → See the problem chart DIFFICULTY IN FINDING A PARTNER, p.292.

NO ↓

Do you form friendships quite easily but find that you 'block' when it comes to sexual relationships?

YES → The problem chart DIFFICULTY IN FORMING SEXUAL RELATIONSHIPS, p.294, analyzes some of the reasons behind the inability to make this transition.

NO ↓

Do you feel no strong drive to form sexual relationships because you have never been particularly interested in sex?

YES → You may simply have a low sex drive, although sometimes the guilt instilled by an overstrict upbringing can lead to a repression of sexual feelings. If your lack of interest in sex has caused problems with partners in the past, see DEALING WITH A SEX-DRIVE DISCREPANCY, p.272, and OVERCOMING INHIBITIONS, p.224.

NO ↓

Do you prefer a series of casual sexual encounters to committing yourself to one relationship?

YES → This may simply be the sexual lifestyle that appeals to you at the moment. But if you have never found it easy to develop the emotional side of your relationships, see OVERCOMING THE FEAR OF INTIMACY, p.226. This, together with the problem chart DIFFICULTY IN SUSTAINING RELATIONSHIPS, p.296, may help you achieve more balanced and satisfying long-term partnerships. You will also find guidance in the problem chart LACK OF EMOTIONAL INVOLVEMENT, p.184.

NO ↓

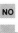

Do you have a relationship which works well but to which you are hesitant to commit yourself on a long-term basis?

NO

YES

There is no way of guaranteeing a happy-ever-after partnership. But **Factors which make a relationship work or fail**, p.301, indicates the main pointers to success or failure, so that you can at least establish the odds.

Do your relationships usually start well but end disastrously time after time?

NO

YES

If your relationships never last, it may be that you are not choosing well, or that you are not yet clear about the things that matter most to you. Consult the problem chart DIFFICULTY IN SUSTAINING RELATIONSHIPS, p.296.

Do you have a very clear image of the kind of partner you want, so that you 'screen' women you meet almost entirely by their looks, and do few of them measure up to this ideal?

NO

YES

The more rigid your blueprint for a prospective partner, the less likely it is that you will find a woman to match it. WHAT KIND OF PARTNER ARE YOU LOOKING FOR?, p.298, should enable you to see whether you are limiting your options by being inflexible.

Do you find that most of the women you are attracted to are involved with someone else?

YES

NO

If this happens often it suggests that you do not want to get involved just yet. This tactic provides the safest way of looking as though you are trying while ensuring that you do not succeed. It also points to a reluctance to let yourself become emotionally close to people. You will need to overcome this reserve if you are to make a lasting relationship. See OVERCOMING THE FEAR OF INTIMACY, p.226.

You are probably single because at the moment it suits you. Perhaps it is because you want a break from relationships or because you are giving so much of your time and energy to something else – work, for example – that you cannot make a full-time commitment. Solitude can become a habit though, so if you want eventually to share your life with someone, try not to remain detached from close relationships for long.

CELIBACY

Many men go through periods when for various reasons they need to be alone or free from sexual involvement. Such periods of abstinence can often prove beneficial to you, and you may find that you miss the warmth and the closeness of a partner more than sex. However, self-imposed abstinence of longer than a few months suggests that there is another reason for your lack of interest in sex (see problem chart LACK OF INTEREST, p.180) or that you are using celibacy to opt out of close relationships (see problem chart LACK OF EMOTIONAL INVOLVEMENT, p.184).

DIFFICULTY IN FINDING A PARTNER

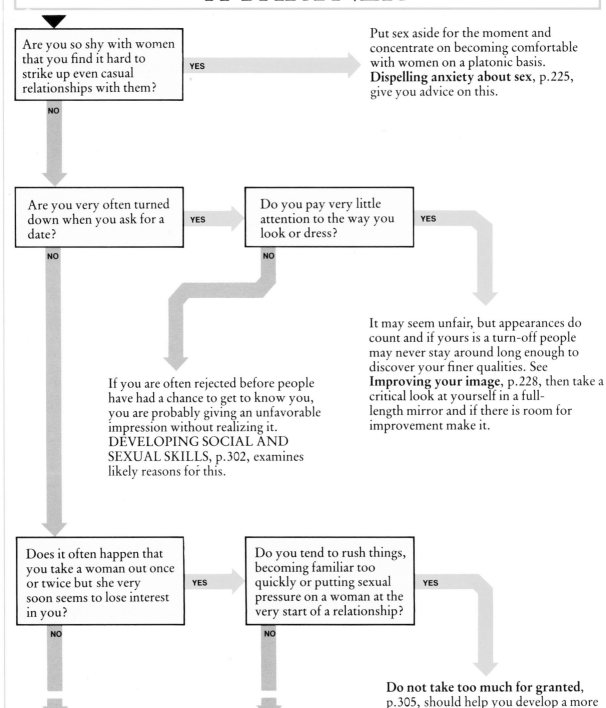

Are you so shy with women that you find it hard to strike up even casual relationships with them?

YES → Put sex aside for the moment and concentrate on becoming comfortable with women on a platonic basis. **Dispelling anxiety about sex**, p.225, give you advice on this.

NO

Are you very often turned down when you ask for a date?

YES → Do you pay very little attention to the way you look or dress?

YES → It may seem unfair, but appearances do count and if yours is a turn-off people may never stay around long enough to discover your finer qualities. See **Improving your image**, p.228, then take a critical look at yourself in a full-length mirror and if there is room for improvement make it.

NO → If you are often rejected before people have had a chance to get to know you, you are probably giving an unfavorable impression without realizing it. DEVELOPING SOCIAL AND SEXUAL SKILLS, p.302, examines likely reasons for this.

NO

Does it often happen that you take a woman out once or twice but she very soon seems to lose interest in you?

YES → Do you tend to rush things, becoming familiar too quickly or putting sexual pressure on a woman at the very start of a relationship?

YES → **Do not take too much for granted**, p.305, should help you develop a more sensitive approach.

NO

NO

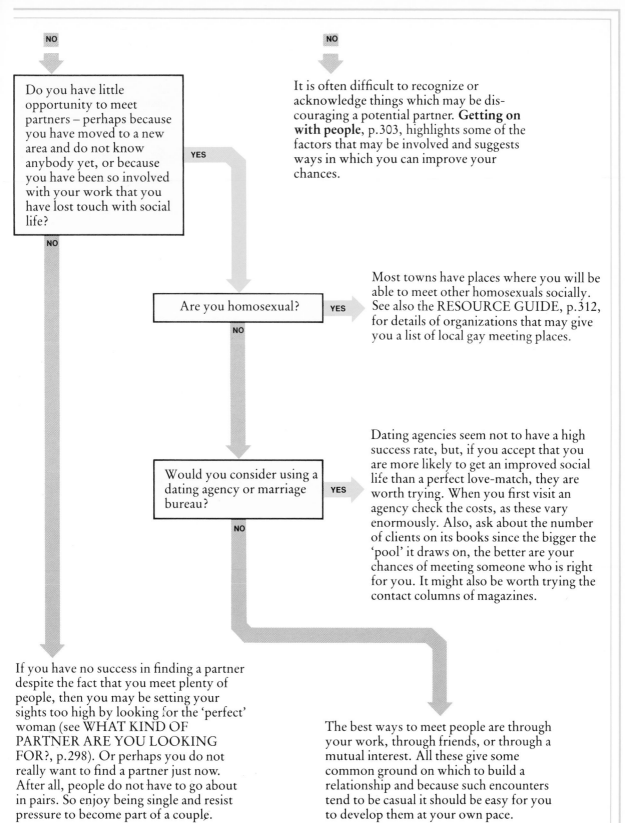

Do you have little opportunity to meet partners – perhaps because you have moved to a new area and do not know anybody yet, or because you have been so involved with your work that you have lost touch with social life?

YES

It is often difficult to recognize or acknowledge things which may be discouraging a potential partner. **Getting on with people**, p.303, highlights some of the factors that may be involved and suggests ways in which you can improve your chances.

NO

Are you homosexual? **YES**

Most towns have places where you will be able to meet other homosexuals socially. See also the RESOURCE GUIDE, p.312, for details of organizations that may give you a list of local gay meeting places.

NO

Would you consider using a dating agency or marriage bureau? **YES**

Dating agencies seem not to have a high success rate, but, if you accept that you are more likely to get an improved social life than a perfect love-match, they are worth trying. When you first visit an agency check the costs, as these vary enormously. Also, ask about the number of clients on its books since the bigger the 'pool' it draws on, the better are your chances of meeting someone who is right for you. It might also be worth trying the contact columns of magazines.

NO

If you have no success in finding a partner despite the fact that you meet plenty of people, then you may be setting your sights too high by looking for the 'perfect' woman (see WHAT KIND OF PARTNER ARE YOU LOOKING FOR?, p.298). Or perhaps you do not really want to find a partner just now. After all, people do not have to go about in pairs. So enjoy being single and resist pressure to become part of a couple.

The best ways to meet people are through your work, through friends, or through a mutual interest. All these give some common ground on which to build a relationship and because such encounters tend to be casual it should be easy for you to develop them at your own pace.

DIFFICULTY IN FORMING SEXUAL RELATIONSHIPS

Are you hesitant about making the first sexual move? — YES → **Is this because you are not really attracted to the woman in question?** — YES →

NO ↓   NO ↓

The only good reason for having sex is because you want to. If very few women excite you sexually, the reason may be a low sex drive or powerful inhibitions (see **Inhibitions and your sex drive**, p.272). Also, check your rating on the questionnaire ORIENTATION, p.175. It may be that you prefer men to women as sexual partners.

Is it because you are not sure whether she is attracted to you? — YES →

NO ↓

This is largely a matter of being able to 'read' your partner's body language. **Learning body language**, p.302, and **Judging her response**, p.305, will help you recognize the signs that she is ready to move on to the next stage of the relationship. **The importance of timing**, p.304, will then prove particularly useful.

Are you nervous about making a move because you are very inexperienced sexually? — YES →

NO ↓

It is normal to feel nervous at first. Concentrate on being sensual rather than sexual, until you feel more sure of yourself. If you are nervous, it often helps to simply spend the night together, without making love. See **Your first sexual experience**, p.305.

Are you reluctant to move the relationship onto a sexual footing because you have had sexual problems in the past and are afraid that they may recur? — YES →

See **Dispelling sexual anxiety**, p.225, which suggests ways of overcoming this problem.

NO ↓   NO ↓

Are you worried that if you embark on a sexual relationship your partner might become too emotionally involved?

YES → This is always a risk in any sexual encounter, but it is your partner's risk as much as yours. Be honest about the way you feel, then it is up to her whether she is prepared to take that risk. See OVERCOMING THE FEAR OF INTIMACY, p.226.

When you do make a sexual move, are you often rejected?

YES → Do you tend to rush things, suggesting sex very soon after you meet a woman?

YES → Take a look at **Do not take too much for granted**, p.305. Most people find sex more satisfying with someone they know and like, so get to know your partner first and give her the chance to get to know you. You will probably find that this way you are rejected less often.

Do you often suggest sex just because you think it is expected of you?

YES → Making an automatic pass because you feel it is expected of you is nearly always a mistake. It can happen when a new relationship has intensified more quickly than you would have liked, so that you are thrown into sex before you are ready. Be guided by your own feelings – you may both like to spend more time developing a sensual relationship, perhaps sleeping together without having sex, before starting a sexual one.

Do you see sex as the inevitable conclusion to a date with a new partner?

YES → Sex is only inevitable if you both want it. See **Do not take too much for granted**, p.305.

If you find that your relationships fail repeatedly before you have an opportunity to put them on a sexual footing, the problem chart DIFFICULTY IN SUSTAINING RELATIONSHIPS, p.296, will help you by suggesting possible reasons. DEVELOPING SOCIAL AND SEXUAL SKILLS, p.302, offers further advice on ending repeated sexual rejection.

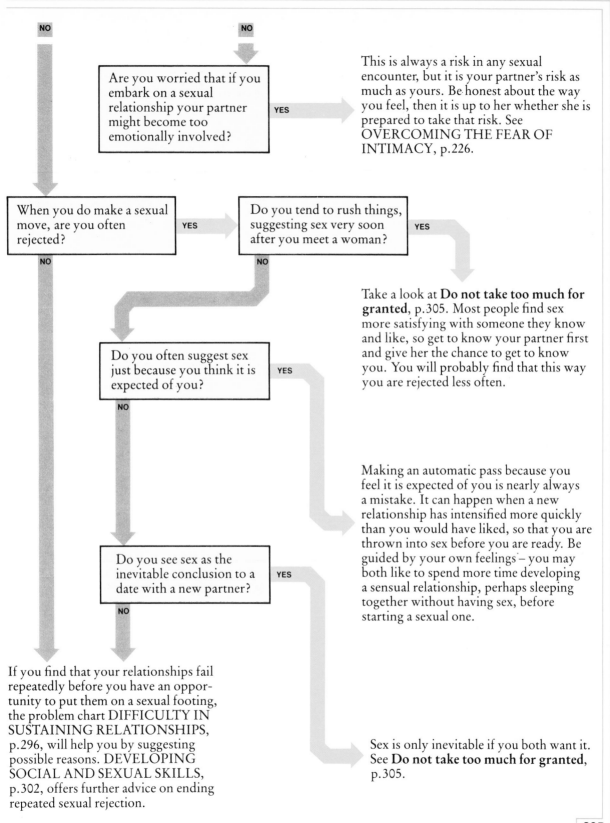

DIFFICULTY IN SUSTAINING RELATIONSHIPS

Are most of the women you become involved with different from you in some fundamental respect? Are they far more or less intelligent, for example, or do they have a totally different outlook on life?

YES → It is easier to make a lasting relationship with someone with whom you have a lot in common. The more similar you are in personality, background, and attitudes, the fewer sources of friction there will be. See **Look for similarity**, p.300.

NO ↓

Do you tend to get involved with women who have practical or personality problems or who seem very dependent on you?

YES → You are choosing partners who lack the emotional stability which is an essential ingredient of successful long-term relationships, perhaps because you need to feel the stronger partner. Be sure that this is what you really want and do not expect, each time, that your partner will change or mature. The chances are high that she will not. See **Look for emotional maturity**, p.300.

NO ↓

Do you always set your sights low because you are afraid of being rejected by women you find really attractive?

YES → In going for what you really want, you need to risk a bit more to gain a bit more. Even if you are rejected sometimes, the relationships you do make will be more satisfying and probably more lasting. See WHAT KIND OF PARTNER ARE YOU LOOKING FOR?, p.298.

NO ↓

Are you emotionally very reserved, finding it hard to show love or affection?

YES → Your partner will get very little emotional feedback from you and may find the relationship unsatisfying. The problem chart LACK OF EMOTIONAL INVOLVEMENT, p.184, analyzes reasons for this and suggest other parts of the book you may find helpful.

NO ↓

Are the emotional ties between you and your parents very strong and is it important for you to have their support and approval in everything you do? **YES** → Unless you can achieve real emotional independence, your adult relationships will always be at risk. See **Learning to be more assertive**, p.229, for advice on how to become more independent.

NO

Do you get very jealous of anyone your partner shows even a slight interest in or liking for? **YES** → Your relationships might last longer if you had more confidence in your own ability to sustain them. IMPROVING YOUR SELF-ESTEEM, p.227, should help you to achieve this.

NO

Do you feel that whatever goes wrong in your relationships must be your fault? **YES** ↑

NO

Are you very moody or inclined to lose your temper easily? **YES** → Anger is one of the most destructive elements in any relationship. **Dealing with anger**, p.271, discusses ways of expressing this feeling that will not hurt or alienate your partner irretrievably.

NO

Do you find that although you are very attracted to a partner at first, you lose interest as soon as the relationship shows signs of becoming serious? **YES** → This reluctance to commit yourself may be because you fear a close relationship. See OVERCOMING THE FEAR OF INTIMACY, p.226, which analyzes some of the reasons for this and directs you to parts of the book that may be helpful.

NO

If you are still uncertain about why your relationships tend to fail, see **Factors which make a relationship work or fail**, p.301. This suggests other factors to consider if you are starting a relationship which you hope will last.

MEN ♂ 5 THE SINGLE MAN

WHAT KIND OF PARTNER ARE YOU LOOKING FOR?

For some men, sexual interest is so easily awakened that they are attracted to any number of women, and it is not a problem to find a desirable partner. By complete contrast, a few spend years searching for their ideal woman with the same success as if they were questing for the unicorn.

Looks are of paramount importance in sexual attraction for some men, while for others personality is more crucial. For most, though, sexual interest is stimulated by a partner's physical appearance and will then either intensify or die away as her personality reveals itself. Accordingly, you probably have your physical preferences – blondes rather than brunettes, for example, or rounded women rather than angular ones. You may even have a mental image of your ideal partner, but even if, on rare occasions, reality and imagination have a transitory meeting, you cannot expect this to happen often. What is much more common is that you find yourself attracted to someone who bears only a passing resemblance to your perfect woman.

The dangers of inflexibility

Problems may arise, however, when you have such strong ideas about what your partner should be like that you cannot feel attracted to someone who does not conform to them. Obviously, the more rigid your requirements, the less chance there is of finding someone to suit you. Inflexibility is a disadvantage in a long-term relationship too. People change, and your partner will grow older, possibly fatter, certainly grayer. If this matters a great deal to you it may endanger the relationship. The personality too is subject to change, and this becomes particularly apparent if you were both young when you met and have matured together.

The danger in holding out for the perfect partner, quite apart from the fact that she probably does not exist, is that it will prevent you from making the most of the relationships you do have. You may never feel able to make a proper commitment and put everything into a relationship if you are perpetually hoping that something better will come along.

ASSESSING YOUR FLEXIBILITY

The following set of exercises will help you judge whether you are limiting yourself and your sexual opportunities by being too rigid and demanding in your preferences.

1 PHYSICAL PREFERENCES

The aim of the first exercise is to discover which physical characteristics influence your choice of a partner, and how important they are to you.

1 Make a list of ten women you consider physically attractive. They need not be women you know well, or feel a strong sexual attraction to, but simply females whose looks you admire.

2 Next make a list of ten women you do not consider attractive. (Remember, all you are concerned with in these two lists is physical appearance.)

3 Now try to find one quality you really like about each of the women in the first list. List these preferred qualities under the heading 'Positive'.

Then, returning to the list of women you find unattractive, compile a list under the heading 'Negative' of ten physical attributes that you see as unattractive in those women. It may occur that you include the opposite of a quality you write down in the preceding list: 'fat', for example, in the second list, while you put 'slim' in the list of positive attributes. This does not matter.

4 Work through the lists of positive and negative attributes carefully, deciding how important each attribute is to you. Put a mark beside those which, in either a positive or a negative way, are essential to your sexual interest. For example, if one of your preferences is height, put a mark beside that, while if red hair is such a turn-off for you that you could never feel attracted to a redhead, mark that characteristic. Do not mark attributes that you consider important but not indispensable.

Now go on to the second exercise, in which you are asked to apply a similar vetting procedure to personality traits.

2 PERSONALITY PREFERENCES

Even when you meet someone you think looks attractive, she does not necessarily excite you sexually. Nearly always it is some personality trait that tips the balance. You can analyze which of these 'turn-ons' and 'turn-offs' are important to you just as you did previously with physical attributes.

1 Think of the women you know reasonably well and consider to be physically attractive.

2 Now, of these women, select and list ten who arouse you sexually, or have done at some time, and then in a second list ten who, despite their looks, have never excited any real sexual feelings in you.

3 Next, find ten personality traits among the first ten women that you consider attractive and list these under all the heading 'Positive'. Then list ten unattractive personal characteristics that you find in the second group, listing these under 'Negative'.

4 Decide which of these positive and negative traits are so important as to be indispensable to your sexual interest and put a mark beside them.

Your lists of attractive and unattractive qualities, both physical and personal, constitute your own blueprint for sexual attraction. These qualities are what is needed (though not, of course, *all* that is needed) if you are to be sexually attracted to a woman. The number of marks you have put down indicates how rigid this blueprint is. Even one or two emphasized preferences on each list implies that you are to some extent limiting your choice of potential partners. Most men can feel attracted to a woman provided she satisfies at least some of their 'turn-on' requirements, and as long as these outweigh the 'turn-offs' there will probably be at least some sexual interest. The fewer marks there are, the more flexible you are and the more women you will find suitable as prospective sexual partners.

Making yourself more flexible

If your blueprint is very inflexible, it is probably worth trying to change your expectations. The best way to do this is to concentrate your attention on the things about your present partner (or a woman you are currently interested in) that do appeal to you. You will probably find that these are qualities that you have listed in the preceding exercises as important but not vital to your sexual interest. You will probably be able to discover additional qualities you may not have listed as important but which seem special in this person. It is a question of focusing on the positive aspects and of turning your attention back to them when it wanders off.

An alternative is to try to modify your partner so that she fits your blueprint. A tactful man may suggest some change of hair color or style, or diet, but change is not always possible and even if it is, your partner may be happy as she is. If you want to try this, the only fair way is to propose a trade-off. Therefore be prepared to do what you can to alter your own appearance so that it fits your partner's sexual blueprint (which she too may want to check by modifying the above method) more accurately.

MAKING A LASTING RELATIONSHIP

It is difficult to predict the chances of success of any relationship, for the most unlikely partnerships survive for years, while others collapse which seem to have everything in their favor. Nevertheless, the observations of marriage guidance counselors and studies of the causes of marital breakdown suggest that certain factors predispose a relationship to either success or failure. If you are wondering about your chances of making a lasting partnership, below are some of the most important factors to consider.

☐ *Do not commit yourself too young.* Youthful marriages run the greatest risks of all. Every major study of marriage shows that commitments made before the age of 19 are the least likely to survive (especially if embarked upon because the woman is pregnant). As you mature, you will change, developing different needs and interests from one another. It is possible for two people to move in more or less the same direction, continuing to meet each other's changing needs, but far more likely that you will grow apart.

☐ *Do not commit yourself too soon.* You should not consider making a relationship permanent until you have known each other for at least nine months. It takes most people that long to get to know the best and worst of each other, and living with someone is the best way to discover whether your partnership is likely to stand the test of time. A stormy involvement is a danger sign. If you have frequent quarrels and, even worse, if one or other has broken off the relationship more than once, it augurs badly for the future, for the pattern is one that is likely to become established. Protracted dating can be suspect too. If you have been talking about, but postponed, a permanent relationship for a couple of years or more, look carefully at your motives. It may be that you are not yet really ready to lose your independence.

☐ *Look for similarity.* Studies have shown that there is a tendency for people of similar disposition to marry. While some marriages of opposites do succeed, living together without friction is obviously easier for the couple who have similar interests and attitudes and want much the same things from life. It helps to have at least one or two major interests in common and it is probably best to be similar in age as well. If there is a difference of more than ten years between you, it is likely that there will be differences in outlook that are too great for an easy relationship to develop.

☐ *Look for sexual compatibility.* Sex will not prove the binding force it can be if your attitudes toward it are very different, or if it plays a much more (or much less) important part in your life than it does in your partner's. Sexual compatibility is not a matter of technique, and the mechanics of successful lovemaking can be learned as a couple adjust to each other. But it is important that you are truly attracted to and aroused by each other, for it is only on this basis that you will be able to accommodate each other's sexual needs. Given a background of mutual attraction and love, nearly all sexual problems are soluble; without it most are likely to prove insurmountable.

☐ *Look for emotional maturity.* Some personality traits seem to bode particularly ill for the future of a long-term relationship. Frequent expressions of anger, whether they are in the form of rages, the desire to dominate, or a tendency to be hypercritical, are the worst danger sign. And while a relationship may just be able to survive with one partner who feels like this, two will almost certainly doom it to failure. Low self-esteem also signals trouble, as it produces the insecurity and jealousy that will make a loving and trusting relationship hard to attain.

Overdependence can make an adult and lasting relationship impossible. A partner who is still very reliant on parental support and approval may demand more reassurance from you than you have time or, indeed, are prepared, to give. And on the inevitable occasions when you are the one who needs, if only temporarily, to be dependent and supported, she may be quite unable to take the responsibility.

☐ *Make sure that your partner can provide physical closeness and affection.* A person who is emotionally isolated and finds it hard to show affection or to accept it, has poor prospects of sustaining a fulfilling relationship.

□ *Look for flexibility.* The ability to adapt to change is one of the most important attributes to look for in a partner. Neither individuals nor partnerships are static, and a person who is uncompromising may find it hard to meet the changing needs and circumstances of a long-term relationship. It is a good sign if, for example, she is willing to think about new ideas or try new activities, or can adapt easily to last-minute or altered plans.

□ *Do not expect your partner to change.* If you have serious doubts about the relationship, forget it. It is a mistake to enter an unpromising relationship in the hope that your partner will change. If you can live with her as she is now, fine. But if you find yourself hoping that she will become, under your own moderating influence, less moody or extravagant, slower to anger, or less prone to jealousy, you are running a considerable risk. Some people have a great capacity for change, others are the opposite. So if the change matters to you, look for signs of it before you commit yourself, not after.

One ingredient essential for success is not listed above because it requires special emphasis. This is your own certainty about the relationship and the resultant determination to make it work. If you have reservations about your partner, they are likely to grow, and will prevent you from giving the relationship the 100 per cent commitment which more than anything will help it to overcome problems and survive.

Use the chart below to assess the chances of your relationship. In the column on the left are the bonus factors that are likely to increase your chances of success. These do not guarantee bliss, of course, but they do mean that you are likely to have a more contented life together. In the right-hand column are the risk factors. It seems easier to predict disaster than contentment, partly at least because it attracts more attention: more research has been carried out into the reasons for the break-up of relationships than into the factors which help couples to stay happily together. So it is more a cause for concern if you check several items on the 'risk' list than if you fail to check many bonus items.

FACTORS WHICH MAKE A RELATIONSHIP WORK OR FAIL

BONUS FACTORS		RISK FACTORS	
□ Successful cohabitation for at least six months	□ Emotional stability	□ Marrying too young (before 19 years of age)	□ Anger
□ Similar educational and social backgrounds	□ Similar need and enthusiasm for sex	□ Premarital pregnancy	□ Emotional coldness
□ Similar intelligence	□ Flexibility and adaptability	□ Marrying to escape an unhappy home	□ Poor self-image – reflected in low self-confidence
□ Less than ten years difference in age	□ Emotional self-sufficiency	□ Marrying 'on the rebound'	□ Fear of independence
□ Similar attitudes on major issues	□ Ability to give and receive affection	□ Short involvement (under nine months)	□ Possessiveness or extreme jealousy
□ Shared interests and activities	□ Consideration for others	□ Frequent friction or break-ups	□ Selfishness or self-centeredness
□ Similar ambitions and enjoyment of similar lifestyle	□ Similar physical attractiveness	□ Emotional instability	□ Substantial diff-erence in physical attractiveness

DEVELOPING SOCIAL AND SEXUAL SKILLS

The term 'social skill' simply means the art of getting along with people, making them feel by what you say and the way you behave that you like them – and that you are likeable too. Your social skill determines how well you carry off a first meeting, how easy you find it to make friends, and how smoothly you manage to make the transition from a social to a sexual relationship. The handling of this last situation calls for another set of skills, which we shall examine after looking at ways in which you can acquire an easy social manner.

Learning body language

Much of the time, especially at the beginning of a relationship, words are too crude a tool to convey the subtle shades of feeling passing between two people. When you scarcely know each other, the messages 'I like you', 'I'd like to get to know you better', 'Let's take this a stage further' are largely conveyed by body language, a system of communication based on the way you stand, move, and look at each other. You will both respond to this, although you may be unaware of doing so.

Everyone uses body language, but because it can as easily convey negative as positive messages, not everyone uses it to his or her best advantage. Shy people, for example, often send out the wrong signals without realizing it, producing the wrong response in others. What is really only shyness is often interpreted by strangers, and sometimes acquaintances, as boredom, lack of interest, or even hostility. So learning to read, and to use, body language is an important part of being socially adept.

Eye contact

Always look at the person you are talking to, not over his shoulder (which suggests that you are bored or inattentive) or down at the floor (which indicates that you are shy or even shifty). If he drops his eyes you are probably holding your own gaze for rather too long. What most people find comfortable is intermittent eye contact, for about five seconds in every half minute. This shows that you are interested but not putting the other person under uncomfortably close scrutiny.

When you are sexually interested in a woman, eye contact is one of the simplest and most unmistakable ways of showing it. Hold your glance longer than you would in an ordinary social situation, but again, do not overdo it. You will be able to judge her feelings by the way she responds. If she returns your gaze steadily, this could be an indication of her own interest. If she drops her eyes or shifts her gaze away it could mean that she is not interested, although it may simply be a sign that she is shy and that you are moving too fast. Watch movies or television if you want to see how it is done, for successful actors have long relied on the sustained, smouldering look to express interest in the opposite sex.

Facial expression

It is all too true that you are usually taken at face value. If you look miserable or worried, people will assume that this is the way you feel. If you are often asked if you are feeling OK or are worried about something when in fact you are fine, then your face is not giving the message you want to convey. Smiling is especially important for it is the most direct way of telling a woman that you like her, or that you find her attractive. At the very least, it makes you look friendly and responsive and opens up the possibility of greater closeness.

Gestures

Use your hands to add emphasis and interest to what you are saying. This is something that is often easiest to learn by watching others. There is no need to be dramatic as quite small movements are usually all that is necessary. Head movements are important when you are listening because they encourage the other person to continue speaking as well as indicating your own interest.

Posture

You will give an impression of self-confidence – however you feel – if you stand straight and hold your head up. When you first meet someone, it is best not to stand either too close or too far away. Many people feel uneasy if a stranger stands right next to them since it seems like an invasion of their personal space. On the other hand, physical proximity is a sign of attraction and it is one of the cues you can give when you want to advance a relationship and put it on a more intimate footing. By contrast, standing much farther away often gives an impression of aloofness or even mistrust.

Touching

Use a discreet touch as another signal that you find a woman attractive. Watch carefully for the response you get so that you do not overstep the line between showing interest, which is usually welcome, and 'pawing', which is not. Gentle pressure on a woman's hand or arm as you greet her or say goodbye, for example, is more affectionate and less formal than a handshake, but less intimate than a kiss. Once you have established contact you can step up the relationship by more prolonged or more frequent touching. Move from 'safe' gestures – a brief touch on her knee to emphasize a point as you are talking, brushing her hand with your own as you pass her something, holding it for a moment or two as you say goodbye – to more overtly sexual ones. Hold her hand in the cinema or as you walk down the street. If she does not draw away, and especially if she is starting to make the same gestures to you, the chances are that you will soon be able to move to the next stage, the hugging and kissing that lead to exploration and caressing of each other's bodies.

Listen to your voice

Your voice, after your appearance, makes the strongest initial impact on the people you meet. You can get an impression of how others hear you by listening to a tape recording of yourself. Few people like the sound of their own voice at first, but try to pick out the characteristics that might make it difficult or irritating for others to listen to and that you may be able to modify. Do you mumble, for example? Resolve to speak more clearly and loudly enough to be heard easily without creating a harsh effect. Does your voice sound high-pitched or monotonous? Try to lower it a little or to vary the tone. Put expression into your speech, but do not overemphasize individual words. Conversation, not oratory, is what you need to become proficient in. Try also to identify and eliminate irritating mannerisms such as frequent hesitation or nervous giggles.

Getting on with people

Conversation is the prime ingredient of social success. If you can handle it well, you will make a good first impression on people you meet and it will carry you with confidence through the opening stages of a new relationship. If you find it hard to talk to people, or if they seem unresponsive to you or seldom follow up the first encounter, it is possible that you have unwittingly developed some bad conversational habits. The following notes will help you if this is the case.

☐ Keep the conversation fairly neutral at first, so that either of you can back off easily if you want to. Talk about things which could not possibly offend or lead to heart-searching before moving on to more personal matters. It is a mistake to tell too much too soon. If you embark on an immediate outpouring of the intimate details of your personal life you will frighten off the other person with your intensity.

☐ Do not, when you first meet someone, either undersell or oversell yourself. It is normal to try to present yourself in a flattering light, but remember that a false image may be difficult to live up to (or hard to live down).

☐ Do not wander off the point of conversation, talk too much about yourself, or interrupt continually when someone else is talking.

☐ Never answer a question with a flat yes or no. This ends a conversation as soon as it has started. Expand your answer somehow, giving the other person a cue to continue the discussion.

☐ Talk about what really interests you and be positive in what you say. It is even better if you can find something you have in common – a shared interest or a mutual friend – to get the conversation going.

☐ Try not to let lengthy pauses develop. If you cannot think of a new topic, follow up what the other person last said with a comment or, preferably, a question that renews the discussion.

☐ When you are listening, remember that this is not a totally passive role. Every now and then make some encouraging response to stress that you are listening. When it is your turn to speak, take the opportunity of confirming first of all that you have understood and enjoyed what the other person has said.

☐ At the end of a conversation, ask yourself how balanced it has been. Have you done all the talking? Or practically none of it? Do you feel you know much more about the other person than he or she knows about you, or vice versa? Ideally, you should balance your disclosures so that neither of you feels that the other is holding back. Nor should you feel that the other person is disclosing more personal information than you are prepared to give away about yourself.

☐ When you first meet someone, it is not a good idea to prolong the conversation longer than feels comfortable, or, if you are at a party or other social gathering, to cling to the person you have just met like a limpet. It is better to move on when things are still going well, leaving your new acquaintance free to meet other people. If you like him or her enough, say something that will make it obvious that you have enjoyed the conversation and would like to follow up the meeting ('It's been nice talking to you', 'Perhaps we'll meet again later').

Being sexually successful

Many men feel unhappy or frustrated because they consider themselves unsuccessful with women. This sense of failure is made worse by the fact that some men seem to have no difficulty at all in attracting any number of willing partners. But the most apparently successful men are not necessarily those who especially like women or have the best sex life. Their main pleasure is usually not derived from a caring and sharing sensuality, but from making sex into a competitive sport. Pleasure for these men is in the chase, or in being able to flaunt a beautiful new partner in public. It melts away once they have achieved their objective, so that they develop no real commitment to, or concern for, their partner and can move smoothly to the next port of call. To the onlooker, such easy promiscuity may seem enviable, but it is not a particularly satisfying way of life.

True sexual success depends on such things as self-esteem, assertiveness, the ability to relax, and a genuine liking and consideration for women. The following advice will help you move in this direction. Remember that however average or undistinguished you believe yourself to be, some women will have a preference for *you*, for the kind of person *you* are. If you are aware of this you will not always have to do all the pursuing.

What to do on the first date

It is usually best not to make the first date with a partner too 'heavy'. You may both be more comfortable if it is casual and informal – lunch or coffee during the day, for example, so that you can get to know each other without either of you wondering about what is going to happen afterward. Do not expect to be asked inside if you meet at her place, and do not turn up too early or late. Do not be stingy, but do not spend rashly either. Never fuss about the price when you are paying for a meal. If she offers to buy you a drink or to pay her way, accept. It will make the relationship more equal and let her know that she has a choice about what you do. If you think she is offering out of politeness, do not accept immediately. If she really wants to pay, she will insist, and then you should let her.

Spend time and energy, as well as money, planning where to go and what to do. Try to picture the kind of things she might enjoy. Offer to cook for her, for example, and set the scene with soft lights, good music, comfortable and tidy surroundings. Find out what music she likes and get some suitable records or tapes. Or watch a good movie on TV together. If you go to a restaurant, choose one with atmosphere. But do not suggest anything that might make her feel uneasy on a first date. She might get worried, for example, if a picnic takes you to some very remote or deserted spot. Be flexible about meetings – if a last minute change of plan is unavoidable, or if she wants to cancel the date, be flexible about it. And never, when you are with her, show too much interest in other women you meet or see.

The importance of timing

Assuming that you continue meeting after the first date, the question will arise sooner or later of whether you are going to enter into a sexual relationship. The early stages of such a relationship are a game in which each of you makes moves to which the other responds, ideally with the situation developing at a pace which suits you both. A sense of timing is crucial, so that you can judge the right moment to accelerate the pace or to draw back a little and consolidate the position you hold.

If your timing is wrong it is probably because you have tried to act independently, either ignoring or misreading the signals your partner sends which tell you she is ready for the next move. Move too slowly and she is likely to become irritated or lose interest. Move too fast and you may put her under too much pressure. This may force her into a situation where she rejects you or backs away because she is not yet ready to go further and feels that this course is the only one you have left open to her.

Often, what you take to be a personal rejection by someone you have tried to date may simply be a matter of bad or unlucky timing. You may have chosen a time when she was involved with someone else, or caught her in the aftermath of a relationship when she needed to be free from involvement for a while to recover her emotional equilibrium. If you think there is a chance that this may be so, then do not be too discouraged. Keep your options open by maintaining casual contact with her and trying your luck again later. If you get the same message a second time, then accept defeat and move on.

Judging her response

Provided that your timing has been fortunate and that you are sending out the right signals through body language, you should be able to 'read' your partner's responses and judge when she is ready for you to step up the pace. Raised eyebrows, eyes wide open, and dilated pupils all indicate an encouraging response. If you find you are looking into each other's eyes for longer and longer periods, this is also a definite 'come-on' signal. Be appreciative if she stands close to you, or at least does not move away when you draw closer to her. You are getting a favorable response, too, if she nods her head in enthusiastic agreement with what you are saying, or occasionally touches you to emphasize a point she is making.

Do not take too much for granted

If your sexual advances are often rebuffed, it may be that you are assuming sex is your right, thereby reducing your partner's freedom of choice, so that rejection is likely, even inevitable. The following advice will help you to reassess your situation and probably to improve your success with prospective sexual partners.

☐ Do not look on every woman as a sex object or prize as soon as you meet her. The man who says, 'Your place or mine?' as soon as he has been introduced may win a few but he will lose many more.

☐ Do not assume that social responsiveness is the same as sexual encouragement. Because a woman is polite, or even friendly, this does not necessarily mean that she is ready to go to bed with you – or, at least, not yet. Look for definite signs of sexual interest before making a move.

☐ Do not expect every encounter, every date, to lead to sex. Keep your first dates casual so that you can get to know each other first.

☐ Do not be too familiar too soon. Show admiration in the way you look at her and interest in what she says and does. But unless you are very sure of your ground, do not use verbal endearments or physical caresses at a first meeting.

Sexual good manners

When it becomes clear that a sexual relationship is on the cards, remember that sensitivity plays as important a part in a new sexual encounter as it does at the beginning of any other relationship. By adopting the following advice you should avoid the worst breaches of sexual etiquette and so safeguard your developing relationship.

☐ Carry a packet of condoms with you so that if you find your partner is unprotected (you should always ask her whether she has any form of contraception) you can allay any fears of pregnancy.

☐ Make sure the sheets are clean if the venue is your bedroom. Reassure your partner if she has her period, that this need not prohibit sex as far as you are concerned, but do not press her if she prefers to wait until it is over. If she is willing, provide a clean towel for her to lie on.

☐ Suggest a bath, shower, or massage together first, especially if either of you is tense or nervous.

☐ Ask her how and where she likes to be touched and find out exactly what she wants to do. She may prefer to be the sexually active partner, or conversely, just to cuddle or sleep beside you the first time, rather than have sex.

☐ Do not in any circumstances resort to sexual blackmail by saying you love her if you do not or by making her feel that just because you are aroused she has an obligation to do something about it.

☐ Do not try so-called aphrodisiacs. They do not work and some are even dangerous. The most potent aphrodisiac of all is to be made to feel truly desirable. So tell your partner how much you admire and desire her and *never* criticize any imperfections in her looks or figure.

Your first sexual experience

Even if you are sexually experienced you may have problems at first with a new partner. You will be anxious to make a good impression, and may be so tense or nervous that you cannot get an erection, however much you want her. If you do get an erection you may lose it, or climax too soon through overexcitement. The situation may be very similar if it is your first ever sexual experience, except that in this case your problems will probably be compounded by the fact that your partner is equally inexperienced and nervous. Whatever happens, do not feel that you have failed if it is not quite as you hoped it would be, and do not take it too seriously, for the situation will improve as you gain confidence.

The following suggestions should help to make your sexual initiation more enjoyable.

☐ Never contemplate sex with a woman if you do not find her attractive.

☐ Make sure you have time, comfort, and privacy. Five minutes in the back of a car with an ever-present threat of discovery may rid you of your virginity, but it will not give you a true idea of how good sex can be.

☐ Do not be in too much of a hurry, especially if your partner is also sexually inexperienced. Make sure she is fully aroused, by caressing and stimulating her for at least ten minutes before you enter her. When she is fully aroused, her natural vaginal lubrication will make penetration easier. If she is tense because this is her first time too, it will probably be more comfortable for both of you if you use saliva or an artificial lubricant as well.

☐ Choose a man-on-top position (see SEXUAL POSITIONS, p.211) and put a pillow beneath your partner's hips so that it is easier to enter her. Spread her vaginal lips gently with your fingers and guide your penis between them.

☐ Push gently but firmly. You may need to apply some pressure if she is a virgin, but do not thrust hard. The hymen forms no real barrier since it is a very thin membrane that only partially covers the vaginal entrance. There will be very little pain and virtually no loss of blood when it is broken.

☐ Now begin to thrust lightly (but not deeply if it is her first time). Neither of you should feel let down if she does not reach orgasm; few women do the first few times they have sex and some rarely do, even with regular intercourse. For most women, being able to experience orgasm through intercourse is something that has to be learned and is not automatic as it is for men.

▽ **First intercourse**
The first time you have intercourse, it will probably be quite unlike what you imagined. But you should not take any disappointment too seriously, since you have plenty of time in which to learn the varied skills of lovemaking.

APPENDICES
SEX AND HEALTH

It is difficult for anyone to enjoy sex – and sometimes even to function sexually – if they are feeling ill or off-color. Any chronic or painful illness, for example, will almost always tend to decrease your capacity and desire for sex. If you are convalescing after an acute illness, you will probably find that your sexual appetite is reduced. Sometimes the drugs you have to take can affect sex drive and performance.

If your general life style is an unhealthy one, this too is often reflected in your sex-life. Heavy smoking and drinking can both lead to erection problems, for example. A serious weight problem means that in all probability you will be breathless, less mobile and therefore less sexually vigorous. Your mental state is important too. A depressive illness can affect your self-esteem and lower your sexual confidence. It is also likely to cause erection problems and a loss of sexual interest.

Some medical problems cause specific sexual difficulties – but often these are remediable. A few of the most common medical conditions that affect sexual functioning are discussed below. Your doctor may be able to give you further practical advice, and advise you about the side effects of particular drugs.

Diabetes mellitus

The condition can lead to erection problems, which are more severe the older you are and the longer you have the disease. You are less likely to develop the problem if the diabetes is treated by diet alone.

What you should do

Try not to dwell on the possibility – often if there is a problem it is mild, but worry may make it worse and can lead eventually to a loss of sexual interest.

Heart attack

Erection problems are quite common both immediately before and for some time after a heart attack, probably because the blood supply to the erectile tissue decreases. But the main problem is the anxiety that sex may bring on another attack.

What you should do

☐ Be reassured, if your doctor says it is alright to take moderate exercise, that sex will be safe.

☐ Get accustomed to masturbating once more before resuming sex with a partner.

☐ Keep your sexual encounters as stress-free as possible. New partners or illicit relationships may make you more anxious than a trusted partner in familiar surroundings.

☐ Take things easily at first, with occasional rest and no sexual gymnastics. After about 6 months your sexual activity should be back to normal.

Multiple sclerosis

Erection problems are common and sensation in the penis and the ability to ejaculate may be lost. However, in some cases increased sensitivity makes orgasm and even touch unpleasant.

What you should do

Use direct stimulation to produce an erection as this often works when fantasy does not.

Arthritis

Reduced mobility and the restriction of sexual activity are usually associated with this condition and others that cause stiff or painful joints.

What you should do

☐ Choose the time of day when you have least pain to make love.

☐ Take painkillers, if you use them, half an hour before making love.

☐ Before making love, rest and take a warm bath.

☐ Experiment to discover the most comfortable position. If movement is a problem, choose a position in which your partner can do most of the work. But if you cannot support her weight, use a rear-entry or side-by-side position (see SEXUAL POSITIONS, p.211).

Ileostomy/colostomy

Erection problems and, occasionally, ejaculatory difficulties or retrograde ejaculation (into the bladder) may follow these operations, especially in older men who have had the rectum removed.

Embarrassment about the condition and a fear of leakage may diminish sexual enjoyment.

What you should do

☐ First of all, make quite sure that your bag fits well and securely.

☐ Learn to predict when your bag will be full and adjust your lovemaking accordingly. You will probably find it best, for example, not to make love for an hour or two after you have eaten.

☐ If the bag seems to get in the way, try a different position. It may seem less intrusive if your partner is on top, for example.

☐ Tell a new partner about your condition *before* you make love for the first time. Reassure her that sex will not harm the stoma (artificial orifice) or create any other medical problems.

☐ With a new partner, or until you are so accustomed to your bag that you can forget about it, you may feel more comfortable wearing something over it.

Spinal injuries

Erection may be impaired – the degree depends on the site and severity of the injury. But often it can be obtained by either physical or psychic (mental) stimulation. Ejaculation is often lost and fertility may be diminished in those men who can ejaculate.

What you should do

If you have a partial erection:

☐ Use any method that works to maintain it. If direct stimulation is used, make sure your partner realizes that she should continually stimulate your penis to maintain the erection.

☐ Experiment to discover the position in which an erection is most easily sustained. Often one in which the woman squats astride the man is the most suitable.

☐ With your partner's help you may be able to ease your penis into her. Then hold the base and move it around in her vagina.

If you have no erection:

☐ Remember that you and your partner can still make love using your hands and mouth (see STIMULATION TECHNIQUES p.206). You may discover that the sensitivity of other parts of your body, especially just above your genitals, seems to increase in a compensatory way.

☐ Artificial aids such as vibrators may be helpful. If you both like the idea, try an artificial penis. These are strapped to your body and are either solid or hollowed out so that your penis fits inside.

☐ In some cases mechanical aids may be used to support the penis. These either produce a permanent erection or are hinged so that the penis can hang down when not in use.

THE SEXUAL SIDE-EFFECTS OF DRUGS

Few drugs enhance sexual functioning, but many drugs have adverse effects on it, and often on sex drive as well. For example anti depressants may reduce sexual functioning, while anticonvulsants reduce both sex drive and sexual functioning.

Of the 'recreational' drugs, some, including alcohol (in small doses), amphetamines, cocaine and marijuana, increase sexual desire, but nearly all – including tobacco – have an adverse effect on a person's ability to become aroused, reach orgasm and generally enjoy sex.

SEXUALLY TRANSMITTED DISEASES

Sexually transmitted diseases (also referred to as STD or, decreasingly, as venereal diseases or VD) are nearly always transferred from person to person through vaginal or anal intercourse or oral-genital contact. Most of the organisms that cause these diseases thrive only in warm, moist conditions and cannot survive outside the body for more than a few minutes. Therefore it is virtually impossible to contract an STD through contact with, say, a lavatory seat, although infection may occasionally be spread via a towel handled immediately after use by an infected person.

It is essential to seek medical help promptly either from your doctor or from a special clinic if you think you may have a sexually transmitted disease. Treatment is simple and effective provided it is started early enough. You should have no sexual relationships until you are cured, and it is important that your recent sexual partners contact a doctor immediately too, since during the incubation period you may have infected others.

Non-specific urethritis (NSU)

This is the most common sexually transmitted disease and 80 per cent of sufferers are male. About 45 per cent of cases are probably caused by a bacterium called chlamydia, but other microbes are also believed to cause the disease.

Symptoms Tingling in the tip of the penis, sometimes accompanied by a scant clear discharge. Both are most noticeable first thing in the morning and appear 1-5 weeks after the infection is contracted.

Treatment By antibiotics. Your partner should also be treated, even if she has no symptoms. You should not have sex until the treatment is complete.

Gonorrhea

One person in 100 develops gonorrhea (often called 'the clap') each year. It is more common in people who have many sexual partners, and two-thirds of sufferers are male. The disease is caused by a bacterium transmitted through vaginal or anal intercourse or oral sex.

Symptoms Discomfort in urination and a slight discharge of pus. Symptoms appear within 2-10 days of infection. Untreated, the disease may spread through the sexual organs, and obstruct the flow of urine. It can also lead to sterility. Anal infection may cause moistness and pain in the rectum; oral infection may result in mouth ulcers or a sore throat.

Treatment By antibiotics. You must abstain from sex until you are free of symptoms.

Genital herpes

A viral disease transmitted by direct body contact. Not everyone who comes into contact with herpes develops the disease, and many people have symptomless attacks and acquire immunity. The first bout of herpes may last 2-3 weeks. About half of all sufferers have subsequent attacks, but these tend to be shorter and less severe. Attacks tend to recur when the sufferer is physically run down or under stress.

Symptoms A genital rash of red patches with white, itching blisters which may burst to form shallow, painful ulcers. There may be tenderness and swelling in the groin, pain or a burning sensation during urination, fever, and general discomfort. Symptoms appear 2-20 days after contact.

Treatment There is at present no effective treatment, although a drug, acyclovir, reduces the period for which you are infectious. An analgesic such as aspirin or local anesthetic will reduce severe pain. Cold compresses and ice-packs ease discomfort, and painting the area with gentian violet may help. Wear cotton boxer-style briefs and avoid tight pants. Abstain from sex while you have symptoms, and use condoms for about 4 weeks after the symptoms have vanished. A condom will protect your partner only if it covers the infected area.

Syphilis

Syphilis is rare. Most sufferers are male and most are homosexual. The disease organism usually enters through the urethra, rectum or mouth.

Symptoms The first sign is a hard, painless, highly infectious sore on the penis and anus. It takes 9-90 days to appear and disappears spontaneously after a few weeks. The disease can be successfully treated with antibiotics; if untreated, a non-irritant rash, and swollen lymph glands, may develop some weeks later. Warty lumps may appear around the anus if it was the site of original infection. The disease then enters a symptom-free stage. More serious symptoms, leading eventually to death, may develop years later.

Genital warts

These appear as small cauliflower-like growths on the genitals or around the anus. They are caused by a virus that is transmitted by direct body contact, and appear between one and six months after the infection.

Treatment Application of a caustic substance, or by freezing or electrical cauterization.

Pubic lice ('crabs')

Minute blood-sucking insects which appear in the pubic or anal hair. The lice appear several weeks after the infection and may cause severe itching, especially at night.

Treatment Application of a special cream or lotion.

AIDS

AIDS – Acquired Immune Deficiency Syndrome – is caused by the human immunodeficiency virus (HIV). The virus is present in body fluids – blood, semen, and sometimes saliva, though in saliva the quantities are probably too small to cause infection. AIDS is primarily a sexually transmitted disease, but

---

GUIDELINES FOR SAFER SEX

Sex does not cause AIDS. Being frightened of the disease does not mean you have to give up sex, nor does it mean avoiding physical contact with an infected person. It is safe to live with someone who has AIDS, to sleep in the same bed, share the same household utensils, and hug them. The danger lies in allowing an infected person's body fluids – blood, semen, vaginal fluids and (to a much lesser extent) saliva to enter your own body through a cut or an abrasion.

The table below puts various sexual activities into categories according to the risk they involve. It is important to realise that in our present state of knowledge it is impossible to say with absolute certainty exactly how risky any form of sex is. The virus has been found in saliva, for example, and although there is no evidence as yet that AIDS has ever been acquired by kissing, one can't say with certainty that this is impossible. We can, however, say that it is unlikely. So it is that on a balance of possibilities – erring on the cautious side – that the risks of various sexual activities have been assessed.

In general, 'safer sex' means using a barrier during sexual activities which involve an exchange of body fluids, or avoiding those activities altogether. The HIV virus cannot penetrate the latex of which condoms are made, so using latex as a barrier between you and your partner's body fluids is an effective safety measure. Condoms should be used during intercourse (extra-strong ones during anal intercourse). Nonoxynol-9, an ingredient of most spermicides, kills the HIV

virus, so use spermicide as well as a condom as an additional safety measure. Alternatively, buy a brand of condom which is itself lubricated with nonoxynol-9.

If you are infected yourself, 'safe sex' precautions are still sensible even if your only sexual partner is another infected person. A characteristic of the HIV virus is that it constantly changes its structure within the body. Someone who is re-infected with a variation of the virus may develop a new and different set of symptoms.

Monogamy is the best guarantee of a really safe sex life. If you change partners often, or if your regular partner has other sexual contacts, the only sensible policy is always to use a condom and spermicide whenever you have intercourse.

NO RISK

Solo and mutual masturbation; body massage (excluding the genital area); using unshared sex toys (e.g. vibrators, dildoes).

LOW RISK

Intercourse (anal or vaginal) with a condom and spermicide; fellatio ("sucking") without ejaculation, or wearing a condom; anilingus ("rimming") i.e. oral-anal sex, through a latex barrier.

HIGH RISK

Anal and vaginal intercourse without a condom; "Fisting" – insertion of the hand into the rectum (the risk is lessened if a latex glove is worn); using shared sex toys; any sex act which draws blood.

it can also be passed on by transfusion with infected blood, or by the shared use of a hypodermic needle or syringe among intravenous drug users.

Once inside the body, the virus penetrates and multiplies inside the T4 white blood cells which play a vital part in the body's defences against some infections and cancers. Eventually the cells burst, releasing HIV particles into the blood which can then infect more T4 blood cells. As cells are gradually destroyed, the person becomes more prone to infections of the lungs, gut, or brain, or to various forms of cancer, such as Kaposi's sarcoma, a rare form of skin cancer. At the moment it seems probable that between 1 in 10 and 1 in 3 of those infected with the virus will eventually develop AIDS.

AIDS cannot be transmitted by casual social contact; to cause infection, the virus must actually enter the body through a cut or abrasion in the skin or the mucous membranes which line the rectum, vagina or mouth. The rectum is especially vulnerable because its lining is thin and delicate, so anal intercourse carries a higher risk than most other forms of sexual activity. However, the disease can also be spread by vaginal intercourse. Use of a condom helps to prevent infection (see **Guidelines for safer sex**, p.310). Most doctors believe that the chances of catching AIDS from a single sexual encounter with an infected person are very small. It is repeated sexual contact with an infected person or persons that is likely to lead to infection. The HIV virus cannot survive for long outside the body, and is destroyed by ordinary household bleaches and disinfectants, or by detergent diluted in hot water. If the blood of an infected person is spilt, it can be safely cleaned up using any of these. Unless the infected blood actually enters your own bloodstream through some skin lesion it cannot harm you.

Symptoms Some people infected with the HIV virus do not develop symptoms, though they can still infect others. A few people develop a mononucleosis-like illness soon after infection, which clears up without treatment, but most feel perfectly well. People who have had the infection for some months or years may develop permanently swollen lymph glands, and tend to develop common skin infections. Some people go on to develop a variety of symptoms, including fever, weight loss, diarrhea and oral thrush, which are known as the AIDS-related complex, or ARC. ARC is not itself fatal, but people who develop it are more likely to develop full-blown AIDS. This usually has a pattern of repeated infections, weight loss, weakness and eventual death. On average, about 3-4 years elapse between infection and the development of AIDS.

Treatment Although there is no vaccine or cure for AIDS at present, the conditions associated with it can often be treated. Early trials suggest that in a few cases the drug Retrovir (AZT) may 'buy time' by slowing down the progress of the disease, though the drug has very unpleasant side-effects.

TESTING FOR AIDS

When someone is infected with the HIV virus that causes AIDS, their body develops antibodies against the virus. A blood test for the presence of HIV antibodies provides a fairly reliable indication as to whether or not the person is infected with the virus. If you are in a 'high risk' group (that is, if your partner is an active homosexual, if you or your partner have many casual sexual relationships, or are intravenous drug users), you may wonder whether to take the antibody test. It may seem easier to know, so you can face the fact that you are antibody positive (if that is what the test indicates), rather than have to cope with the uncertainty of not knowing.

However, testing does not always provide conclusive proof that you either will or will not develop AIDS. Although the test is reliable, it is not 100 per cent reliable; a second, different type of test is usually carried out on any positive sample to confirm the result. Moreover, the HIV antibodies take a few weeks (or even months) to develop, so a test carried out shortly after you have been infected will give a negative result. Finally, although a positive antibody test shows that you have been exposed to the virus, it does not mean that you will inevitably develop AIDS.

A positive test result has important implications, so counseling is advisable for anyone who is considering having the test. People who are antibody positive are usually advised only to tell those who actually need to know – their doctor, dentist, close friends, and of course their sexual partner. Sadly, there are still many misconceptions about AIDS, and there is unnecessary discrimination against people who have the disease or are antibody positive.

RESOURCE GUIDE

RECOMMENDED READING

General

Comfort, A. *The joy of sex*. New York, NY, Simon and Schuster, 1974

Fettner, A. Guidici and Check, W. A. *The truth about AIDS* (revised and updated edition). New York, NY, Holt, Rinehart and Winston, 1985

Kubler-Ross, E. *AIDS: The ultimate challenge*. New York, NY, Macmillan, 1988

Nowinski, J. *Becoming satisfied: A man's guide to sexual fulfillment*. Englewood Cliffs, New Jersey, Prentice-Hall, 1980

Silver, S.J. *The male: From infancy to old age*. New York, NY, Charles Scribner & Sons, 1981

Westheimer, W. *Dr Ruth's guide to good sex*. New York, NY, Warner, 1984

Zilbergeld, B. *Male sexuality*. New York, NY, Bantam Books, 1981

For couples

Barbach, L. *For each other: Sharing sexual intimacy*. New York, NY, Doubleday, 1982

Gochros, H.L. and Fischer, J. *Treat yourself to a better sex life*. Englewood Cliffs, New Jersey, Prentice-Hall, 1980

McCarthy, B. and McCarthy, E. *Sexual awareness: Enhancing sexual pleasure*. New York, NY, Carroll & Graf Publishers, 1984

Phillips, D. and Judd, R. *Sexual confidence*. New York, NY, Bantam Books, 1982

For older readers

Butler, R.N. & Lewis, M.I. *Love and sex after sixty: A guide for men and women in their later years*. New York, NY, Harper & Row, 1976

Schover, L.R. *Prime time: Sexual health for men over fifty*. New York, NY, Holt, Rinehart & Winston, 1984

For disabled or handicapped readers

Bullard, D.G. & Knight, S.E. (editors) *Sexuality and physical disability: Personal perspectives*. St. Louis, Mo., C.V. Mosby, 1981

Kempton, W. *Sex education for persons with disabilities that hinder learning*. N. Scituate, Mass. Duxbury Press, 1975

Sex therapy and education

For information on sex therapy clinics and sex education programs, contact:

American Association of Sex Educators, Counselors, and Therapists (AASECT) 600 Maryland Avenue SW, Washington, DC 20024.

Information services for homosexuals

The following organizations provide information and advice for homosexual men and women:

Div. 44, Gay and Lesbian Concerns, American Psychological Associations, 1200 17th Street NW, Washington, DC 20036.

Institute for Human Identity, 490 West End Avenue, New York, NY 10024.

Los Angeles Gay and Lesbian Community Services Center, 1213 N. Highland Avenue, Los Angeles, CA 90038.

Gay Men's Health Crisis (GMHC), 254 West 18th Street, New York, NY 10011

NAME   DATE OF BIRTH   DATE

Your Sexual Profile Chart

Use the chart below to create your own sexual profile. See p.176 for instructions.

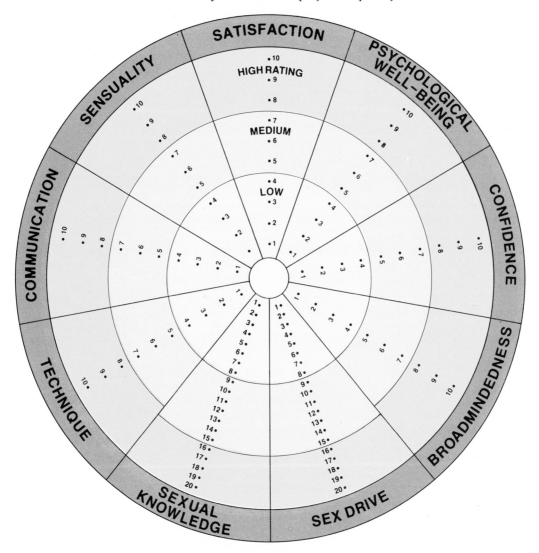

KEY TO ORIENTATION QUESTIONNAIRE (p.175)

☐ **A** You are exclusively heterosexual.

☐ **B** You are predominantly heterosexual, but under some conditions you may show a flicker of homosexual interest.

☐ **C** You are predominantly heterosexual, but have a strong element of homosexuality.

☐ **D** You are bisexual.

☐ **E** You are predominantly homosexual, but have an element of heterosexuality.

☐ **F** You are predominantly homosexual.

☐ **G** You are exclusively homosexual.

Index

Page numbers in *italics* refer to illustrations and captions

Acknowledgments

Design assistance
Helen Young

Studio services
Fred Ford and Mike Pinney (Radius)

Typesetting
Rowland Phototypesetting (London) Ltd

Reproduction
Repro Llovet, Barcelona

Printing
L.E.G.O., Vicenza